[redacted]

Cub

TAP
TAP
TAP

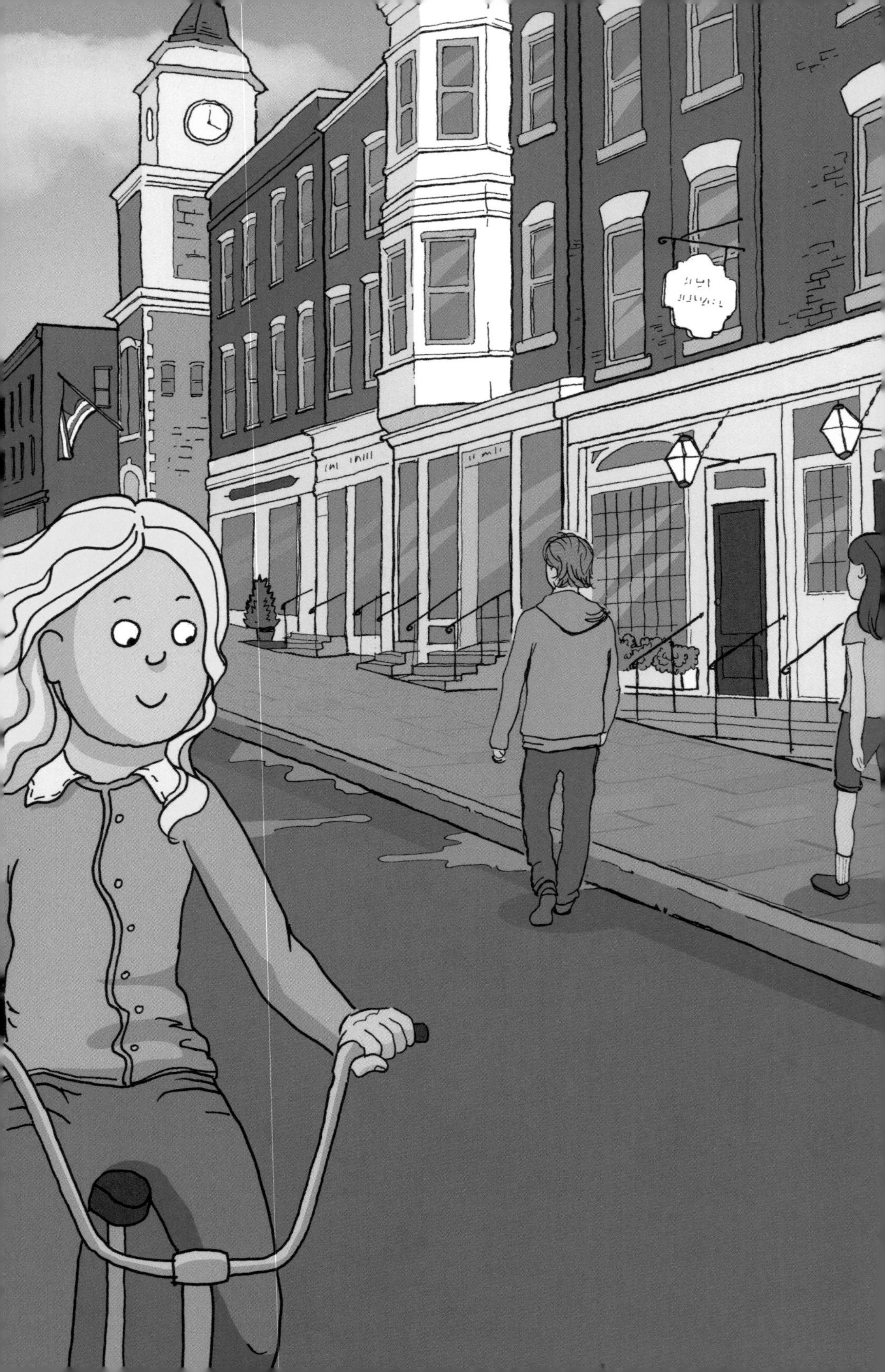

Cub
Cynthia L. Copeland
Colors by Ronda Pattison
ALGONQUIN 2020

ALSO BY CYNTHIA L. COPELAND

REALLY IMPORTANT STUFF MY DOG HAS TAUGHT ME

PUBLISHED BY ALGONQUIN YOUNG READERS
AN IMPRINT OF ALGONQUIN BOOKS OF CHAPEL HILL
POST OFFICE BOX 2225
CHAPEL HILL, NORTH CAROLINA 27515-2225

A DIVISION OF WORKMAN PUBLISHING
225 VARICK STREET
NEW YORK, NEW YORK 10014

PRINTED IN SOUTH KOREA.
PUBLISHED SIMULTANEOUSLY IN CANADA BY THOMAS ALLEN & SON LIMITED.
DESIGN BY NEIL SWAAB.

CATALOGING-IN-PUBLICATION DATA FOR THIS BOOK
IS ON FILE AT THE LIBRARY OF CONGRESS.

10 9 8 7 6 5 4 3 2

FOR MY DAD

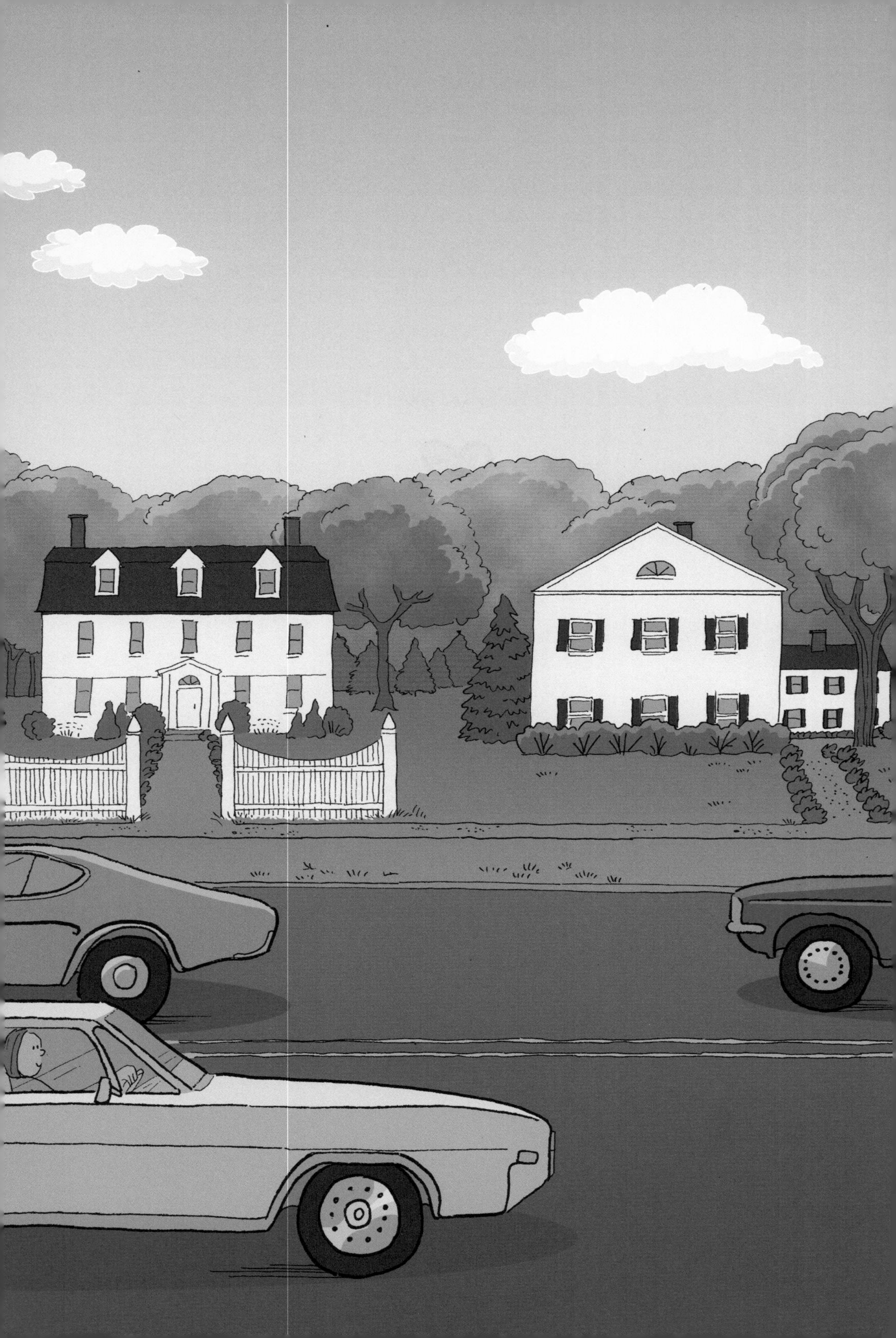

Cub

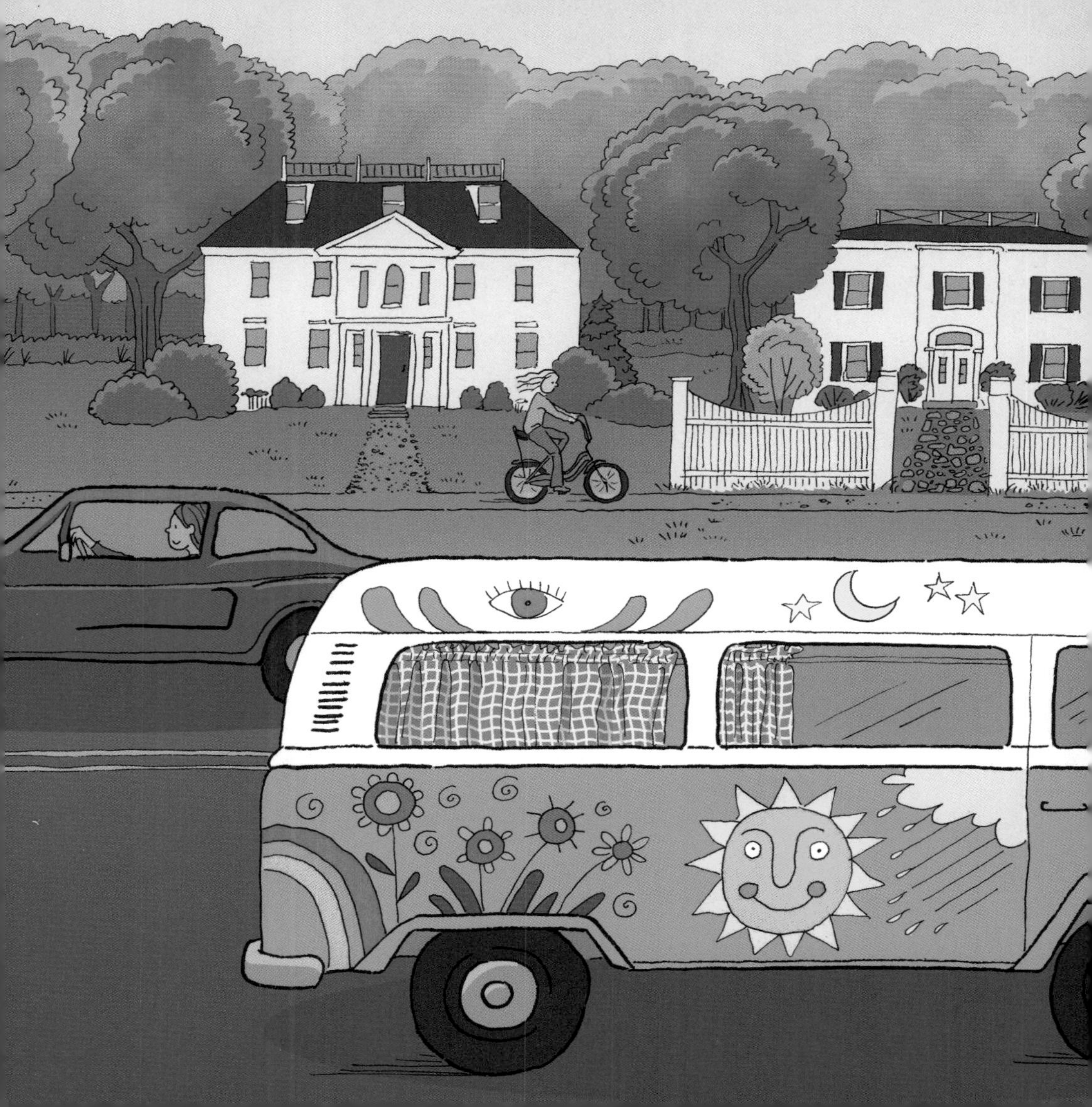

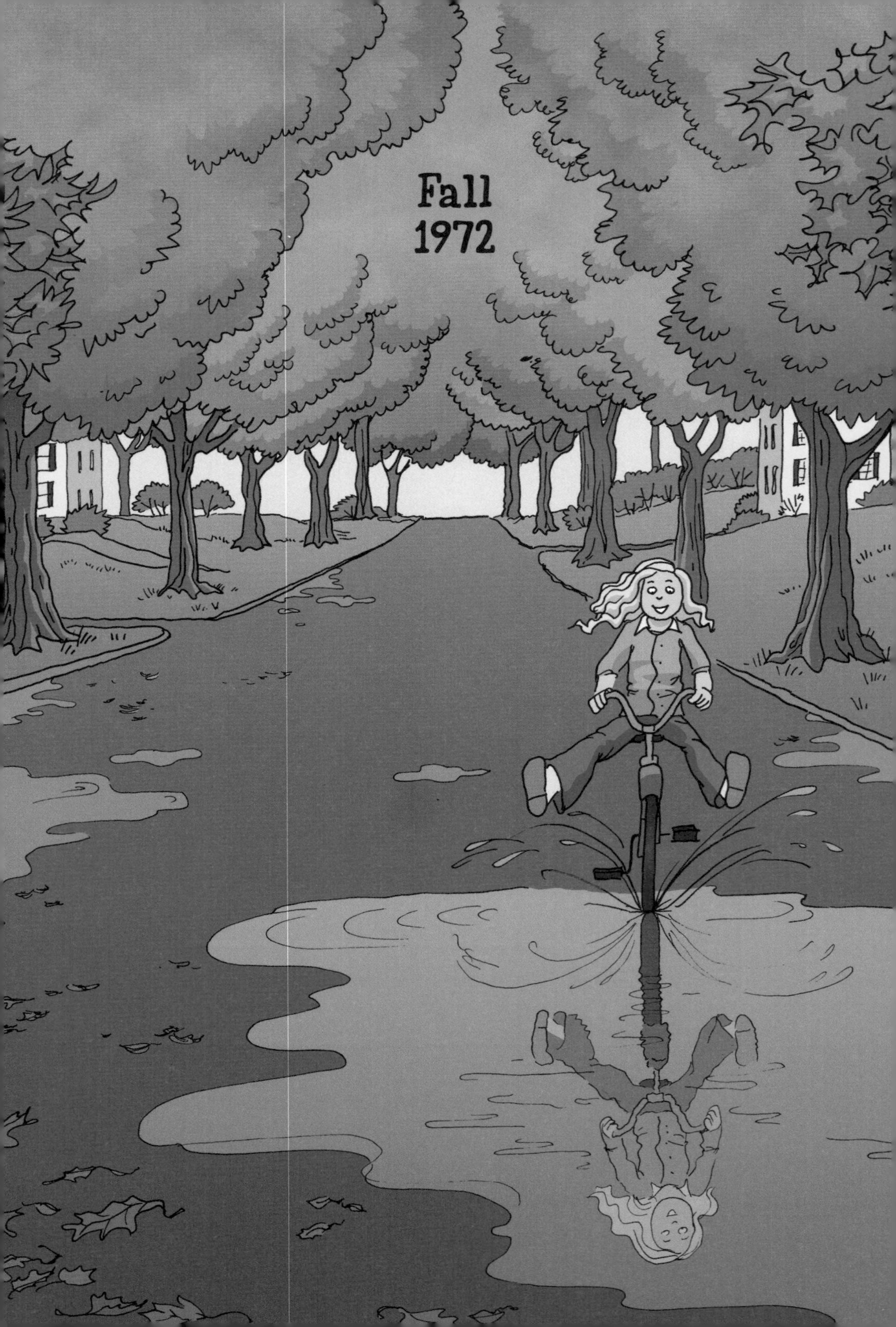
Fall
1972

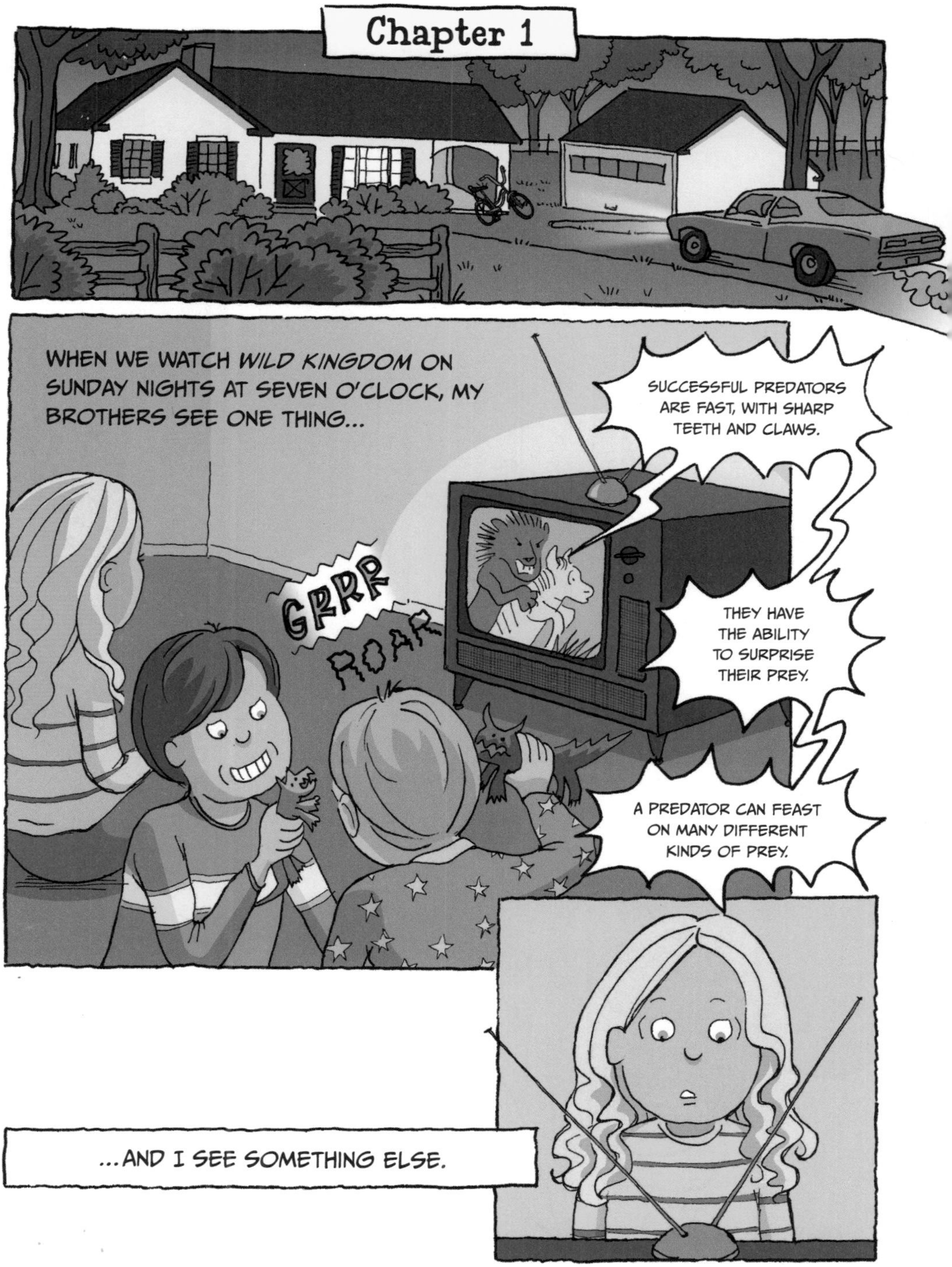
Chapter 1
WHEN WE WATCH WILD KINGDOM ON SUNDAY NIGHTS AT SEVEN O'CLOCK, MY BROTHERS SEE ONE THING...
SUCCESSFUL PREDATORS ARE FAST, WITH SHARP TEETH AND CLAWS.
GRRR
ROAR
THEY HAVE THE ABILITY TO SURPRISE THEIR PREY.
A PREDATOR CAN FEAST ON MANY DIFFERENT KINDS OF PREY.
...AND I SEE SOMETHING ELSE.

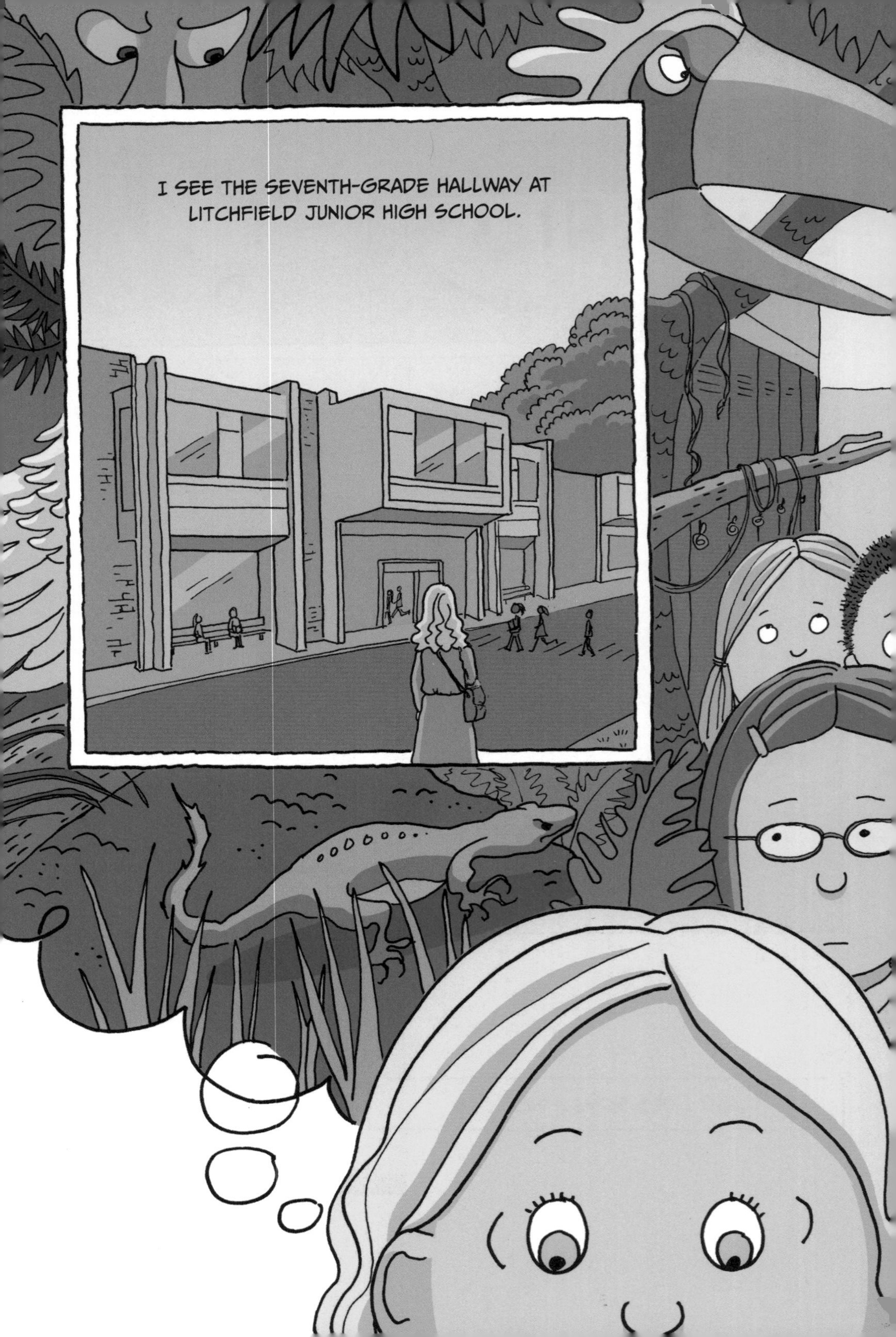
I SEE THE SEVENTH-GRADE HALLWAY AT LITCHFIELD JUNIOR HIGH SCHOOL.

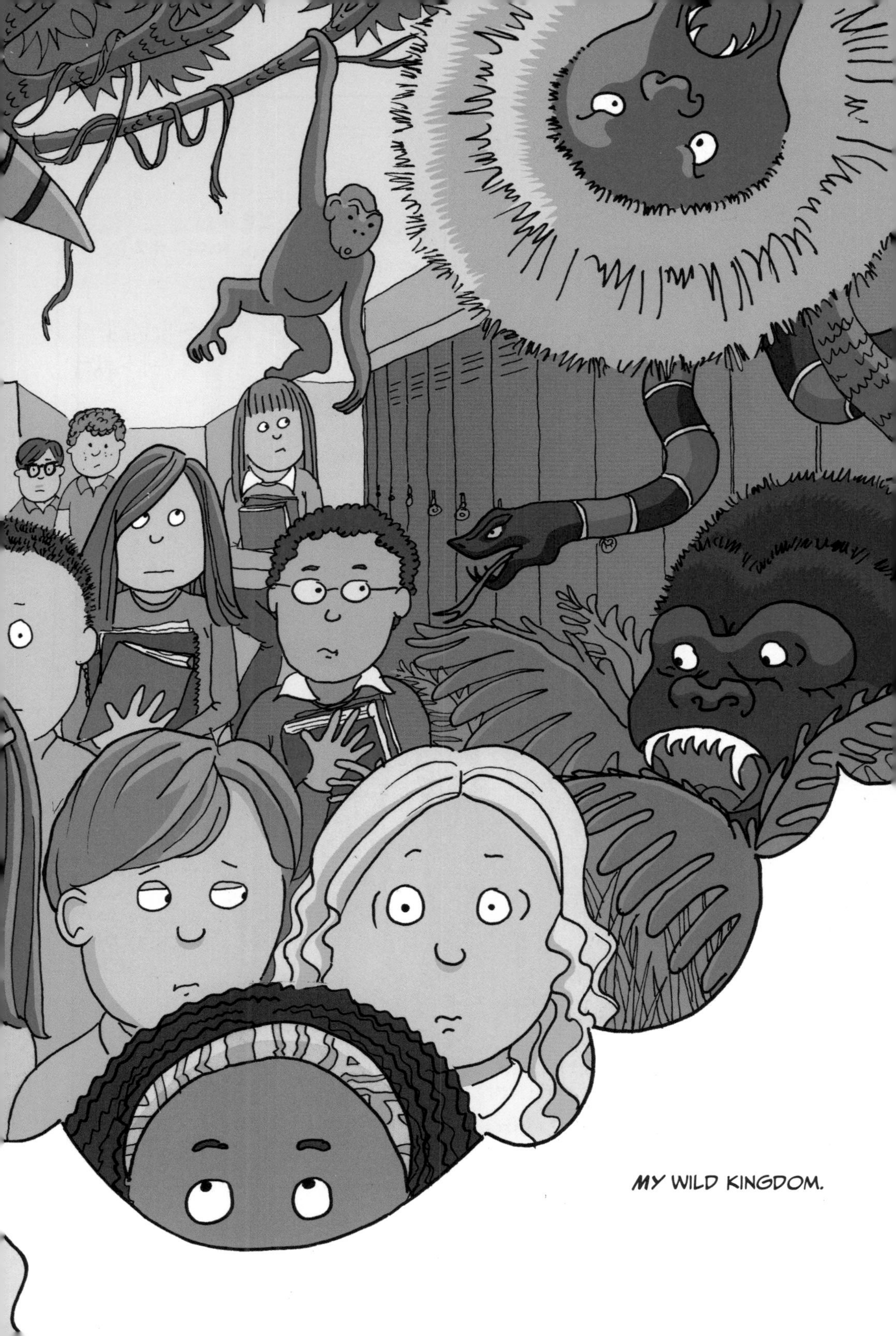

MY WILD KINGDOM.

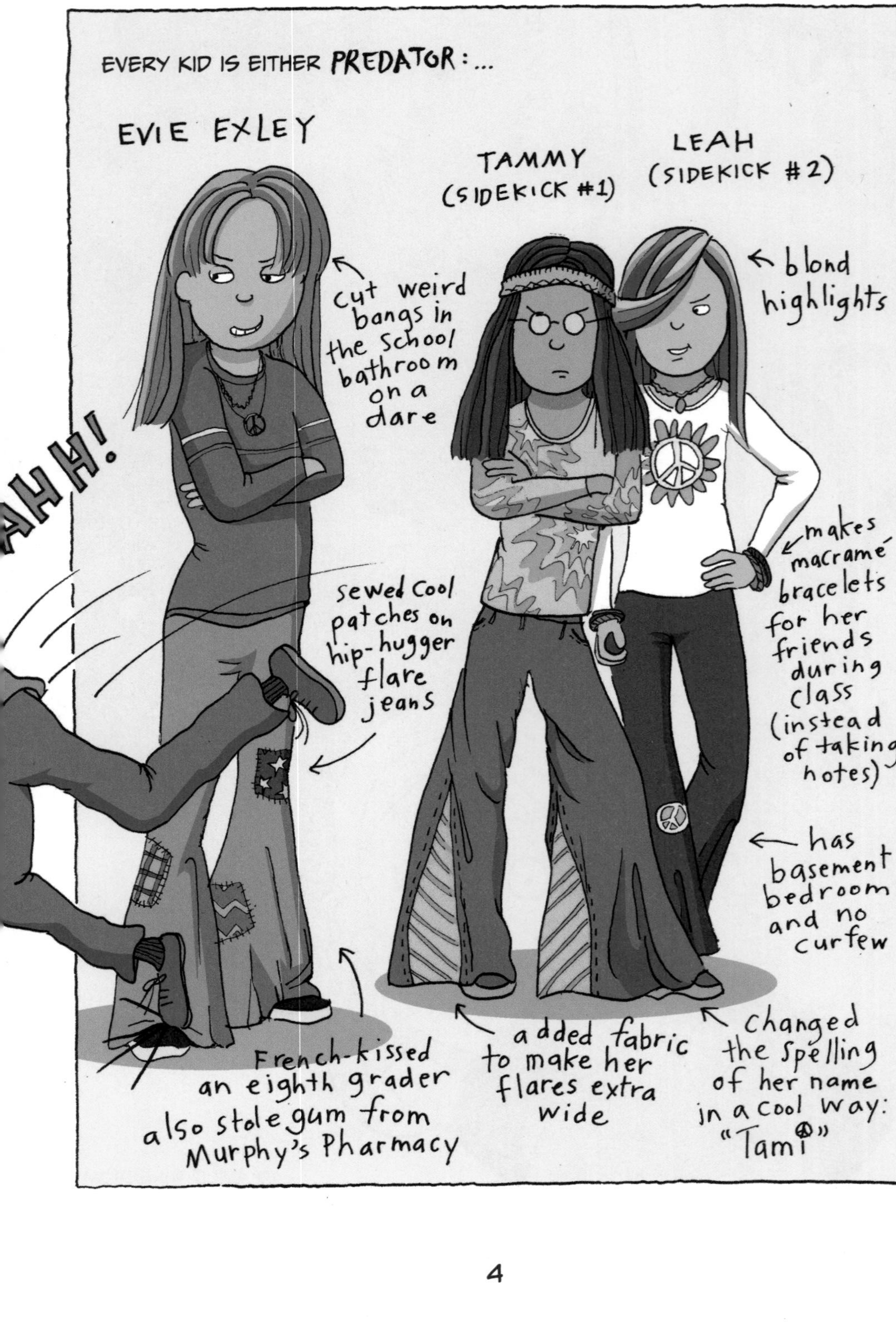
EVERY KID IS EITHER PREDATOR: ...
EVIE EXLEY
TAMMY (SIDEKICK #1)
LEAH (SIDEKICK #2)
AHH!
cut weird bangs in the school bathroom on a dare
sewed cool patches on hip-hugger flare jeans
French-kissed an eighth grader also stole gum from Murphy's Pharmacy
added fabric to make her flares extra wide
blond highlights
makes macramé bracelets for her friends during class (instead of taking notes)
has basement bedroom and no curfew
changed the spelling of her name in a cool way: "Tami"

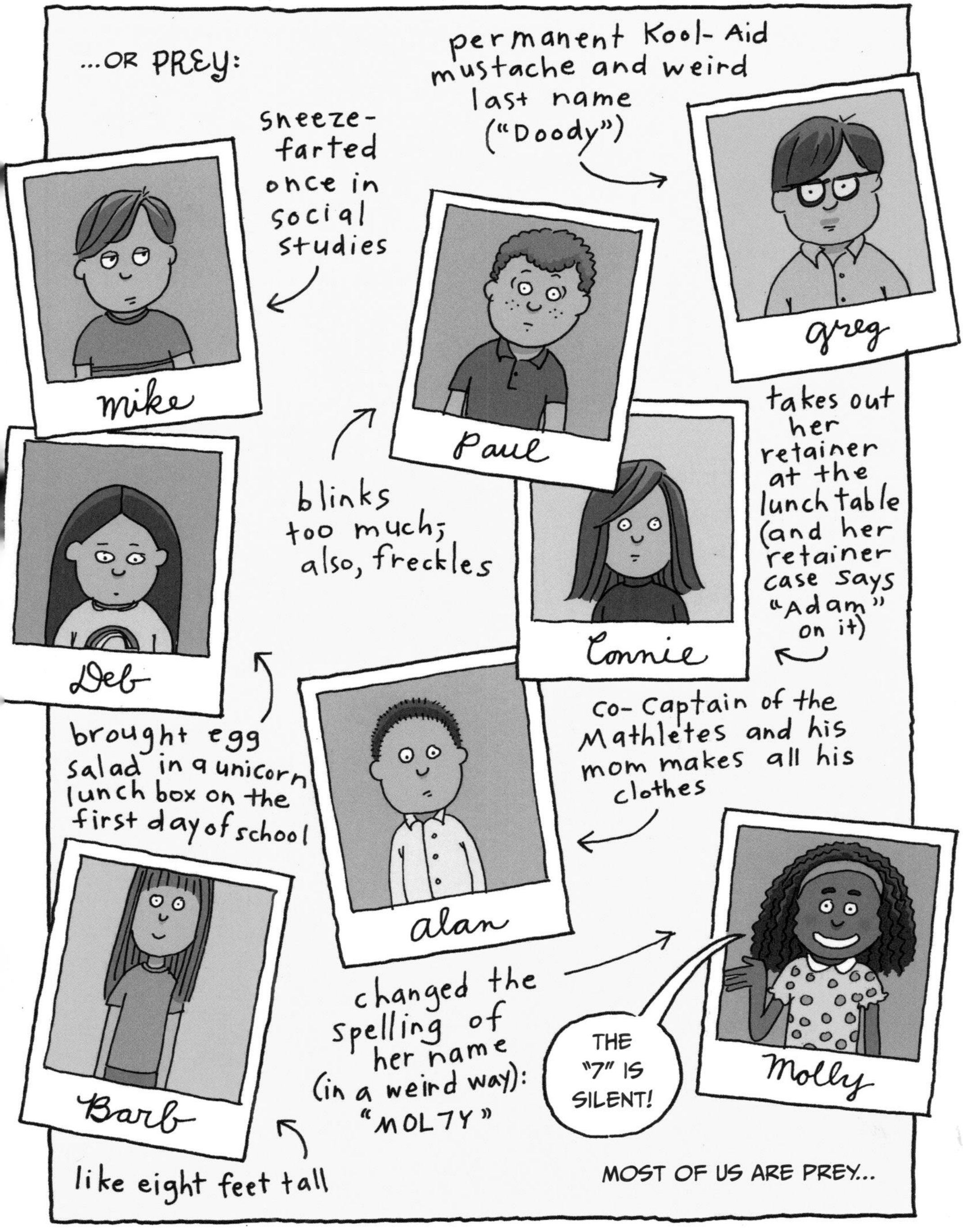
...OR PREY:
sneeze-farted once in social studies
mike
permanent Kool-Aid mustache and weird last name ("Doody")
greg
Paul
blinks too much; also, freckles
takes out her retainer at the lunch table (and her retainer case says "Adam" on it)
Deb
Connie
brought egg salad in a unicorn lunch box on the first day of school
co-captain of the Mathletes and his mom makes all his clothes
alan
changed the spelling of her name (in a weird way): "MOL7Y"
THE "7" IS SILENT!
Molly
Barb
like eight feet tall
MOST OF US ARE PREY...

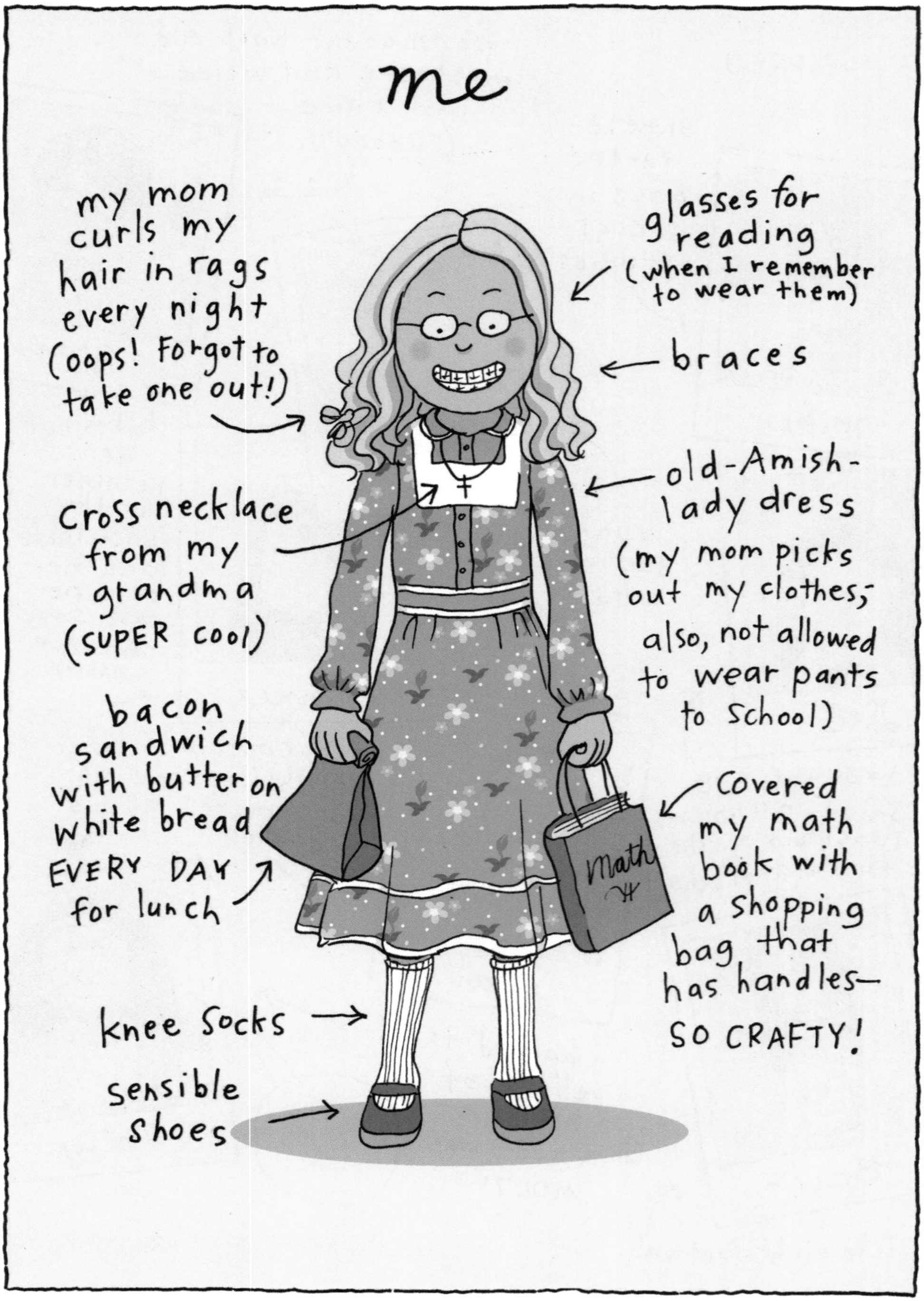
me
my mom curls my hair in rags every night (oops! Forgot to take one out!)
glasses for reading (when I remember to wear them)
braces
Cross necklace from my grandma (SUPER cool)
old-Amish-lady dress (my mom picks out my clothes; also, not allowed to wear pants to school)
bacon sandwich with butter on white bread EVERY DAY for lunch
Covered my math book with a shopping bag that has handles—SO CRAFTY!
Math
knee socks
sensible shoes

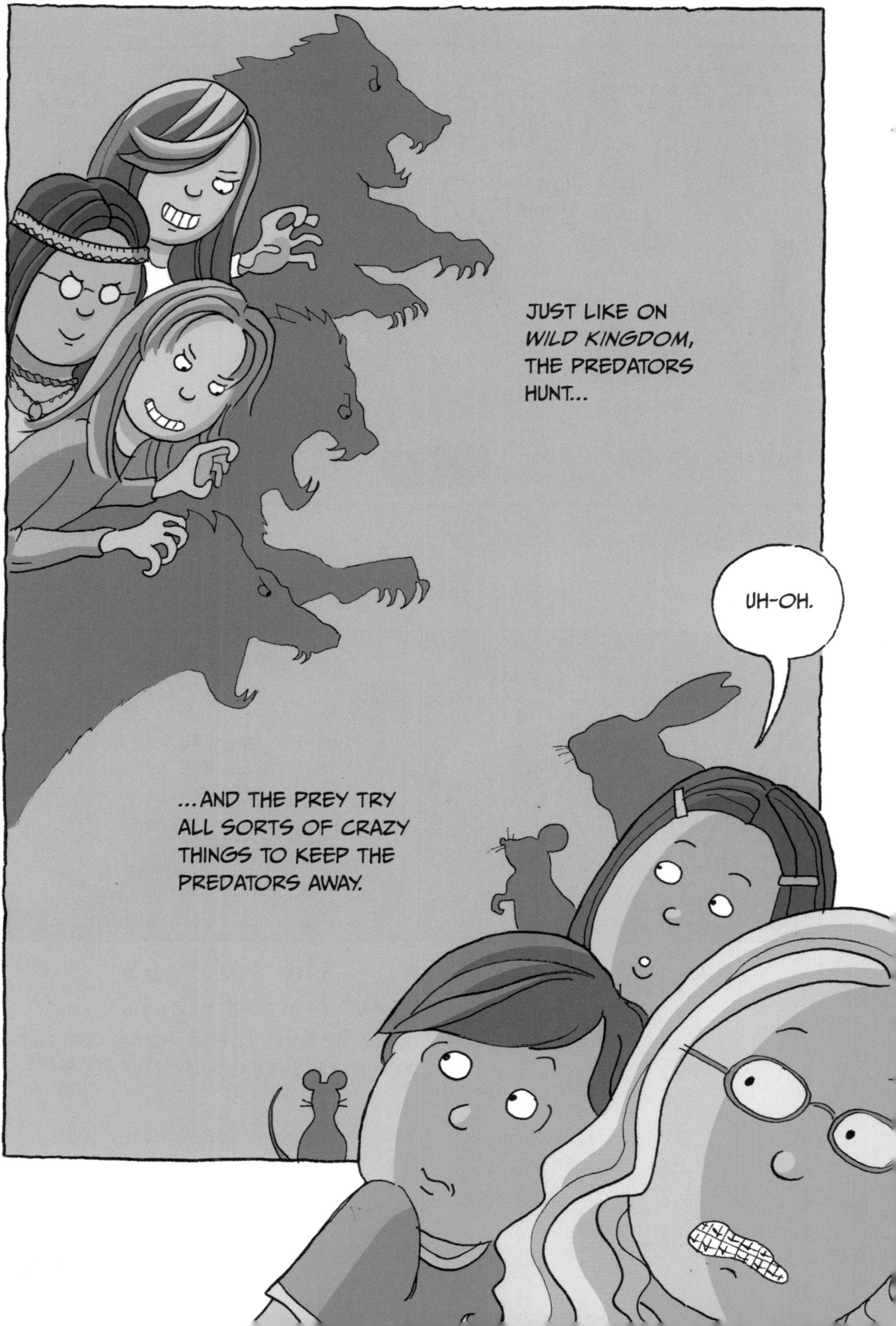
JUST LIKE ON *WILD KINGDOM*, THE PREDATORS HUNT...
...AND THE PREY TRY ALL SORTS OF CRAZY THINGS TO KEEP THE PREDATORS AWAY.
UH-OH.

SOME USE CAMOUFLAGE.

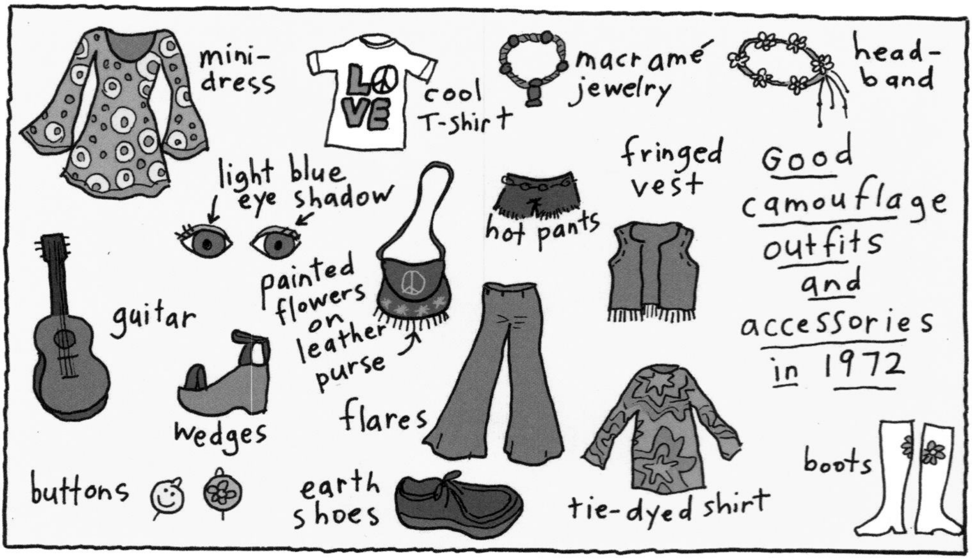
mini-dress
LOVE
cool T-shirt
macramé jewelry
head-band
light blue eye shadow
fringed vest
hot pants
Good camouflage outfits and accessories in 1972
guitar
painted flowers on leather purse
wedges
flares
buttons
earth shoes
tie-dyed shirt
boots

OTHERS USE PREDATOR CONFUSION.*

How it works in the wild:

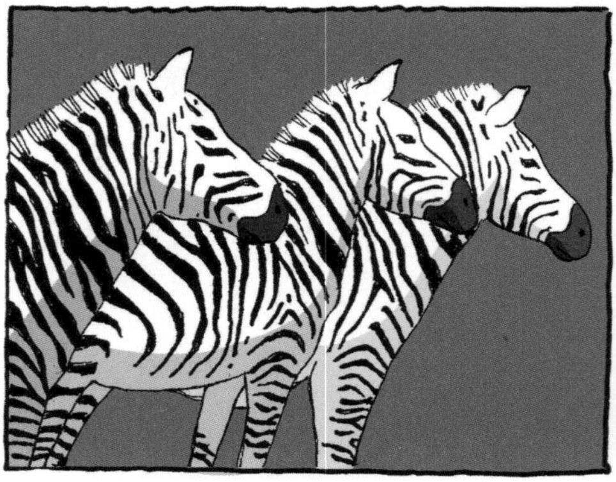

Zebras

How it works in school:

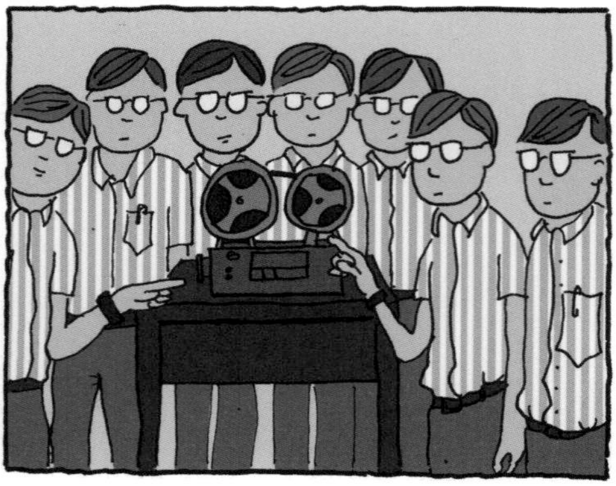

The AV Club

("AV" stands for "Audio visual." Like, before there were computer geniuses, there were these guys.)

*WHEN PREY LOOK THE SAME, THE PREDATORS CAN'T SINGLE OUT JUST ONE TO ATTACK.

SOMETIMES, TO ESCAPE, THEY STARTLE THE PREDATORS...

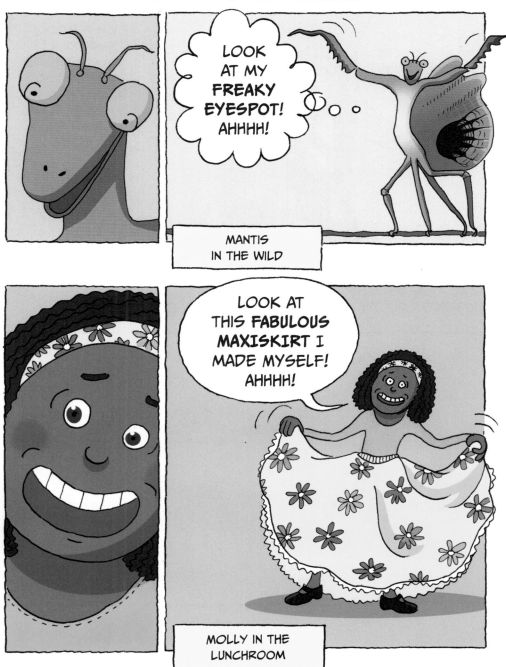

LOOK AT MY **FREAKY EYESPOT!** AHHHH!

MANTIS IN THE WILD

LOOK AT THIS **FABULOUS MAXISKIRT** I MADE MYSELF! AHHHH!

MOLLY IN THE LUNCHROOM

...OR DISTRACT THEM.

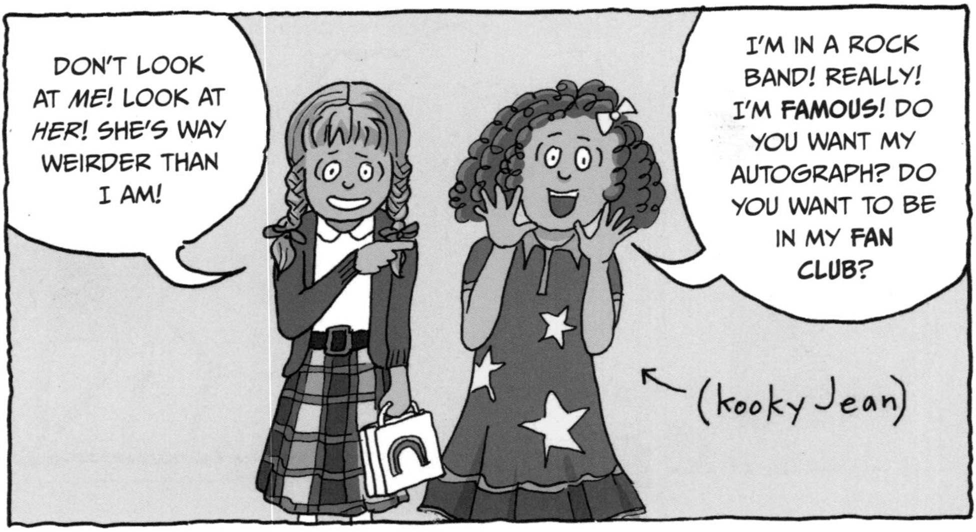
DON'T LOOK AT *ME*! LOOK AT *HER*! SHE'S WAY WEIRDER THAN I AM!
I'M IN A ROCK BAND! REALLY! I'M **FAMOUS**! DO YOU WANT MY AUTOGRAPH? DO YOU WANT TO BE IN MY **FAN CLUB**?
(kooky Jean)

SOME EVEN THROW UP WHEN THEY'RE SCARED (TO GROSS OUT THE PREDATORS).

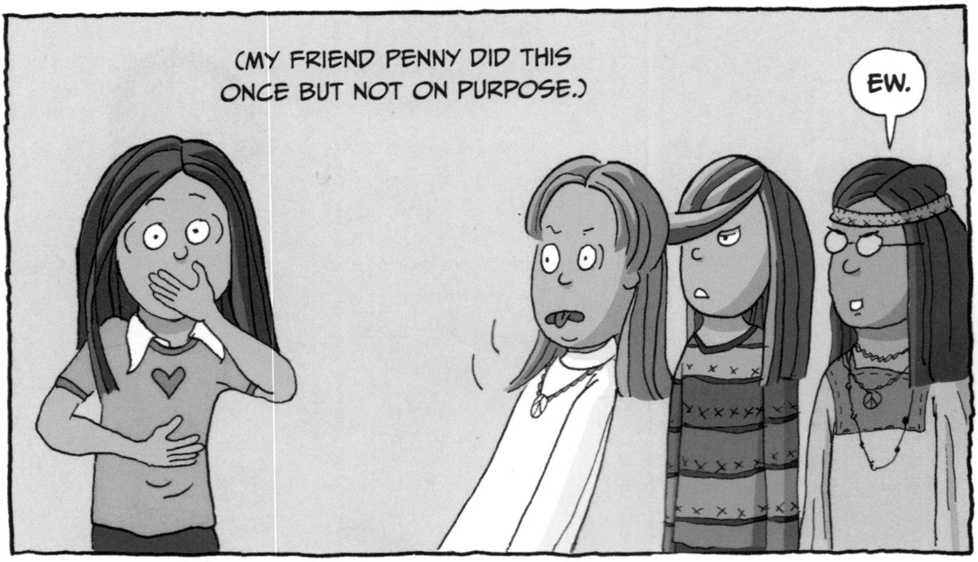
(MY FRIEND PENNY DID THIS ONCE BUT NOT ON PURPOSE.)
EW.

I HAVE A DIFFERENT TACTIC, THOUGH.

I PLAY DEAD.
NOT DEAD LIKE →
BUT DEAD*ISH*.
I JUST ACT SO BORING,
THE PREDATORS LOSE INTEREST IN
ME AND GO AFTER SOMEONE ELSE.

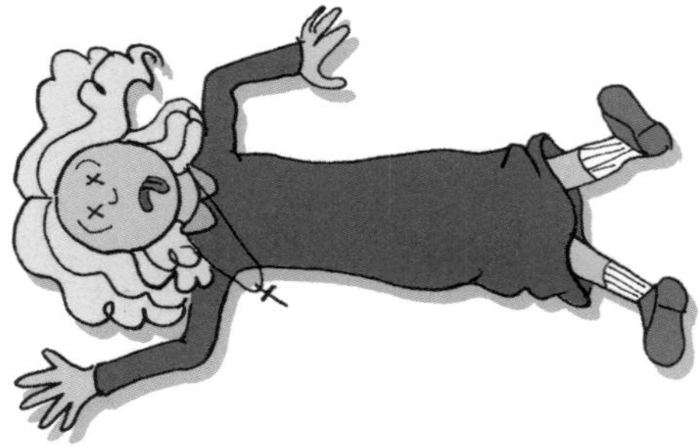

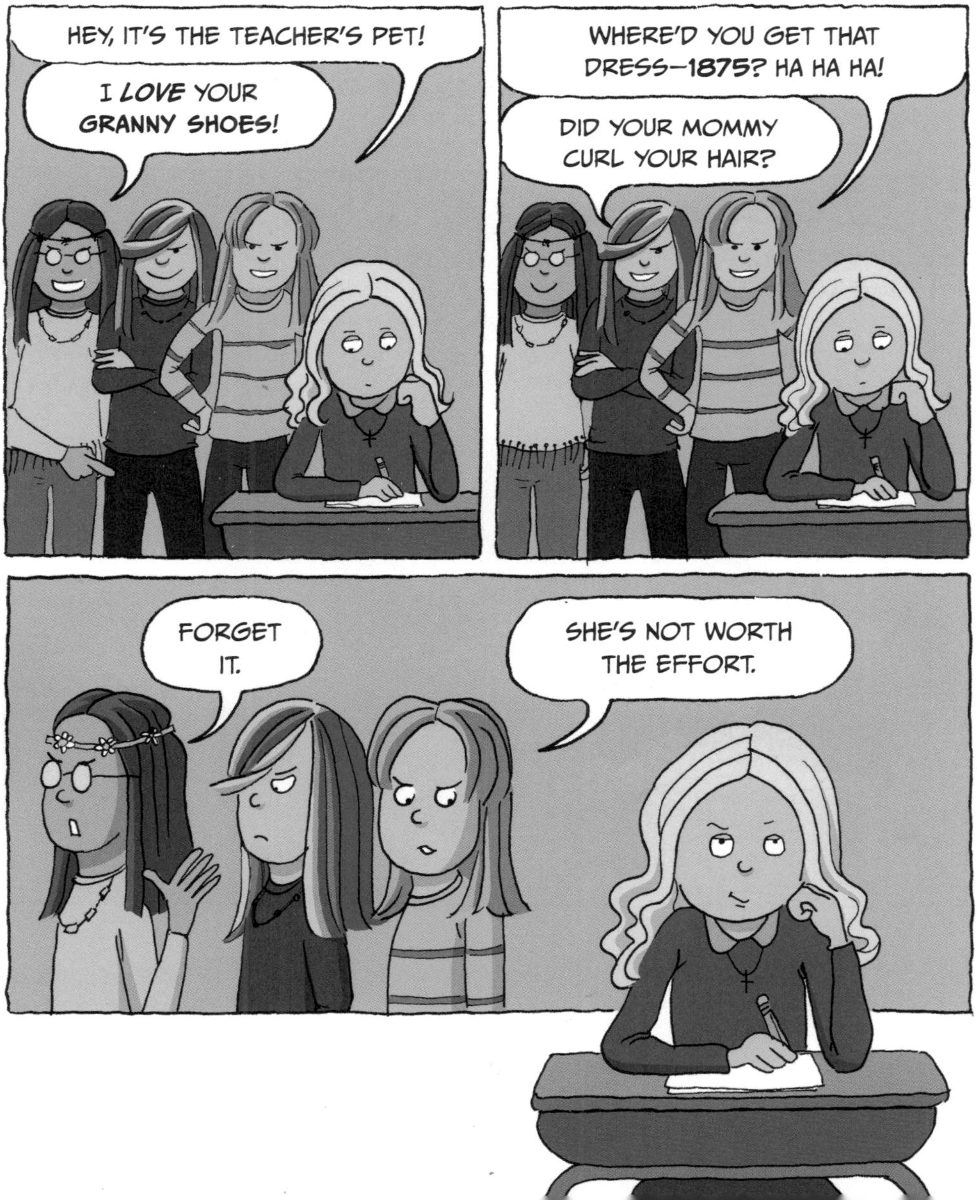
HEY, IT'S THE TEACHER'S PET!
I *LOVE* YOUR GRANNY SHOES!
WHERE'D YOU GET THAT DRESS—1875? HA HA HA!
DID YOUR MOMMY CURL YOUR HAIR?
FORGET IT.
SHE'S NOT WORTH THE EFFORT.

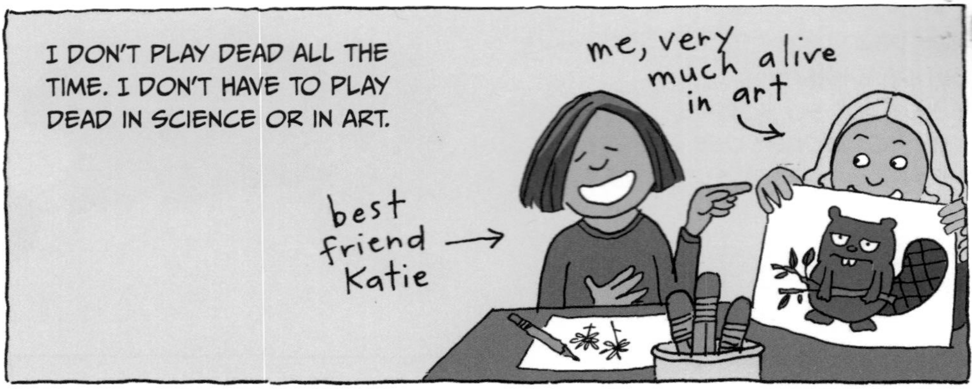

I DON'T PLAY DEAD ALL THE TIME. I DON'T HAVE TO PLAY DEAD IN SCIENCE OR IN ART.
me, very much alive in art
best friend Katie

MOST IMPORTANT OF ALL, I DON'T HAVE TO PLAY DEAD IN ENGLISH: MY VERY FAVORITE CLASS WITH MY VERY FAVORITE TEACHER, MRS. SCHULZ.

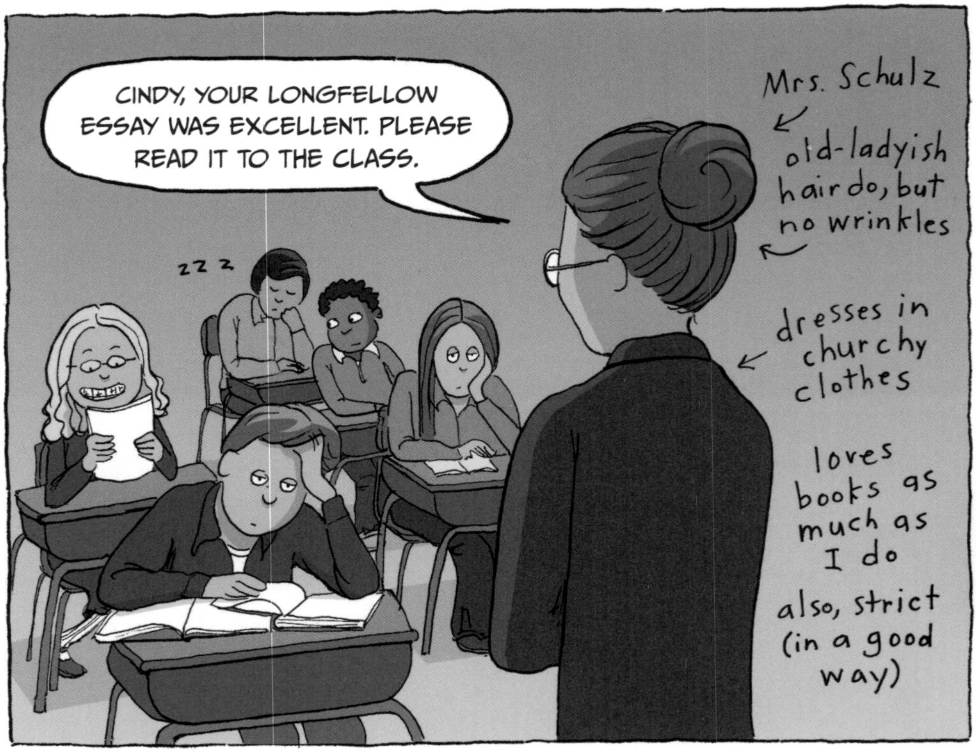

CINDY, YOUR LONGFELLOW ESSAY WAS EXCELLENT. PLEASE READ IT TO THE CLASS.
Mrs. Schulz
old-ladyish hairdo, but no wrinkles
dresses in churchy clothes
loves books as much as I do
also, strict (in a good way)
ZZZ

THANK GOODNESS I DON'T PLAY DEAD IN FRONT OF MRS. SCHULZ.
ESPECIALLY TODAY.

Chapter 2

I HAVE AN ORTHODONTIST APPOINTMENT. MY MOM SAYS SHE'LL PICK ME UP RIGHT AFTER SCHOOL.

SHE WON'T. SHE'LL BE LATE.

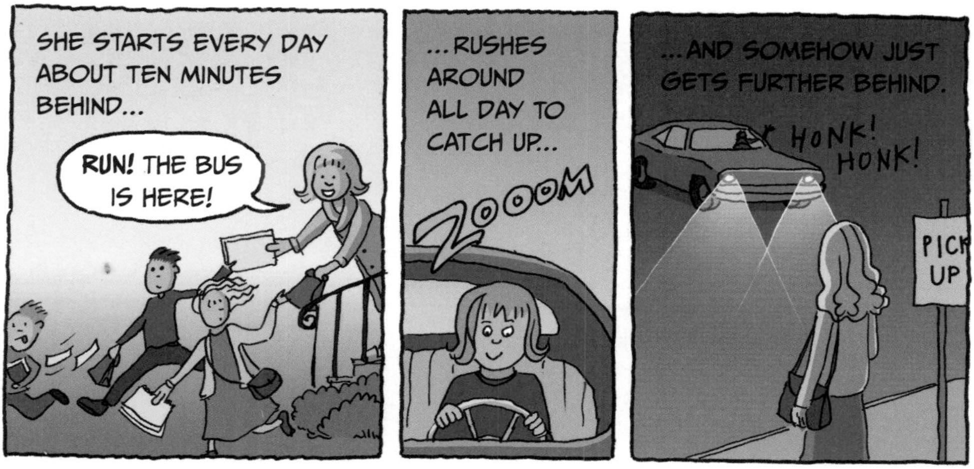
SHE STARTS EVERY DAY ABOUT TEN MINUTES BEHIND...
RUN! THE BUS IS HERE!
...RUSHES AROUND ALL DAY TO CATCH UP...
ZOOOM
...AND SOMEHOW JUST GETS FURTHER BEHIND.
HONK! HONK!
PICK UP

BUT MOST OF THE TIME, BEING THE LAST KID TO GET PICKED UP ISN'T THAT BAD.

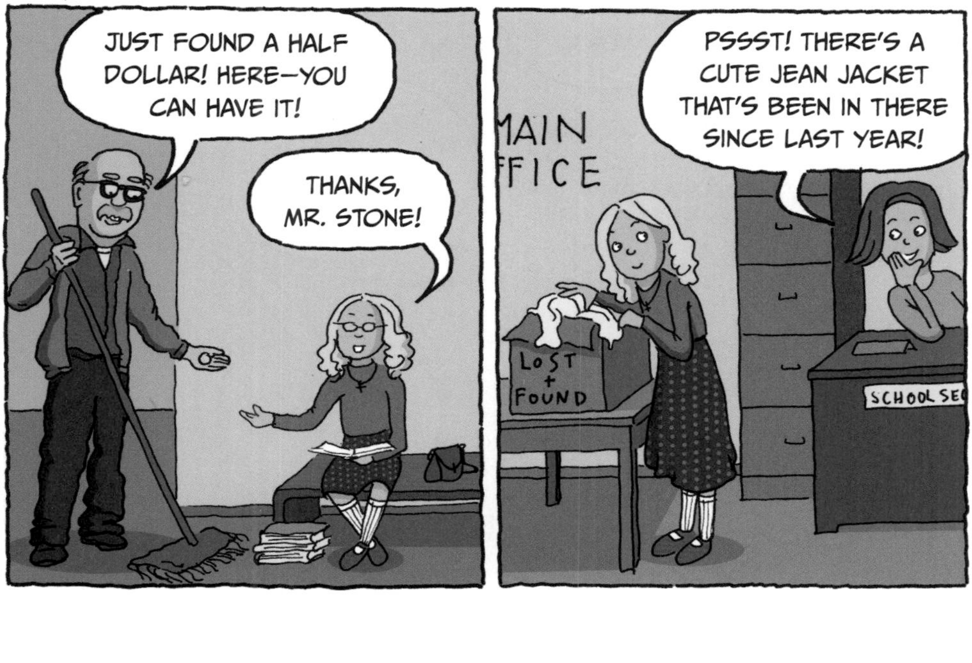
JUST FOUND A HALF DOLLAR! HERE—YOU CAN HAVE IT!
THANKS, MR. STONE!
PSSST! THERE'S A CUTE JEAN JACKET THAT'S BEEN IN THERE SINCE LAST YEAR!
LOST + FOUND

TODAY, IT JUST MIGHT BE THE BEST THING THAT'S EVER HAPPENED TO ME.

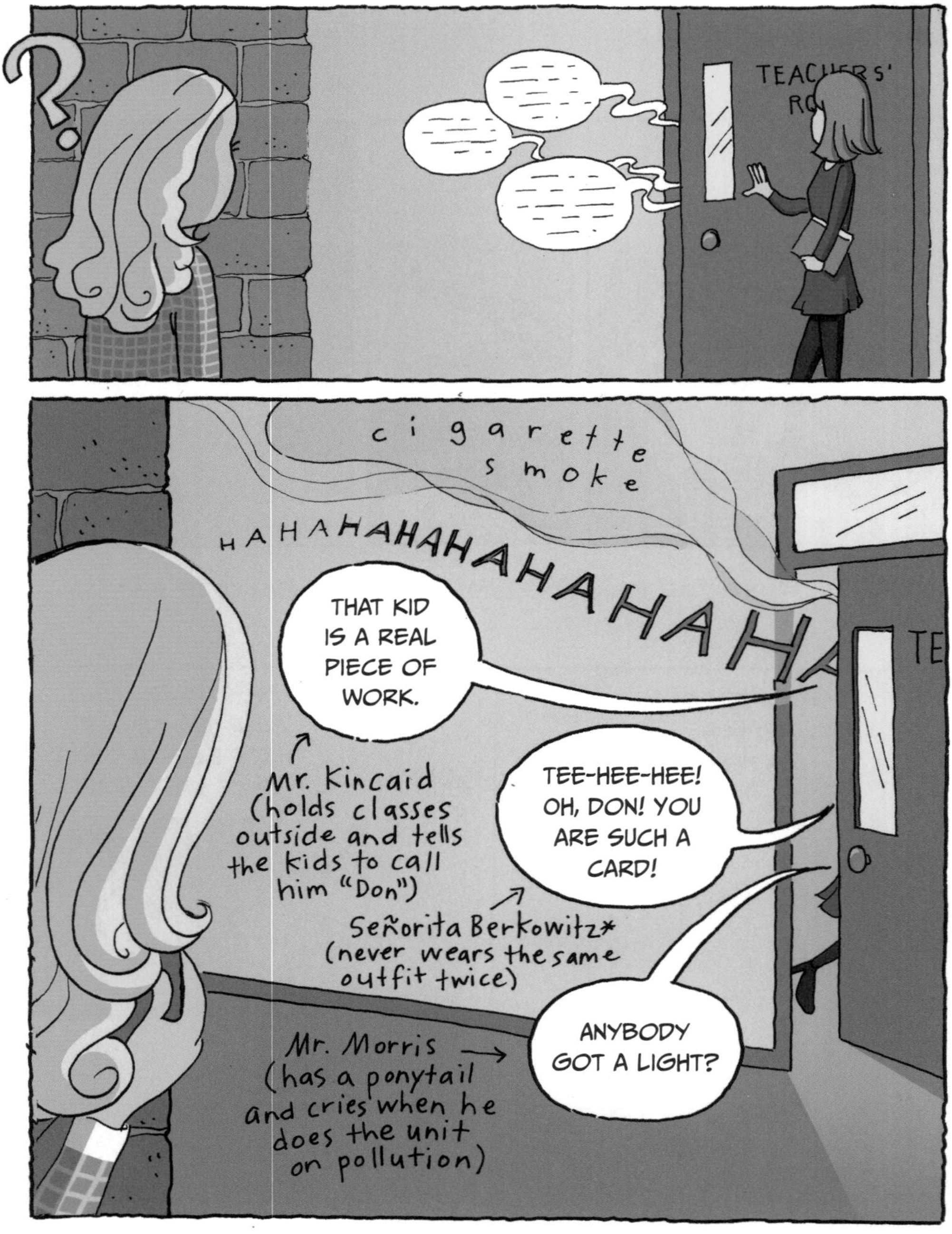
?
cigarette smoke
HAHAHAHAHAHAHAHAHA
THAT KID IS A REAL PIECE OF WORK.
Mr. Kincaid (holds classes outside and tells the kids to call him "Don")
TEE-HEE-HEE! OH, DON! YOU ARE SUCH A CARD!
Señorita Berkowitz* (never wears the same outfit twice)
ANYBODY GOT A LIGHT?
Mr. Morris (has a ponytail and cries when he does the unit on pollution)

*OR MADEMOISELLE BERKOWITZ IF YOU TAKE FRENCH

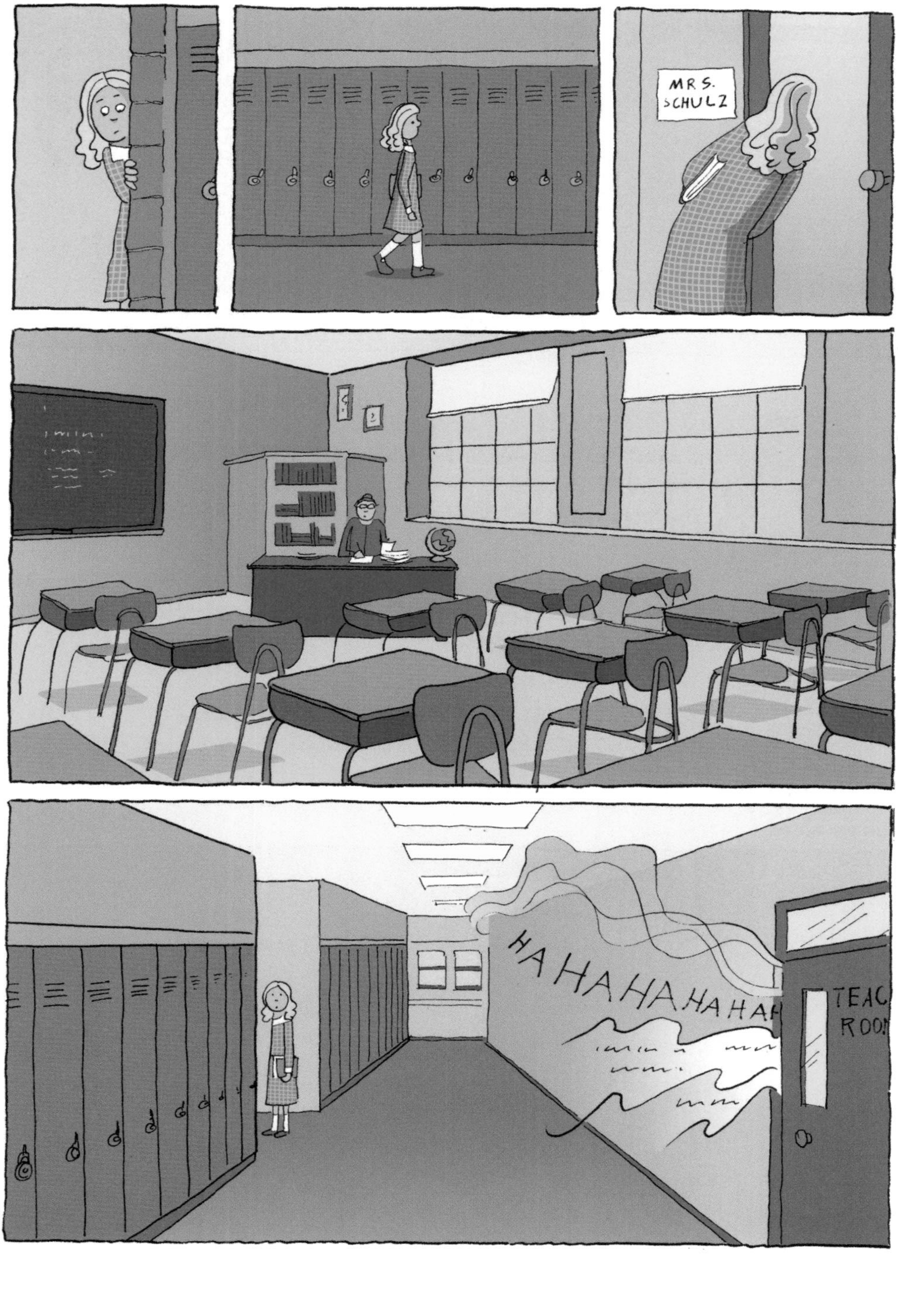
MRS.
SCHULZ
HAHAHAHAHAH
TEAC
ROOM

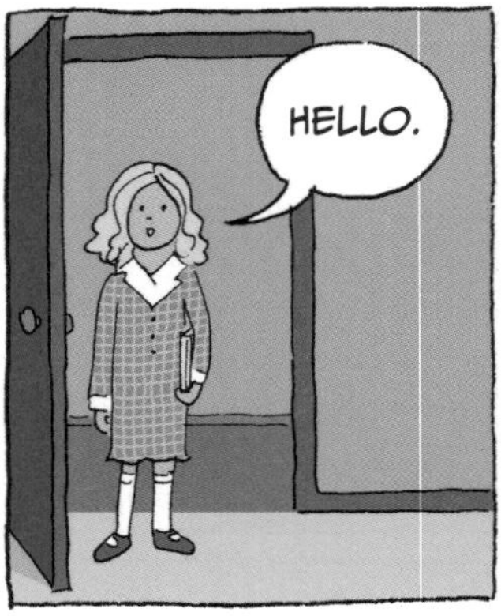
HELLO.

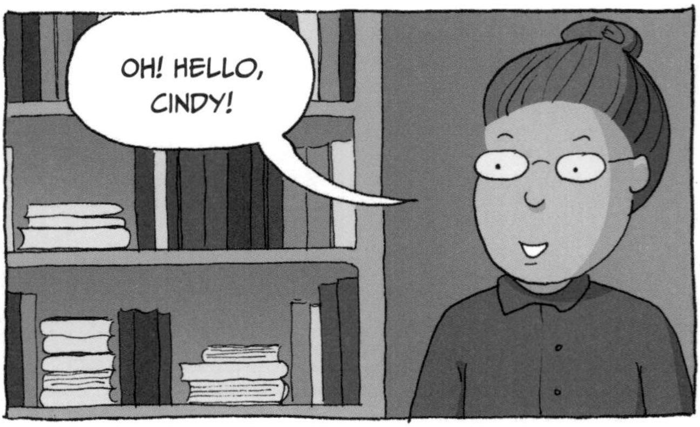
OH! HELLO, CINDY!

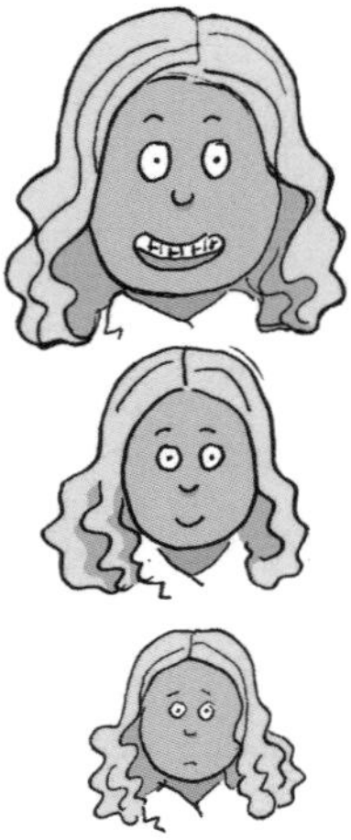

I WANT TO TELL MRS. SCHULZ THAT SHE IS MY VERY FAVORITE TEACHER.
THAT ENGLISH IS THE BEST PART OF EVERY DAY.

THAT I LOVE MADELEINE L'ENGLE AS MUCH AS SHE DOES.
THAT I MEMORIZE ALL THE SUPER NICE COMMENTS SHE WRITES ON MY PAPERS.

BUT I DON'T TELL HER ANY OF THOSE THINGS.
I JUST STAND THERE FEELING WEIRD.

SAYING NOTHING.

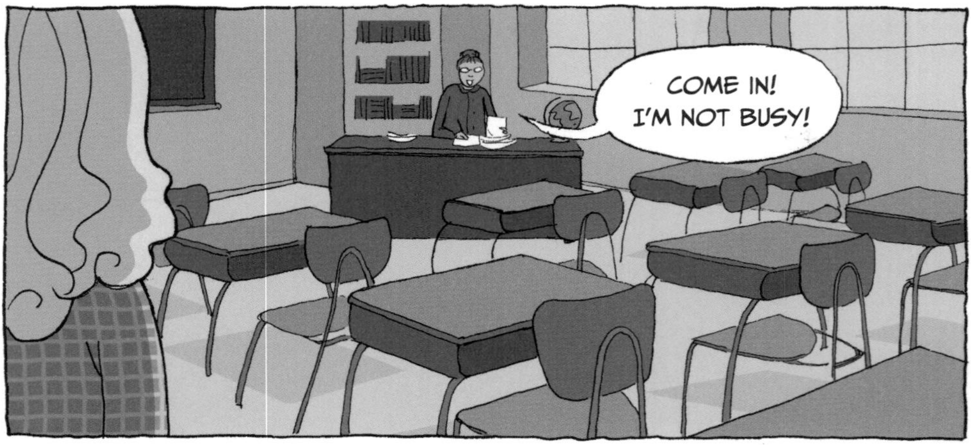
COME IN!
I'M NOT BUSY!

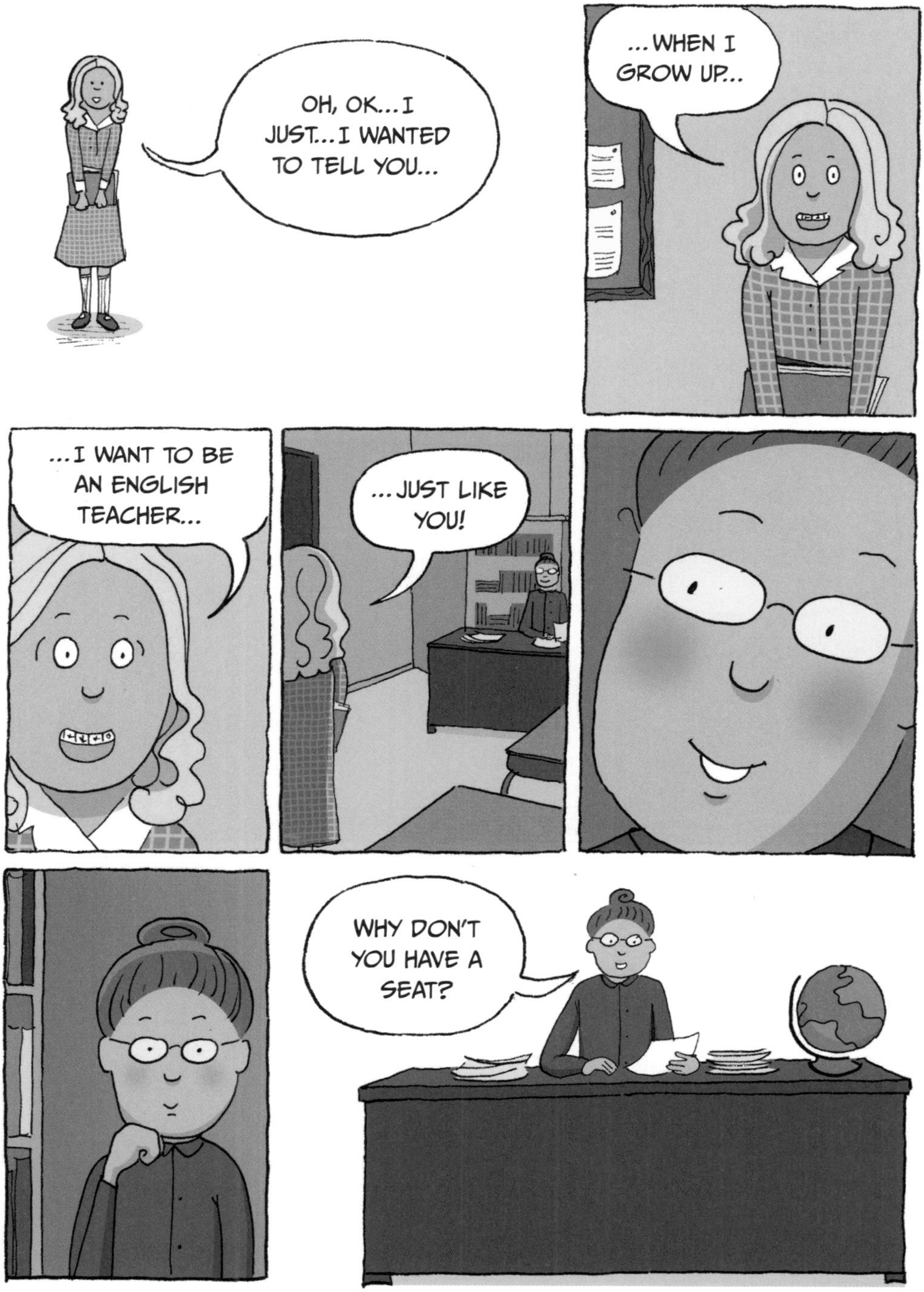
OH, OK... I JUST... I WANTED TO TELL YOU...
...WHEN I GROW UP...
...I WANT TO BE AN ENGLISH TEACHER...
...JUST LIKE YOU!
WHY DON'T YOU HAVE A SEAT?

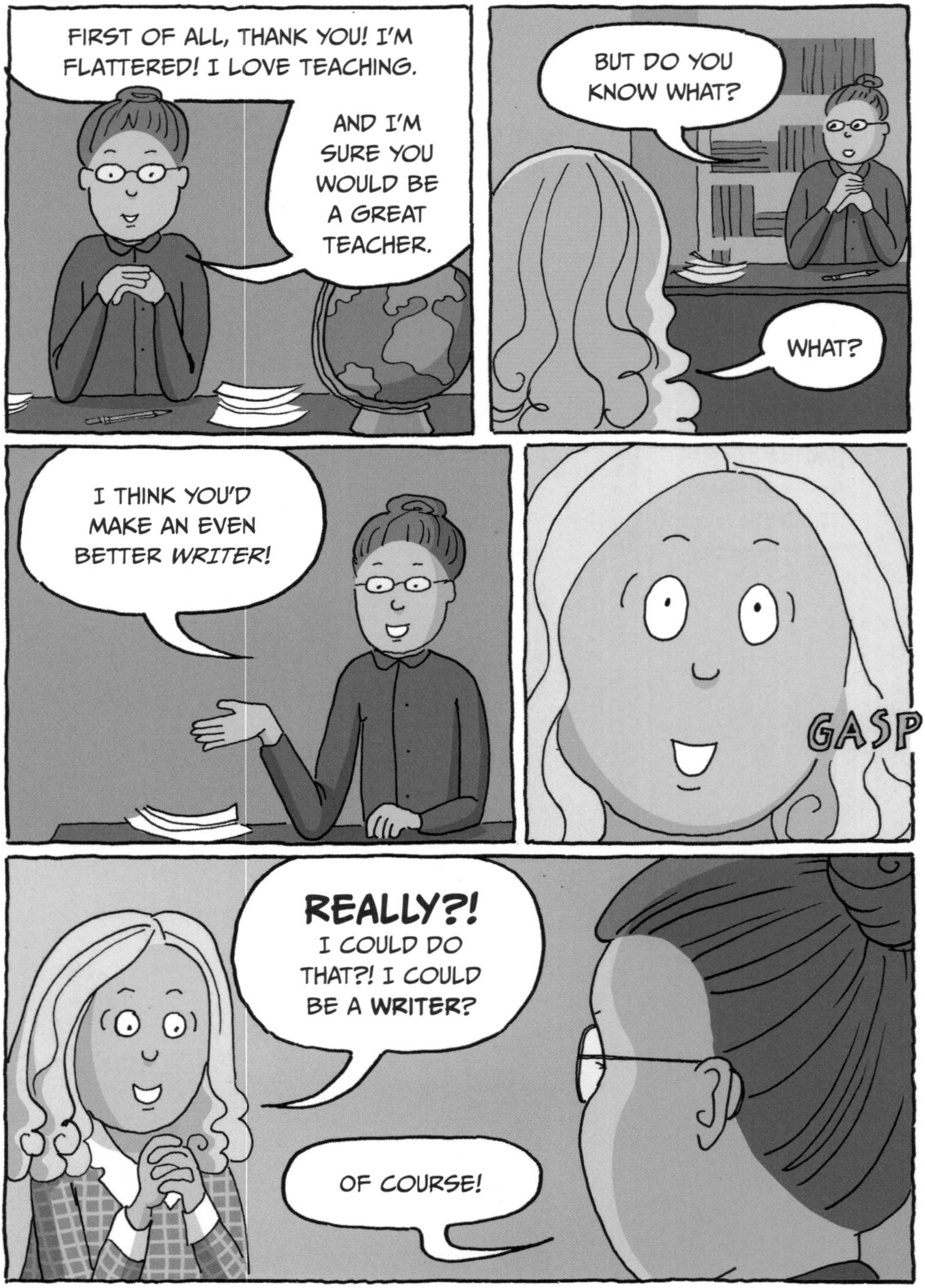
FIRST OF ALL, THANK YOU! I'M FLATTERED! I LOVE TEACHING.
AND I'M SURE YOU WOULD BE A GREAT TEACHER.
BUT DO YOU KNOW WHAT?
WHAT?
I THINK YOU'D MAKE AN EVEN BETTER *WRITER*!
GASP
REALLY?! I COULD DO THAT?! I COULD BE A **WRITER**?
OF COURSE!

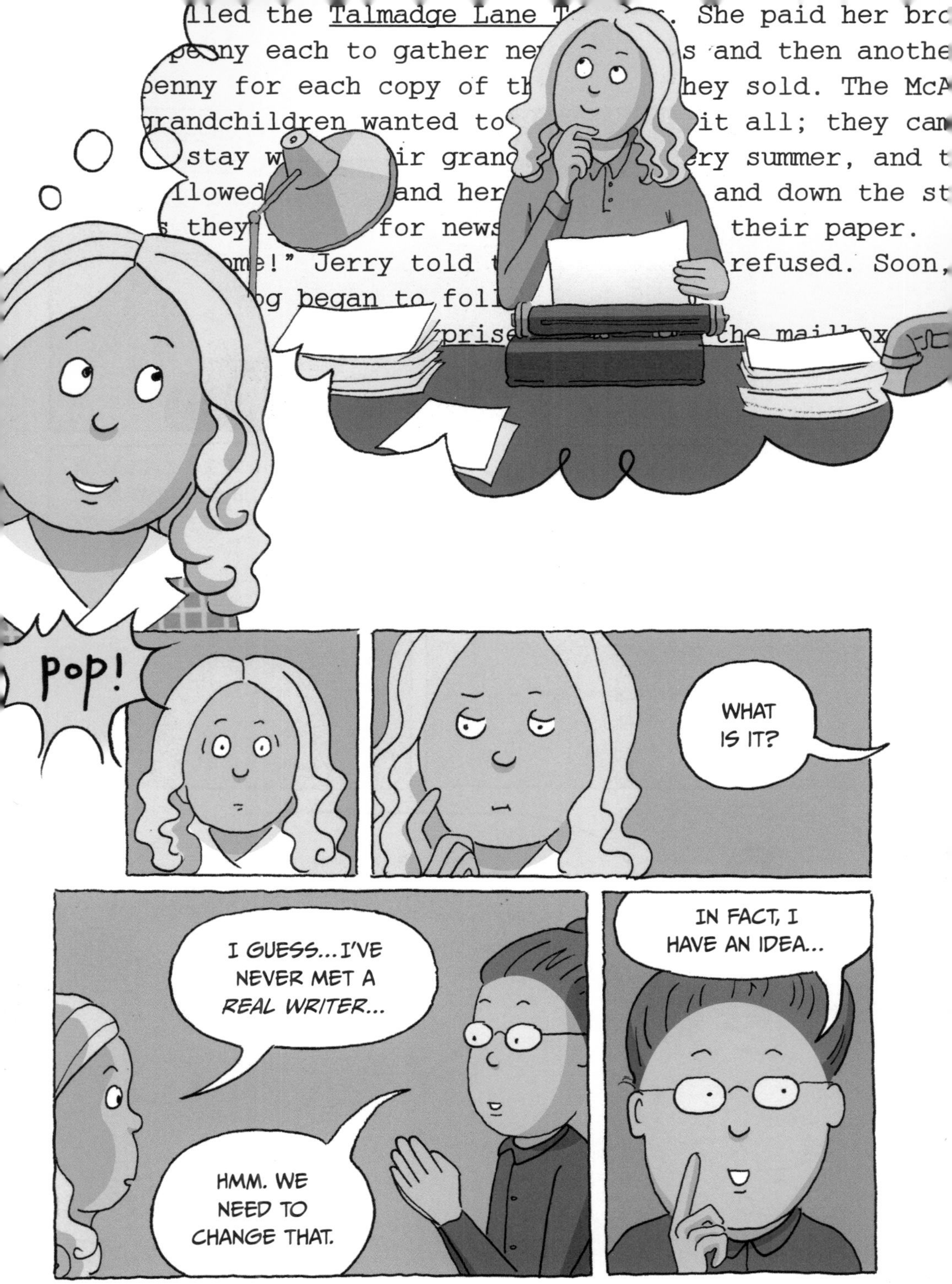

POP!
WHAT IS IT?
I GUESS...I'VE NEVER MET A *REAL WRITER*...
HMM. WE NEED TO CHANGE THAT.
IN FACT, I HAVE AN IDEA...

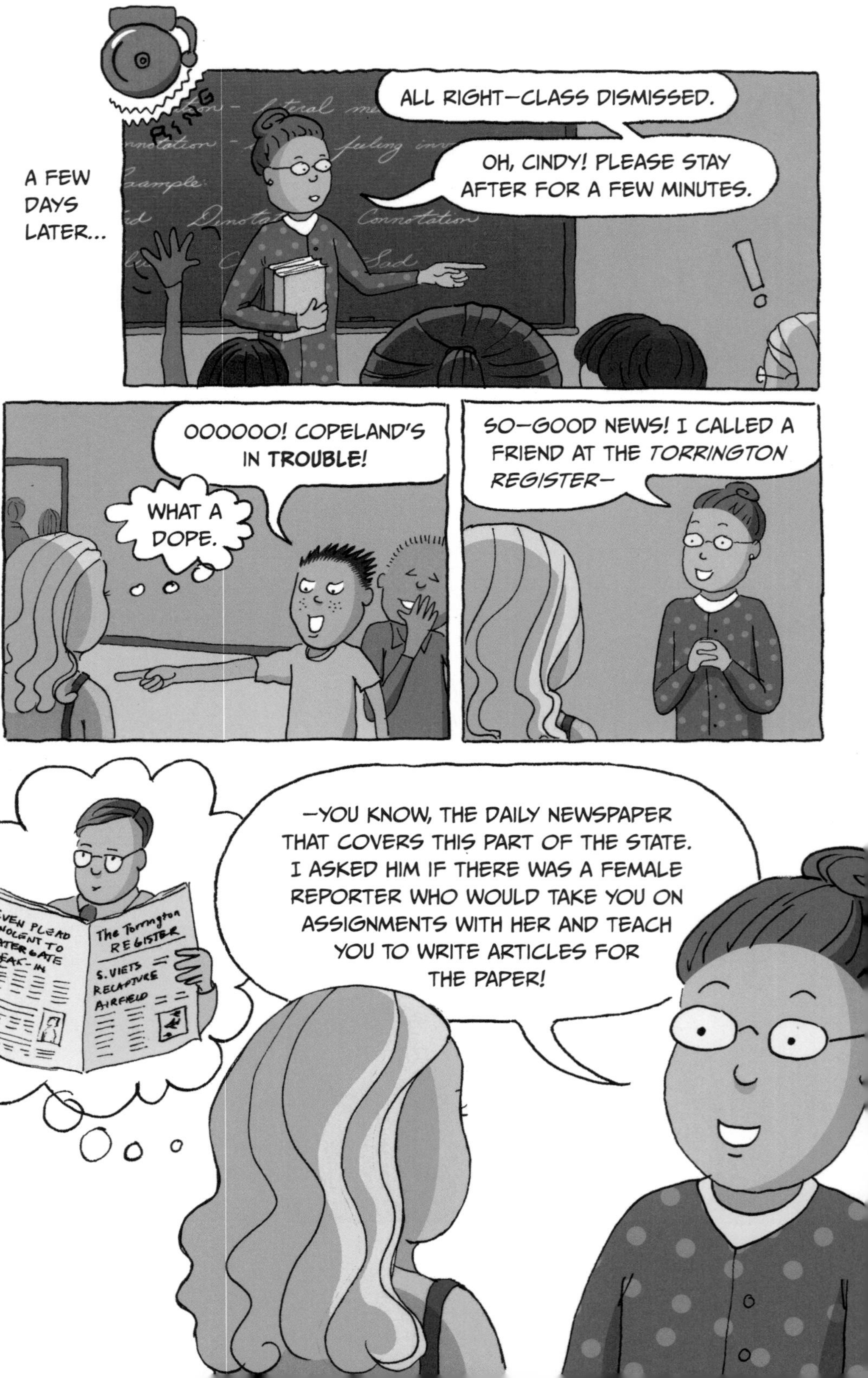
RING
A FEW DAYS LATER...
ALL RIGHT—CLASS DISMISSED.
OH, CINDY! PLEASE STAY AFTER FOR A FEW MINUTES.
!
OOOOOO! COPELAND'S IN **TROUBLE**!
WHAT A DOPE.
SO—GOOD NEWS! I CALLED A FRIEND AT THE *TORRINGTON REGISTER*—
—YOU KNOW, THE DAILY NEWSPAPER THAT COVERS THIS PART OF THE STATE. I ASKED HIM IF THERE WAS A FEMALE REPORTER WHO WOULD TAKE YOU ON ASSIGNMENTS WITH HER AND TEACH YOU TO WRITE ARTICLES FOR THE PAPER!
SEVEN PLEAD INNOCENT TO WATERGATE BREAK-IN
The Torrington REGISTER
S. VIETS RECAPTURE AIRFIELD

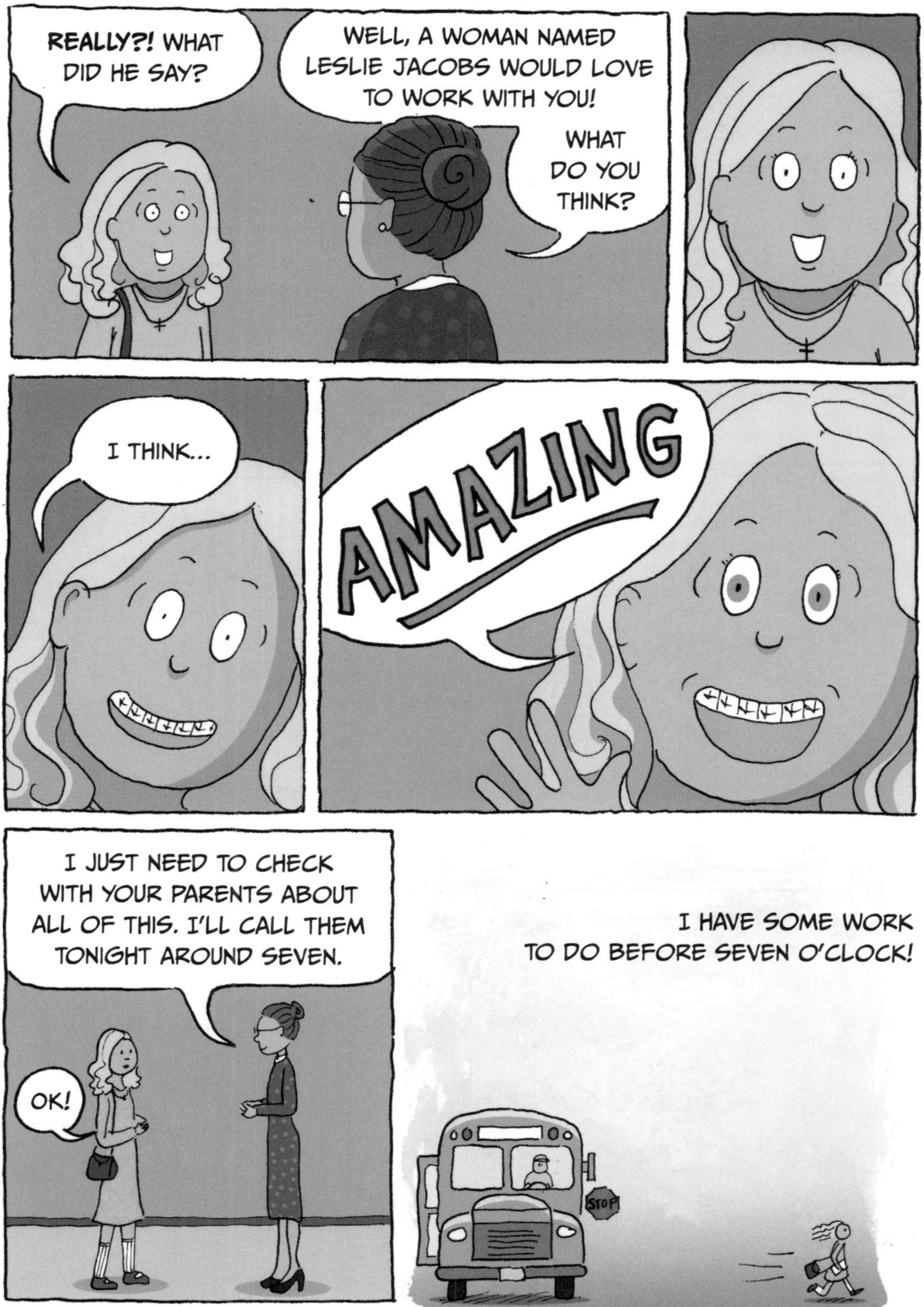
REALLY?! WHAT DID HE SAY?
WELL, A WOMAN NAMED LESLIE JACOBS WOULD LOVE TO WORK WITH YOU!
WHAT DO YOU THINK?
I THINK...
AMAZING
I JUST NEED TO CHECK WITH YOUR PARENTS ABOUT ALL OF THIS. I'LL CALL THEM TONIGHT AROUND SEVEN.
OK!
I HAVE SOME WORK TO DO BEFORE SEVEN O'CLOCK!
STOP

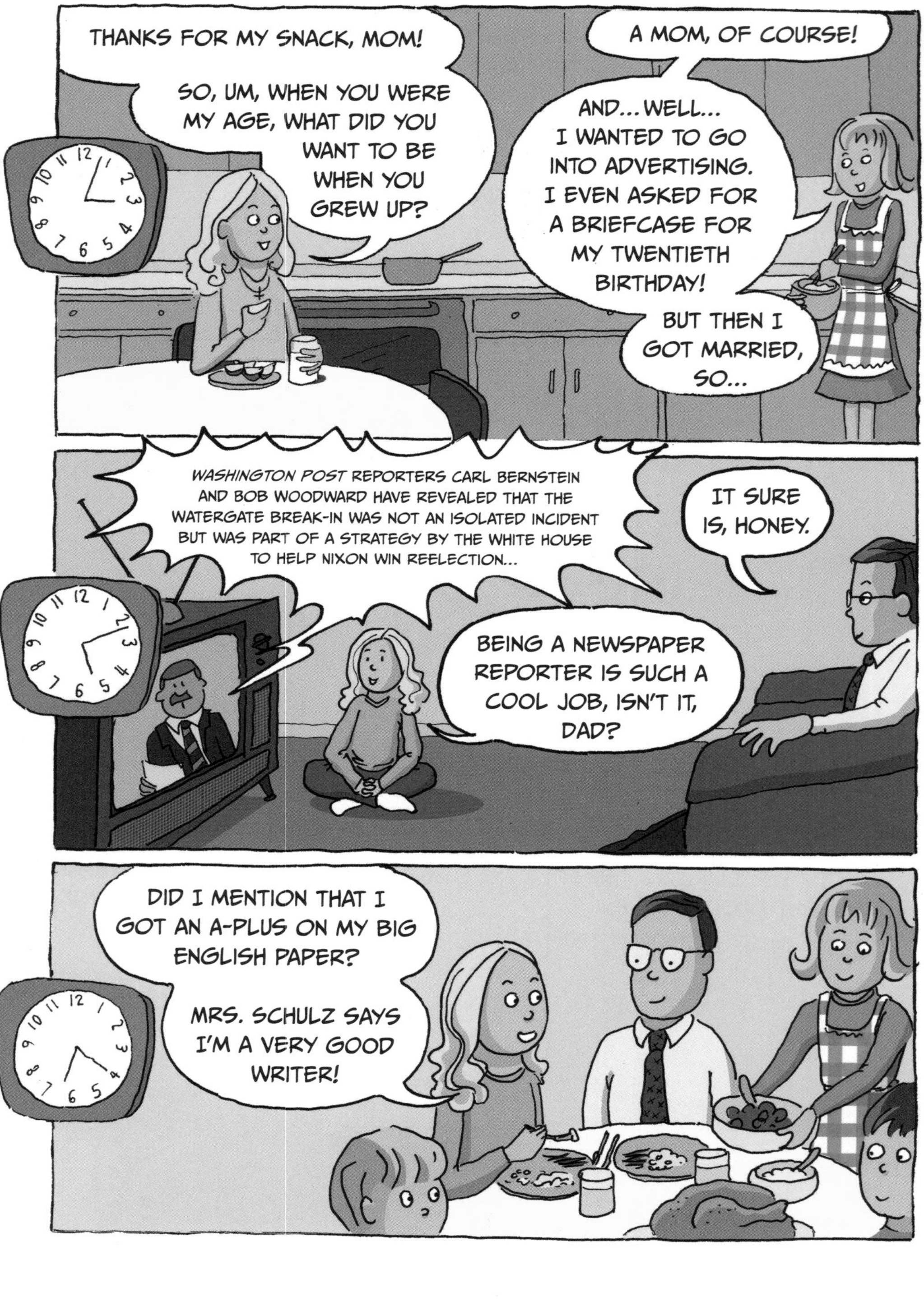
THANKS FOR MY SNACK, MOM!
SO, UM, WHEN YOU WERE MY AGE, WHAT DID YOU WANT TO BE WHEN YOU GREW UP?
A MOM, OF COURSE!
AND... WELL... I WANTED TO GO INTO ADVERTISING. I EVEN ASKED FOR A BRIEFCASE FOR MY TWENTIETH BIRTHDAY!
BUT THEN I GOT MARRIED, SO...
WASHINGTON POST REPORTERS CARL BERNSTEIN AND BOB WOODWARD HAVE REVEALED THAT THE WATERGATE BREAK-IN WAS NOT AN ISOLATED INCIDENT BUT WAS PART OF A STRATEGY BY THE WHITE HOUSE TO HELP NIXON WIN REELECTION...
BEING A NEWSPAPER REPORTER IS SUCH A COOL JOB, ISN'T IT, DAD?
IT SURE IS, HONEY.
DID I MENTION THAT I GOT AN A-PLUS ON MY BIG ENGLISH PAPER?
MRS. SCHULZ SAYS I'M A VERY GOOD WRITER!

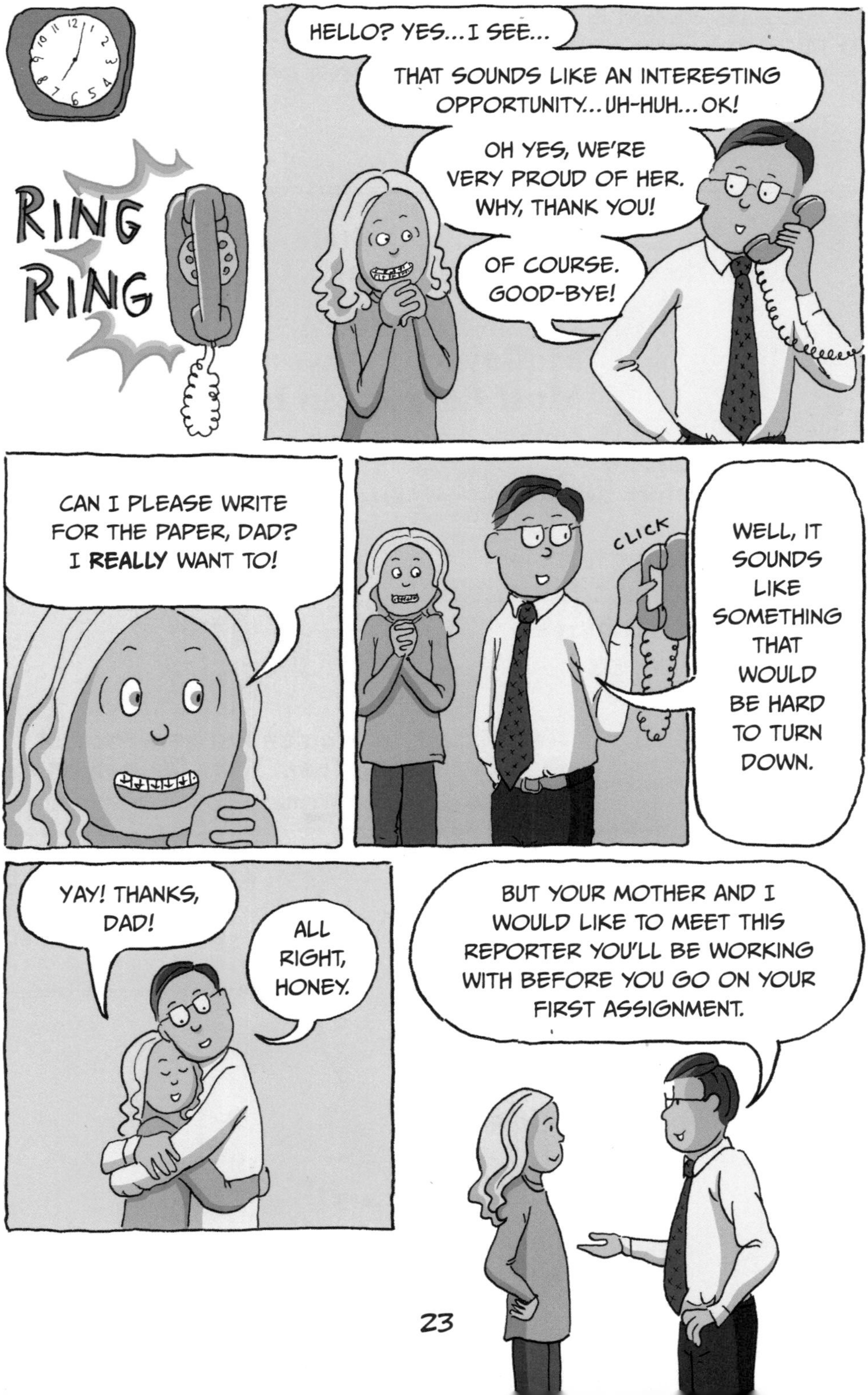
RING
RING
HELLO? YES...I SEE...
THAT SOUNDS LIKE AN INTERESTING OPPORTUNITY...UH-HUH...OK!
OH YES, WE'RE VERY PROUD OF HER. WHY, THANK YOU!
OF COURSE. GOOD-BYE!
CAN I PLEASE WRITE FOR THE PAPER, DAD? I **REALLY** WANT TO!
CLICK
WELL, IT SOUNDS LIKE SOMETHING THAT WOULD BE HARD TO TURN DOWN.
YAY! THANKS, DAD!
ALL RIGHT, HONEY.
BUT YOUR MOTHER AND I WOULD LIKE TO MEET THIS REPORTER YOU'LL BE WORKING WITH BEFORE YOU GO ON YOUR FIRST ASSIGNMENT.

MY FIRST ASSIGNMENT IS **SIX ENTIRE DAYS** AWAY! SO I TRY TO GET READY BY READING AS MANY NEWSPAPERS AS I CAN... EVEN THOUGH I DON'T UNDERSTAND *EVERYTHING* I READ. (OR EVEN MOST OF IT.)

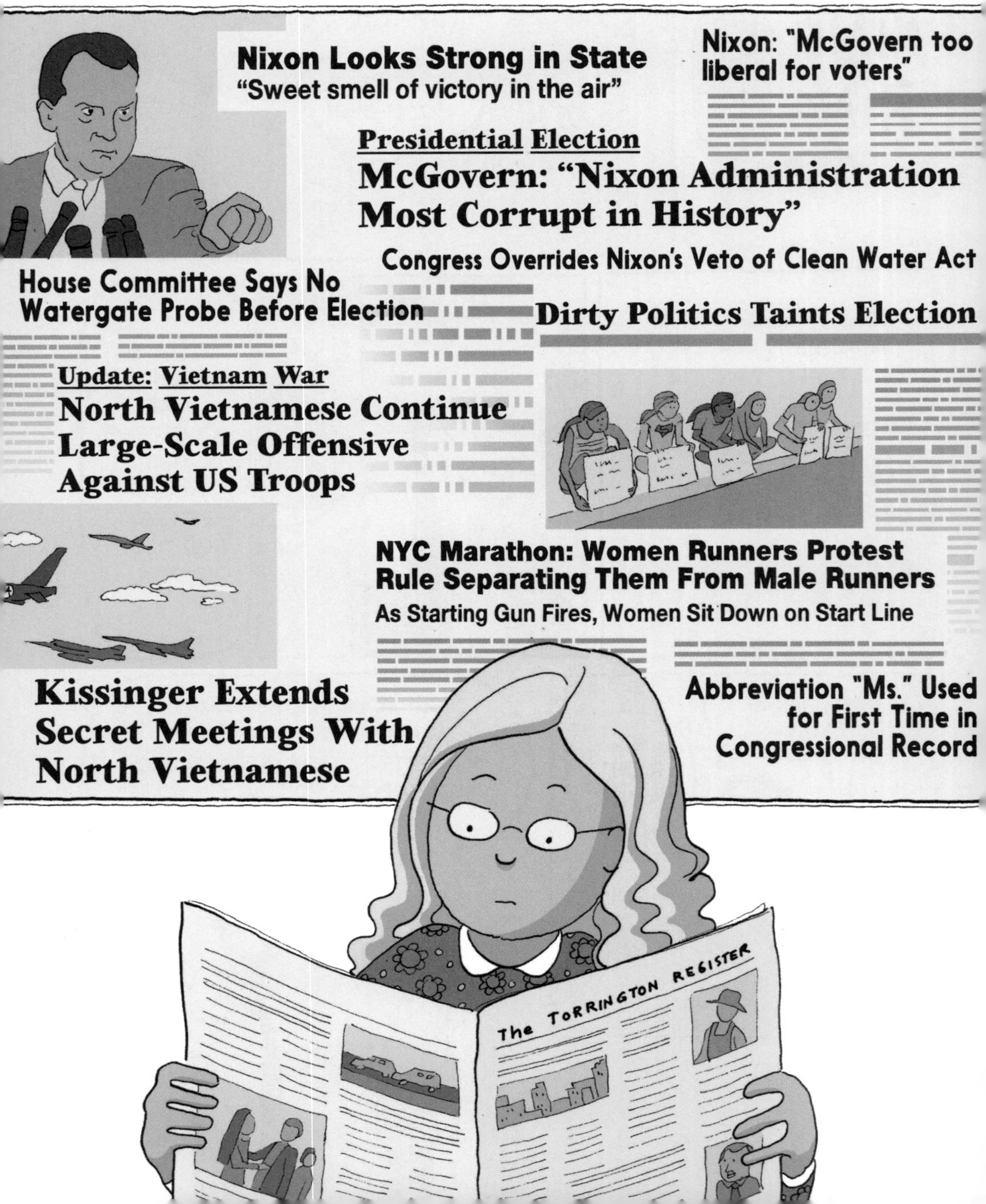
Nixon Looks Strong in State
"Sweet smell of victory in the air"
Nixon: "McGovern too liberal for voters"
Presidential Election
McGovern: "Nixon Administration Most Corrupt in History"
Congress Overrides Nixon's Veto of Clean Water Act
House Committee Says No Watergate Probe Before Election
Dirty Politics Taints Election
Update: Vietnam War
North Vietnamese Continue Large-Scale Offensive Against US Troops
NYC Marathon: Women Runners Protest Rule Separating Them From Male Runners
As Starting Gun Fires, Women Sit Down on Start Line
Kissinger Extends Secret Meetings With North Vietnamese
Abbreviation "Ms." Used for First Time in Congressional Record
The TORRINGTON REGISTER

FINALLY... THE BIG DAY IS HERE!

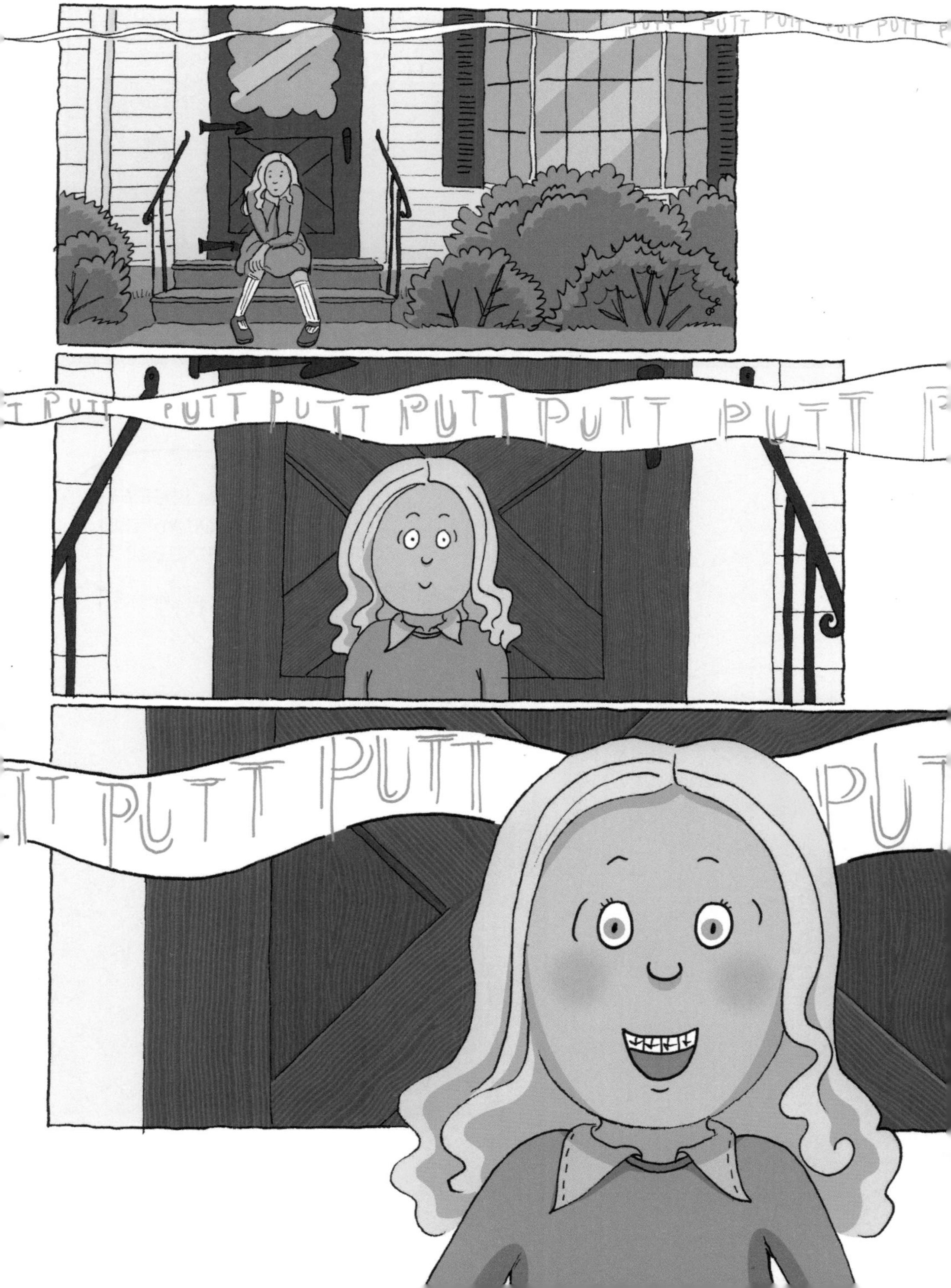
PUTT PUTT PUTT PUTT
PUTT PUTT PUTT PUTT PUTT PUTT
PUTT PUTT PUTT

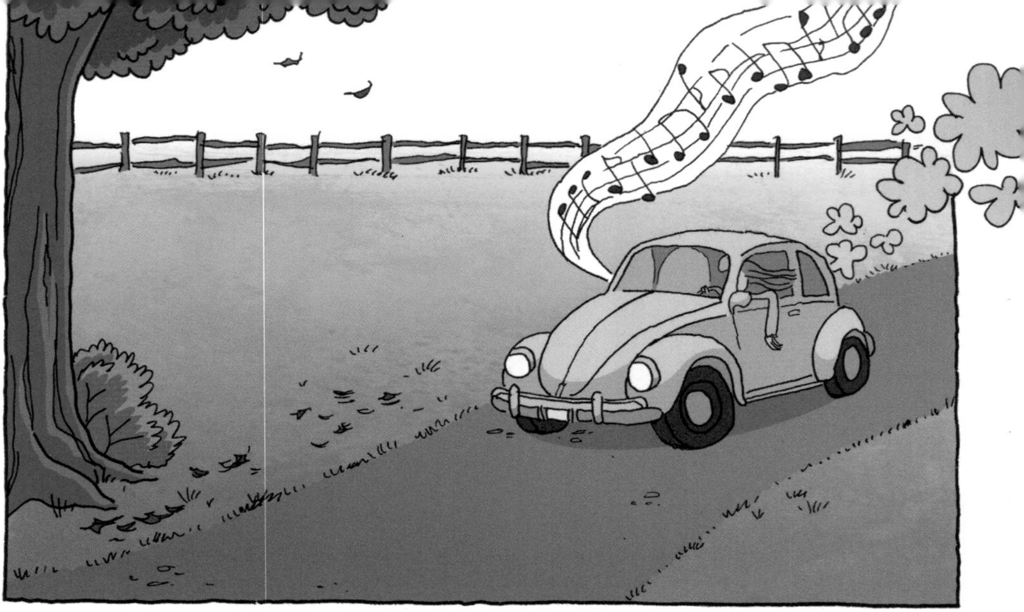

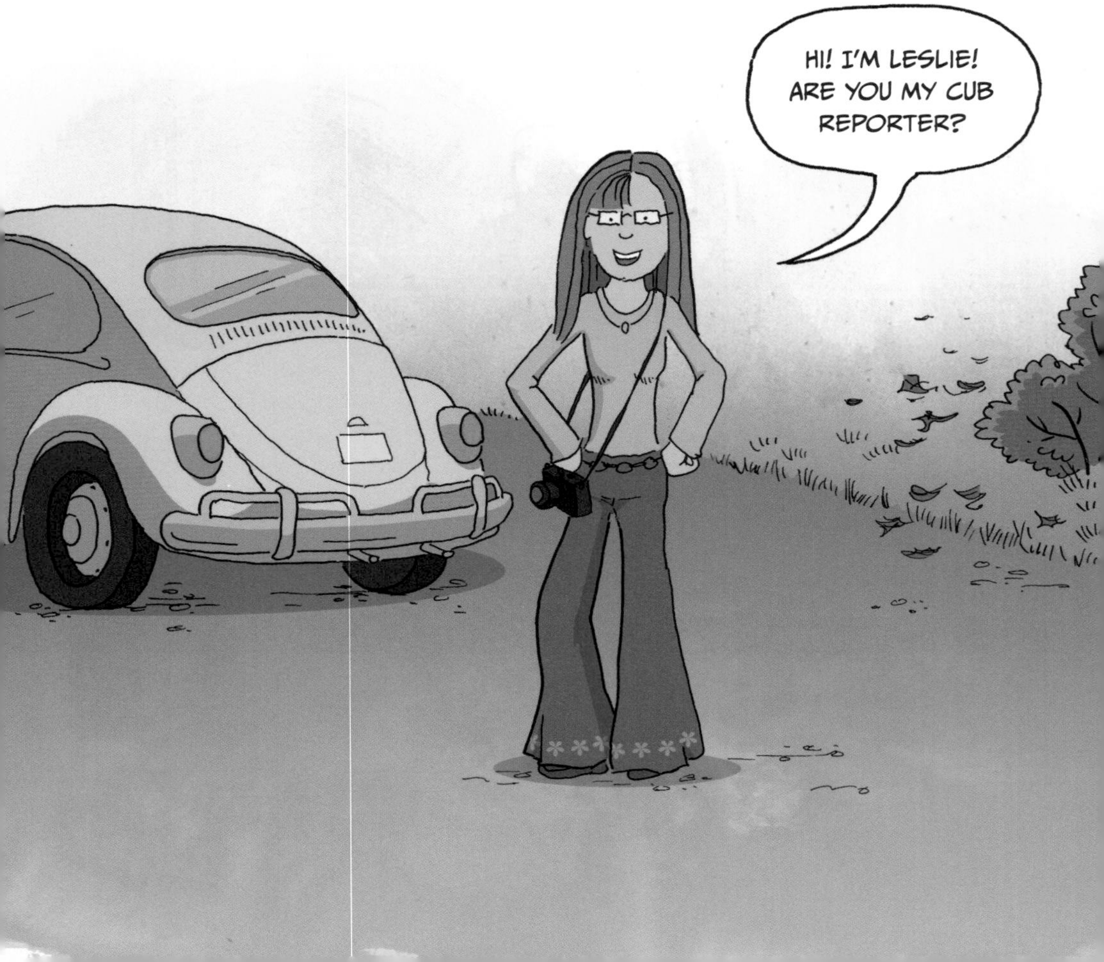
HI! I'M LESLIE! ARE YOU MY CUB REPORTER?

Chapter 3

YOU'LL BE WITH HER AT ALL TIMES DURING YOUR OUTINGS?

OUT ON SCHOOL NIGHTS?

ANY SUPPLIES BESIDES A TYPEWRITER?

SOME O... BE DURIN... ALTHOUGH O... HAPPEN ON...

I DON'T FORESEE ANY OCCASIONS WHEN I WOULDN'T BE WITH HER.

I THINK THA... ALL SHE'LL NE...D FOR NOW...

I HAVE TO WAIT UNTIL LESLIE ANSWERS **AAALL** OF MY PARENTS' QUESTIONS BEFORE WE CAN HEAD OUT ON OUR FIRST ADVENTURE—IN HER VW BEETLE!

WE'RE GOING TO THE BOARD OF EDUCATION'S FINANCE SUBCOMMITTEE MEETING AT THE JUNIOR HIGH SCHOOL!

THIS IS SO COOL!

MEETING ←

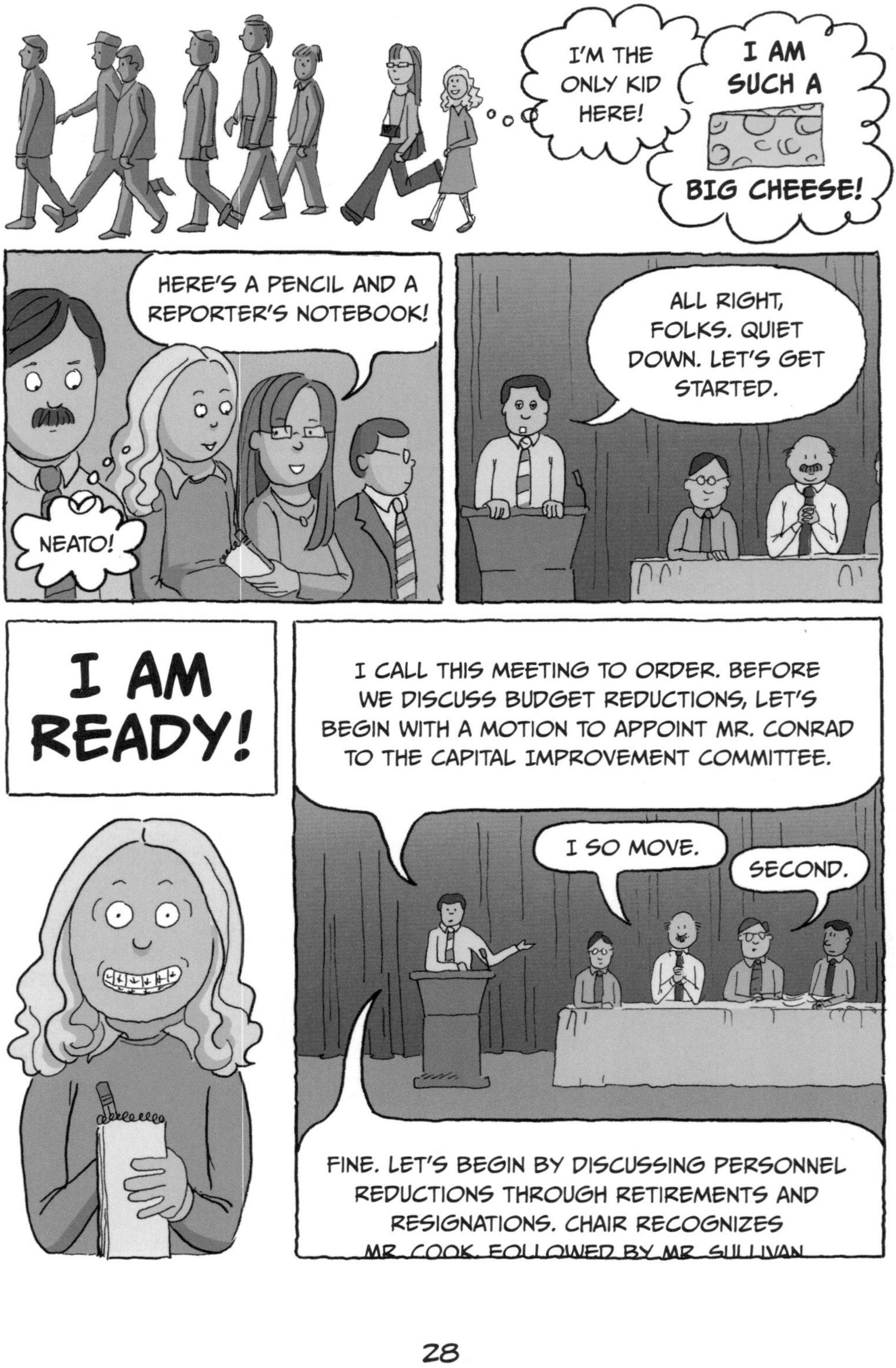
I'M THE ONLY KID HERE!
I AM SUCH A BIG CHEESE!
HERE'S A PENCIL AND A REPORTER'S NOTEBOOK!
NEATO!
ALL RIGHT, FOLKS. QUIET DOWN. LET'S GET STARTED.
I AM READY!
I CALL THIS MEETING TO ORDER. BEFORE WE DISCUSS BUDGET REDUCTIONS, LET'S BEGIN WITH A MOTION TO APPOINT MR. CONRAD TO THE CAPITAL IMPROVEMENT COMMITTEE.
I SO MOVE.
SECOND.
FINE. LET'S BEGIN BY DISCUSSING PERSONNEL REDUCTIONS THROUGH RETIREMENTS AND RESIGNATIONS. CHAIR RECOGNIZES MR. COOK, FOLLOWED BY MR. SULLIVAN

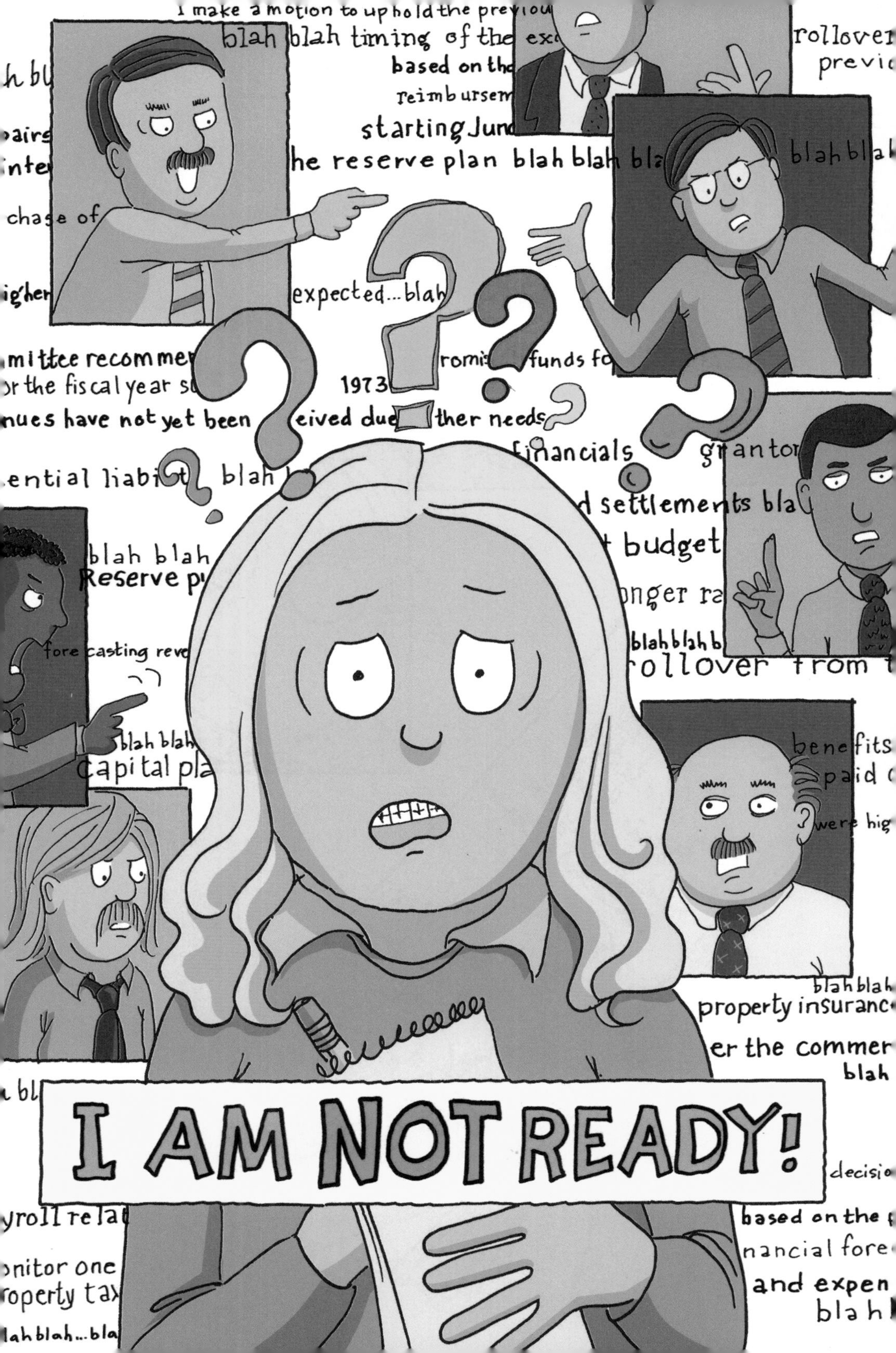
I make a motion to uphold the previou
blah blah timing of the ex
based on the
reimbursem
starting June
he reserve plan blah blah bl
rollover
previ
blah bla
chase of
expected...blah
mittee recommen
r the fiscal year s
1973
funds fo
nues have not yet been
eived due
ther needs
financials
grantor
ential liabi
blah
d settlements bla
budget
blah blah
Reserve p
onger ra
blahblahb
fore casting reve
rollover from
blah blah
capital pla
benefits
paid
were hig
blahblah
property insuranc
er the commer
blah
I AM NOT READY!
decisio
yroll relat
based on the
nancial fore
onitor one
and expen
operty tax
blah
lahblah...bla

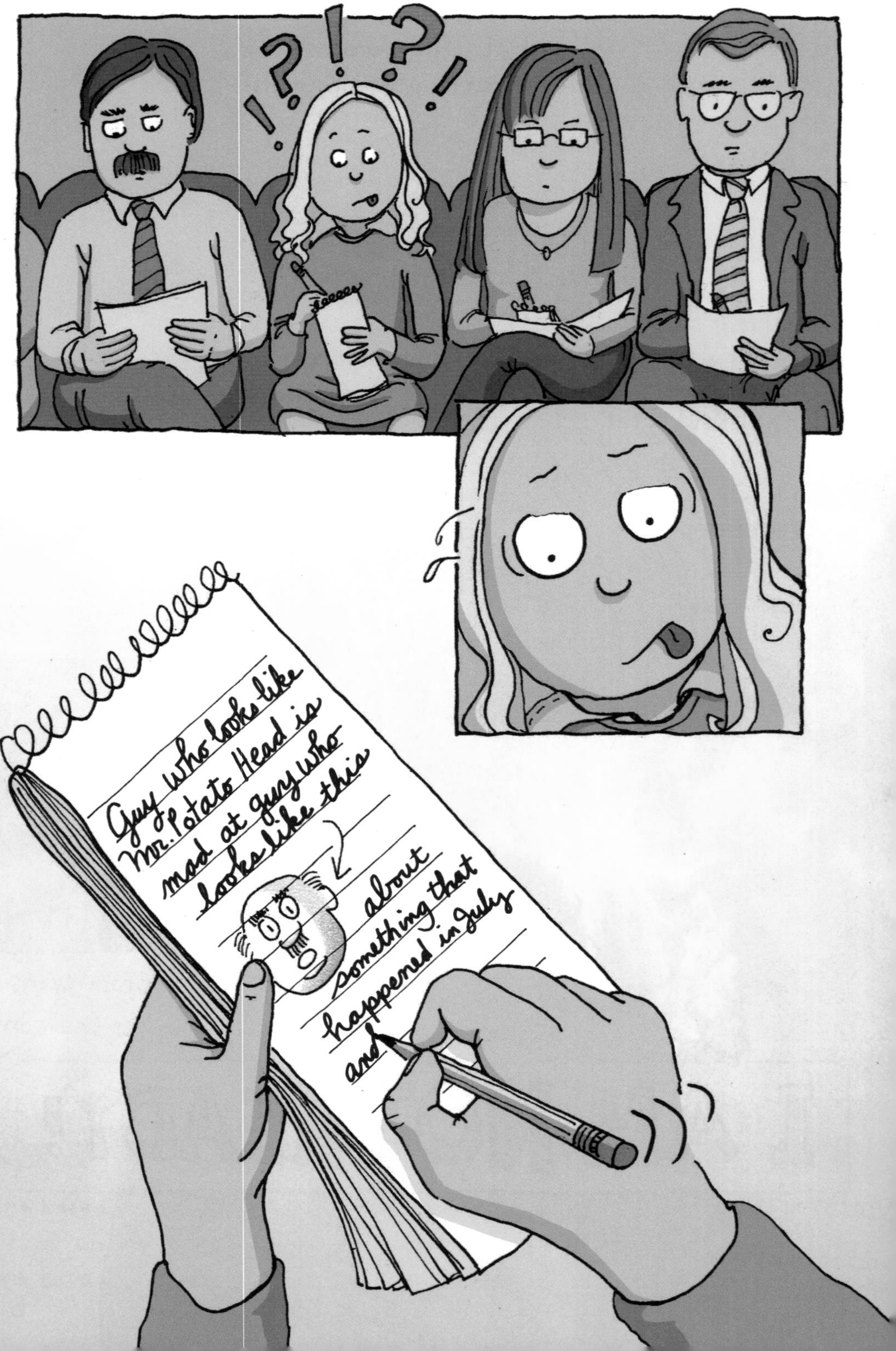
Guy who looks like Mr. Potato Head is mad at guy who looks like this
about something that happened in July
and

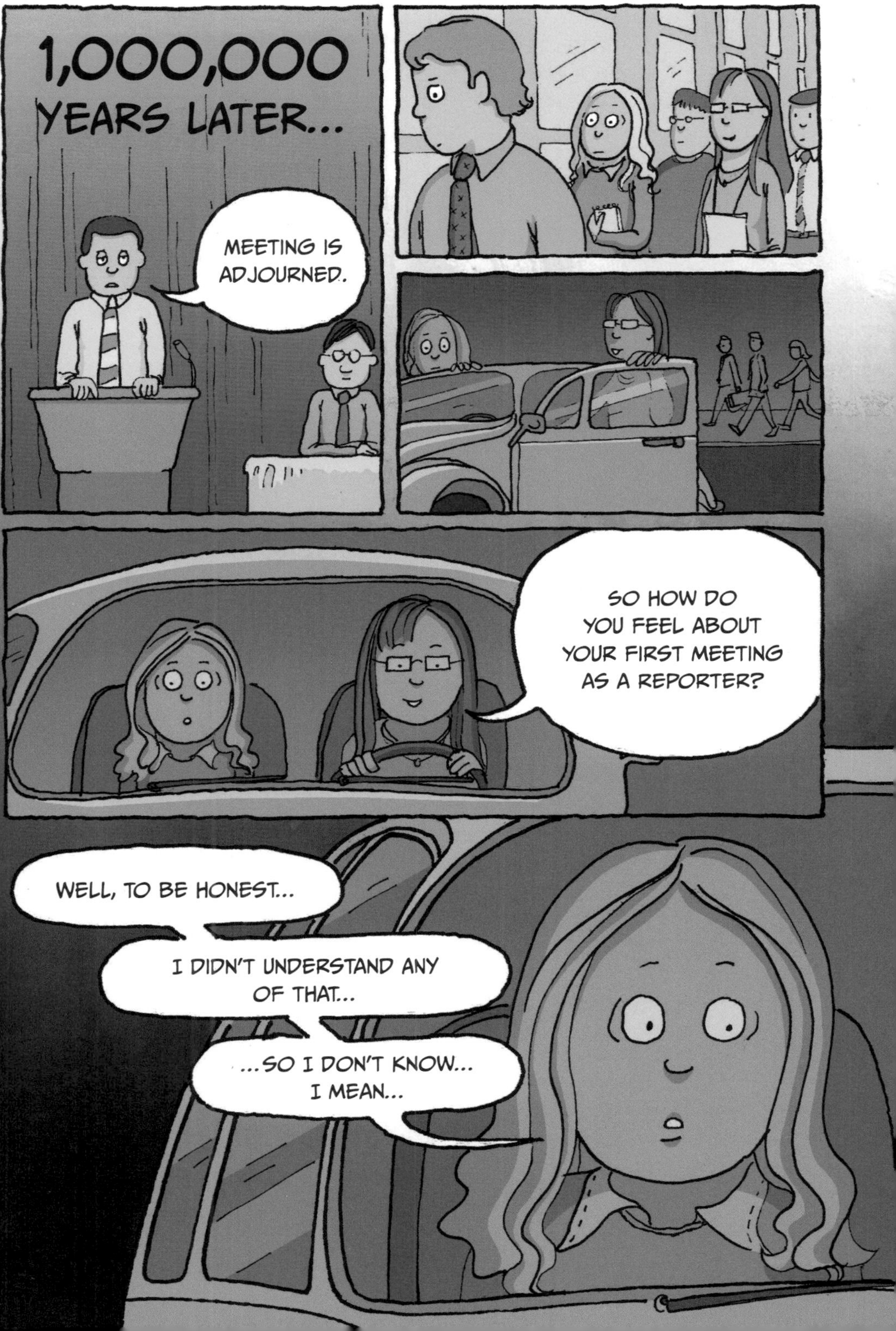
1,000,000 YEARS LATER...
MEETING IS ADJOURNED.
SO HOW DO YOU FEEL ABOUT YOUR FIRST MEETING AS A REPORTER?
WELL, TO BE HONEST...
I DIDN'T UNDERSTAND ANY OF THAT...
...SO I DON'T KNOW... I MEAN...

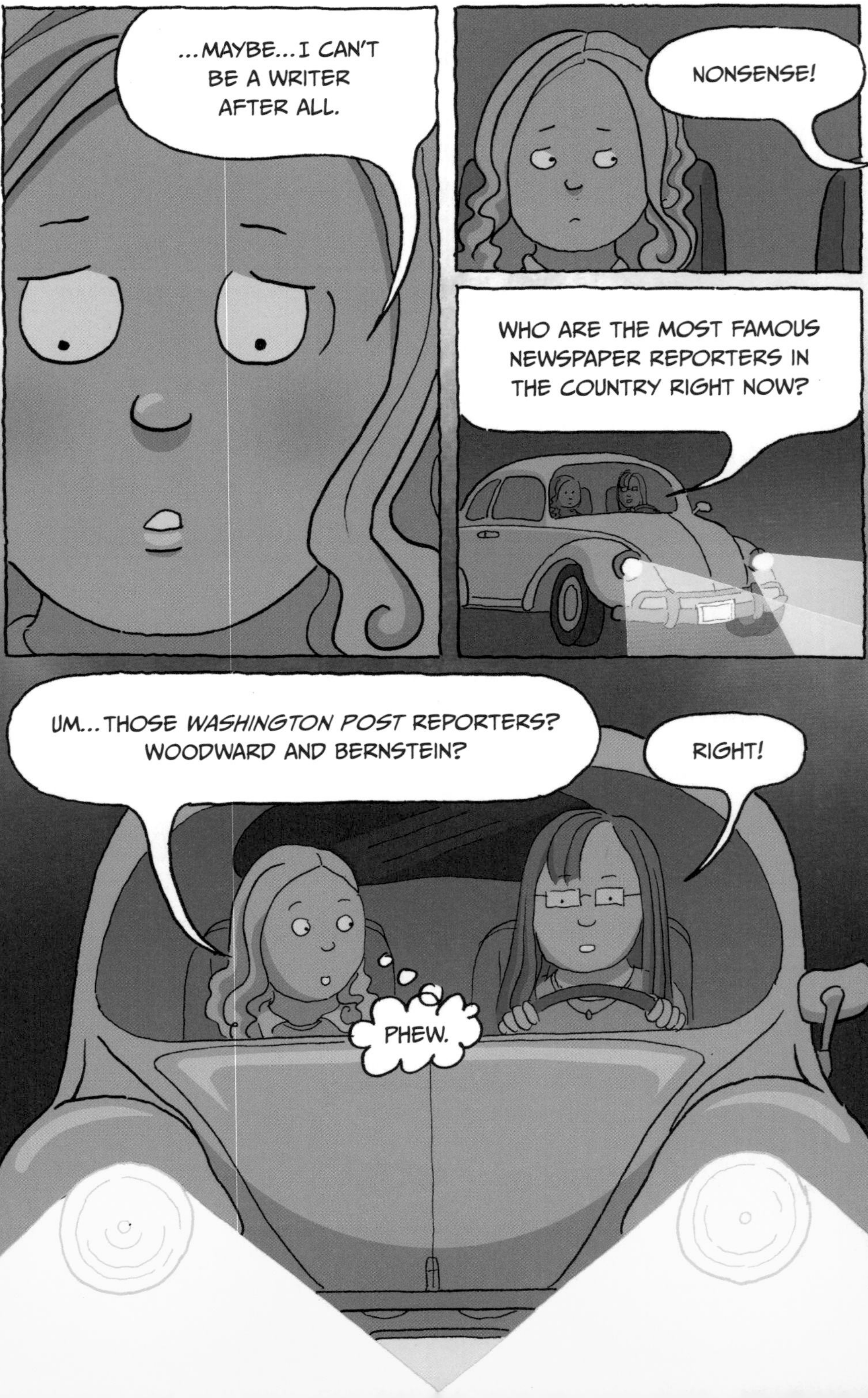
...MAYBE...I CAN'T BE A WRITER AFTER ALL.
NONSENSE!
WHO ARE THE MOST FAMOUS NEWSPAPER REPORTERS IN THE COUNTRY RIGHT NOW?
UM...THOSE *WASHINGTON POST* REPORTERS? WOODWARD AND BERNSTEIN?
RIGHT!
PHEW.

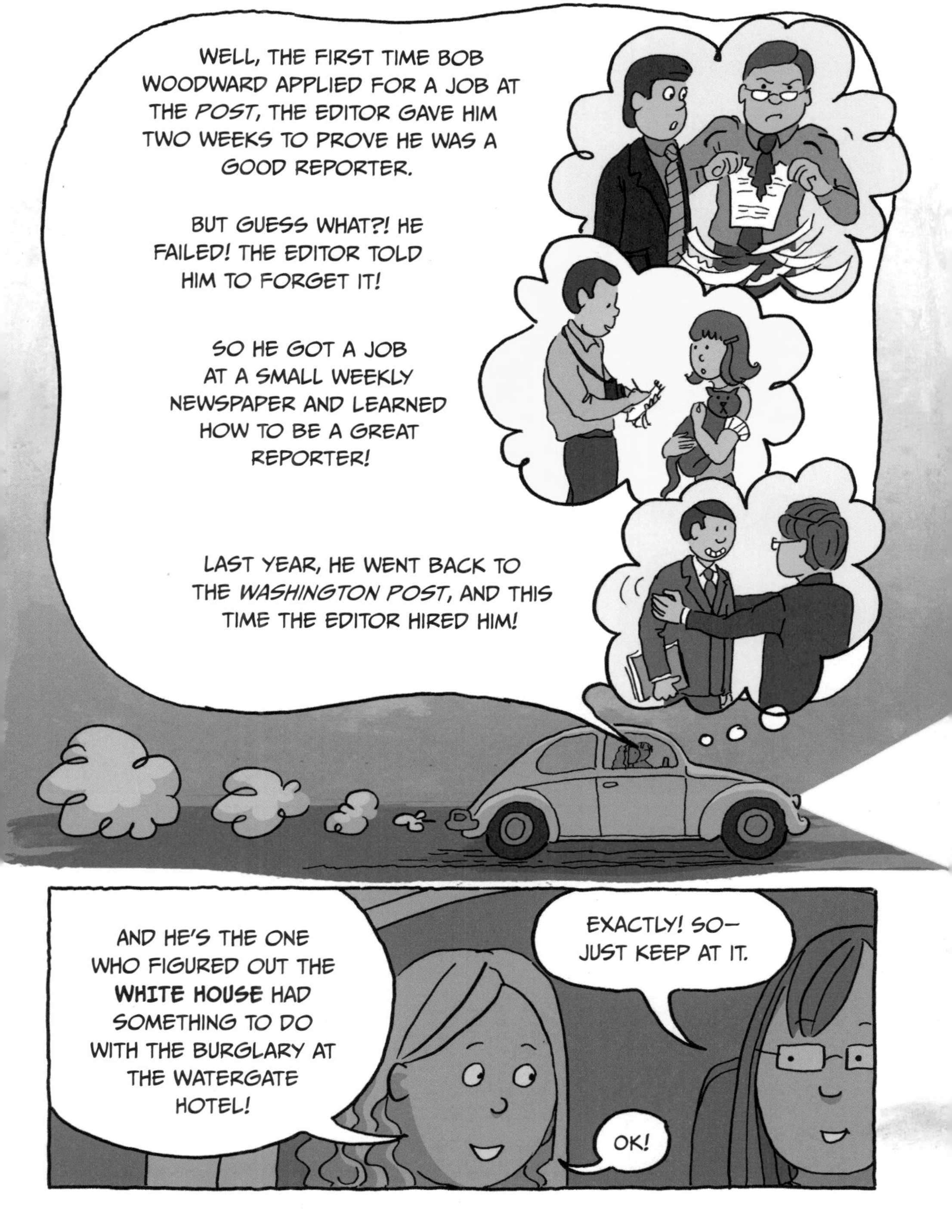
WELL, THE FIRST TIME BOB WOODWARD APPLIED FOR A JOB AT THE *POST*, THE EDITOR GAVE HIM TWO WEEKS TO PROVE HE WAS A GOOD REPORTER.
BUT GUESS WHAT?! HE FAILED! THE EDITOR TOLD HIM TO FORGET IT!
SO HE GOT A JOB AT A SMALL WEEKLY NEWSPAPER AND LEARNED HOW TO BE A GREAT REPORTER!
LAST YEAR, HE WENT BACK TO THE *WASHINGTON POST*, AND THIS TIME THE EDITOR HIRED HIM!
AND HE'S THE ONE WHO FIGURED OUT THE **WHITE HOUSE** HAD SOMETHING TO DO WITH THE BURGLARY AT THE WATERGATE HOTEL!
EXACTLY! SO— JUST KEEP AT IT.
OK!

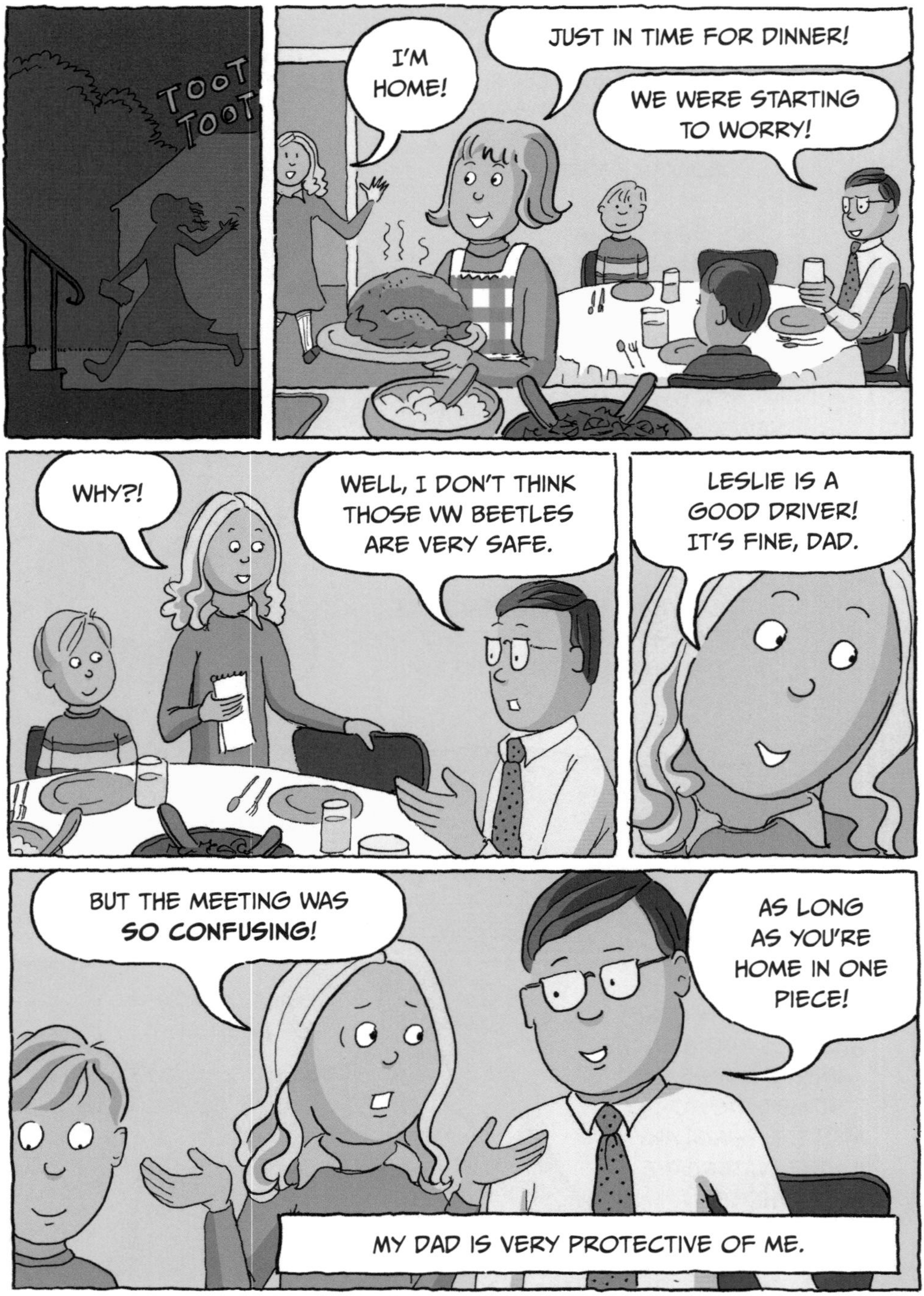
TOOT TOOT
I'M HOME!
JUST IN TIME FOR DINNER!
WE WERE STARTING TO WORRY!
WHY?!
WELL, I DON'T THINK THOSE VW BEETLES ARE VERY SAFE.
LESLIE IS A GOOD DRIVER! IT'S FINE, DAD.
BUT THE MEETING WAS **SO CONFUSING!**
AS LONG AS YOU'RE HOME IN ONE PIECE!
MY DAD IS VERY PROTECTIVE OF ME.

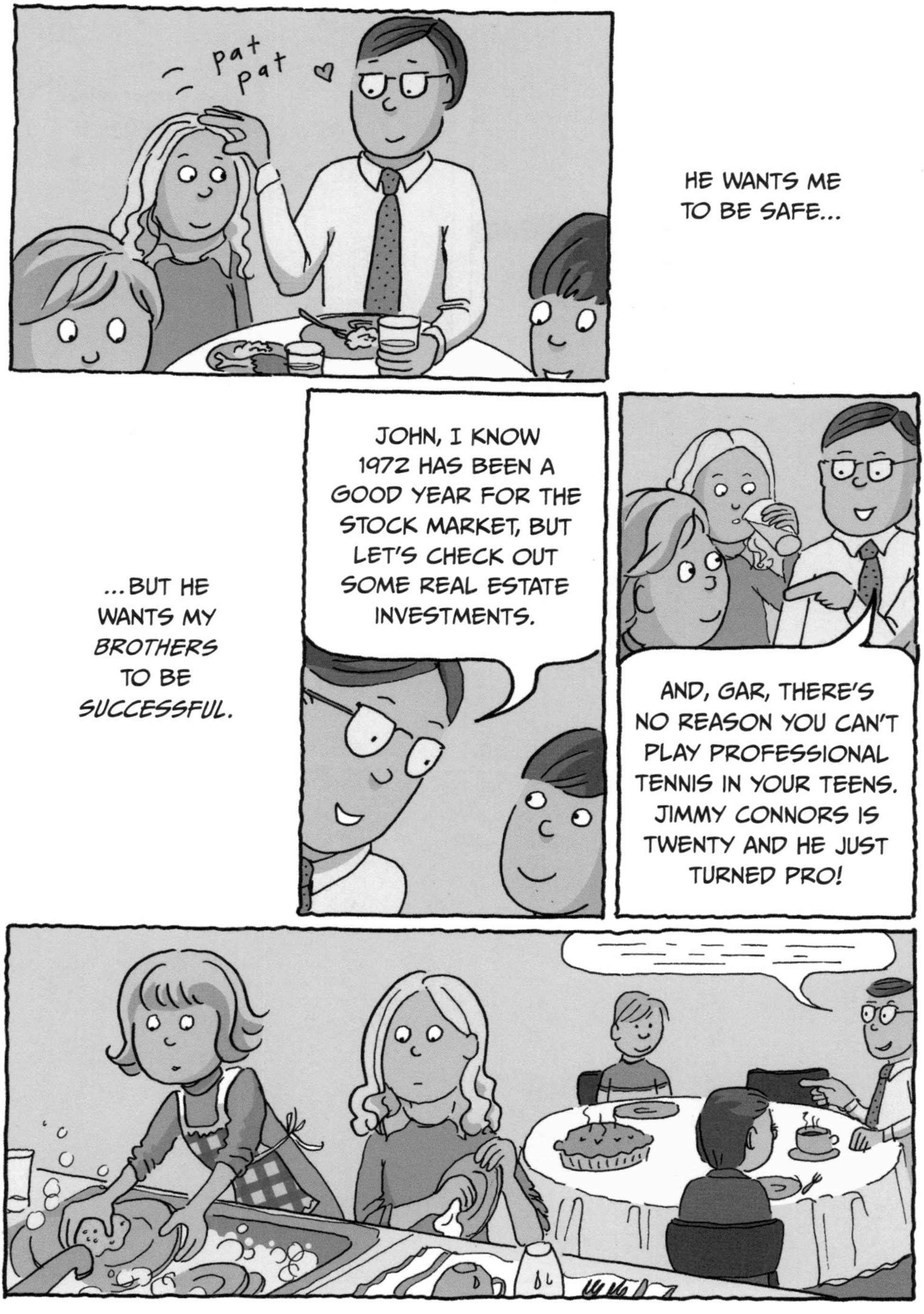
pat pat
HE WANTS ME TO BE SAFE...
...BUT HE WANTS MY *BROTHERS* TO BE *SUCCESSFUL.*
JOHN, I KNOW 1972 HAS BEEN A GOOD YEAR FOR THE STOCK MARKET, BUT LET'S CHECK OUT SOME REAL ESTATE INVESTMENTS.
AND, GAR, THERE'S NO REASON YOU CAN'T PLAY PROFESSIONAL TENNIS IN YOUR TEENS. JIMMY CONNORS IS TWENTY AND HE JUST TURNED PRO!

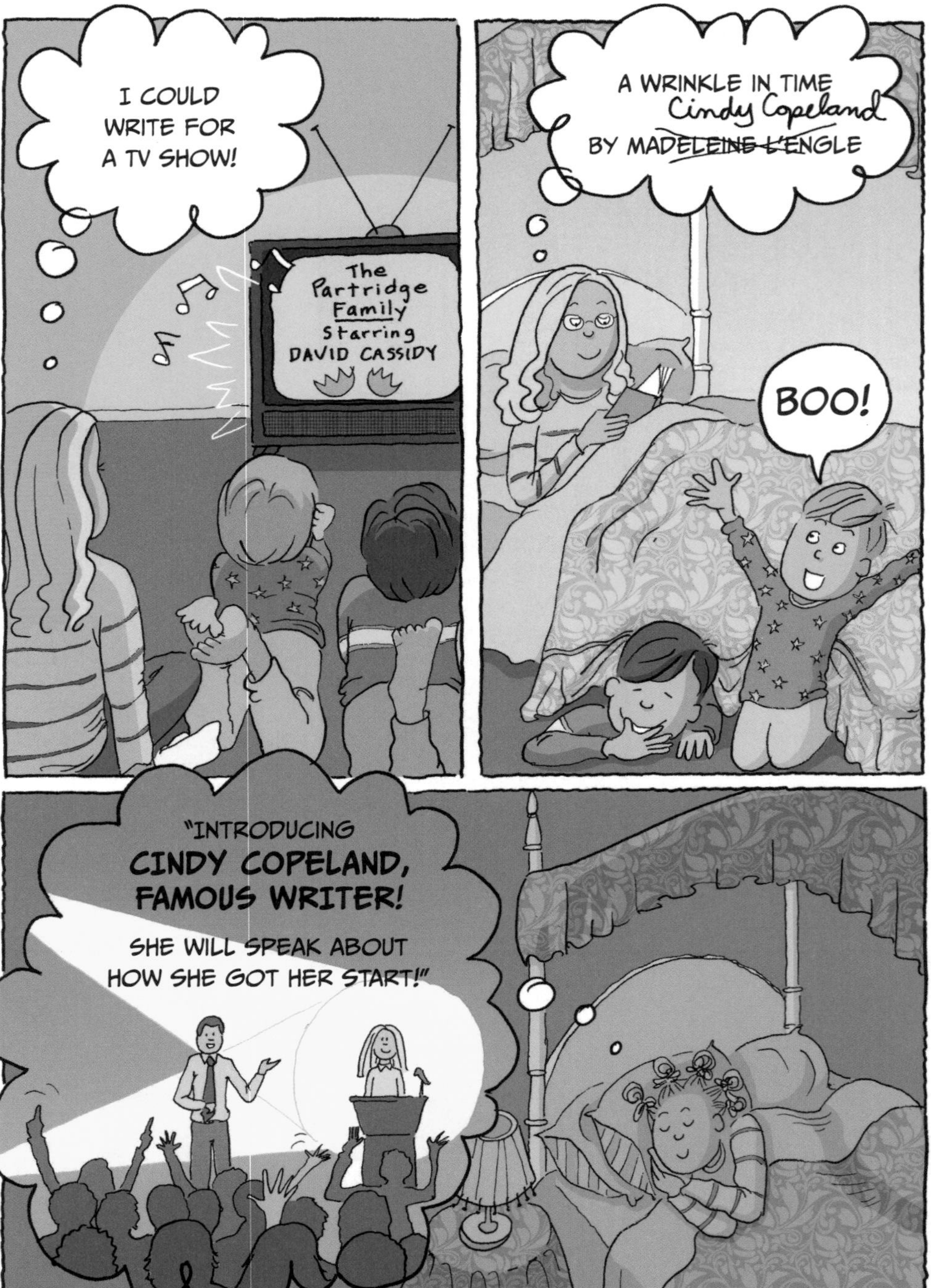
I COULD WRITE FOR A TV SHOW!
The Partridge Family Starring DAVID CASSIDY
A WRINKLE IN TIME
Cindy Copeland
BY MADELEINE L'ENGLE
BOO!
"INTRODUCING CINDY COPELAND, FAMOUS WRITER!
SHE WILL SPEAK ABOUT HOW SHE GOT HER START!"

Chapter 4

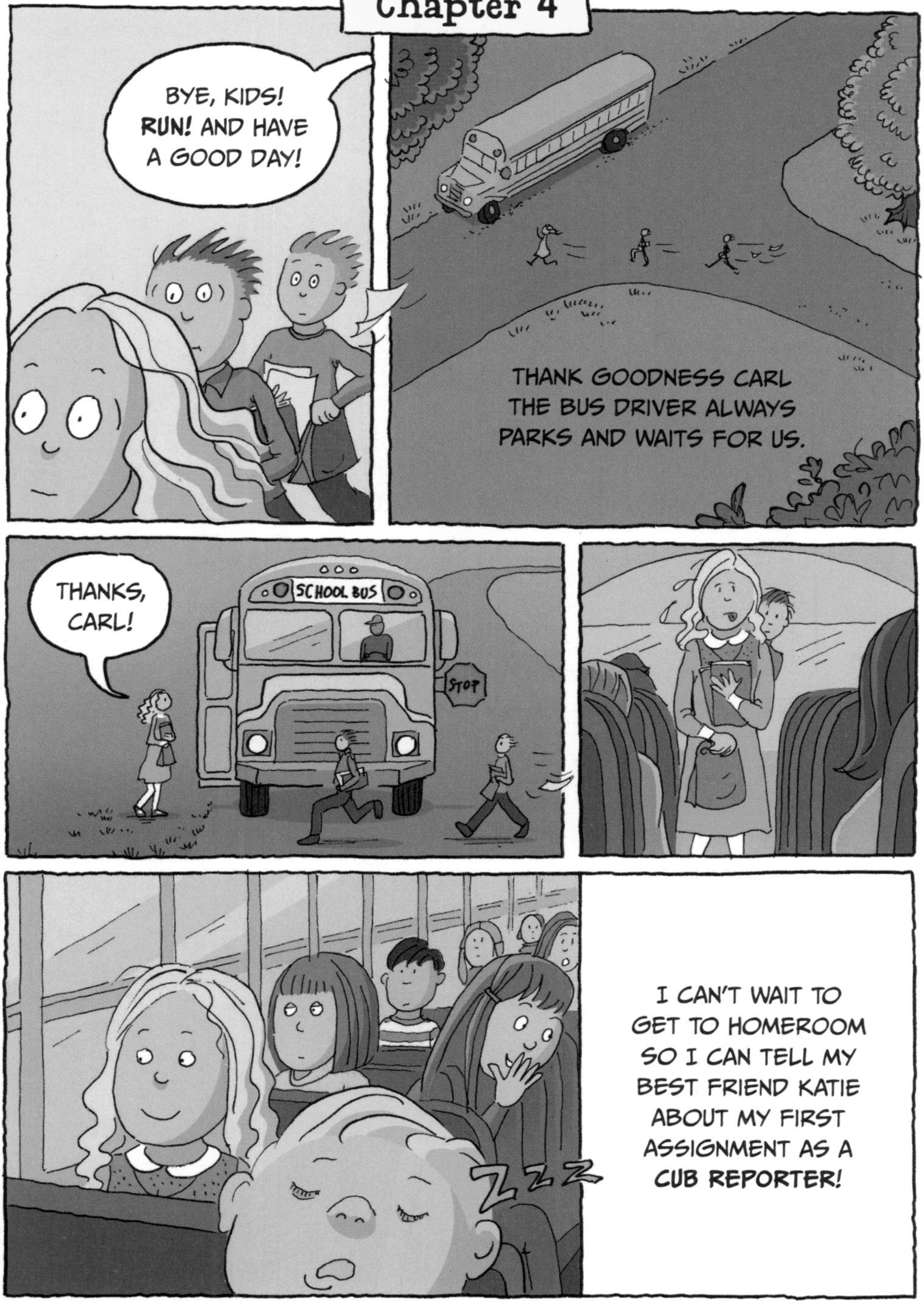
BYE, KIDS! RUN! AND HAVE A GOOD DAY!
THANK GOODNESS CARL THE BUS DRIVER ALWAYS PARKS AND WAITS FOR US.
THANKS, CARL!
SCHOOL BUS
STOP
I CAN'T WAIT TO GET TO HOMEROOM SO I CAN TELL MY BEST FRIEND KATIE ABOUT MY FIRST ASSIGNMENT AS A CUB REPORTER!
ZZZ

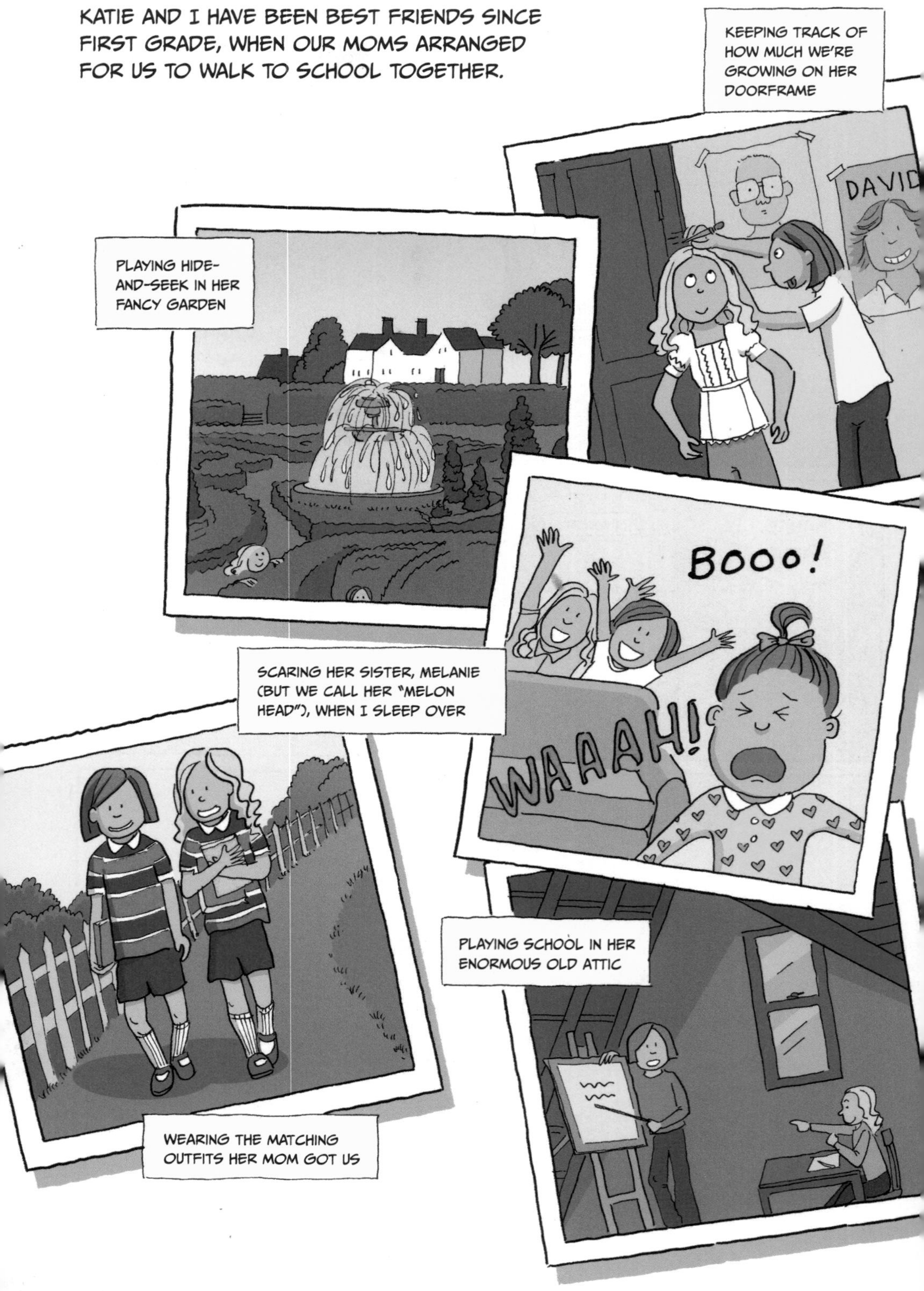
KATIE AND I HAVE BEEN BEST FRIENDS SINCE FIRST GRADE, WHEN OUR MOMS ARRANGED FOR US TO WALK TO SCHOOL TOGETHER.
KEEPING TRACK OF HOW MUCH WE'RE GROWING ON HER DOORFRAME
DAVID
PLAYING HIDE-AND-SEEK IN HER FANCY GARDEN
SCARING HER SISTER, MELANIE (BUT WE CALL HER "MELON HEAD"), WHEN I SLEEP OVER
BOOO!
WAAAH!
WEARING THE MATCHING OUTFITS HER MOM GOT US
PLAYING SCHOOL IN HER ENORMOUS OLD ATTIC

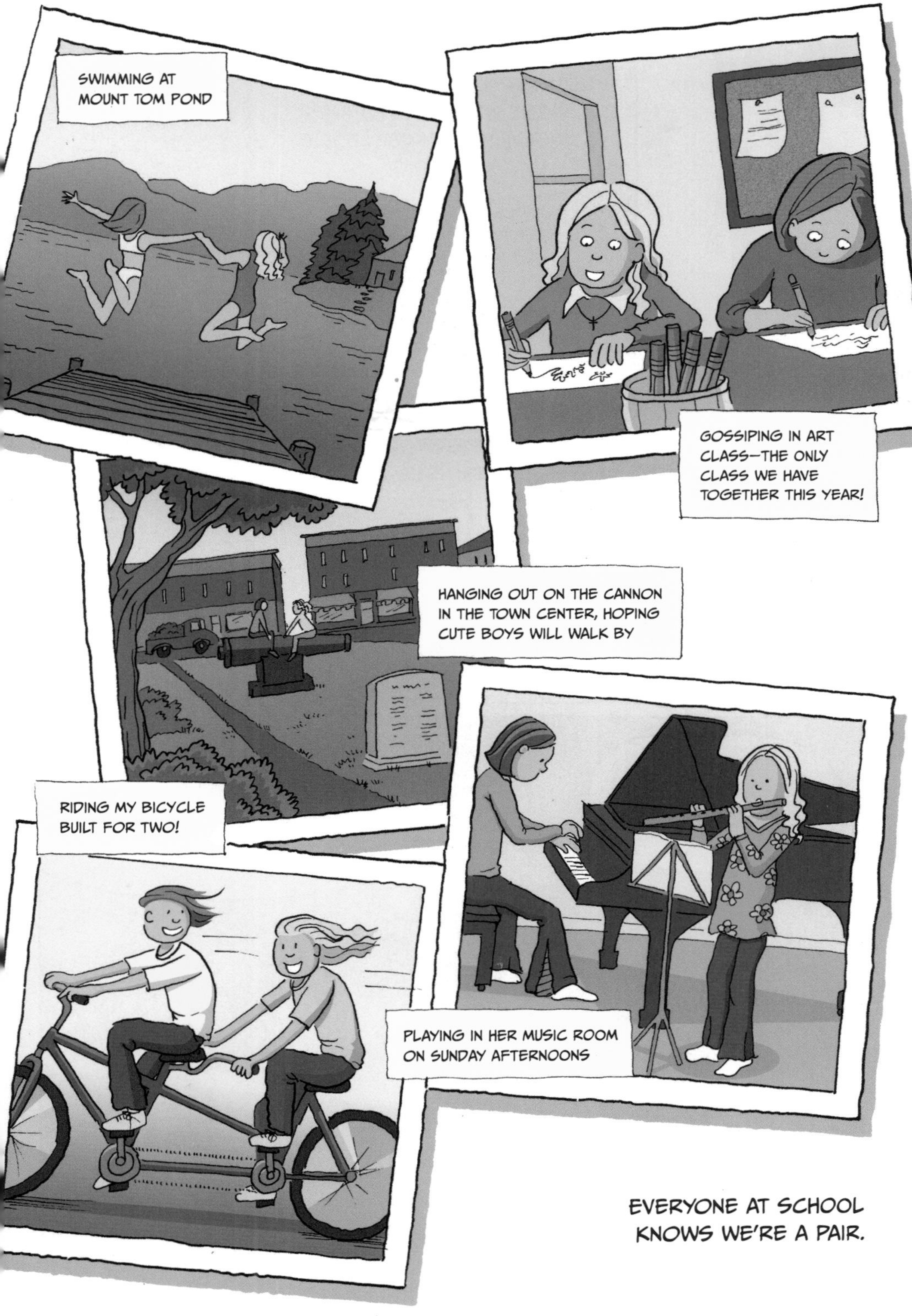
SWIMMING AT MOUNT TOM POND
GOSSIPING IN ART CLASS—THE ONLY CLASS WE HAVE TOGETHER THIS YEAR!
HANGING OUT ON THE CANNON IN THE TOWN CENTER, HOPING CUTE BOYS WILL WALK BY
RIDING MY BICYCLE BUILT FOR TWO!
PLAYING IN HER MUSIC ROOM ON SUNDAY AFTERNOONS
EVERYONE AT SCHOOL KNOWS WE'RE A PAIR.

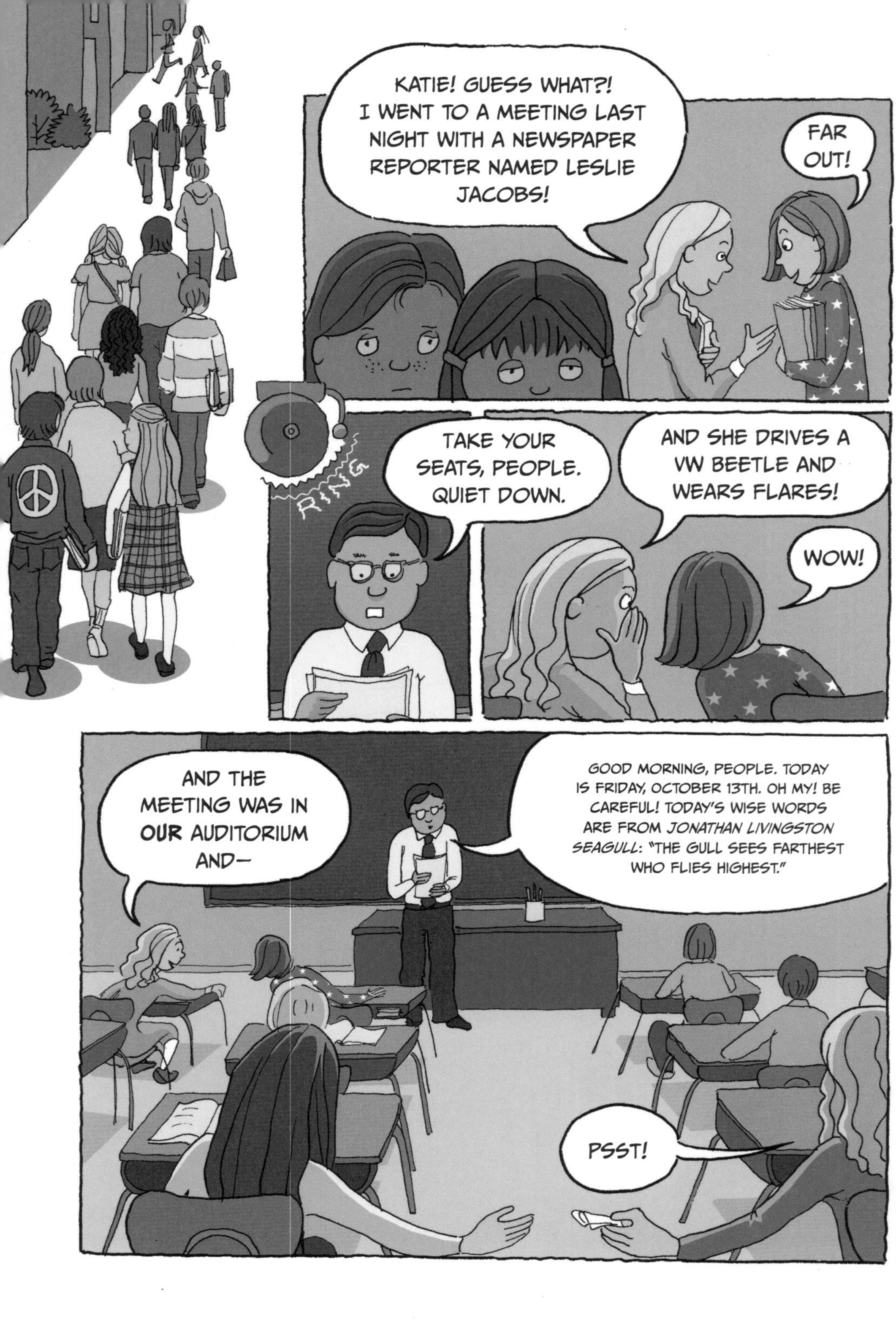
KATIE! GUESS WHAT?! I WENT TO A MEETING LAST NIGHT WITH A NEWSPAPER REPORTER NAMED LESLIE JACOBS!
FAR OUT!
RING
TAKE YOUR SEATS, PEOPLE. QUIET DOWN.
AND SHE DRIVES A VW BEETLE AND WEARS FLARES!
WOW!
AND THE MEETING WAS IN **OUR** AUDITORIUM AND—
GOOD MORNING, PEOPLE. TODAY IS FRIDAY, OCTOBER 13TH. OH MY! BE CAREFUL! TODAY'S WISE WORDS ARE FROM *JONATHAN LIVINGSTON SEAGULL*: "THE GULL SEES FARTHEST WHO FLIES HIGHEST."
PSST!

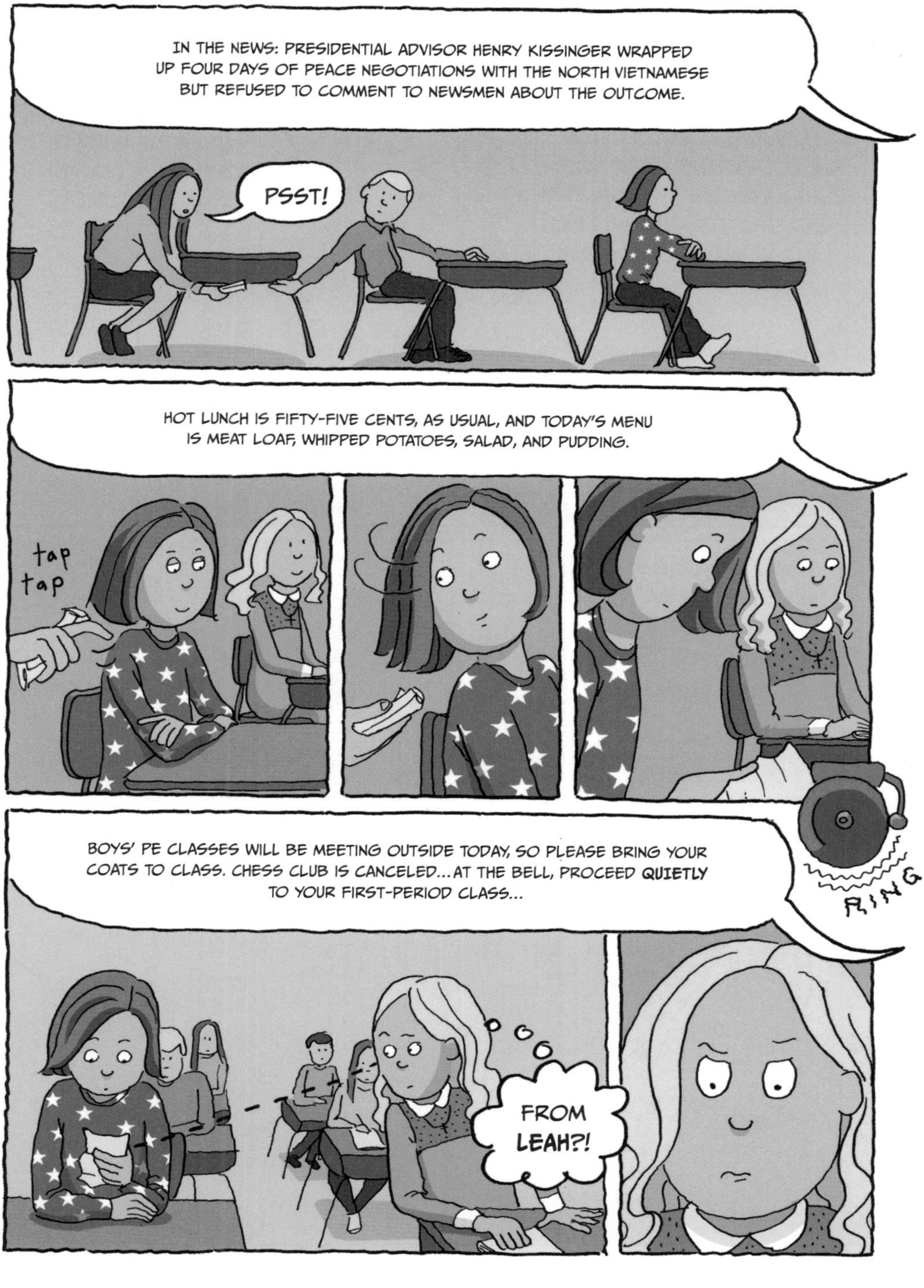
IN THE NEWS: PRESIDENTIAL ADVISOR HENRY KISSINGER WRAPPED UP FOUR DAYS OF PEACE NEGOTIATIONS WITH THE NORTH VIETNAMESE BUT REFUSED TO COMMENT TO NEWSMEN ABOUT THE OUTCOME.
PSST!
HOT LUNCH IS FIFTY-FIVE CENTS, AS USUAL, AND TODAY'S MENU IS MEAT LOAF, WHIPPED POTATOES, SALAD, AND PUDDING.
tap tap
BOYS' PE CLASSES WILL BE MEETING OUTSIDE TODAY, SO PLEASE BRING YOUR COATS TO CLASS. CHESS CLUB IS CANCELED...AT THE BELL, PROCEED **QUIETLY** TO YOUR FIRST-PERIOD CLASS...
RING
FROM **LEAH?!**

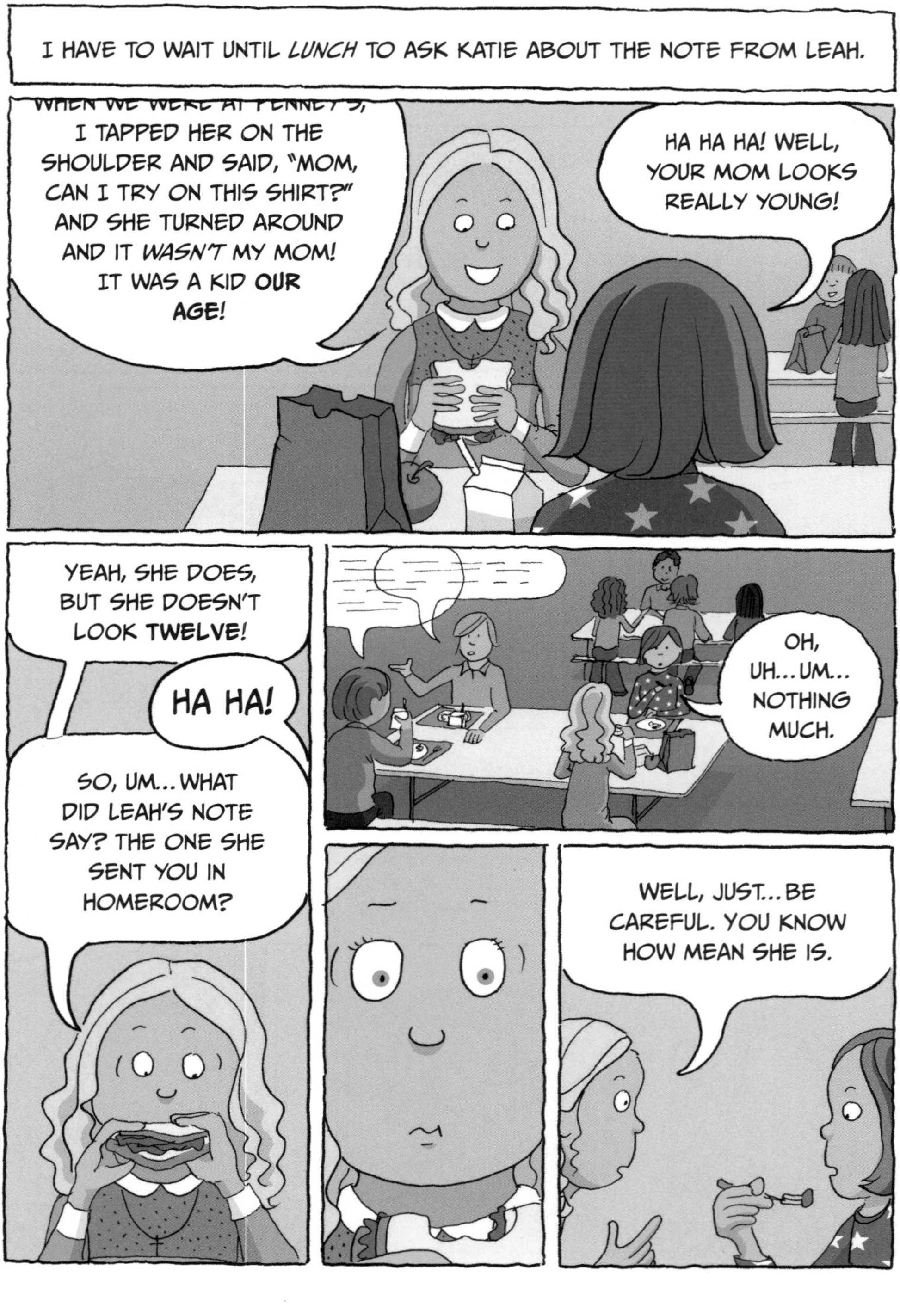
I HAVE TO WAIT UNTIL *LUNCH* TO ASK KATIE ABOUT THE NOTE FROM LEAH.
WHEN WE WERE AT PENNEY'S, I TAPPED HER ON THE SHOULDER AND SAID, "MOM, CAN I TRY ON THIS SHIRT?" AND SHE TURNED AROUND AND IT *WASN'T* MY MOM! IT WAS A KID **OUR AGE!**
HA HA HA! WELL, YOUR MOM LOOKS REALLY YOUNG!
YEAH, SHE DOES, BUT SHE DOESN'T LOOK **TWELVE!**
HA HA!
SO, UM... WHAT DID LEAH'S NOTE SAY? THE ONE SHE SENT YOU IN HOMEROOM?
OH, UH... UM... NOTHING MUCH.
WELL, JUST... BE CAREFUL. YOU KNOW HOW MEAN SHE IS.

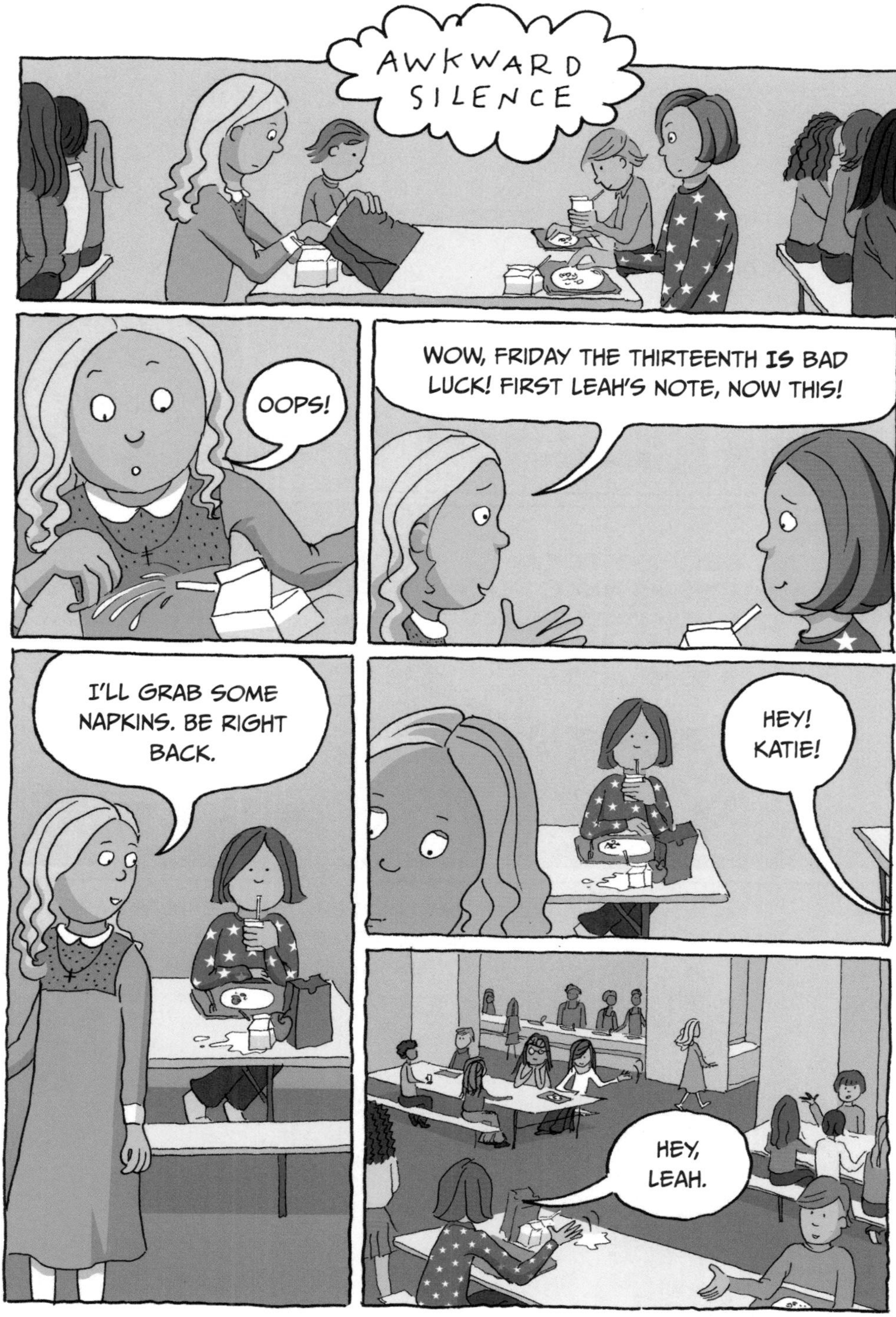
AWKWARD SILENCE
OOPS!
WOW, FRIDAY THE THIRTEENTH IS BAD LUCK! FIRST LEAH'S NOTE, NOW THIS!
I'LL GRAB SOME NAPKINS. BE RIGHT BACK.
HEY! KATIE!
HEY, LEAH.

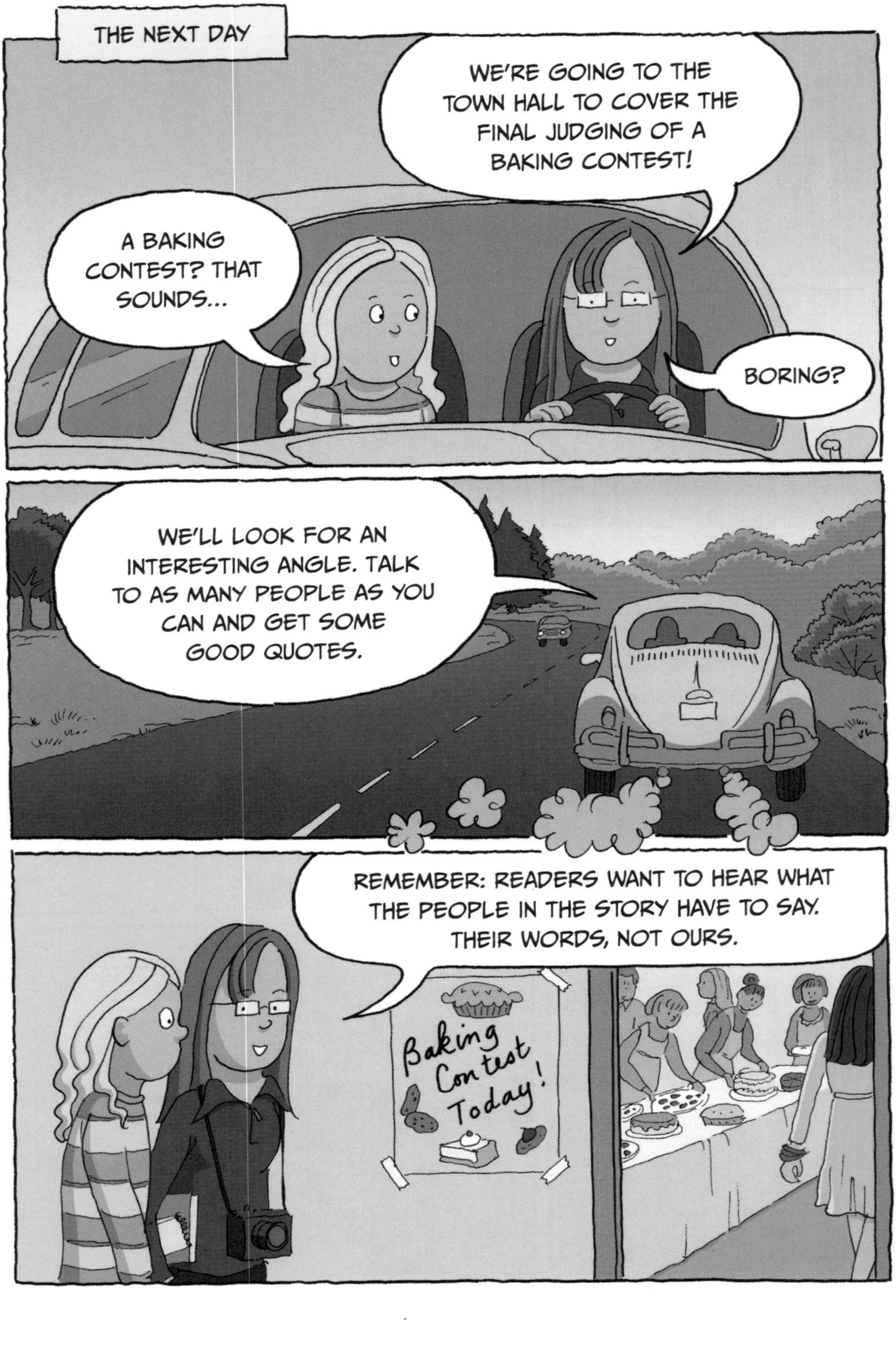
THE NEXT DAY
WE'RE GOING TO THE TOWN HALL TO COVER THE FINAL JUDGING OF A BAKING CONTEST!
A BAKING CONTEST? THAT SOUNDS...
BORING?
WE'LL LOOK FOR AN INTERESTING ANGLE. TALK TO AS MANY PEOPLE AS YOU CAN AND GET SOME GOOD QUOTES.
REMEMBER: READERS WANT TO HEAR WHAT THE PEOPLE IN THE STORY HAVE TO SAY. THEIR WORDS, NOT OURS.
Baking Contest Today!

The editor will write the headline.

BAKING CONTEST WINNER ANNOUNCED

By Cindy Copeland

Where? When?

The Litchfield County Extension Service held a cake baking contest. Miss Nancy Brown and Mrs. Sally Worthington were the lucky judges. The first prize was won by Greg Bennett, a senior at Litchfield High School. Greg is the son of Mr. and Mrs. Samuel Bennett of School Street.

No! The lede needs to catch a reader's attention! Start with: A boy won a baking contest!

Use active voice, not passive voice.

What was the prize? Fill in the holes!

Miss Brown and Mrs. Worthington were surprised to learn that a boy was the one who baked the winning cake! "We didn't say that the contest was limited to girls," Miss Brown commented, "but that's because we never expected any guys to enter!" She said that they had no idea who baked each cake because the names were hidden underneath the cake pans. Miss Brown added that Greg's Midnight Madness chocolate cake was the clear winner. Who wouldn't love a chocolate cake with fudge frosting and pudding in the middle?

Unnecessary!

Opinion, not fact!

As for Greg, he said that the hardest part was not choosing a recipe or baking a cake, but taking all of the teasing from the basketball team. "I had to miss practice on Thursday to bake my cake," he said, "and the other guys gave me a really hard time about it!"

Strong ending!

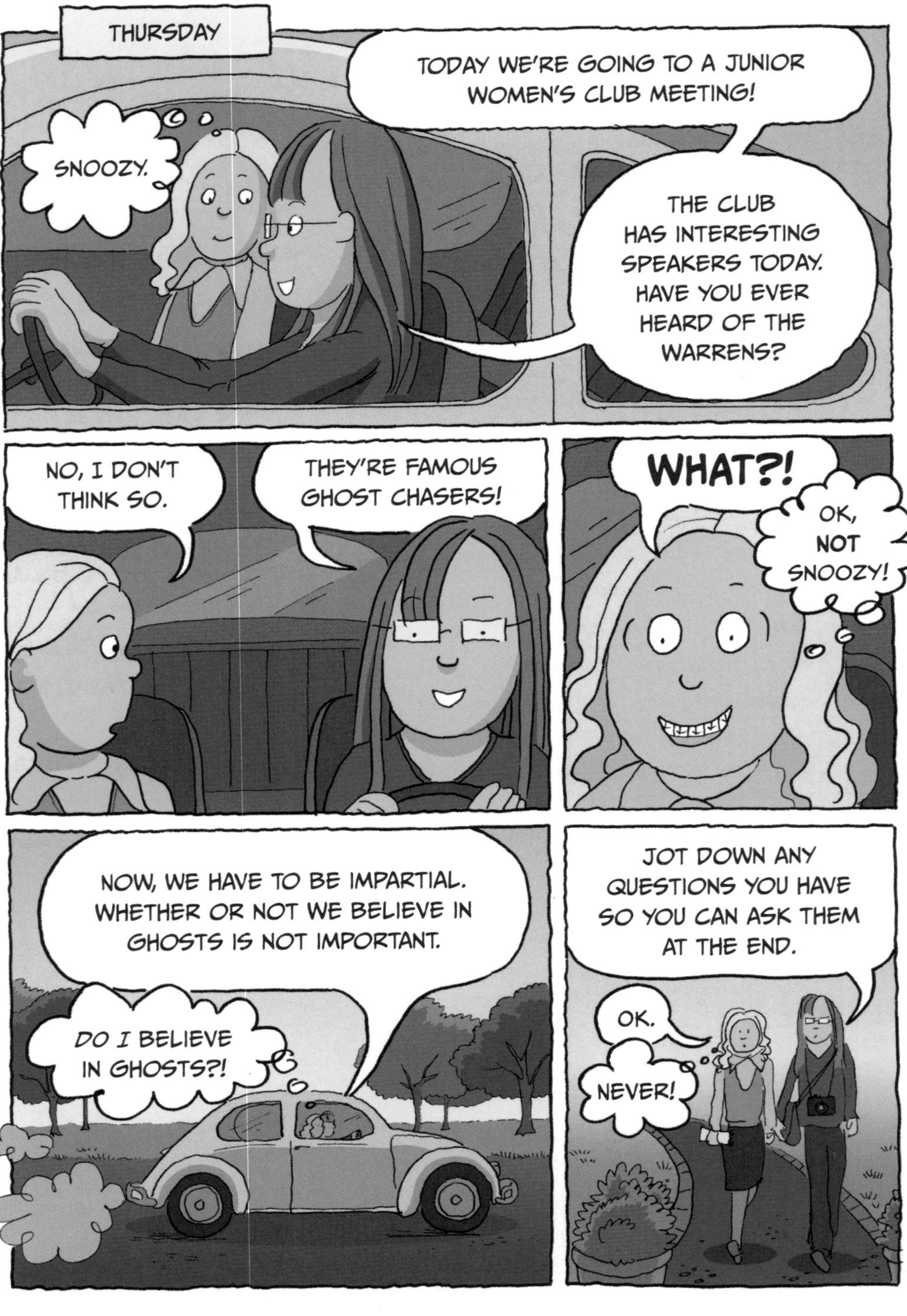
THURSDAY
TODAY WE'RE GOING TO A JUNIOR WOMEN'S CLUB MEETING!
SNOOZY.
THE CLUB HAS INTERESTING SPEAKERS TODAY. HAVE YOU EVER HEARD OF THE WARRENS?
NO, I DON'T THINK SO.
THEY'RE FAMOUS GHOST CHASERS!
WHAT?!
OK, NOT SNOOZY!
NOW, WE HAVE TO BE IMPARTIAL. WHETHER OR NOT WE BELIEVE IN GHOSTS IS NOT IMPORTANT.
DO I BELIEVE IN GHOSTS?!
JOT DOWN ANY QUESTIONS YOU HAVE SO YOU CAN ASK THEM AT THE END.
OK.
NEVER!

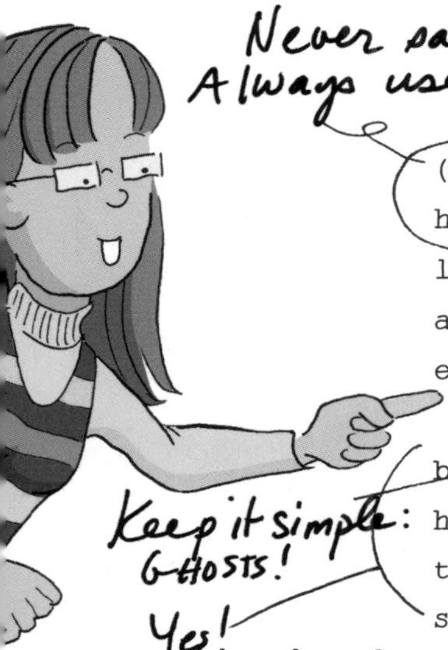

Never say "I"—
Always use third person!

Good lede!

Ed and Lorraine Warren believe in ghosts! (I didn't think I believed in them until I heard the Warrens speak!) The Warrens, who live in nearby Monroe, explained why before a large crowd at a JWC meeting on Saturday evening.

Say "Junior Women's Club"

For almost 30 years, the Warrens have been investigating claims of apparitions and haunted houses. They presented a slide show that featured some of the 300 cases they have studied, many of them in Connecticut.

Keep it simple: GHOSTS!

Yes! You answered who, what, when, where and why!

cut unimportant details

Dressed in a brightly colored shirt, Mr. Warren said that the recent bestseller, The Exorcist, is based on a true story of a boy who became possessed because he used a Ouija board. He warned of potential dangers that amateurs face if they try to contact non-human spirits through witchcraft and black magic. He said that it's very dangerous for people who do not know what they are doing to experiment with such things. Once you have contacted negative beings, he said, "it's not very easy to get rid of them."

Don't repeat yourself! Newspapers don't have extra space!

After the first mention of his name, use "Warren."

Mr. Warren said that he first became interested in supernatural things when he was a child and his family moved into a haunted house.

The couple will be appearing in a TV show based on their research in the coming months.

Good. This can be cut if it won't fit on the page.

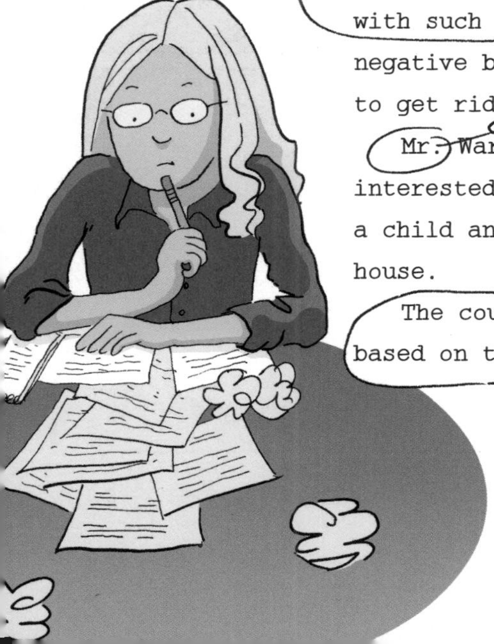

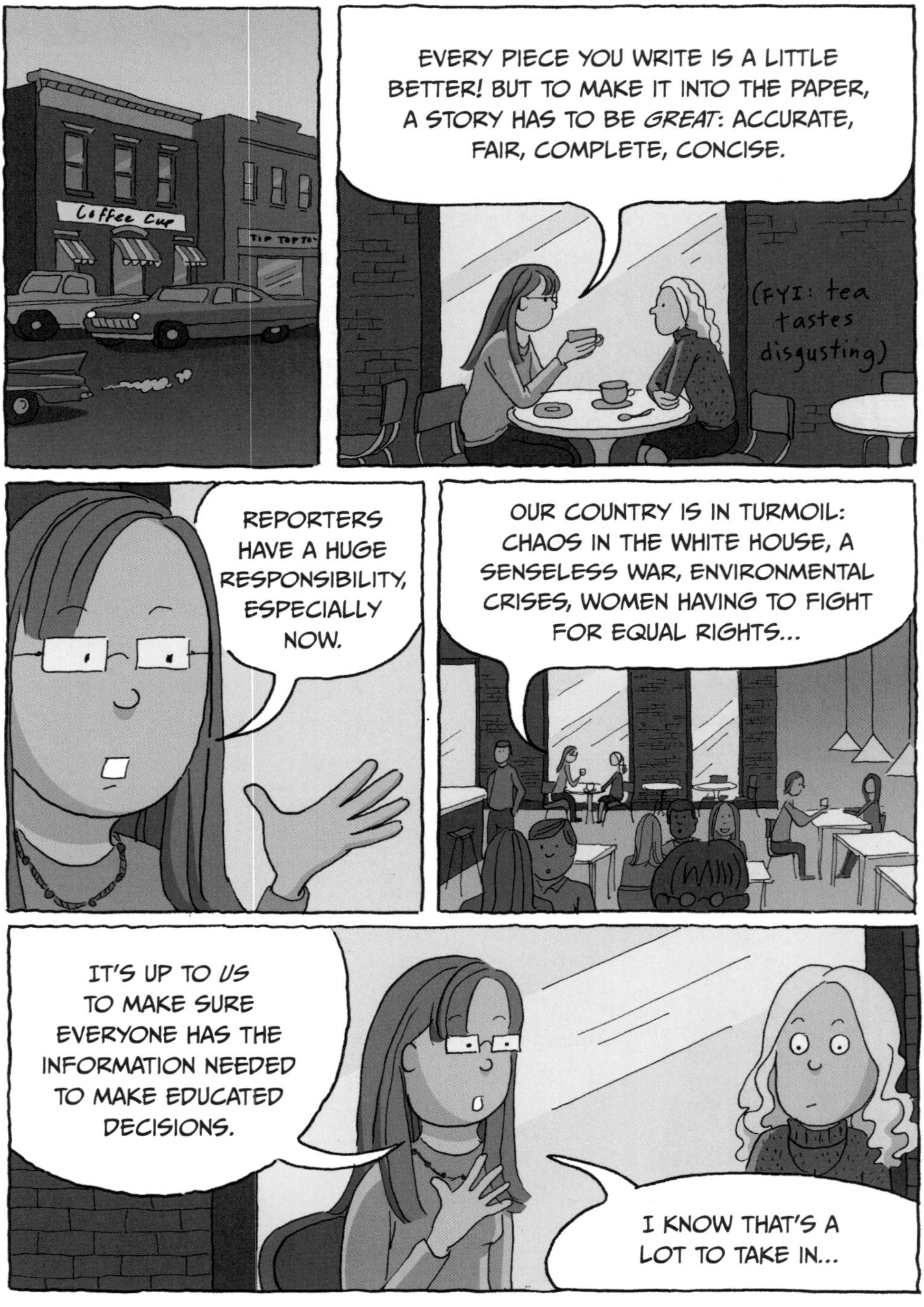
Coffee Cup
EVERY PIECE YOU WRITE IS A LITTLE BETTER! BUT TO MAKE IT INTO THE PAPER, A STORY HAS TO BE *GREAT*: ACCURATE, FAIR, COMPLETE, CONCISE.
(FYI: tea tastes disgusting)
REPORTERS HAVE A HUGE RESPONSIBILITY, ESPECIALLY NOW.
OUR COUNTRY IS IN TURMOIL: CHAOS IN THE WHITE HOUSE, A SENSELESS WAR, ENVIRONMENTAL CRISES, WOMEN HAVING TO FIGHT FOR EQUAL RIGHTS...
IT'S UP TO *US* TO MAKE SURE EVERYONE HAS THE INFORMATION NEEDED TO MAKE EDUCATED DECISIONS.
I KNOW THAT'S A LOT TO TAKE IN...

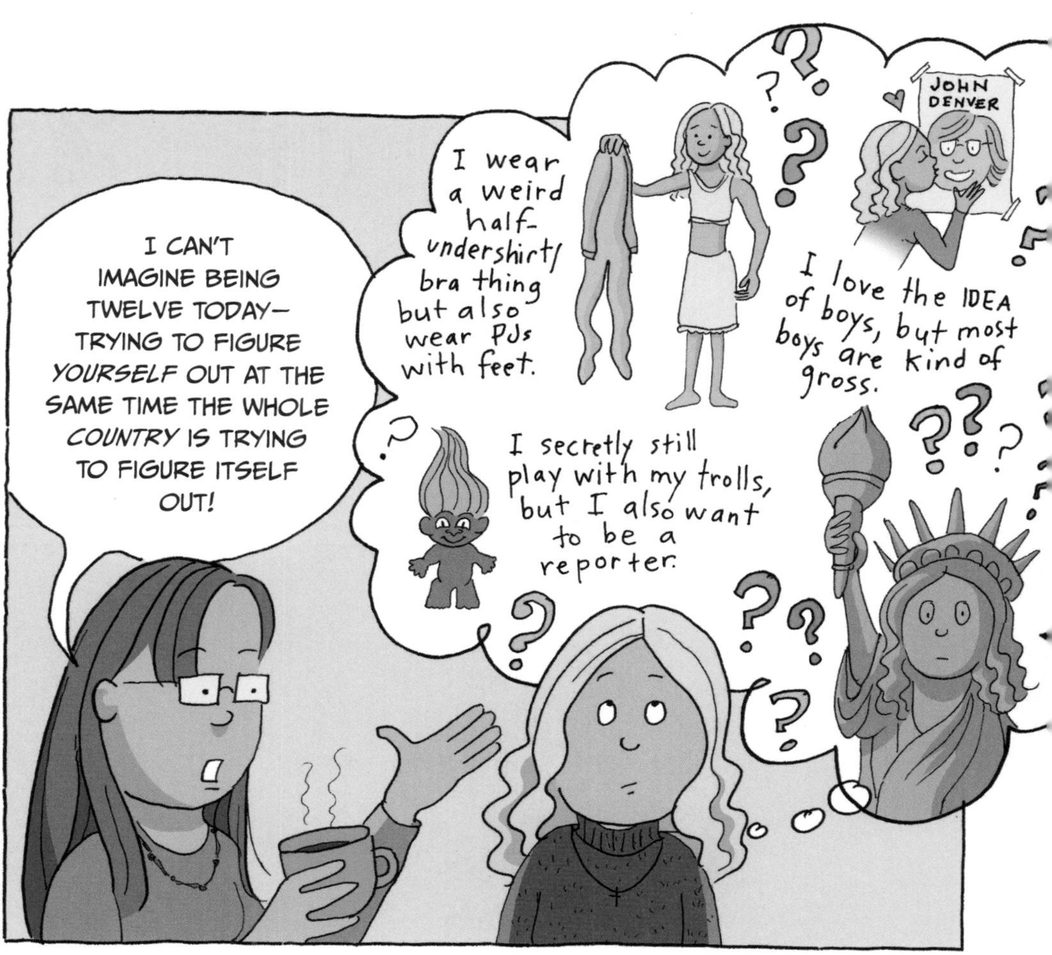
I CAN'T IMAGINE BEING TWELVE TODAY— TRYING TO FIGURE *YOURSELF* OUT AT THE SAME TIME THE WHOLE *COUNTRY* IS TRYING TO FIGURE ITSELF OUT!
I wear a weird half-undershirt/bra thing but also wear PJs with feet.
JOHN DENVER
I love the IDEA of boys, but most boys are kind of gross.
I secretly still play with my trolls, but I also want to be a reporter.

LESLIE'S RIGHT. BEING TWELVE *IS* SUPER WEIRD AND CONFUSING.

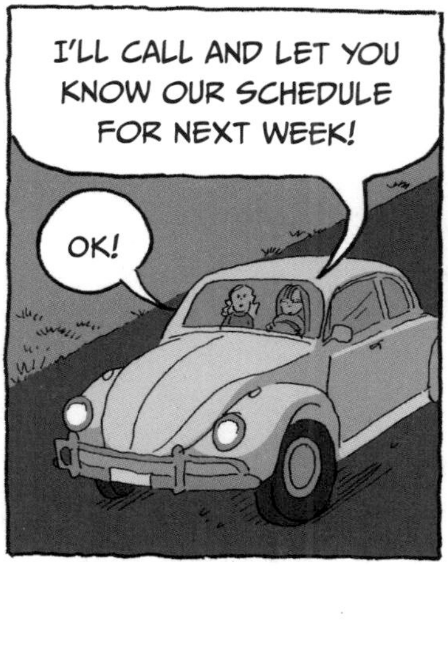
I'LL CALL AND LET YOU KNOW OUR SCHEDULE FOR NEXT WEEK!
OK!

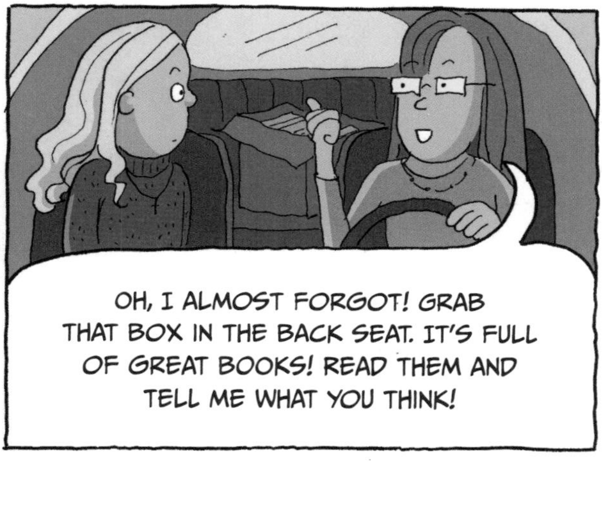
OH, I ALMOST FORGOT! GRAB THAT BOX IN THE BACK SEAT. IT'S FULL OF GREAT BOOKS! READ THEM AND TELL ME WHAT YOU THINK!

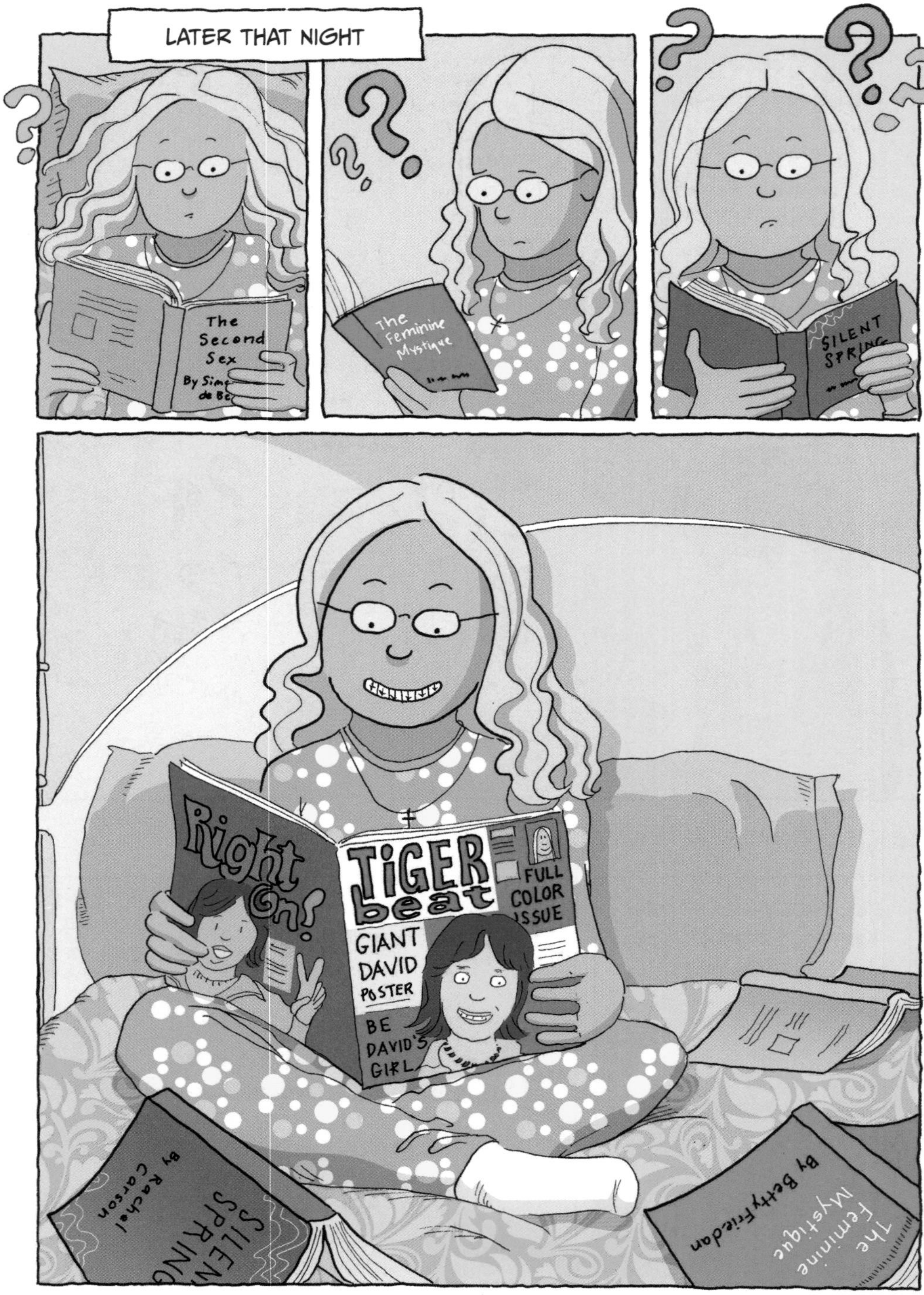
LATER THAT NIGHT
The Second Sex
The Feminine Mystique
SILENT SPRING
Right On!
TIGER beat
FULL COLOR ISSUE
GIANT DAVID POSTER
BE DAVID'S GIRL
SILENT SPRING
By Rachel Carson
The Feminine Mystique
By Betty Friedan

Chapter 5

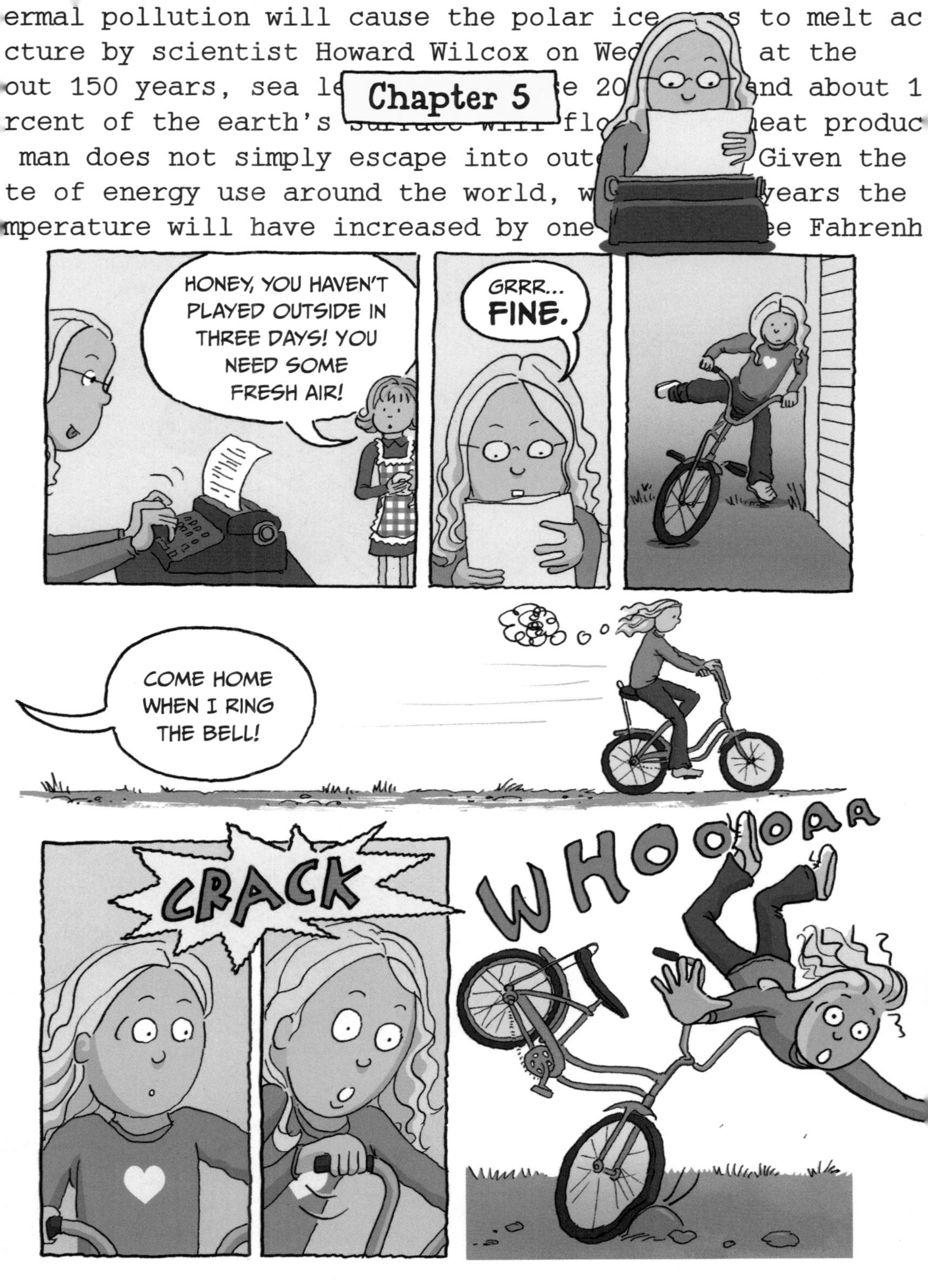
ermal pollution will cause the polar ice
s to melt ac
cture by scientist Howard Wilcox on Wed
at the
out 150 years, sea le
e 20
and about 1
rcent of the earth's
flo
heat produc
man does not simply escape into out
Given the
te of energy use around the world, w
years the
mperature will have increased by one
ee Fahrenh
HONEY, YOU HAVEN'T PLAYED OUTSIDE IN THREE DAYS! YOU NEED SOME FRESH AIR!
GRRR... FINE.
COME HOME WHEN I RING THE BELL!
CRACK
WHOOOOAA

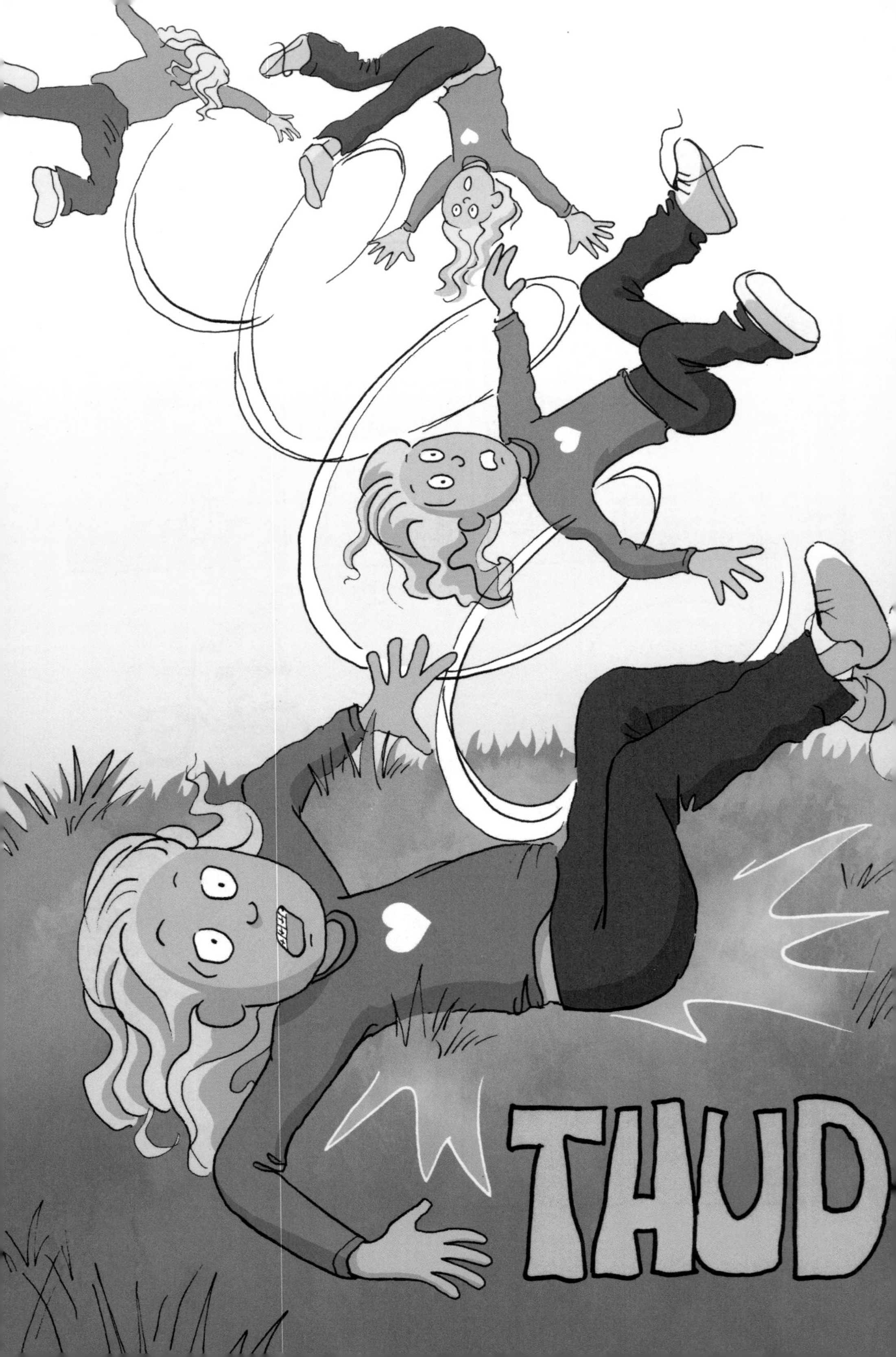
THUD

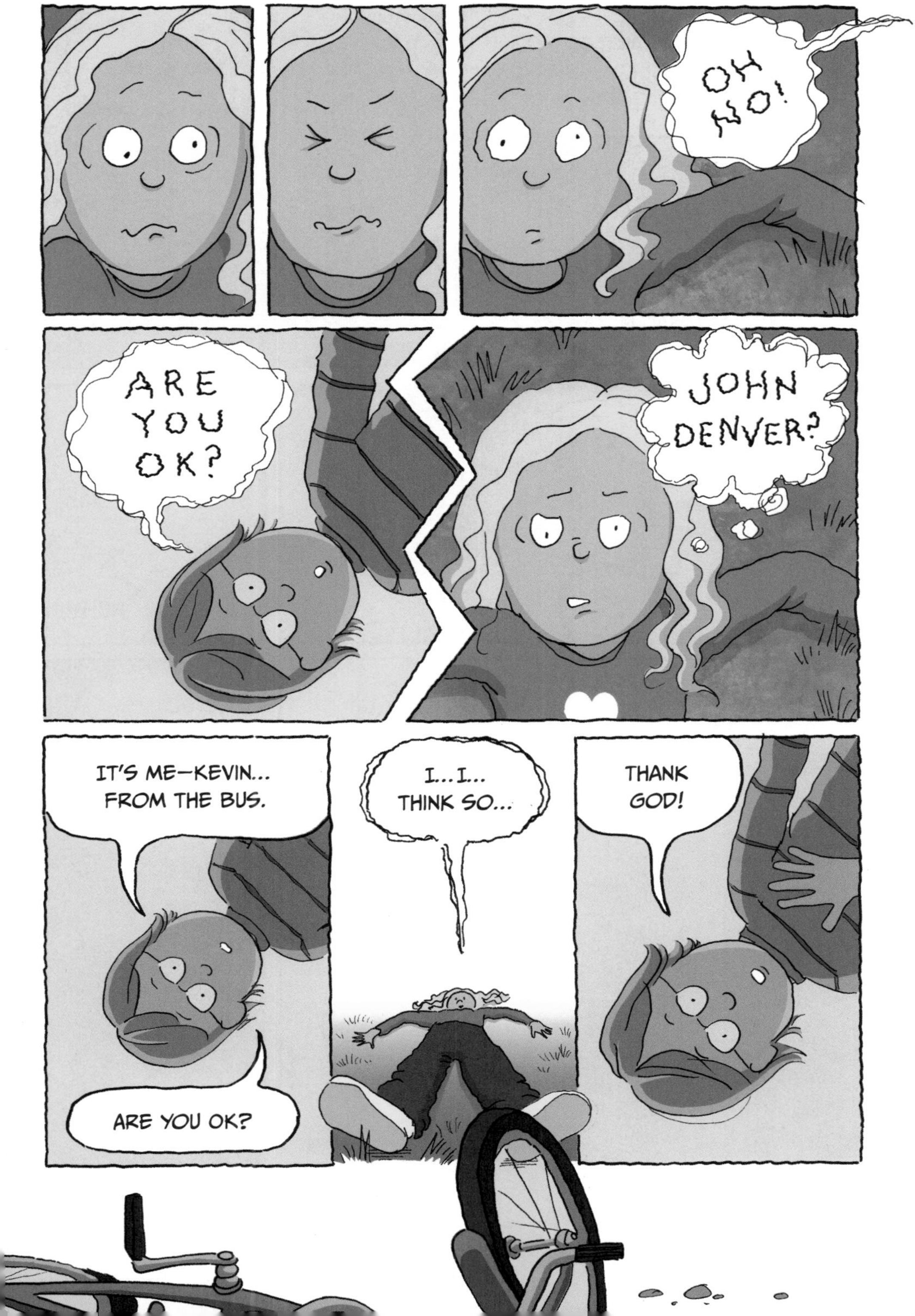
OH NO!
ARE YOU OK?
JOHN DENVER?
IT'S ME—KEVIN... FROM THE BUS.
ARE YOU OK?
I...I... THINK SO...
THANK GOD!

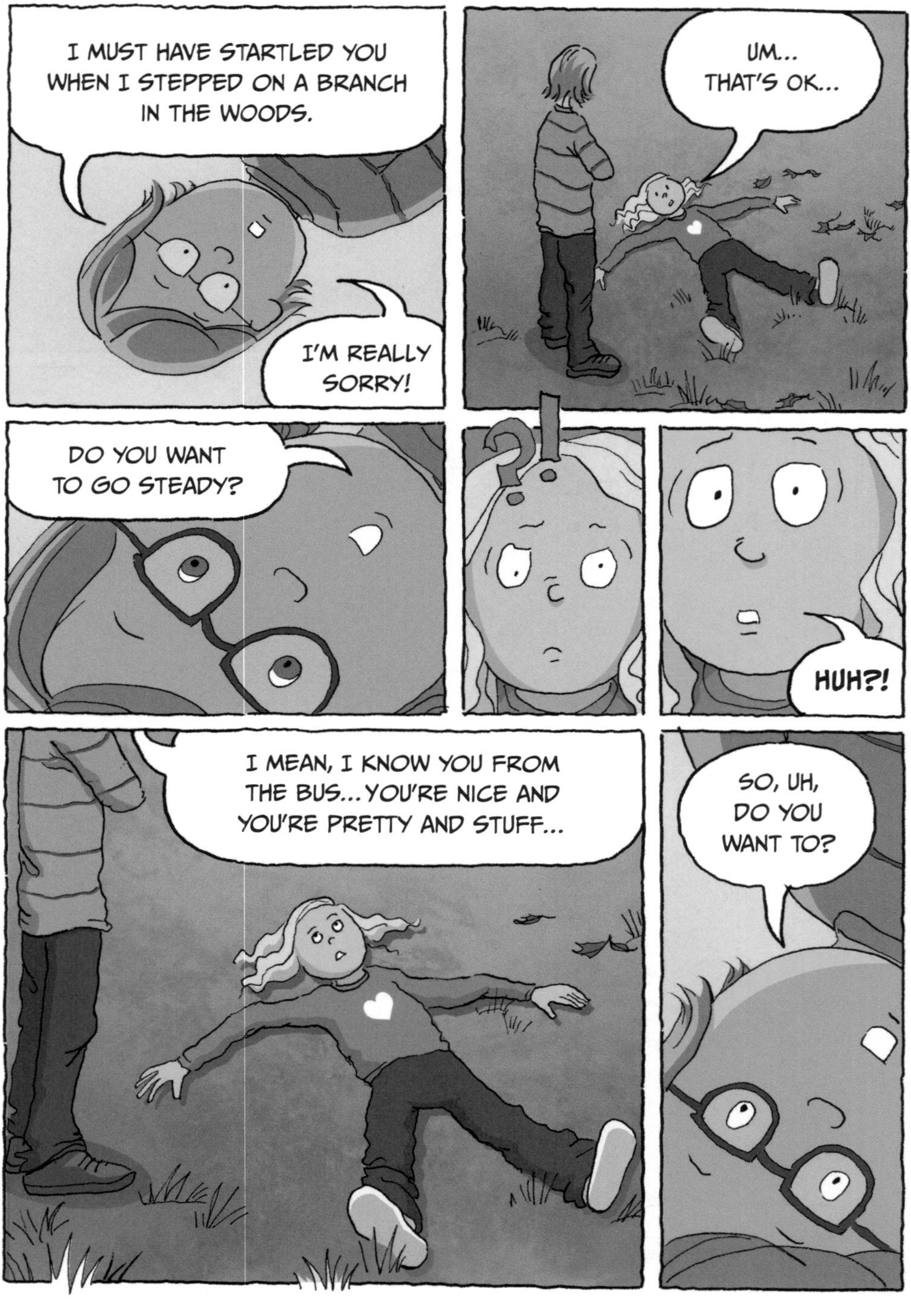
I MUST HAVE STARTLED YOU WHEN I STEPPED ON A BRANCH IN THE WOODS.
I'M REALLY SORRY!
UM... THAT'S OK...
DO YOU WANT TO GO STEADY?
HUH?!
I MEAN, I KNOW YOU FROM THE BUS...YOU'RE NICE AND YOU'RE PRETTY AND STUFF...
SO, UH, DO YOU WANT TO?

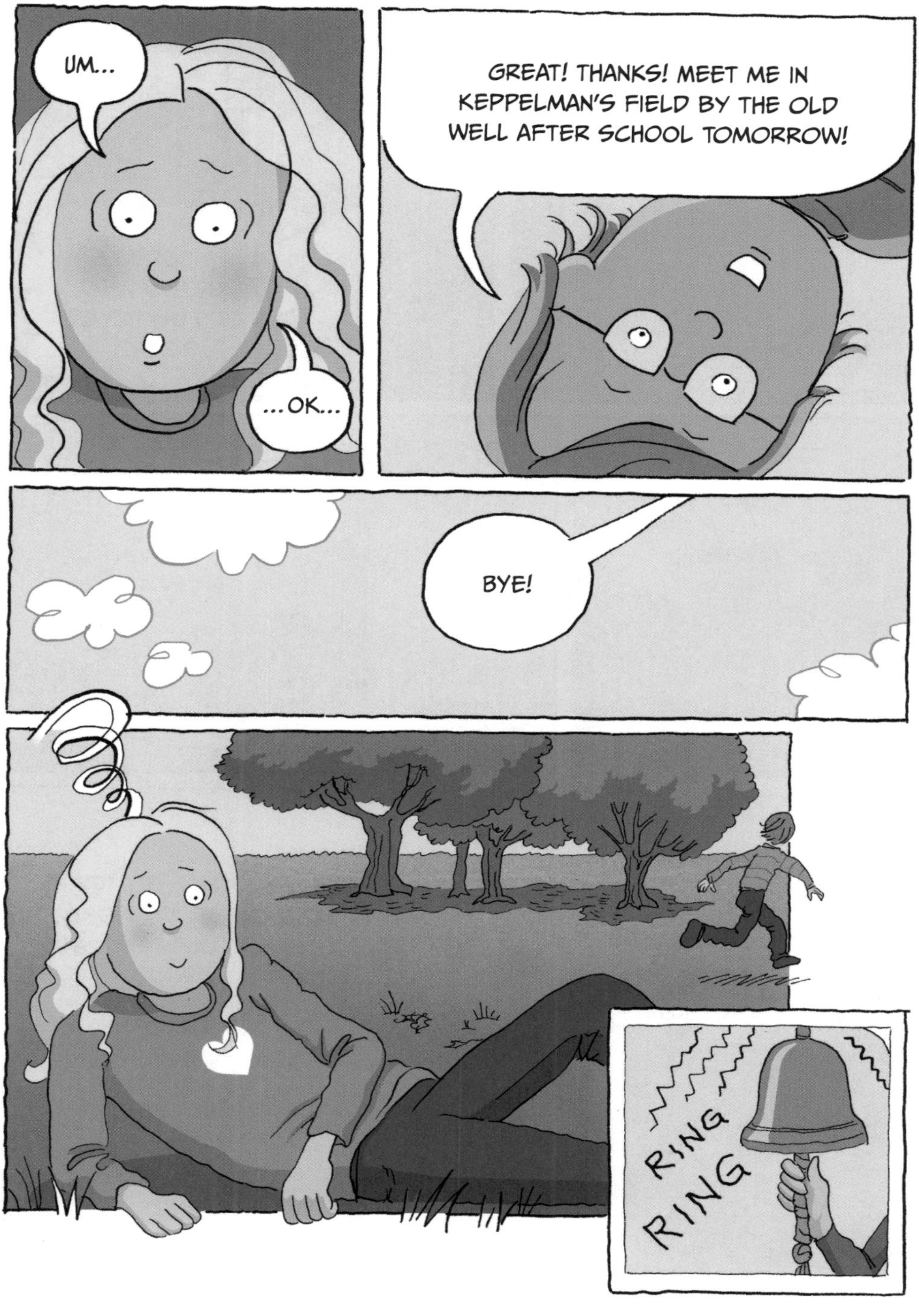

UM...
...OK...
GREAT! THANKS! MEET ME IN KEPPELMAN'S FIELD BY THE OLD WELL AFTER SCHOOL TOMORROW!
BYE!
RING
RING

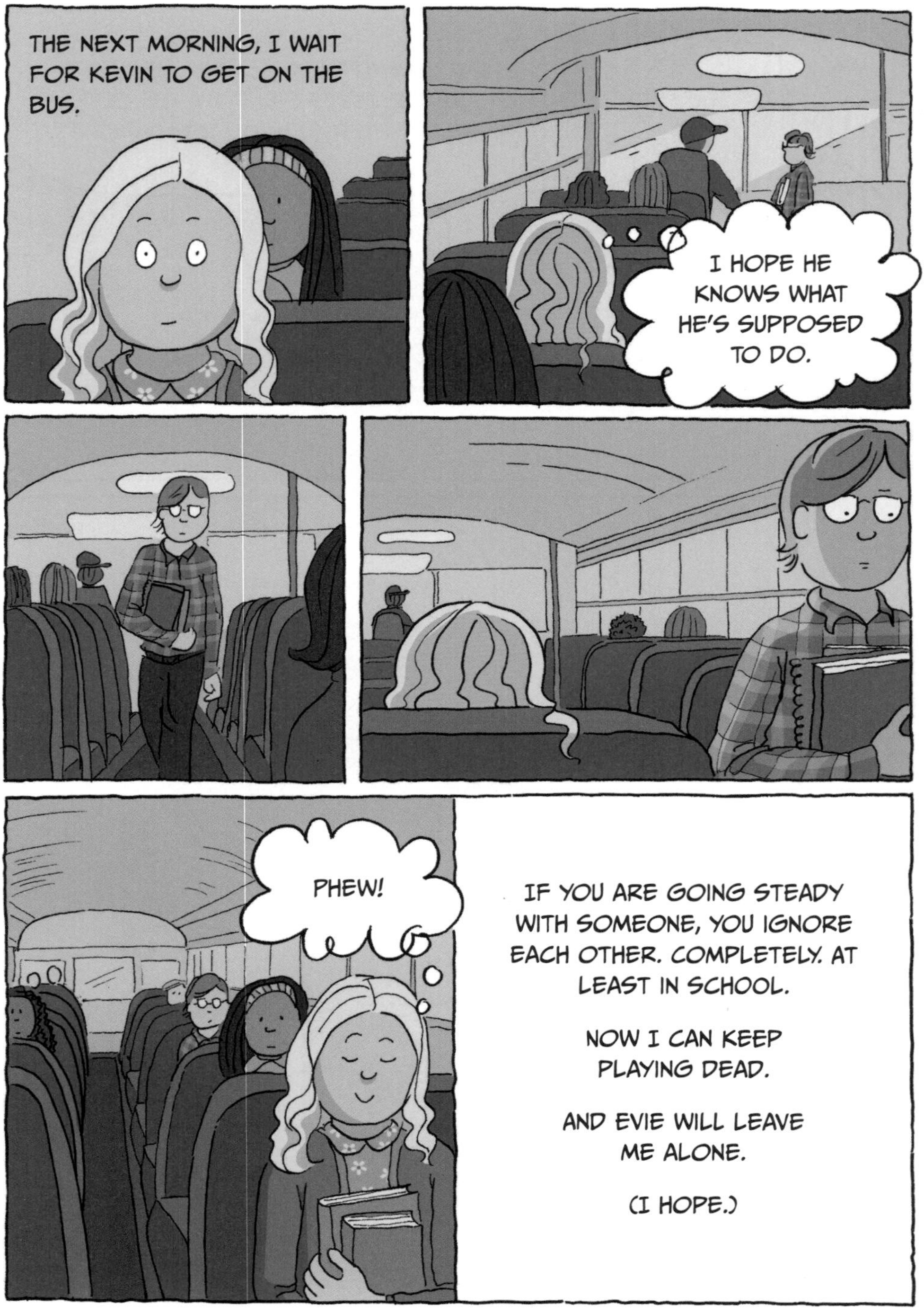
THE NEXT MORNING, I WAIT FOR KEVIN TO GET ON THE BUS.
I HOPE HE KNOWS WHAT HE'S SUPPOSED TO DO.
PHEW!
IF YOU ARE GOING STEADY WITH SOMEONE, YOU IGNORE EACH OTHER. COMPLETELY. AT LEAST IN SCHOOL.
NOW I CAN KEEP PLAYING DEAD.
AND EVIE WILL LEAVE ME ALONE.
(I HOPE.)

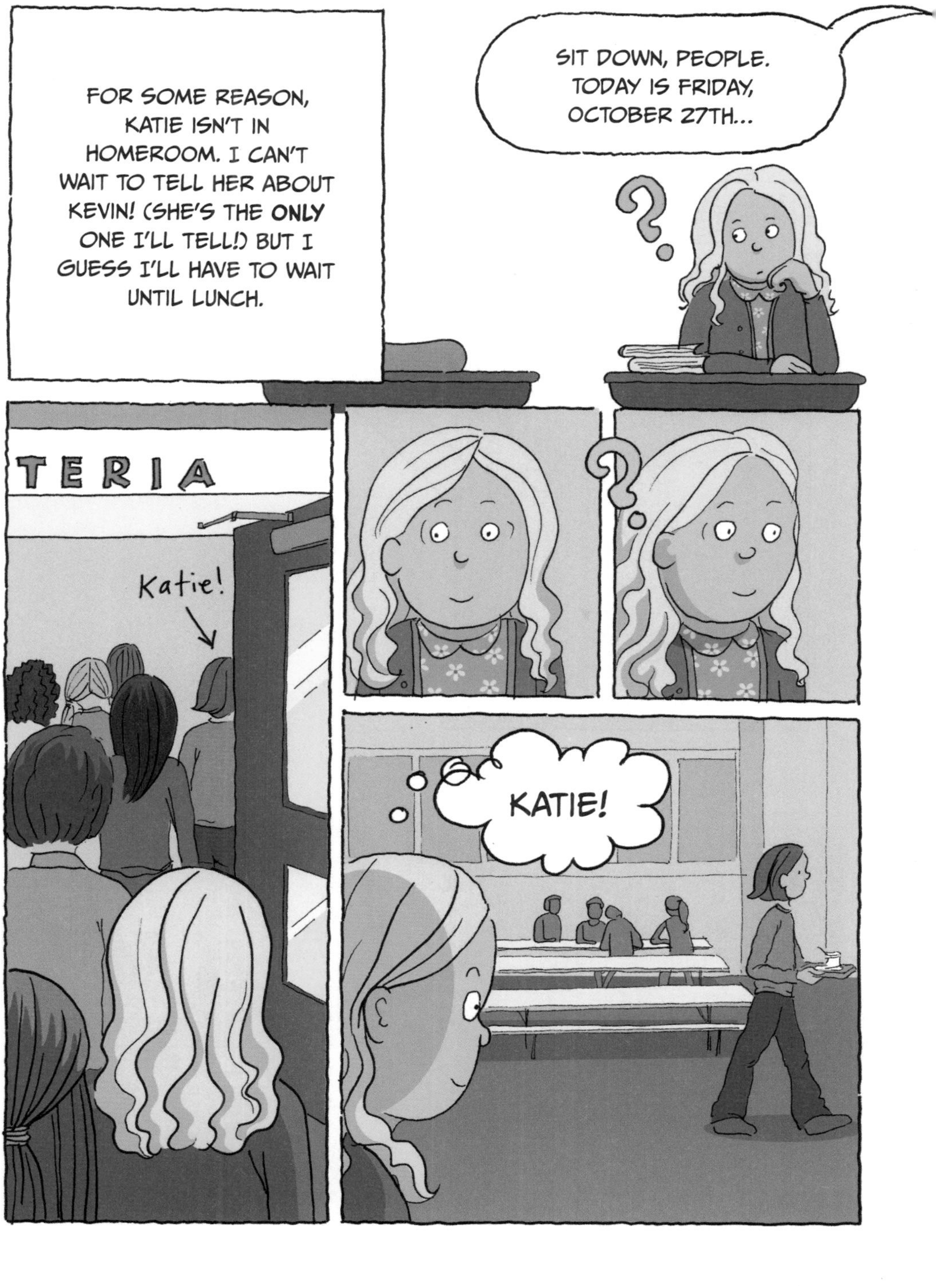
FOR SOME REASON, KATIE ISN'T IN HOMEROOM. I CAN'T WAIT TO TELL HER ABOUT KEVIN! (SHE'S THE **ONLY** ONE I'LL TELL!) BUT I GUESS I'LL HAVE TO WAIT UNTIL LUNCH.
SIT DOWN, PEOPLE. TODAY IS FRIDAY, OCTOBER 27TH...
?
TERIA
Katie!
?
KATIE!

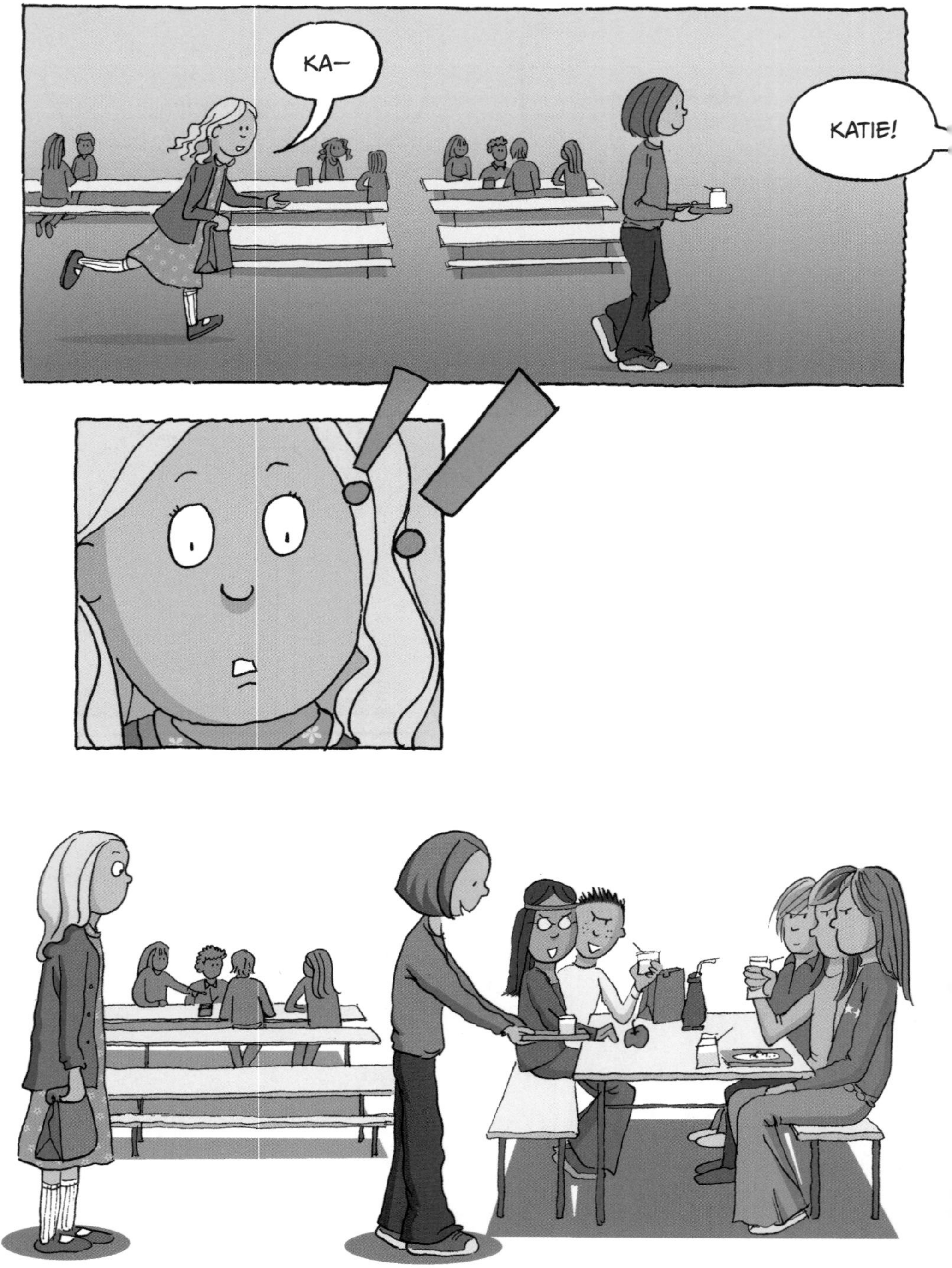
KA—
KATIE!

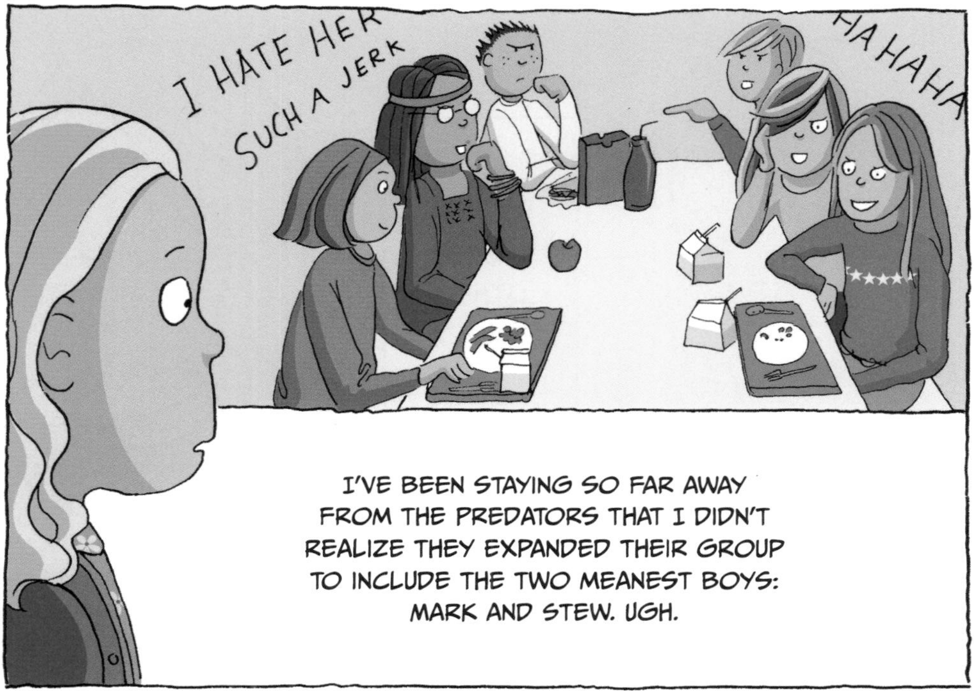
I HATE HER
SUCH A JERK
HAHAHAHA
I'VE BEEN STAYING SO FAR AWAY FROM THE PREDATORS THAT I DIDN'T REALIZE THEY EXPANDED THEIR GROUP TO INCLUDE THE TWO MEANEST BOYS: MARK AND STEW. UGH.

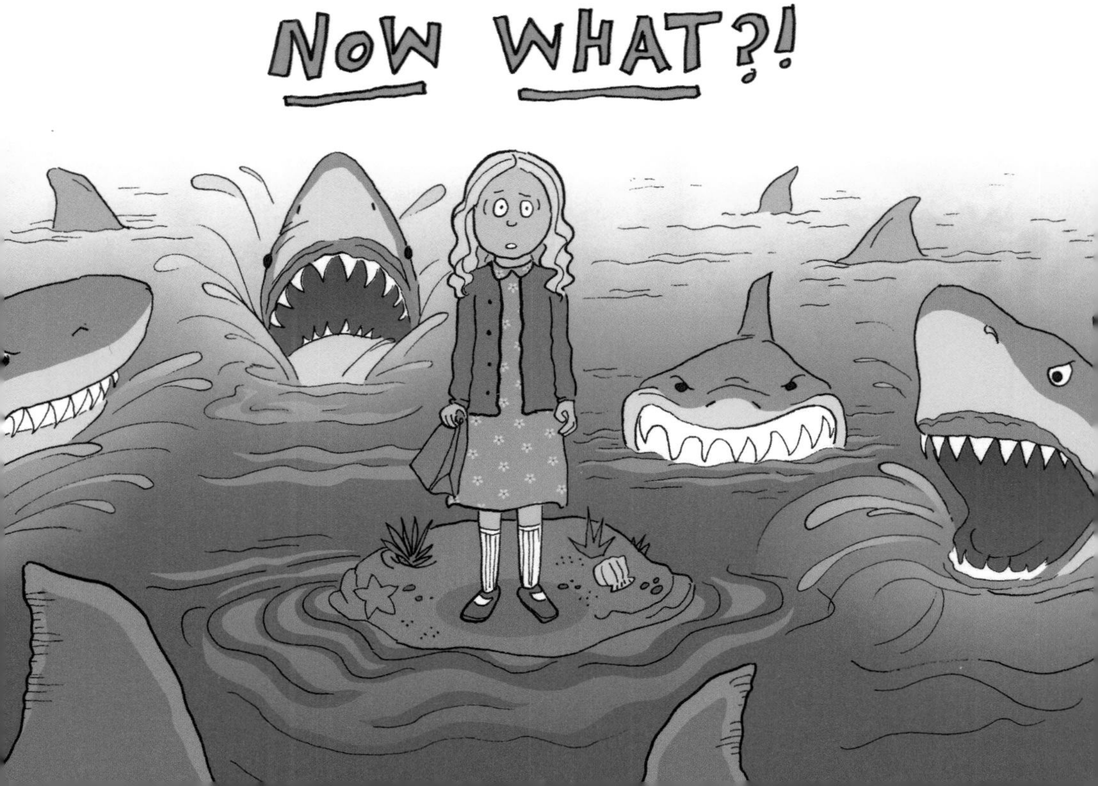
NOW WHAT?!

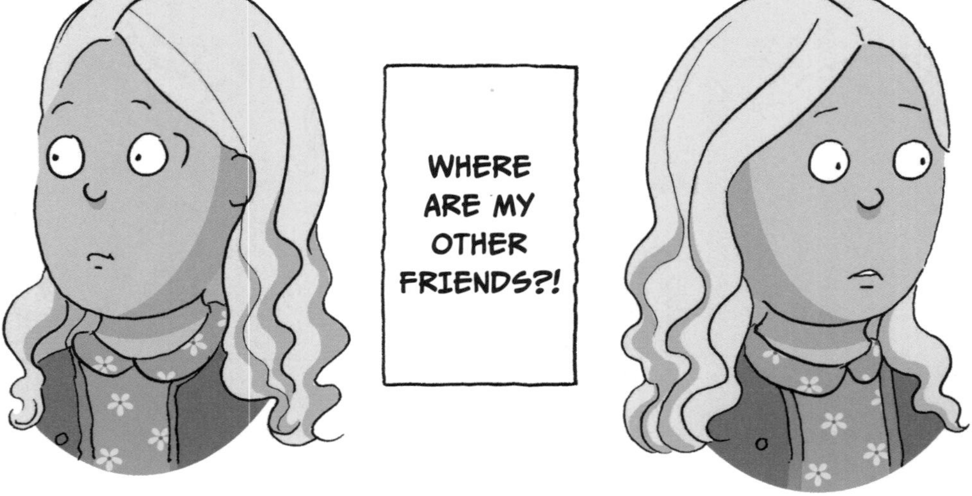
WHERE ARE MY OTHER FRIENDS?!

MOLLY MUST HAVE GONE TO SEÑORITA BERKOWITZ'S ROOM FOR EXTRA HELP IN SPANISH... IS BARB SELLING DONUTS FOR STUDENT COUNCIL? OR DOES SHE ONLY DO THAT *BEFORE* SCHOOL? I DON'T SEE PENNY, MY FRIEND FROM NATURE CAMP AND GIRL SCOUTS...

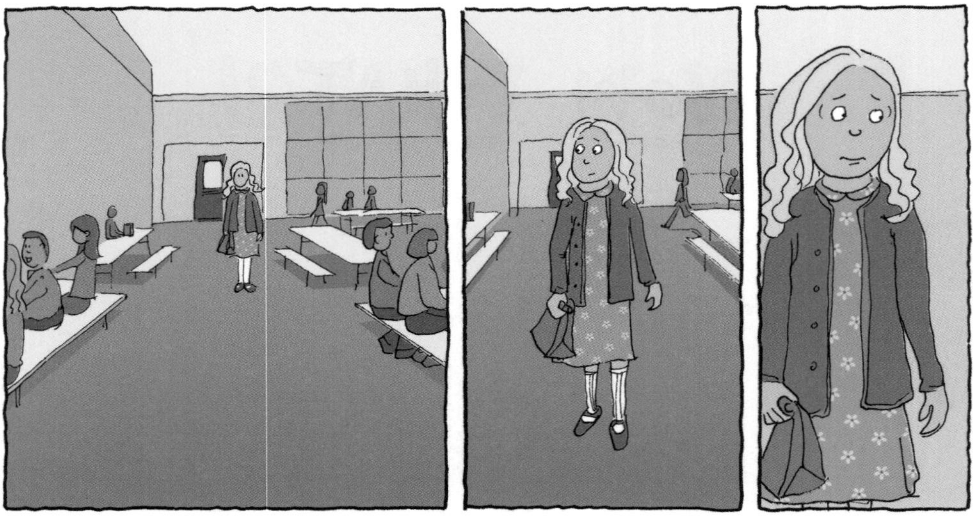

I DON'T SEE ANYONE I CAN SIT WITH...
I'M RUNNING OUT OF OPTIONS...

AND STARTING TO PANIC...

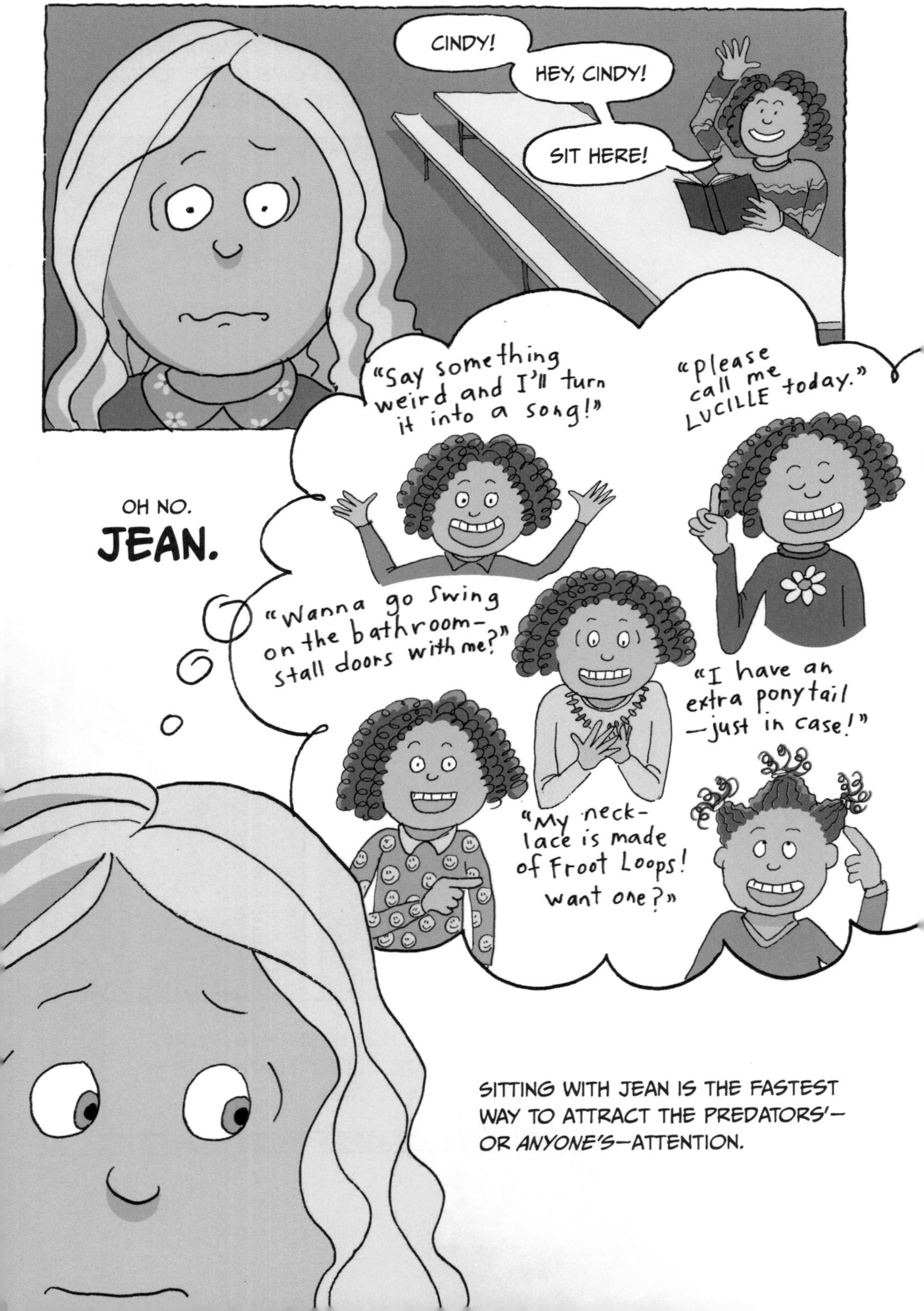
CINDY!
HEY, CINDY!
SIT HERE!
OH NO.
JEAN.
“Say something weird and I'll turn it into a song!”
“please call me LUCILLE today.”
“Wanna go swing on the bathroom-stall doors with me?”
“I have an extra ponytail —just in case!”
“My neck-lace is made of Froot Loops! want one?”
SITTING WITH JEAN IS THE FASTEST WAY TO ATTRACT THE PREDATORS'—OR *ANYONE'S*—ATTENTION.

OH, UM, THANKS ANYWAY, JEAN, BUT I HAVE SOME STUFF TO DO IN THE ART ROOM.

OH, OK!

HAHAHA

HOT LUNCH IS SO GROSS.

HAHA

HAHAHA

I'M NOT HUNGRY ANYMORE, SO I PUT MY LUNCH BACK IN MY LOCKER.

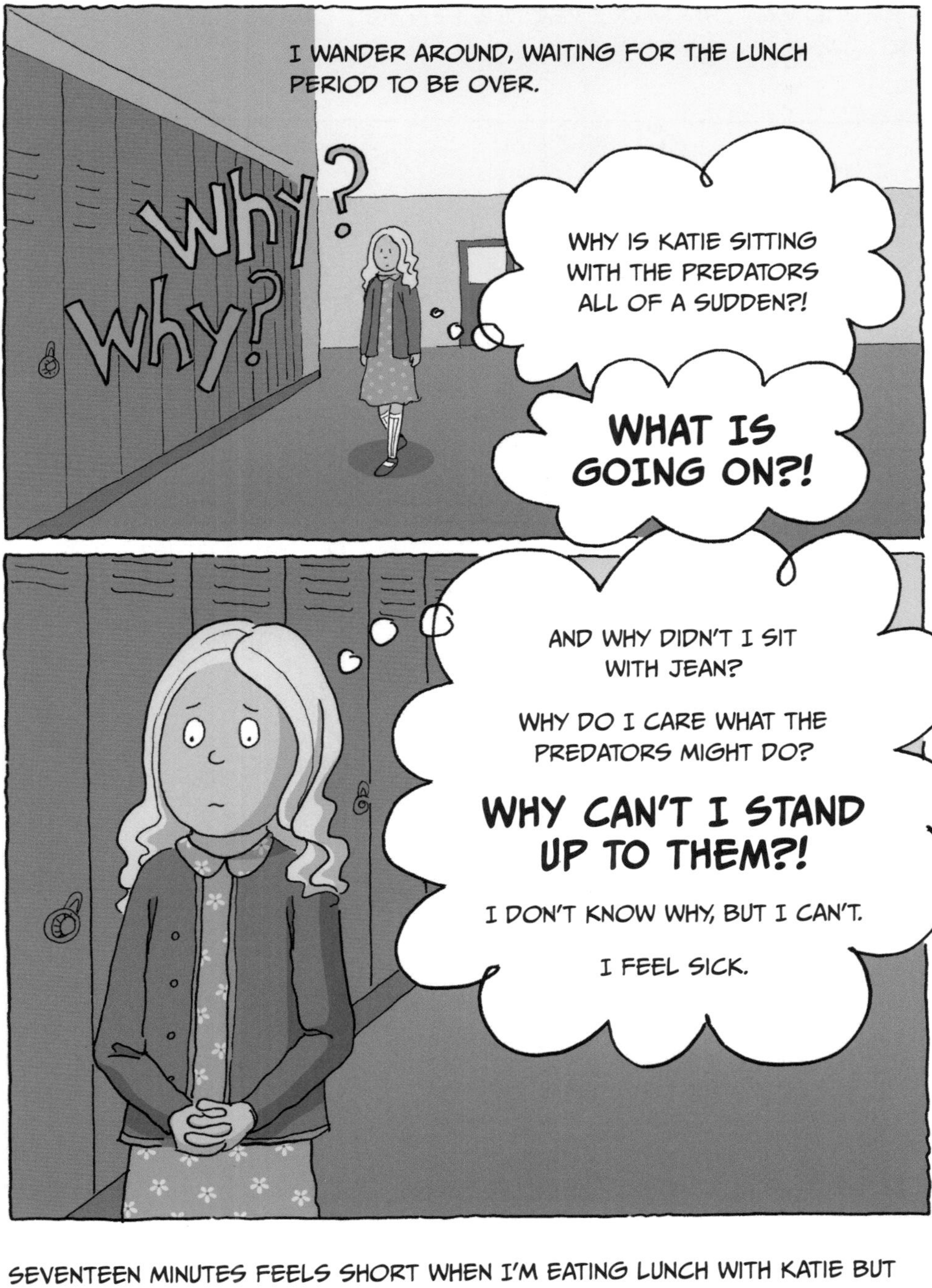
I WANDER AROUND, WAITING FOR THE LUNCH PERIOD TO BE OVER.
WHY? WHY?
WHY IS KATIE SITTING WITH THE PREDATORS ALL OF A SUDDEN?!
WHAT IS GOING ON?!
AND WHY DIDN'T I SIT WITH JEAN?
WHY DO I CARE WHAT THE PREDATORS MIGHT DO?
WHY CAN'T I STAND UP TO THEM?!
I DON'T KNOW WHY, BUT I CAN'T.
I FEEL SICK.

SEVENTEEN MINUTES FEELS SHORT WHEN I'M EATING LUNCH WITH KATIE BUT **VERY LONG** WHEN I'M PACING AND WORRYING.

I HAVE TO WAIT *TWO WHOLE PERIODS* BEFORE I CAN TALK TO KATIE IN ART CLASS.

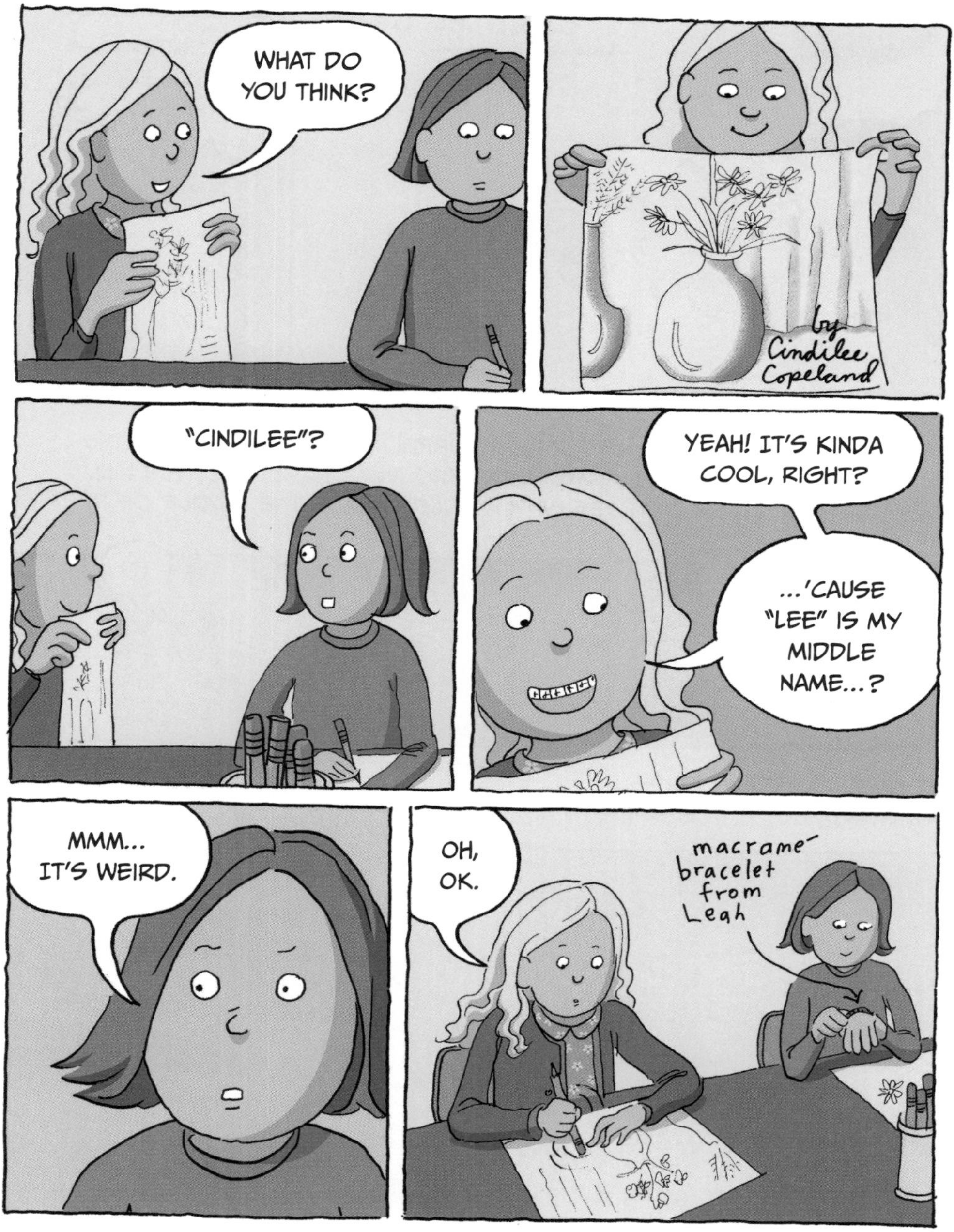
WHAT DO YOU THINK?
by Cindilee Copeland
"CINDILEE"?
YEAH! IT'S KINDA COOL, RIGHT?
...'CAUSE "LEE" IS MY MIDDLE NAME...?
MMM... IT'S WEIRD.
OH, OK.
macrame-bracelet from Leah

I FORGET TO TELL HER ABOUT KEVIN.

Chapter 6

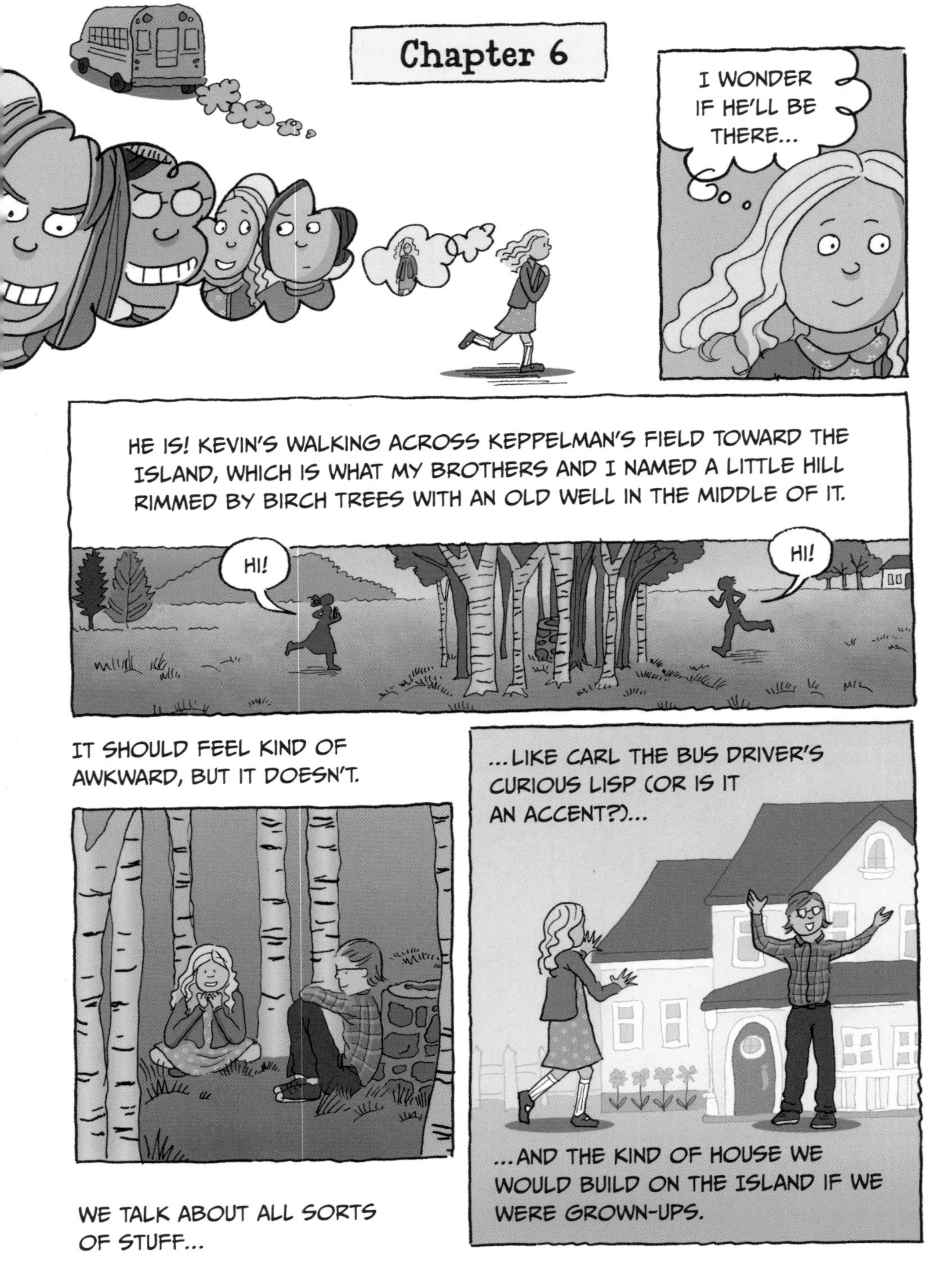

I WONDER IF HE'LL BE THERE...
HE IS! KEVIN'S WALKING ACROSS KEPPELMAN'S FIELD TOWARD THE ISLAND, WHICH IS WHAT MY BROTHERS AND I NAMED A LITTLE HILL RIMMED BY BIRCH TREES WITH AN OLD WELL IN THE MIDDLE OF IT.
HI!
HI!
IT SHOULD FEEL KIND OF AWKWARD, BUT IT DOESN'T.
WE TALK ABOUT ALL SORTS OF STUFF...
...LIKE CARL THE BUS DRIVER'S CURIOUS LISP (OR IS IT AN ACCENT?)...
...AND THE KIND OF HOUSE WE WOULD BUILD ON THE ISLAND IF WE WERE GROWN-UPS.

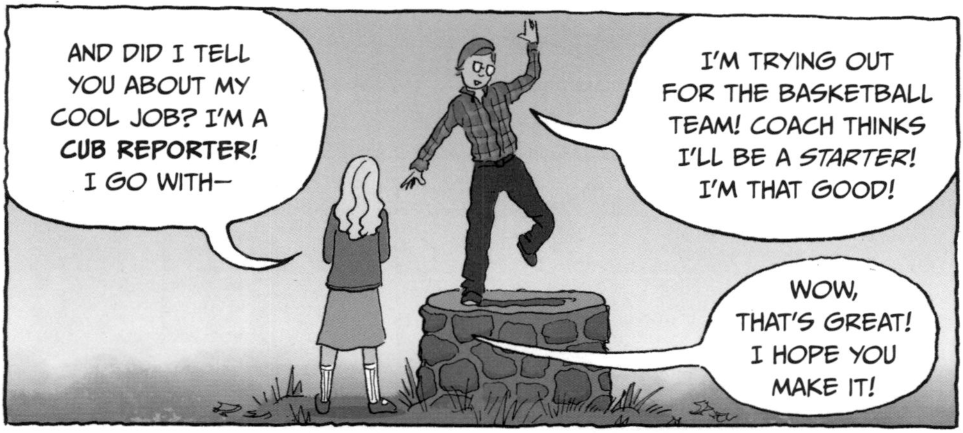
AND DID I TELL YOU ABOUT MY COOL JOB? I'M A **CUB REPORTER!** I GO WITH—
I'M TRYING OUT FOR THE BASKETBALL TEAM! COACH THINKS I'LL BE A *STARTER!* I'M THAT GOOD!
WOW, THAT'S GREAT! I HOPE YOU MAKE IT!

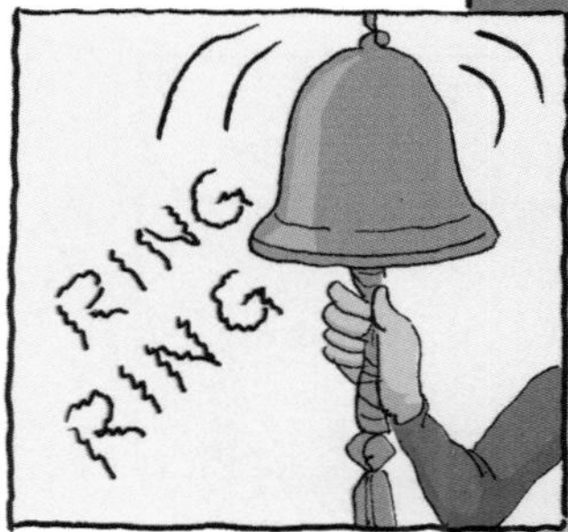
RING
RING

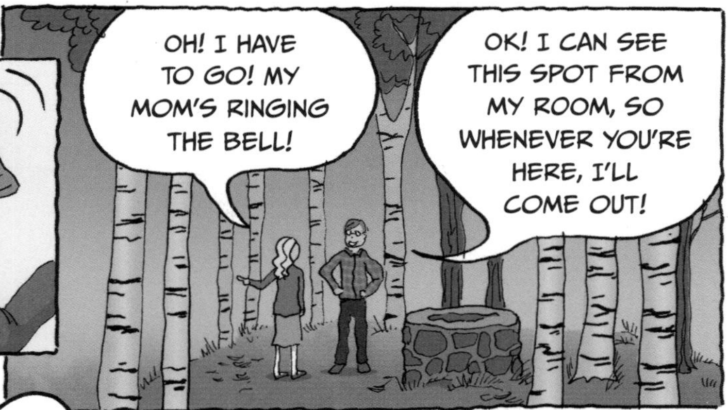
OH! I HAVE TO GO! MY MOM'S RINGING THE BELL!
OK! I CAN SEE THIS SPOT FROM MY ROOM, SO WHENEVER YOU'RE HERE, I'LL COME OUT!

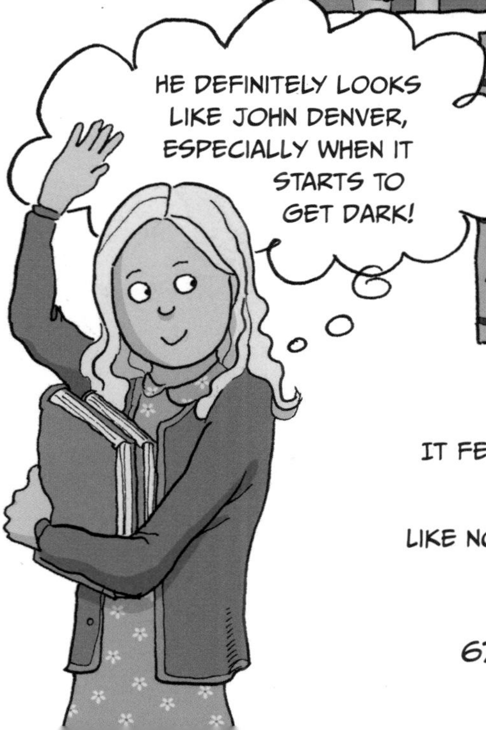
HE DEFINITELY LOOKS LIKE JOHN DENVER, ESPECIALLY WHEN IT STARTS TO GET DARK!

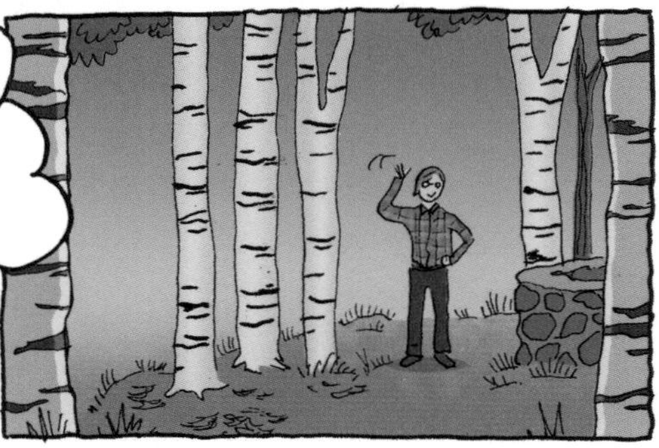

I HATE TO LEAVE.

IT FEELS LIKE WE ARE SO FAR AWAY FROM EVERYONE AND EVERYTHING.

LIKE NOTHING MATTERS BUT THE TWO OF US.

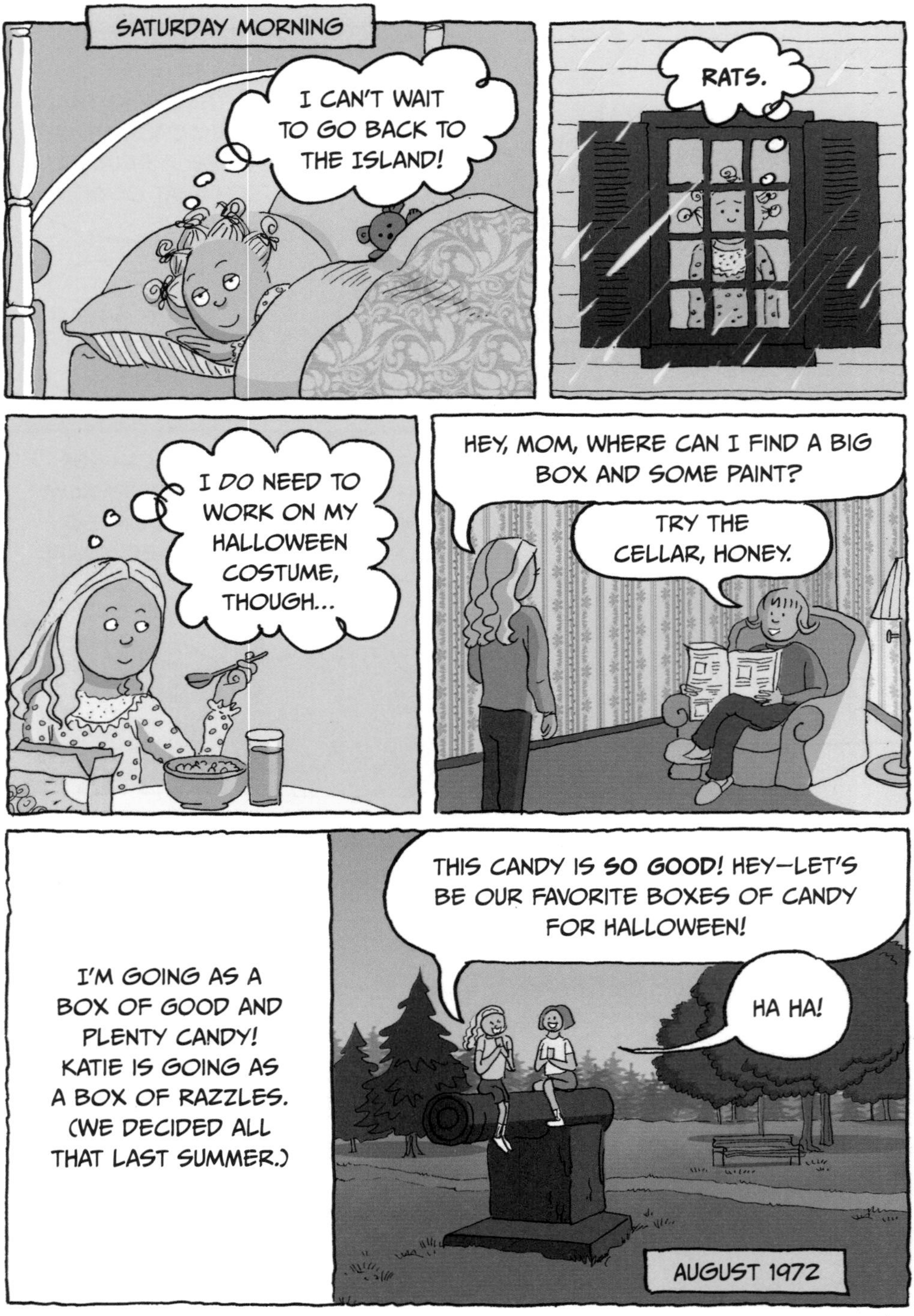
SATURDAY MORNING
I CAN'T WAIT TO GO BACK TO THE ISLAND!
RATS.
I *DO* NEED TO WORK ON MY HALLOWEEN COSTUME, THOUGH...
HEY, MOM, WHERE CAN I FIND A BIG BOX AND SOME PAINT?
TRY THE CELLAR, HONEY.
I'M GOING AS A BOX OF GOOD AND PLENTY CANDY! KATIE IS GOING AS A BOX OF RAZZLES. (WE DECIDED ALL THAT LAST SUMMER.)
THIS CANDY IS **SO GOOD!** HEY—LET'S BE OUR FAVORITE BOXES OF CANDY FOR HALLOWEEN!
HA HA!
AUGUST 1972

WE ALWAYS GO TRICK-OR-TREATING IN COSTUMES THAT GO TOGETHER.

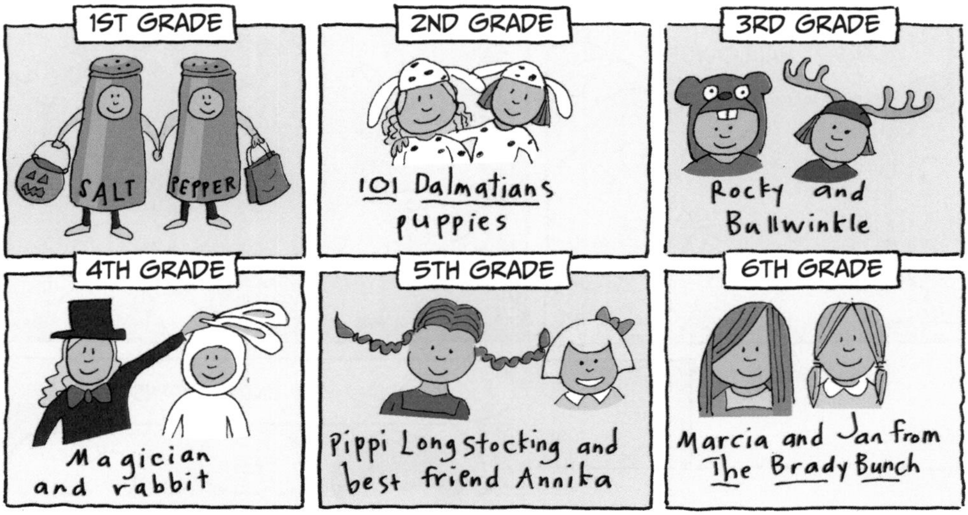
1ST GRADE
SALT
PEPPER
2ND GRADE
101 Dalmatians puppies
3RD GRADE
Rocky and Bullwinkle
4TH GRADE
Magician and rabbit
5TH GRADE
Pippi Longstocking and best friend Annika
6TH GRADE
Marcia and Jan from The Brady Bunch

AND NOW... **SEVENTH GRADE!**

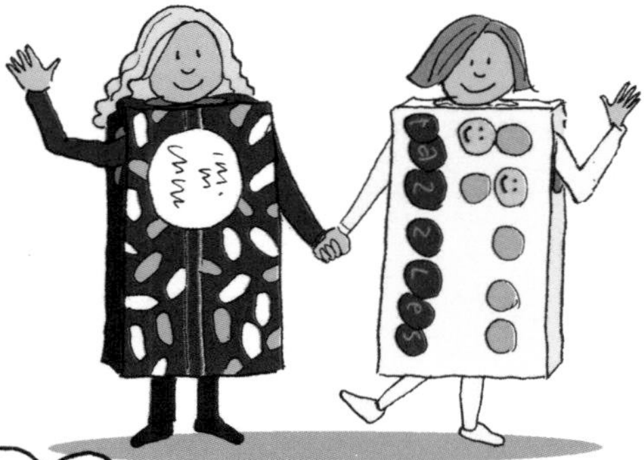

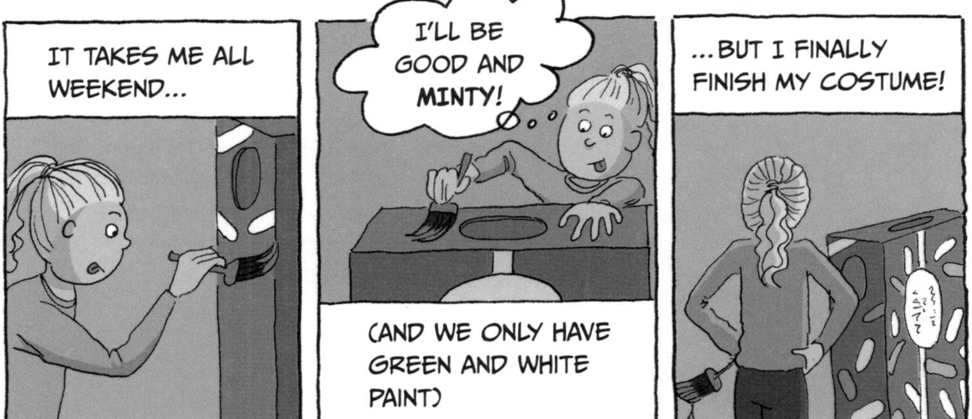
IT TAKES ME ALL WEEKEND...
I'LL BE GOOD AND MINTY!
(AND WE ONLY HAVE GREEN AND WHITE PAINT)
...BUT I FINALLY FINISH MY COSTUME!

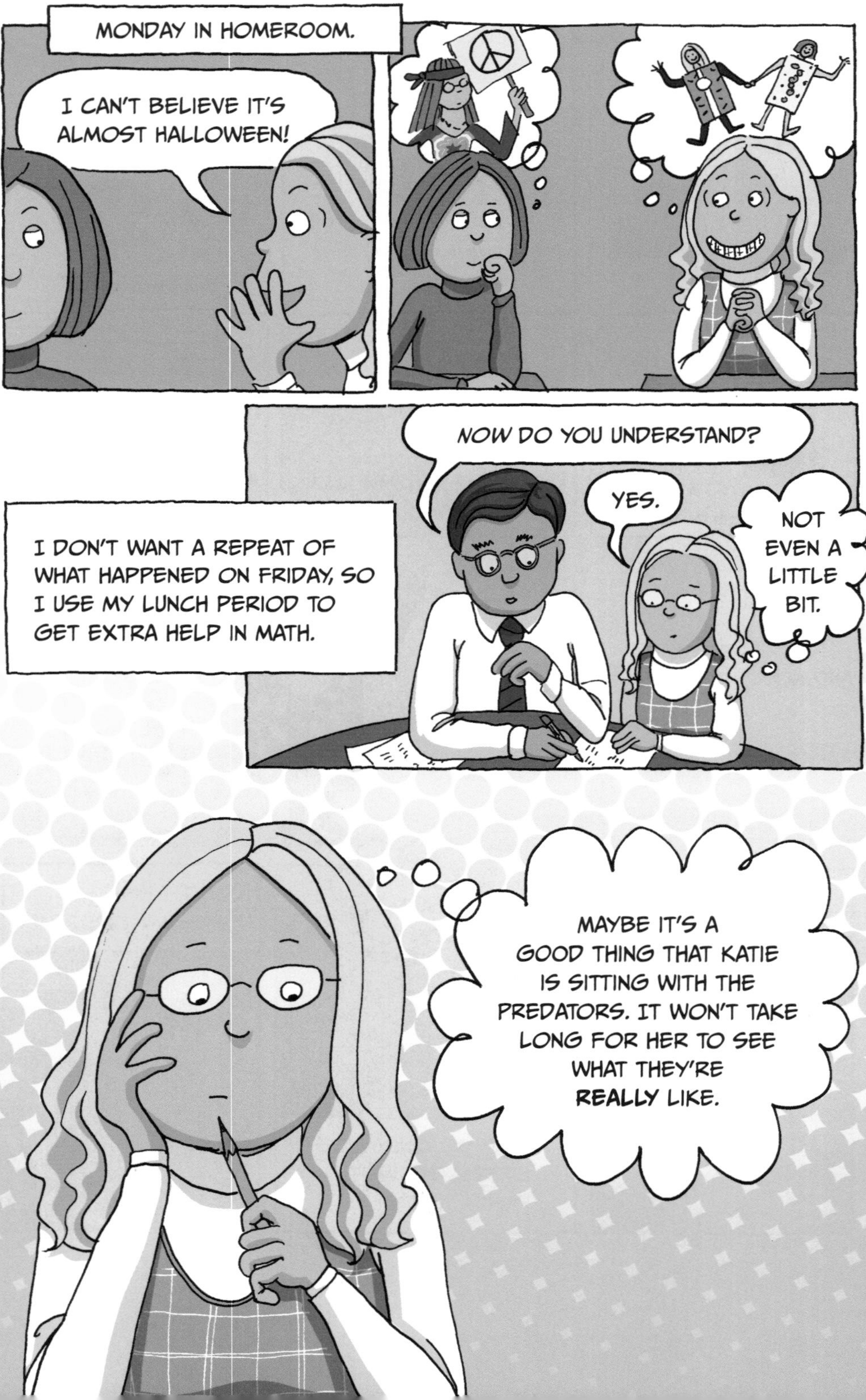
MONDAY IN HOMEROOM.
I CAN'T BELIEVE IT'S ALMOST HALLOWEEN!
NOW DO YOU UNDERSTAND?
I DON'T WANT A REPEAT OF WHAT HAPPENED ON FRIDAY, SO I USE MY LUNCH PERIOD TO GET EXTRA HELP IN MATH.
YES.
NOT EVEN A LITTLE BIT.
MAYBE IT'S A GOOD THING THAT KATIE IS SITTING WITH THE PREDATORS. IT WON'T TAKE LONG FOR HER TO SEE WHAT THEY'RE **REALLY** LIKE.

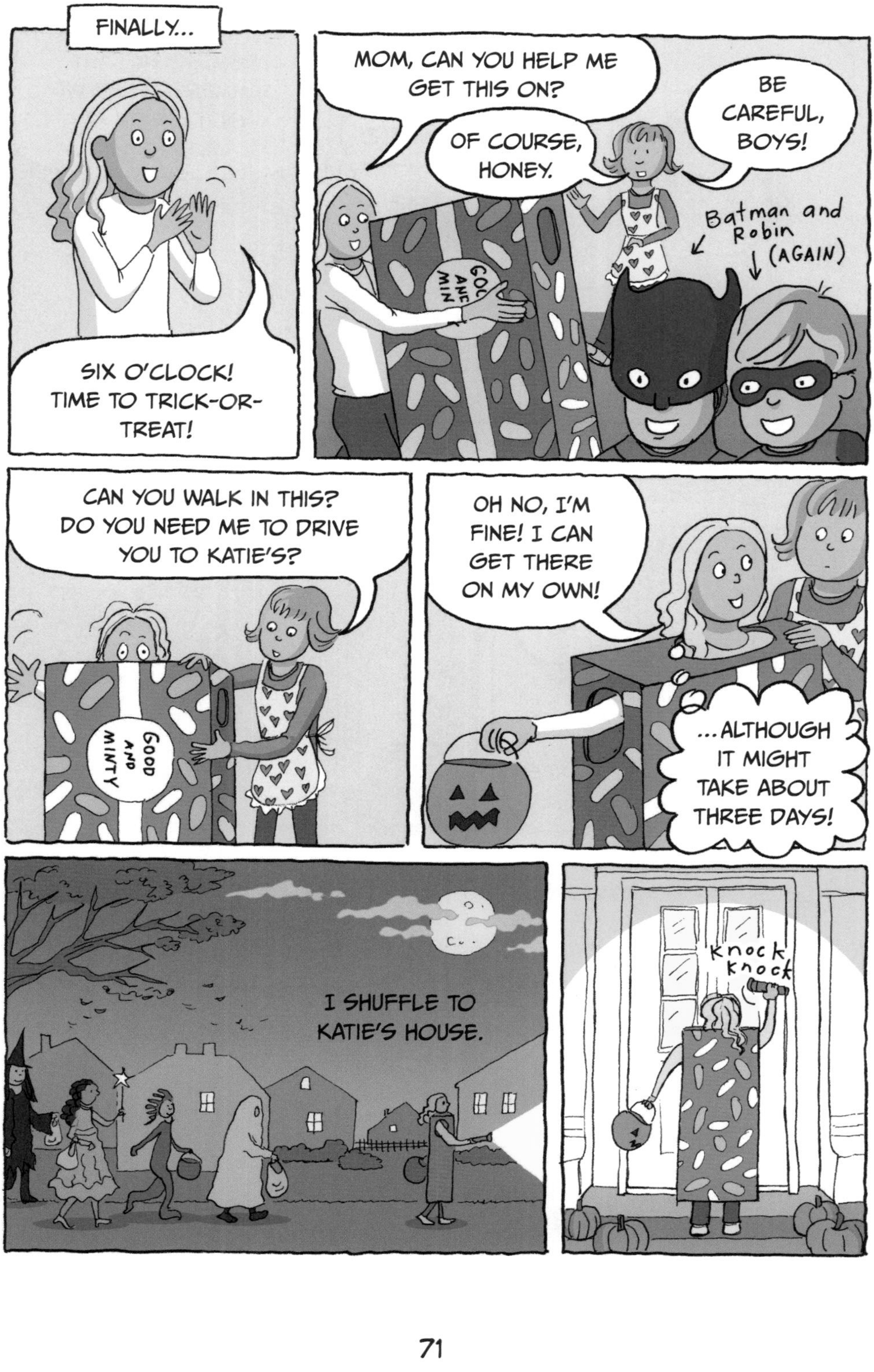
FINALLY...
SIX O'CLOCK! TIME TO TRICK-OR-TREAT!
MOM, CAN YOU HELP ME GET THIS ON?
OF COURSE, HONEY.
BE CAREFUL, BOYS!
Batman and Robin (AGAIN)
CAN YOU WALK IN THIS? DO YOU NEED ME TO DRIVE YOU TO KATIE'S?
GOOD AND MINTY
OH NO, I'M FINE! I CAN GET THERE ON MY OWN!
...ALTHOUGH IT MIGHT TAKE ABOUT THREE DAYS!
I SHUFFLE TO KATIE'S HOUSE.
knock knock

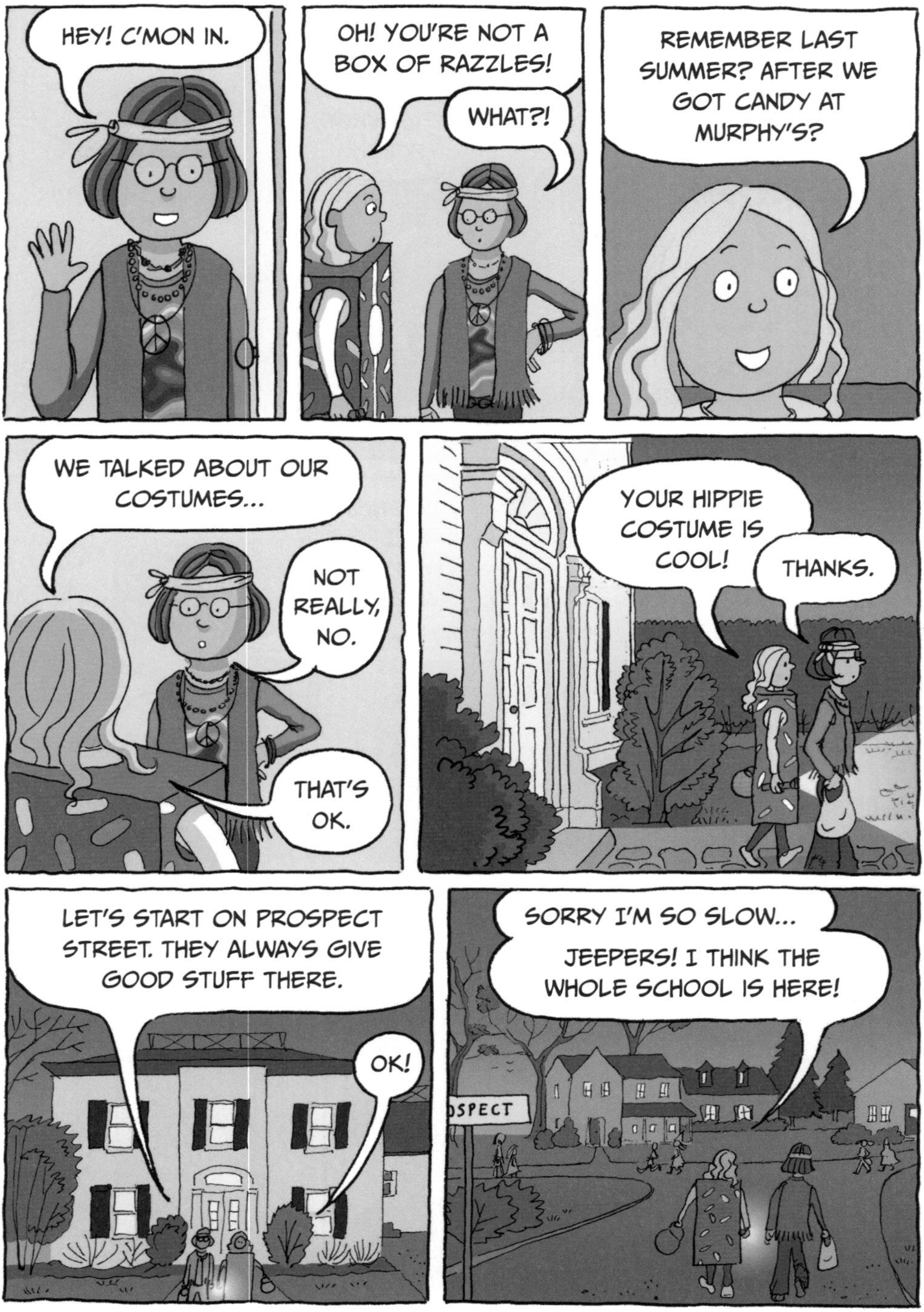
HEY! C'MON IN.
OH! YOU'RE NOT A BOX OF RAZZLES!
WHAT?!
REMEMBER LAST SUMMER? AFTER WE GOT CANDY AT MURPHY'S?
WE TALKED ABOUT OUR COSTUMES...
NOT REALLY, NO.
THAT'S OK.
YOUR HIPPIE COSTUME IS COOL!
THANKS.
LET'S START ON PROSPECT STREET. THEY ALWAYS GIVE GOOD STUFF THERE.
OK!
SORRY I'M SO SLOW...
JEEPERS! I THINK THE WHOLE SCHOOL IS HERE!
OSPECT

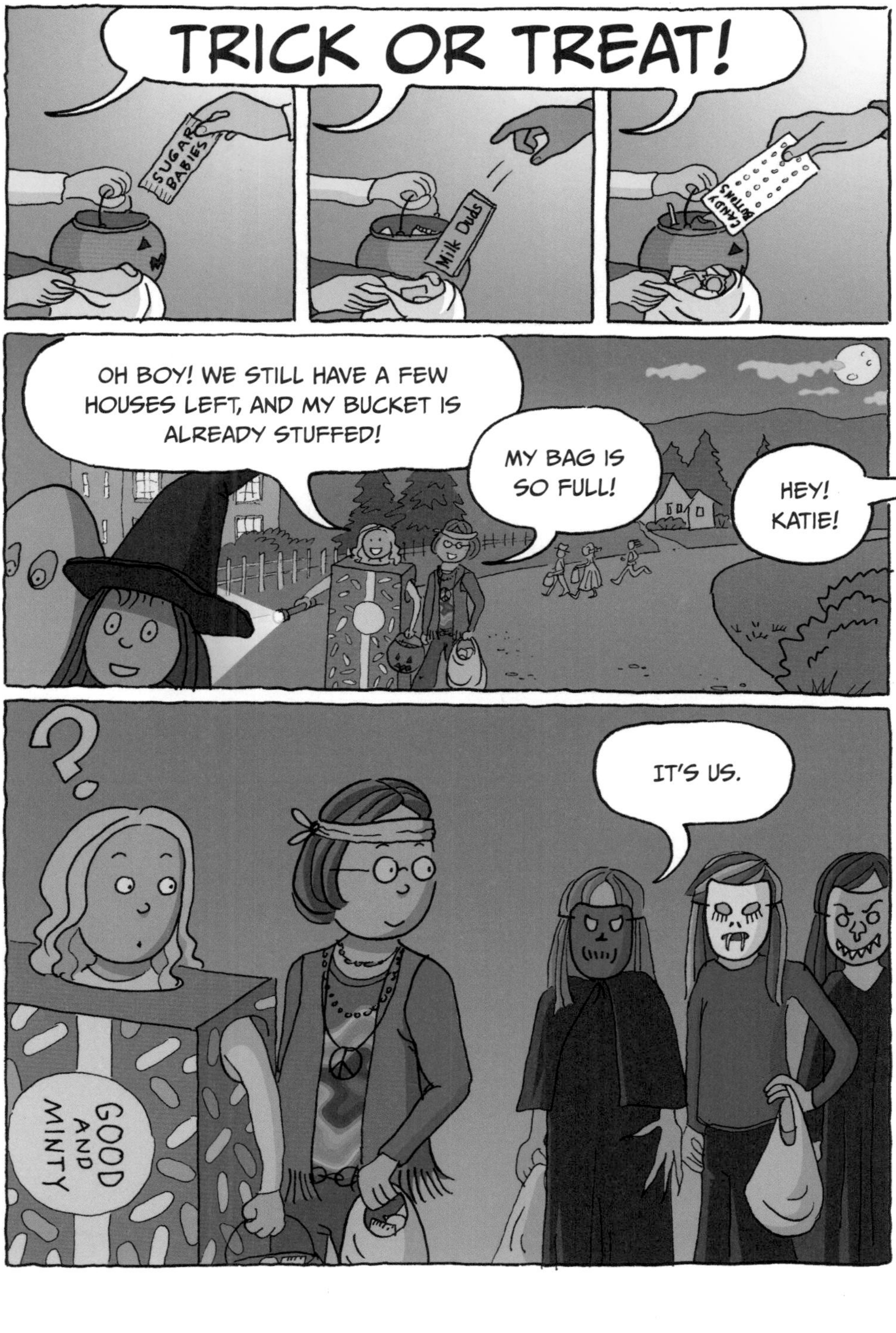
TRICK OR TREAT!
SUGAR BABIES
Milk Duds
CANDY BUTTONS
OH BOY! WE STILL HAVE A FEW HOUSES LEFT, AND MY BUCKET IS ALREADY STUFFED!
MY BAG IS SO FULL!
HEY! KATIE!
?
IT'S US.
GOOD AND MINTY

OH, HEY!

CRAP.

WE HAVE ENOUGH CANDY. WE'RE GOING DOWNTOWN TO HANG OUT ON THE CANNON NOW.

MARK AND STEW ARE MEETING US. YOU WANNA COME...

KATIE?

GOOD

UM...

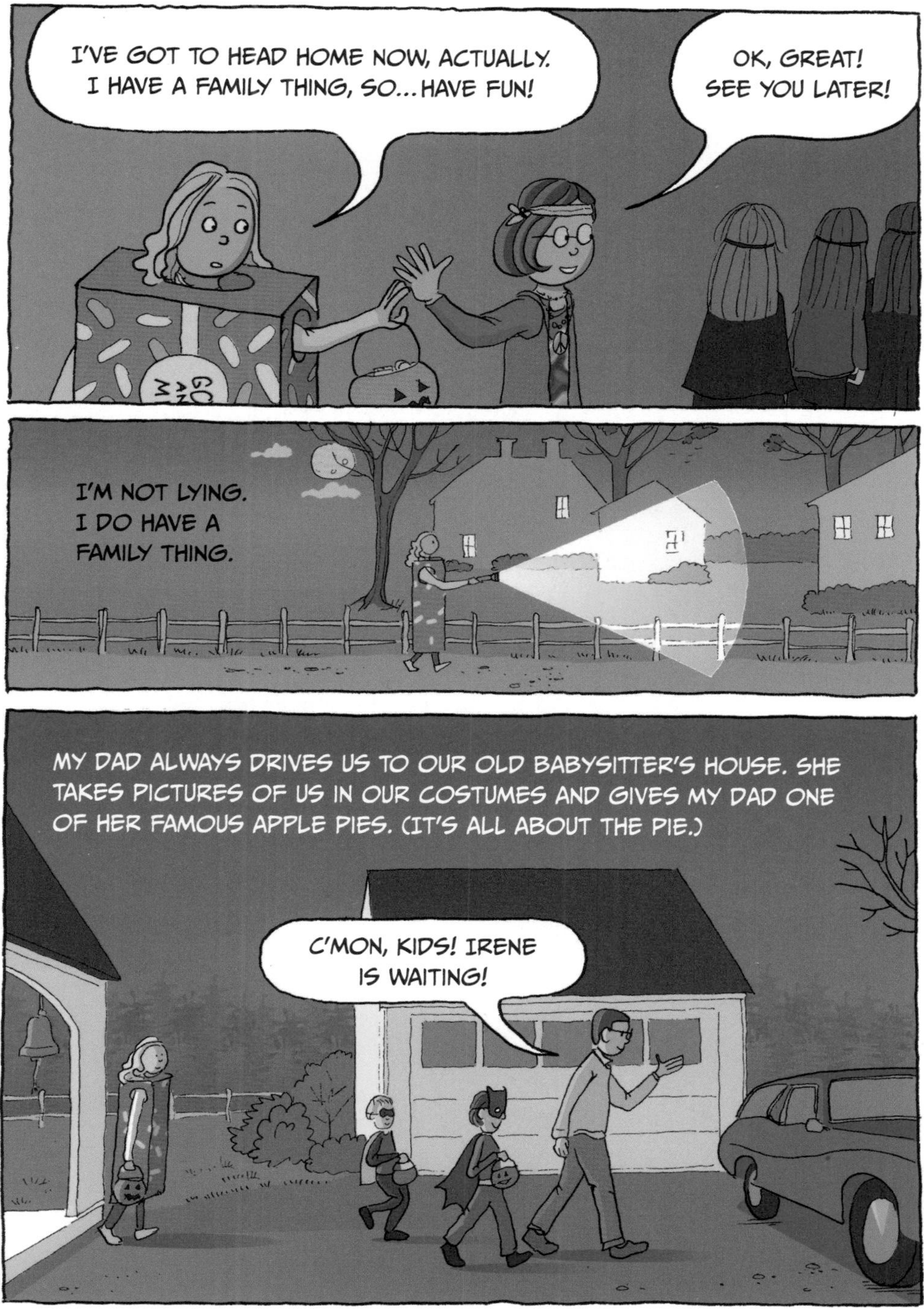
I'VE GOT TO HEAD HOME NOW, ACTUALLY. I HAVE A FAMILY THING, SO... HAVE FUN!
OK, GREAT! SEE YOU LATER!
I'M NOT LYING. I DO HAVE A FAMILY THING.
MY DAD ALWAYS DRIVES US TO OUR OLD BABYSITTER'S HOUSE. SHE TAKES PICTURES OF US IN OUR COSTUMES AND GIVES MY DAD ONE OF HER FAMOUS APPLE PIES. (IT'S ALL ABOUT THE PIE.)
C'MON, KIDS! IRENE IS WAITING!

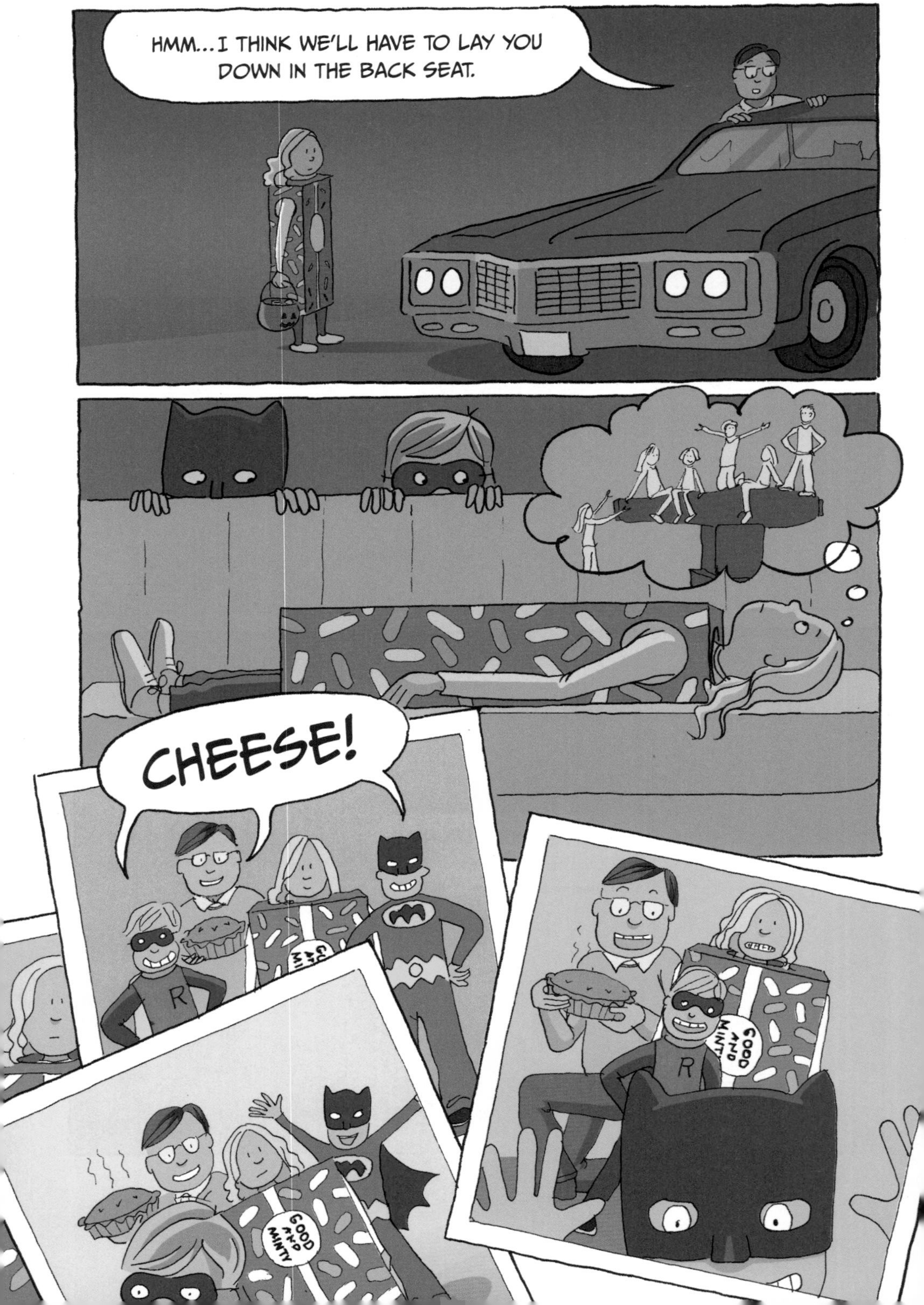
HMM...I THINK WE'LL HAVE TO LAY YOU DOWN IN THE BACK SEAT.
CHEESE!
GOOD AND MINTY

Chapter 7

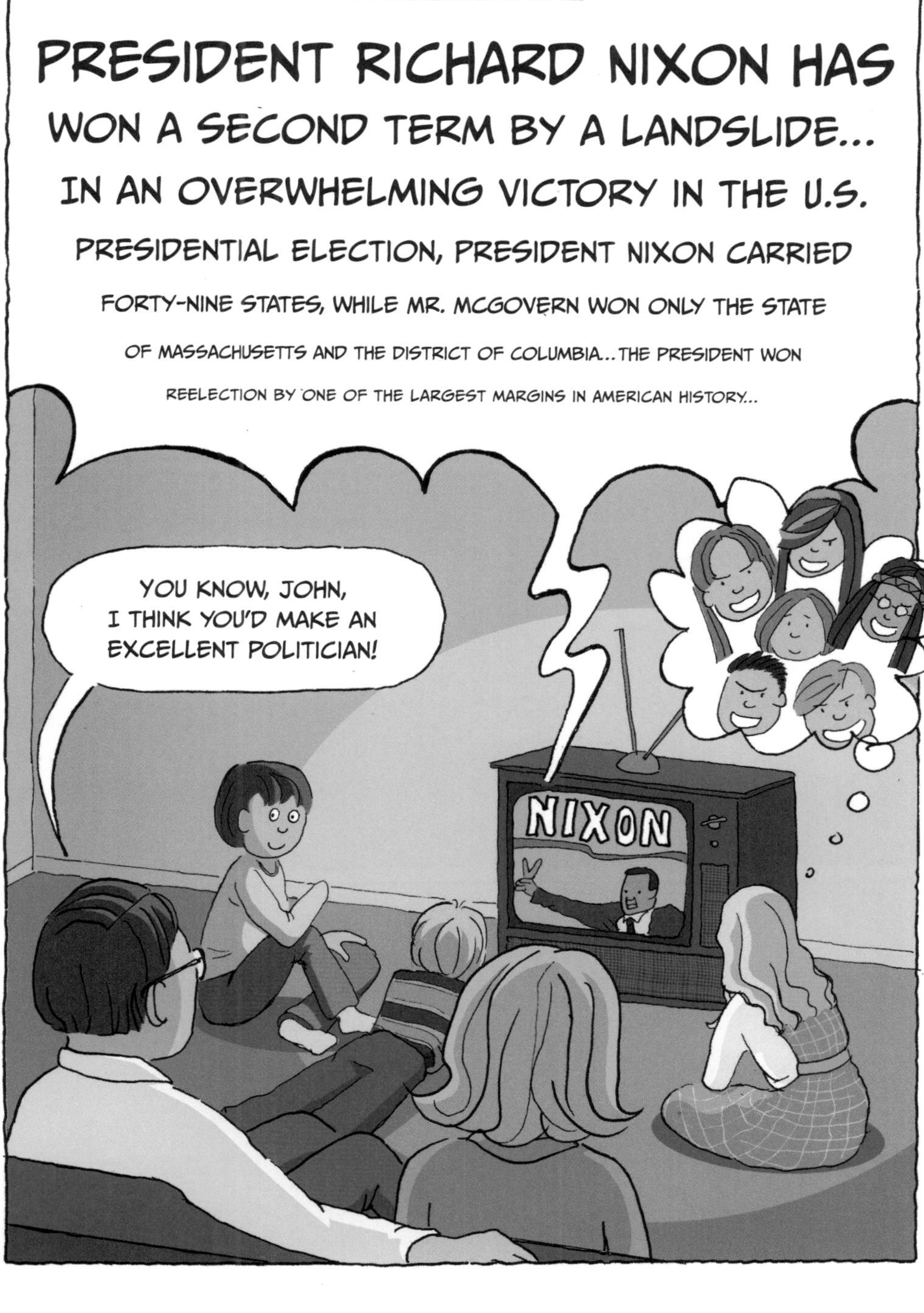
PRESIDENT RICHARD NIXON HAS
WON A SECOND TERM BY A LANDSLIDE...
IN AN OVERWHELMING VICTORY IN THE U.S.
PRESIDENTIAL ELECTION, PRESIDENT NIXON CARRIED
FORTY-NINE STATES, WHILE MR. MCGOVERN WON ONLY THE STATE
OF MASSACHUSETTS AND THE DISTRICT OF COLUMBIA...THE PRESIDENT WON
REELECTION BY ONE OF THE LARGEST MARGINS IN AMERICAN HISTORY...
YOU KNOW, JOHN, I THINK YOU'D MAKE AN EXCELLENT POLITICIAN!
NIXON

ON OUR WAY TO TOWN HALL, LESLIE ONLY WANTS TO TALK ABOUT THE ELECTION. I HAVE MORE IMPORTANT THINGS ON MY MIND. AT LEAST AT FIRST.

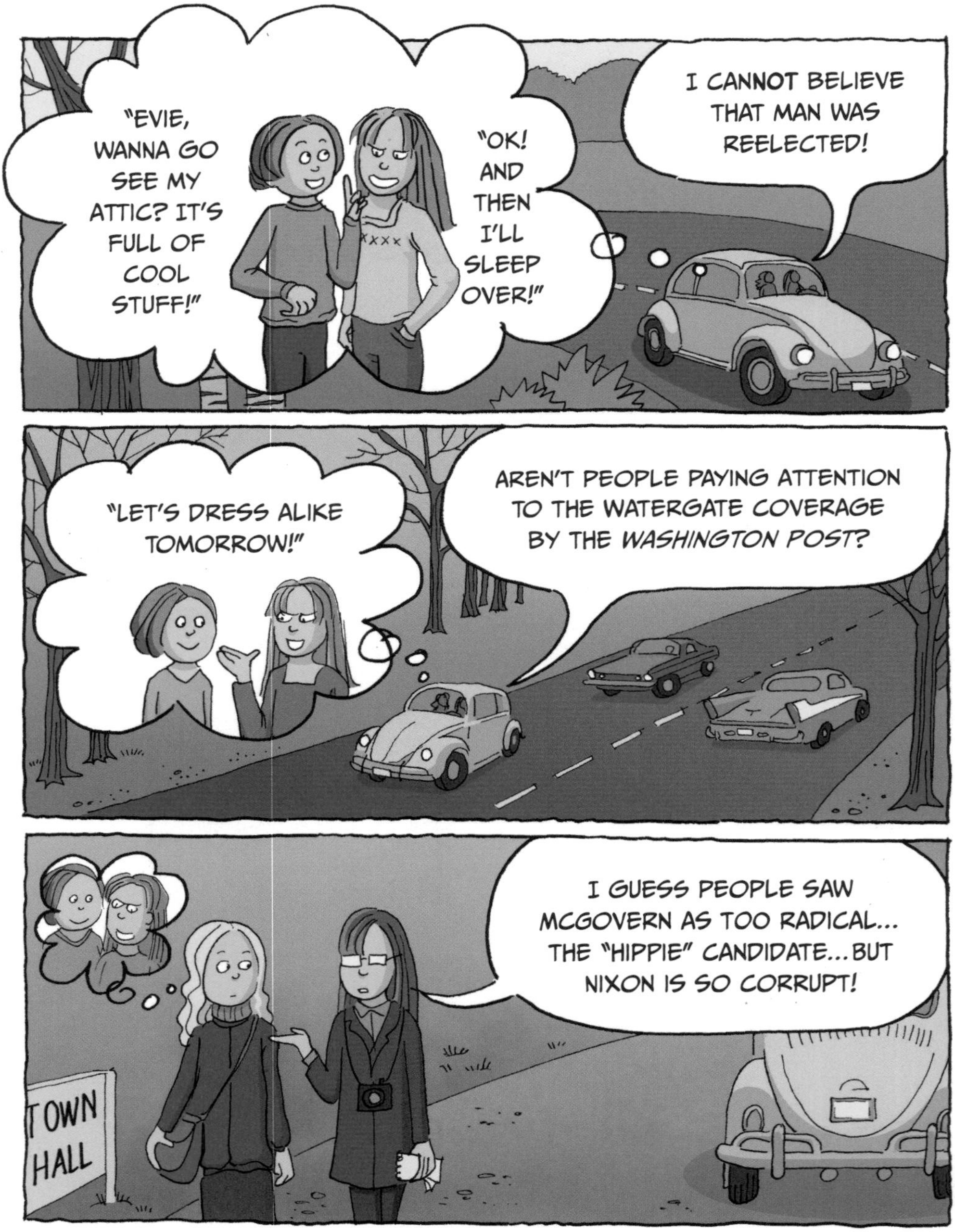

"EVIE, WANNA GO SEE MY ATTIC? IT'S FULL OF COOL STUFF!"
"OK! AND THEN I'LL SLEEP OVER!"
I CANNOT BELIEVE THAT MAN WAS REELECTED!
"LET'S DRESS ALIKE TOMORROW!"
AREN'T PEOPLE PAYING ATTENTION TO THE WATERGATE COVERAGE BY THE *WASHINGTON POST*?
I GUESS PEOPLE SAW MCGOVERN AS TOO RADICAL... THE "HIPPIE" CANDIDATE... BUT NIXON IS SO CORRUPT!
TOWN HALL

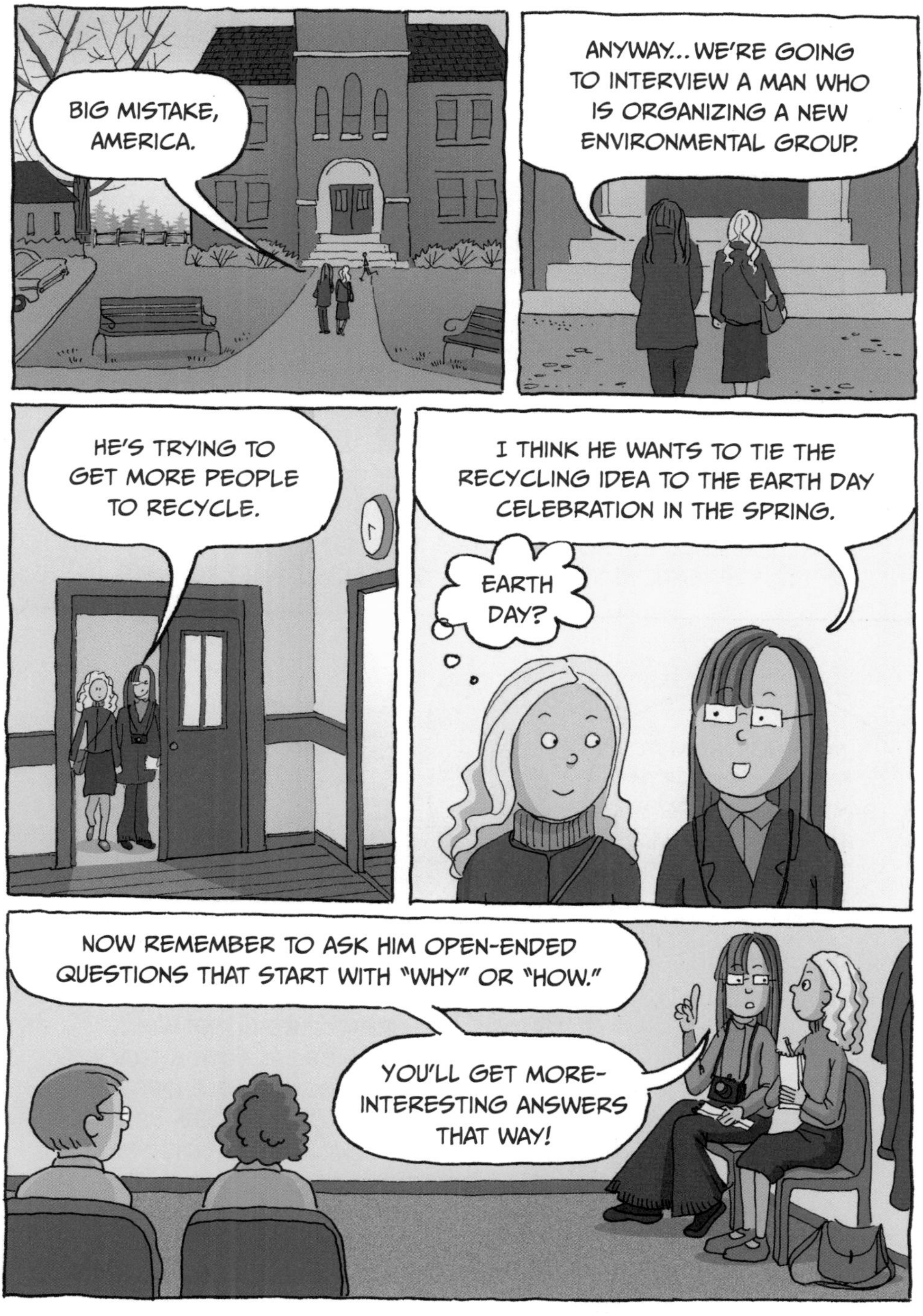
BIG MISTAKE, AMERICA.
ANYWAY... WE'RE GOING TO INTERVIEW A MAN WHO IS ORGANIZING A NEW ENVIRONMENTAL GROUP.
HE'S TRYING TO GET MORE PEOPLE TO RECYCLE.
I THINK HE WANTS TO TIE THE RECYCLING IDEA TO THE EARTH DAY CELEBRATION IN THE SPRING.
EARTH DAY?
NOW REMEMBER TO ASK HIM OPEN-ENDED QUESTIONS THAT START WITH "WHY" OR "HOW."
YOU'LL GET MORE-INTERESTING ANSWERS THAT WAY!

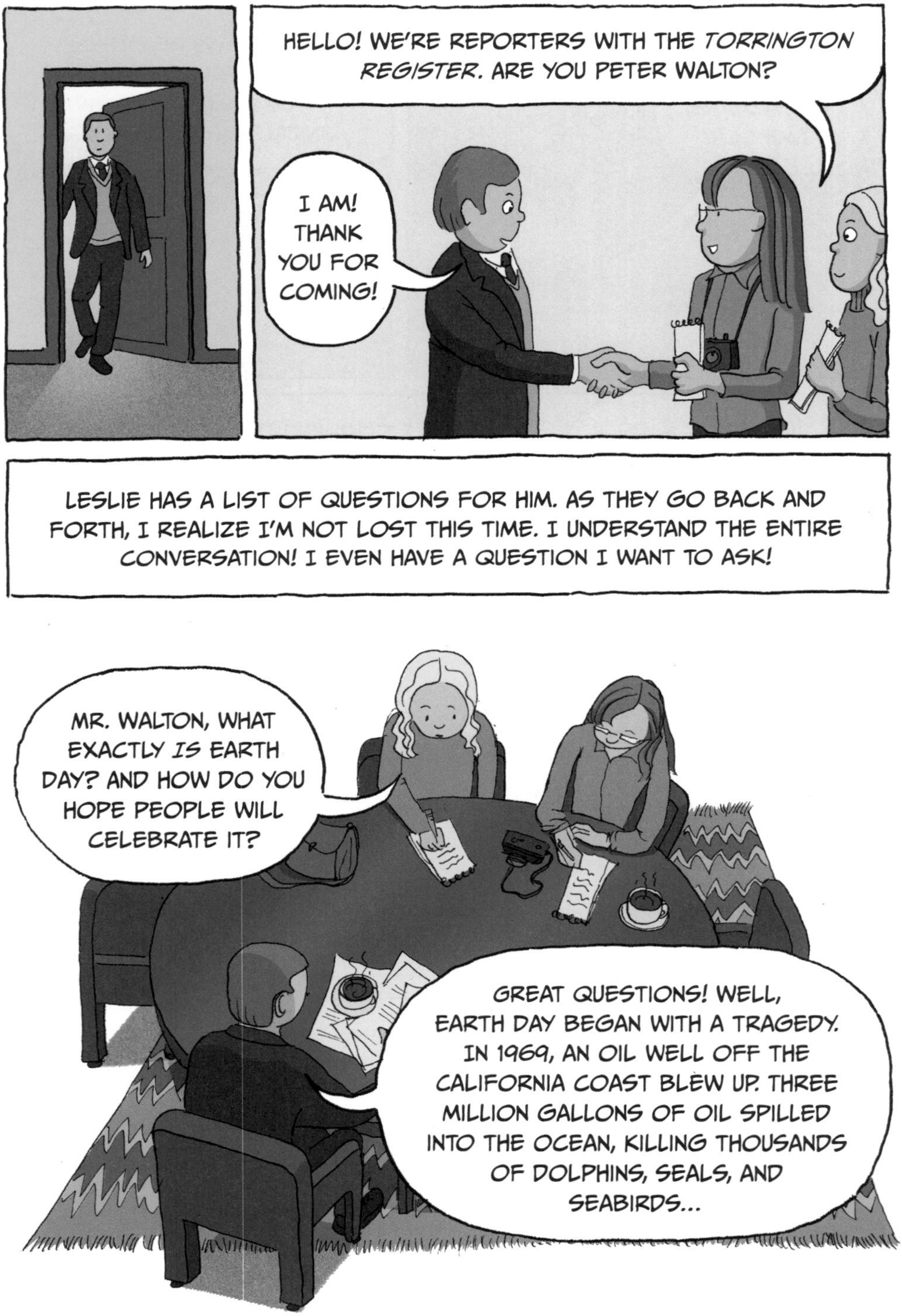
HELLO! WE'RE REPORTERS WITH THE *TORRINGTON REGISTER*. ARE YOU PETER WALTON?
I AM! THANK YOU FOR COMING!
LESLIE HAS A LIST OF QUESTIONS FOR HIM. AS THEY GO BACK AND FORTH, I REALIZE I'M NOT LOST THIS TIME. I UNDERSTAND THE ENTIRE CONVERSATION! I EVEN HAVE A QUESTION I WANT TO ASK!
MR. WALTON, WHAT EXACTLY *IS* EARTH DAY? AND HOW DO YOU HOPE PEOPLE WILL CELEBRATE IT?
GREAT QUESTIONS! WELL, EARTH DAY BEGAN WITH A TRAGEDY. IN 1969, AN OIL WELL OFF THE CALIFORNIA COAST BLEW UP. THREE MILLION GALLONS OF OIL SPILLED INTO THE OCEAN, KILLING THOUSANDS OF DOLPHINS, SEALS, AND SEABIRDS...

tap tap

Nice lede!

The dedicated volunteers who have been operating a make-shift recycling center on Goshen Road want town selectmen to pass a law forcing people to recycle glass and paper.

According to Peter Walton, the chairman of Eco-Action, which runs the center, the volunteer effort proves that there is local interest in recycling. The center is open 24 hours a day, with signs directing people to drop off glass (sorted by color) at a large barn and clean waste paper at a small shed. About 5,000 pounds of glass are crushed at the center every week, he reported.

"The state has said that the dump will be full within two years," Walton said. "I would like to see a government organization handle recycling, but in the meantime, there are many volunteers willing to take on the job."

Walton said that Eco-Action will be helping to organize a parade in the spring on Earth Day to help publicize the group's recycling efforts.

Earth Day is a national event focused on protecting the environment. In 1970, 20 million Americans demonstrated on the first Earth Day, which led to the creation of the Environmental Protection Agency.

MUCH BETTER!

Great!

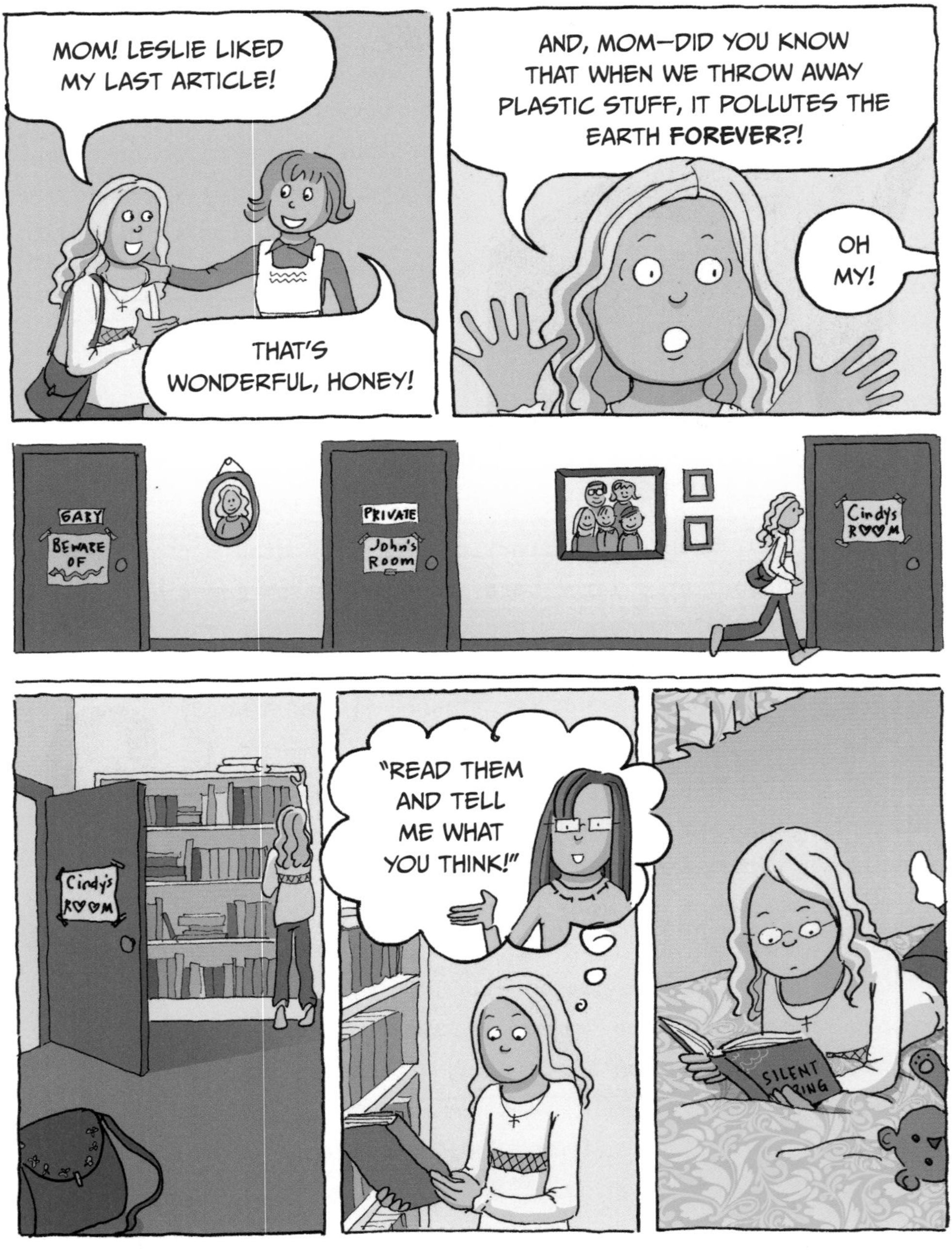
MOM! LESLIE LIKED MY LAST ARTICLE!
THAT'S WONDERFUL, HONEY!
AND, MOM—DID YOU KNOW THAT WHEN WE THROW AWAY PLASTIC STUFF, IT POLLUTES THE EARTH **FOREVER?!**
OH MY!
GARY
BEWARE OF
PRIVATE
John's Room
Cindy's ROOM
Cindy's ROOM
"READ THEM AND TELL ME WHAT YOU THINK!"
SILENT

THANK GOODNESS THINGS ARE GOING WELL *OUTSIDE* OF SCHOOL. BECAUSE RIGHT NOW, BEING *IN* SCHOOL GIVES ME A STOMACHACHE.

TOO MUCH STUFF IS CHANGING.
IT'S JUST... CONFUSING.

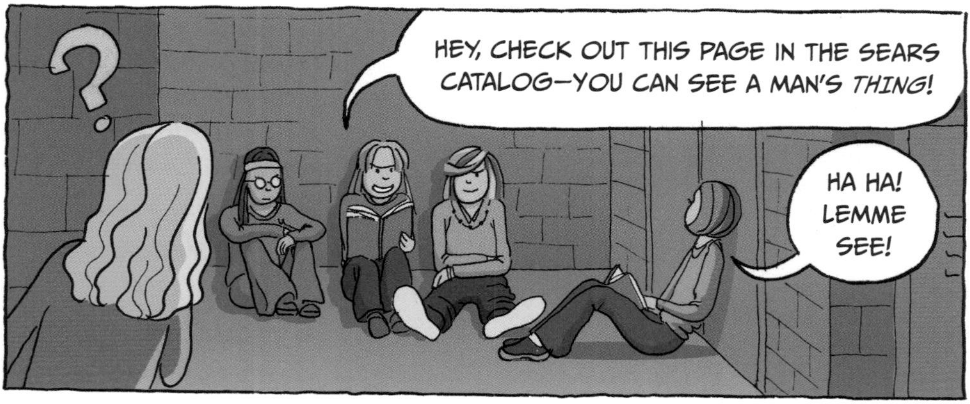
?
HEY, CHECK OUT THIS PAGE IN THE SEARS CATALOG—YOU CAN SEE A MAN'S *THING*!
HA HA! LEMME SEE!

NOW KATIE HANGS OUT WITH THE PREDATORS EVERY MORNING IN THE ELEVATOR ALCOVE. AND SHE ALWAYS SITS WITH THEM AT LUNCH, TOO.

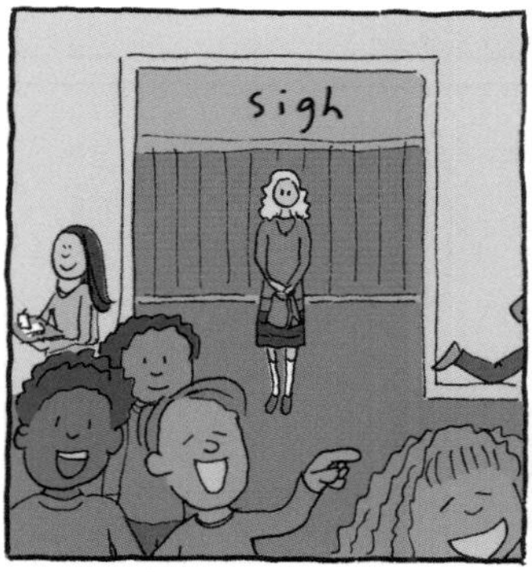
sigh

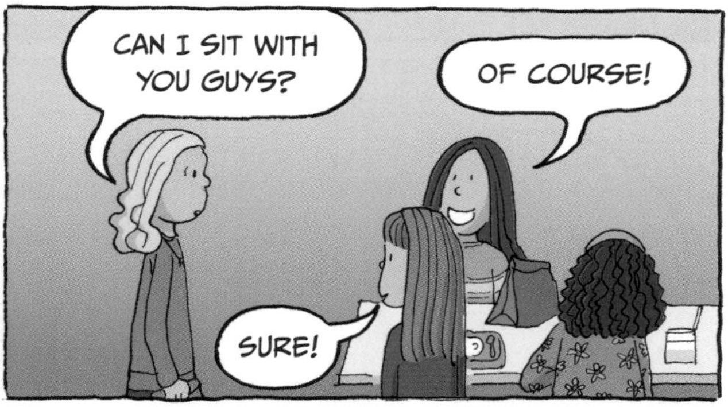
CAN I SIT WITH YOU GUYS?
OF COURSE!
SURE!

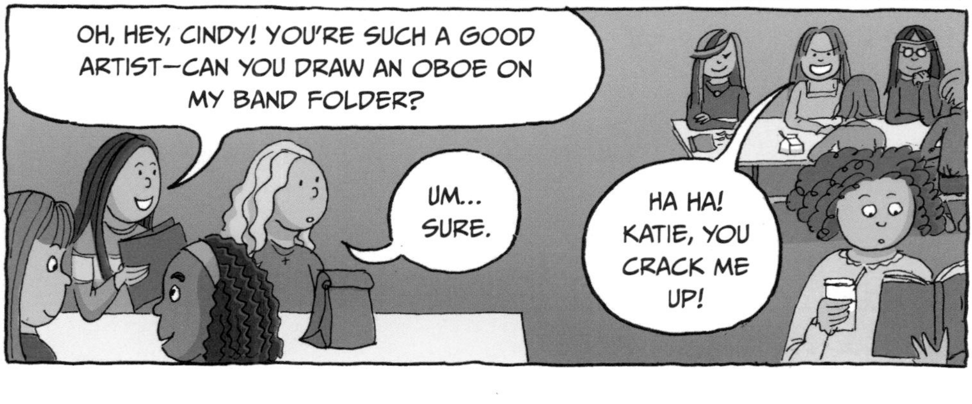
OH, HEY, CINDY! YOU'RE SUCH A GOOD ARTIST—CAN YOU DRAW AN OBOE ON MY BAND FOLDER?
UM... SURE.
HA HA! KATIE, YOU CRACK ME UP!

BUT THEN SOMETIMES IT'S LIKE IT ALWAYS WAS. LIKE *NOTHING* HAS CHANGED.

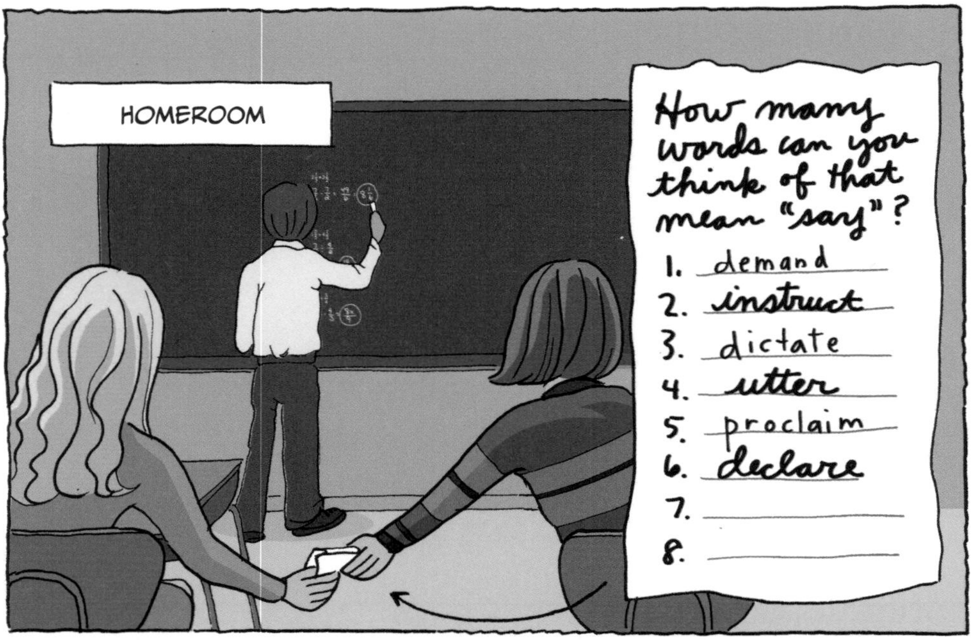
HOMEROOM
How many words can you think of that mean "say"?
1. demand
2. instruct
3. dictate
4. utter
5. proclaim
6. declare
7.
8.

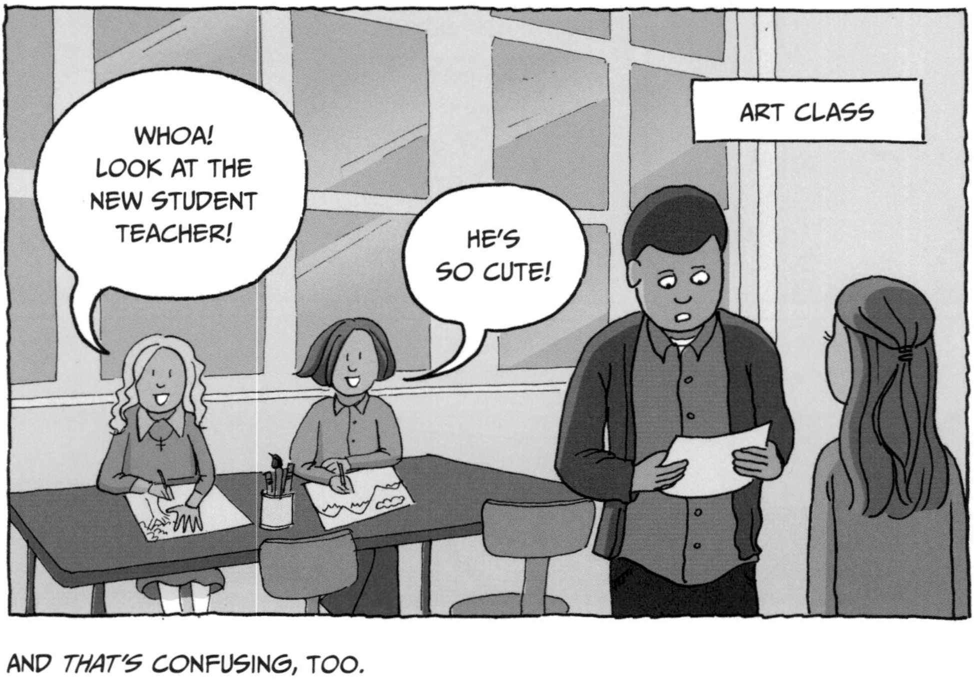
ART CLASS
WHOA! LOOK AT THE NEW STUDENT TEACHER!
HE'S SO CUTE!

AND *THAT'S* CONFUSING, TOO.

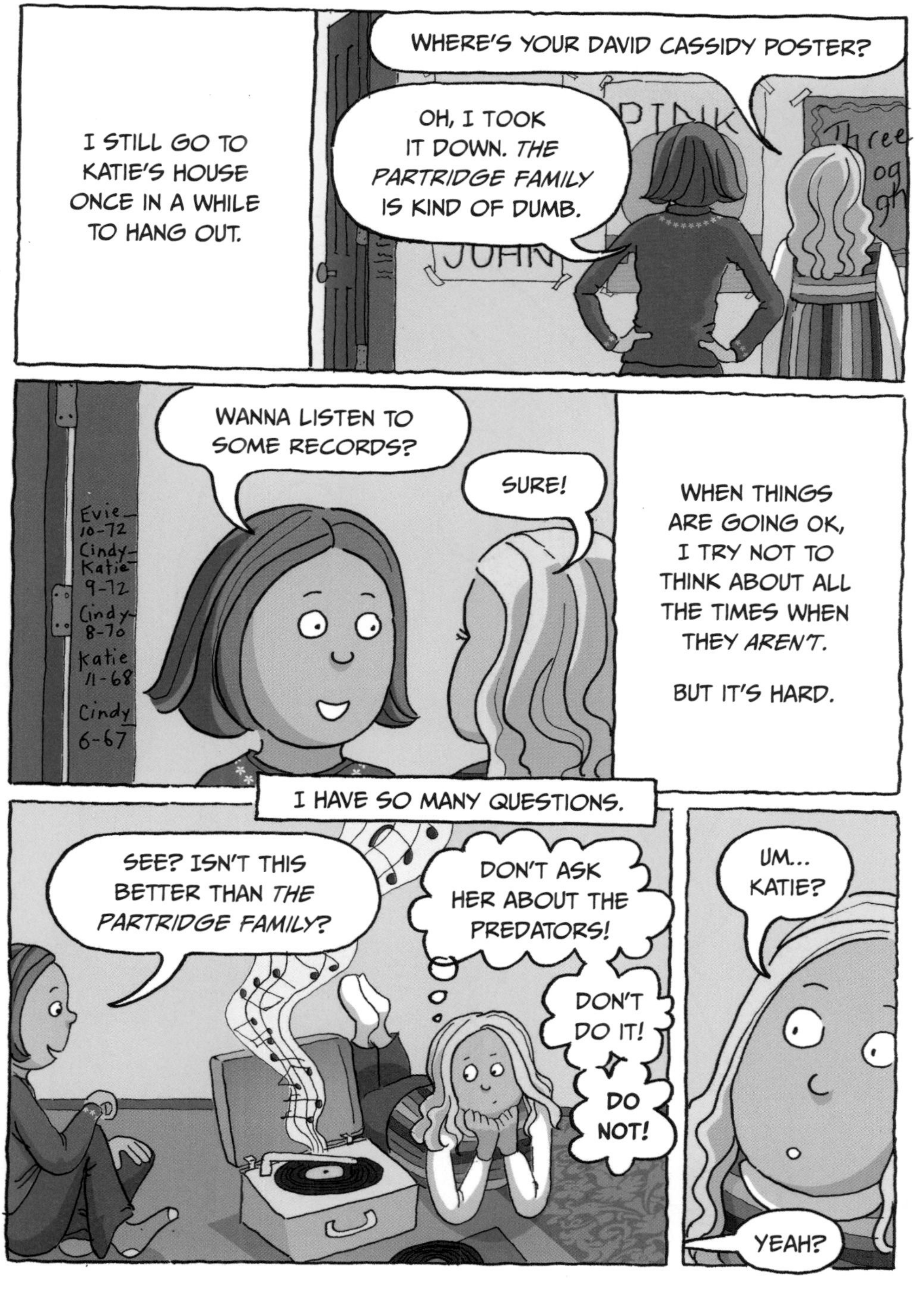
I STILL GO TO KATIE'S HOUSE ONCE IN A WHILE TO HANG OUT.
WHERE'S YOUR DAVID CASSIDY POSTER?
OH, I TOOK IT DOWN. *THE PARTRIDGE FAMILY* IS KIND OF DUMB.
PINK
JOHN
WANNA LISTEN TO SOME RECORDS?
SURE!
Evie 10-72
Cindy 9-72
Katie 9-72
Cindy 8-70
Katie 11-68
Cindy 6-67
WHEN THINGS ARE GOING OK, I TRY NOT TO THINK ABOUT ALL THE TIMES WHEN THEY *AREN'T*.
BUT IT'S HARD.
I HAVE SO MANY QUESTIONS.
SEE? ISN'T THIS BETTER THAN *THE PARTRIDGE FAMILY*?
DON'T ASK HER ABOUT THE PREDATORS!
DON'T DO IT!
DO NOT!
UM... KATIE?
YEAH?

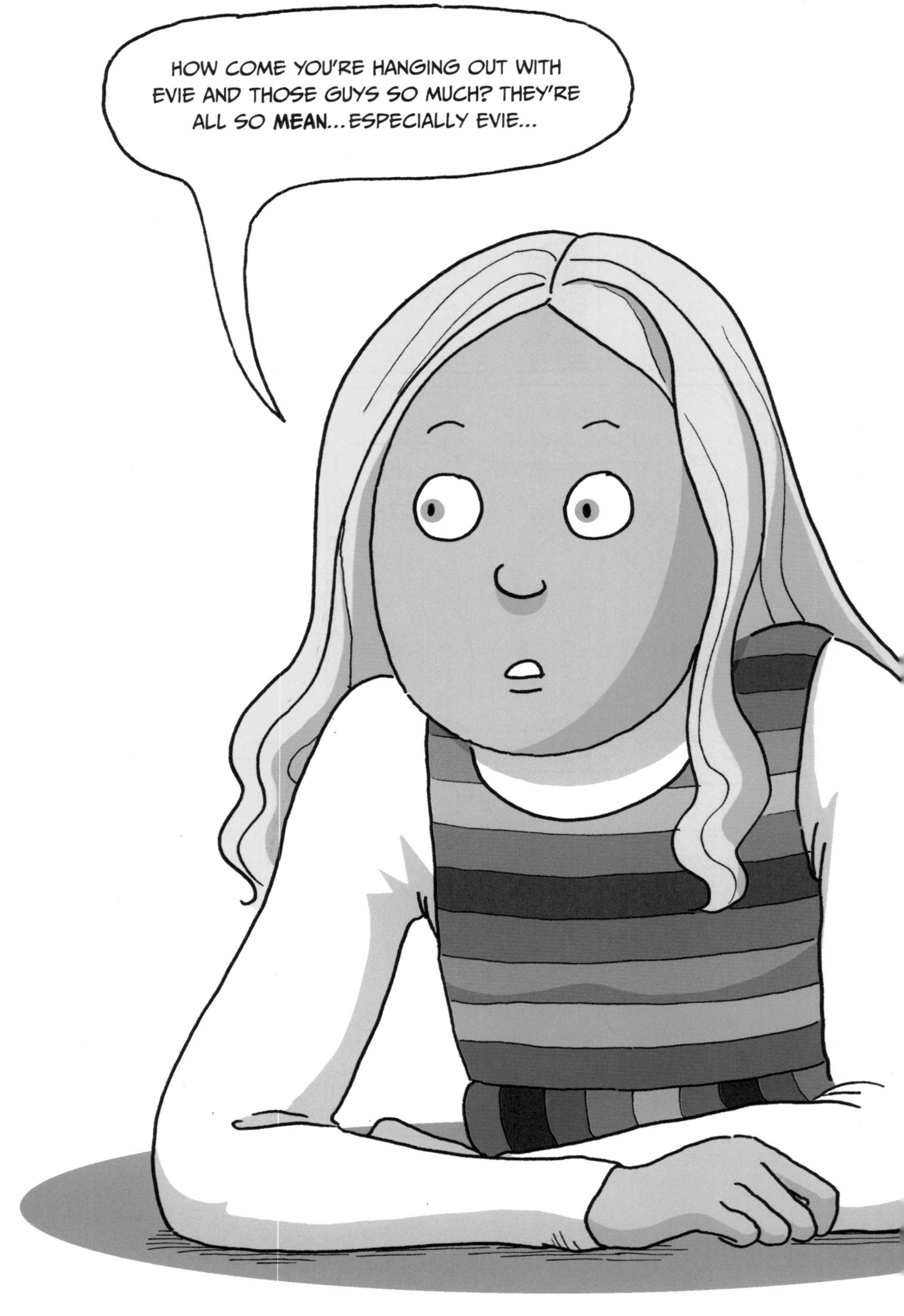
HOW COME YOU'RE HANGING OUT WITH EVIE AND THOSE GUYS SO MUCH? THEY'RE ALL SO **MEAN**...ESPECIALLY EVIE...

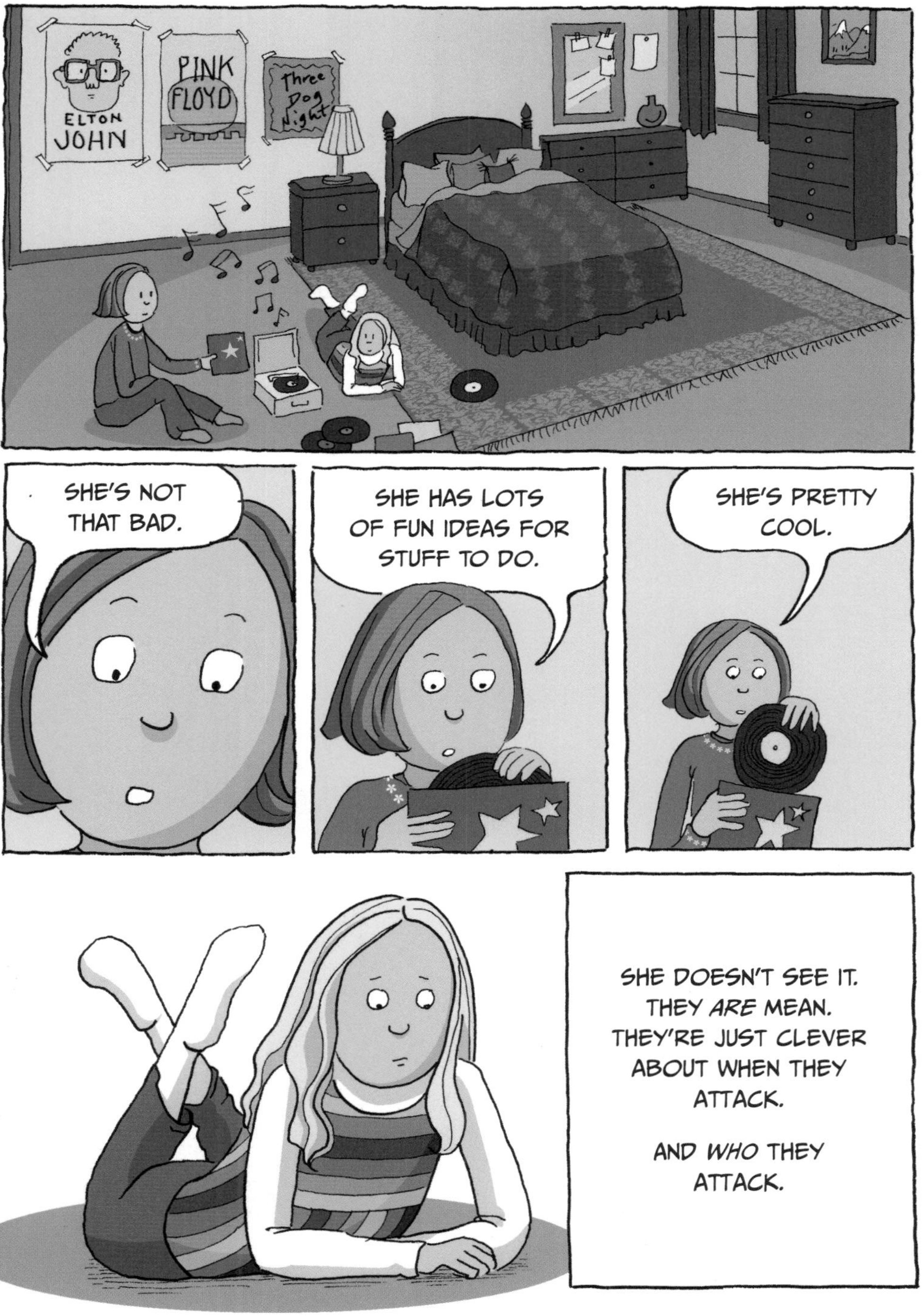
ELTON JOHN
PINK FLOYD
Three Dog Night
SHE'S NOT THAT BAD.
SHE HAS LOTS OF FUN IDEAS FOR STUFF TO DO.
SHE'S PRETTY COOL.
SHE DOESN'T SEE IT. THEY *ARE* MEAN. THEY'RE JUST CLEVER ABOUT WHEN THEY ATTACK.
AND *WHO* THEY ATTACK.

Winter 1972–1973

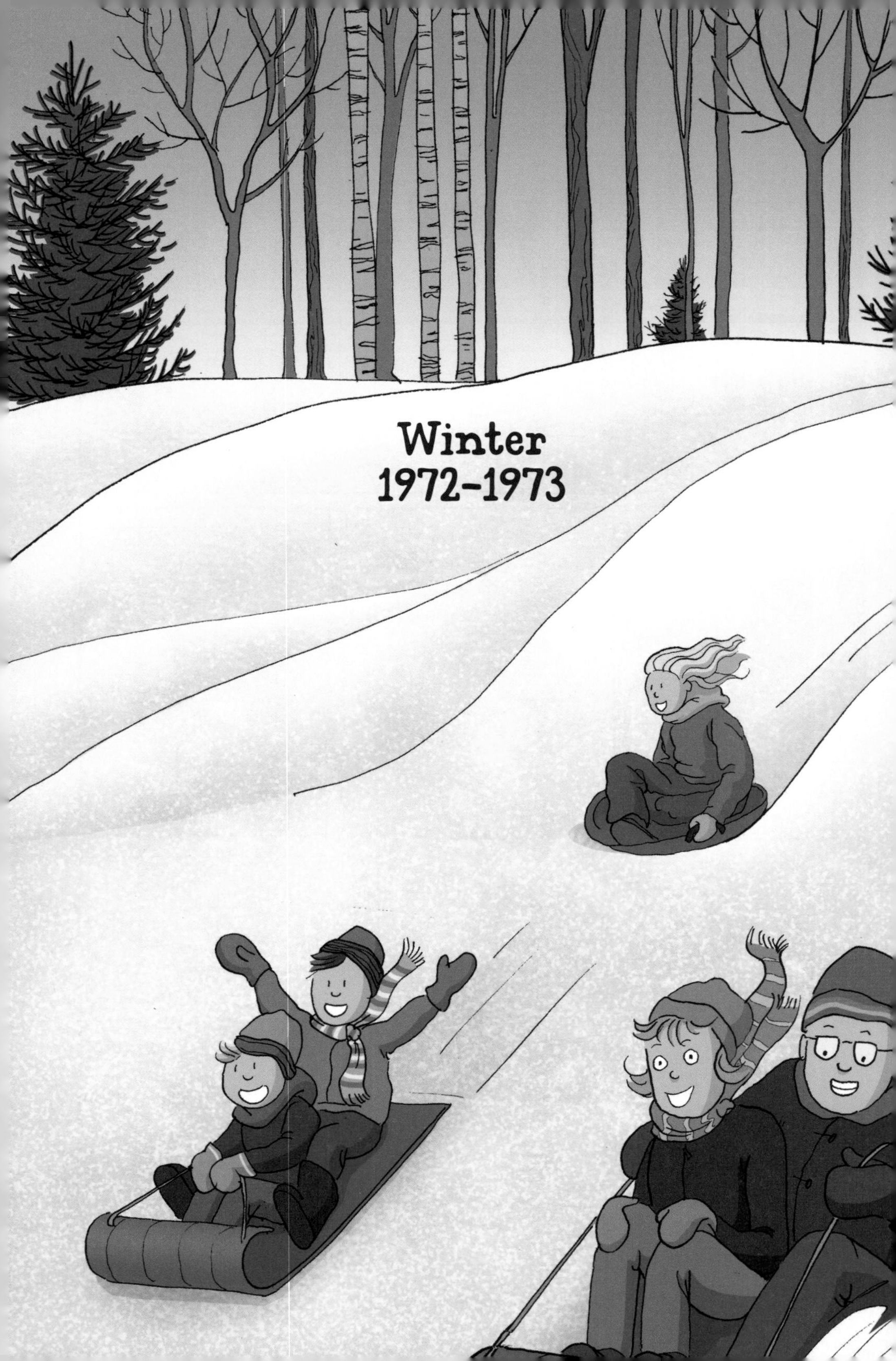

Chapter 8

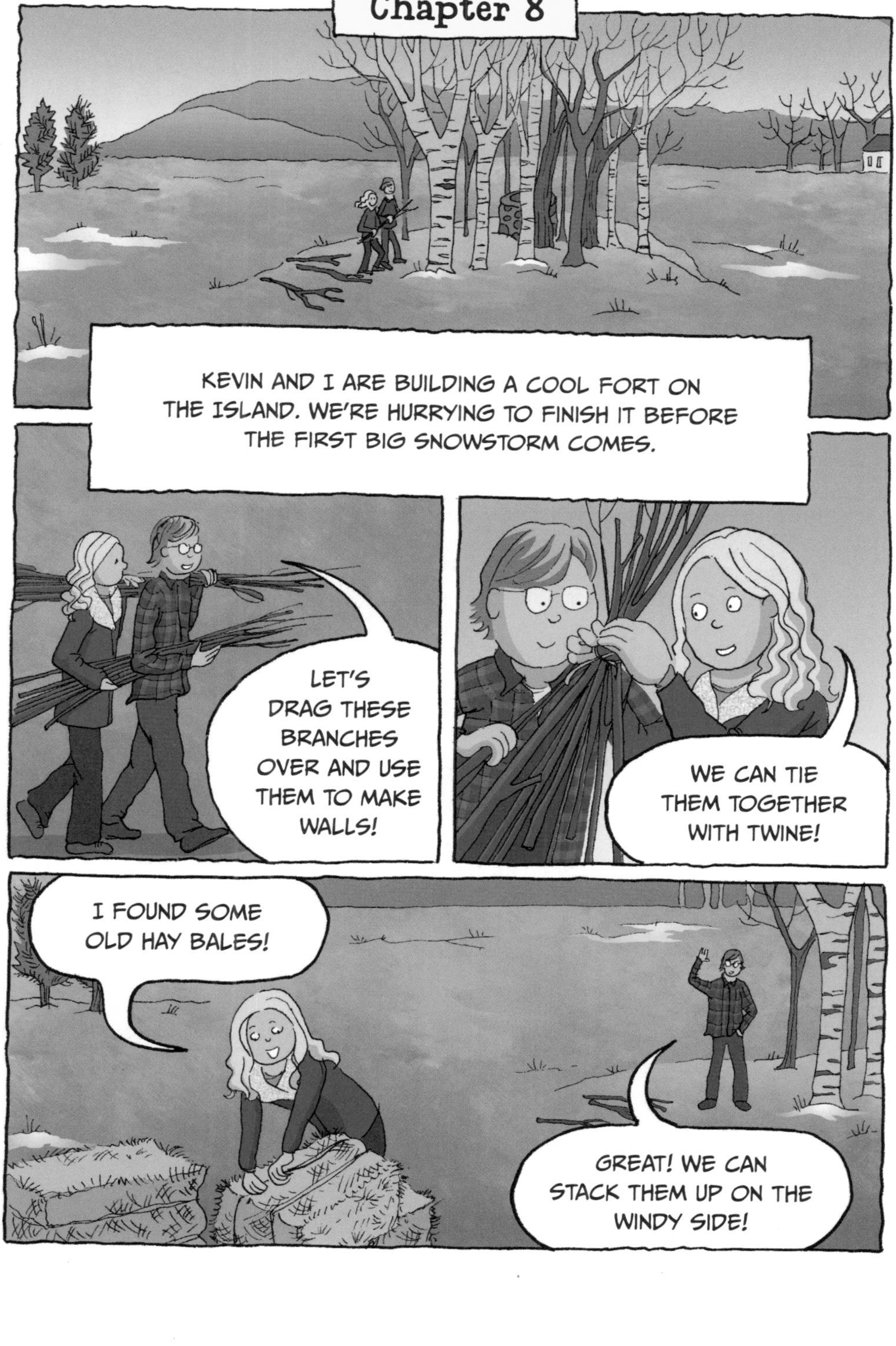
KEVIN AND I ARE BUILDING A COOL FORT ON THE ISLAND. WE'RE HURRYING TO FINISH IT BEFORE THE FIRST BIG SNOWSTORM COMES.
LET'S DRAG THESE BRANCHES OVER AND USE THEM TO MAKE WALLS!
WE CAN TIE THEM TOGETHER WITH TWINE!
I FOUND SOME OLD HAY BALES!
GREAT! WE CAN STACK THEM UP ON THE WINDY SIDE!

guest room
main room
so cozy!
den
MY BROTHERS LIKE TO SPY ON US, SO WE SET TRAPS. IF THEY COME TOO CLOSE, WE KNOW ABOUT IT!
Skunk-cabbage patch stinks if they step in it.
Bell rings if they touch the string.
RING RING

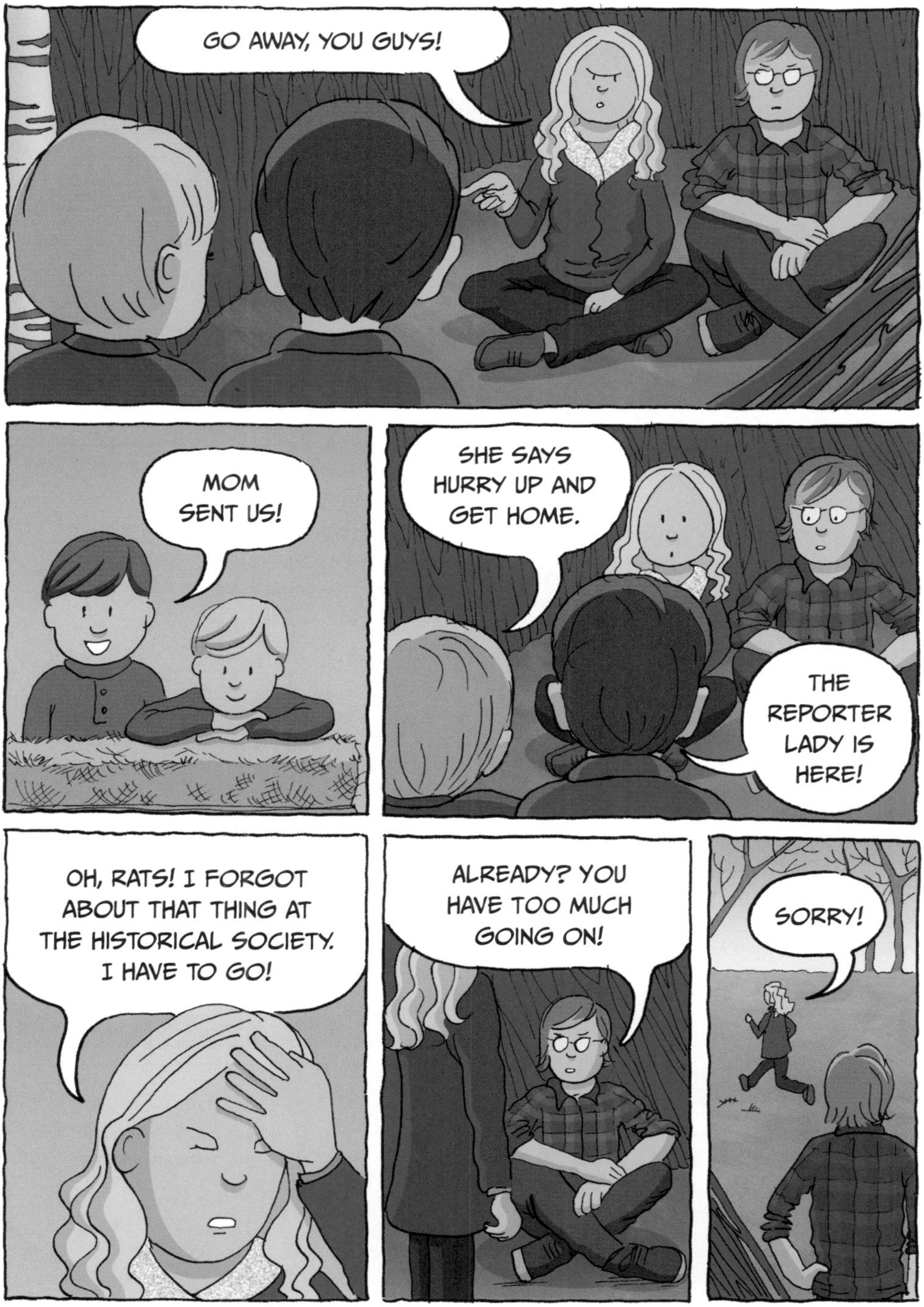
GO AWAY, YOU GUYS!
MOM SENT US!
SHE SAYS HURRY UP AND GET HOME.
THE REPORTER LADY IS HERE!
OH, RATS! I FORGOT ABOUT THAT THING AT THE HISTORICAL SOCIETY. I HAVE TO GO!
ALREADY? YOU HAVE TOO MUCH GOING ON!
SORRY!

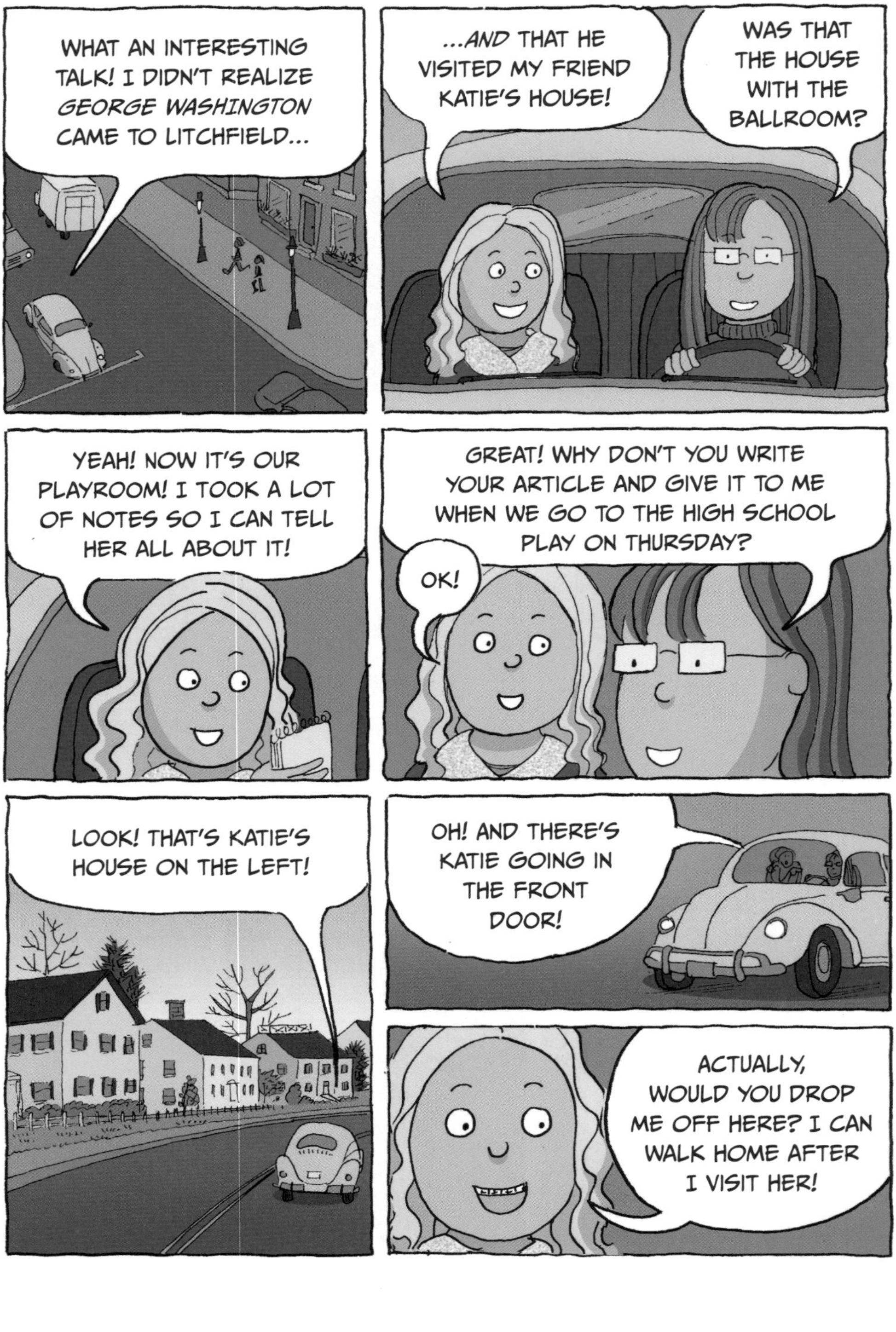
WHAT AN INTERESTING TALK! I DIDN'T REALIZE *GEORGE WASHINGTON* CAME TO LITCHFIELD...
...*AND* THAT HE VISITED MY FRIEND KATIE'S HOUSE!
WAS THAT THE HOUSE WITH THE BALLROOM?
YEAH! NOW IT'S OUR PLAYROOM! I TOOK A LOT OF NOTES SO I CAN TELL HER ALL ABOUT IT!
GREAT! WHY DON'T YOU WRITE YOUR ARTICLE AND GIVE IT TO ME WHEN WE GO TO THE HIGH SCHOOL PLAY ON THURSDAY?
OK!
LOOK! THAT'S KATIE'S HOUSE ON THE LEFT!
OH! AND THERE'S KATIE GOING IN THE FRONT DOOR!
ACTUALLY, WOULD YOU DROP ME OFF HERE? I CAN WALK HOME AFTER I VISIT HER!

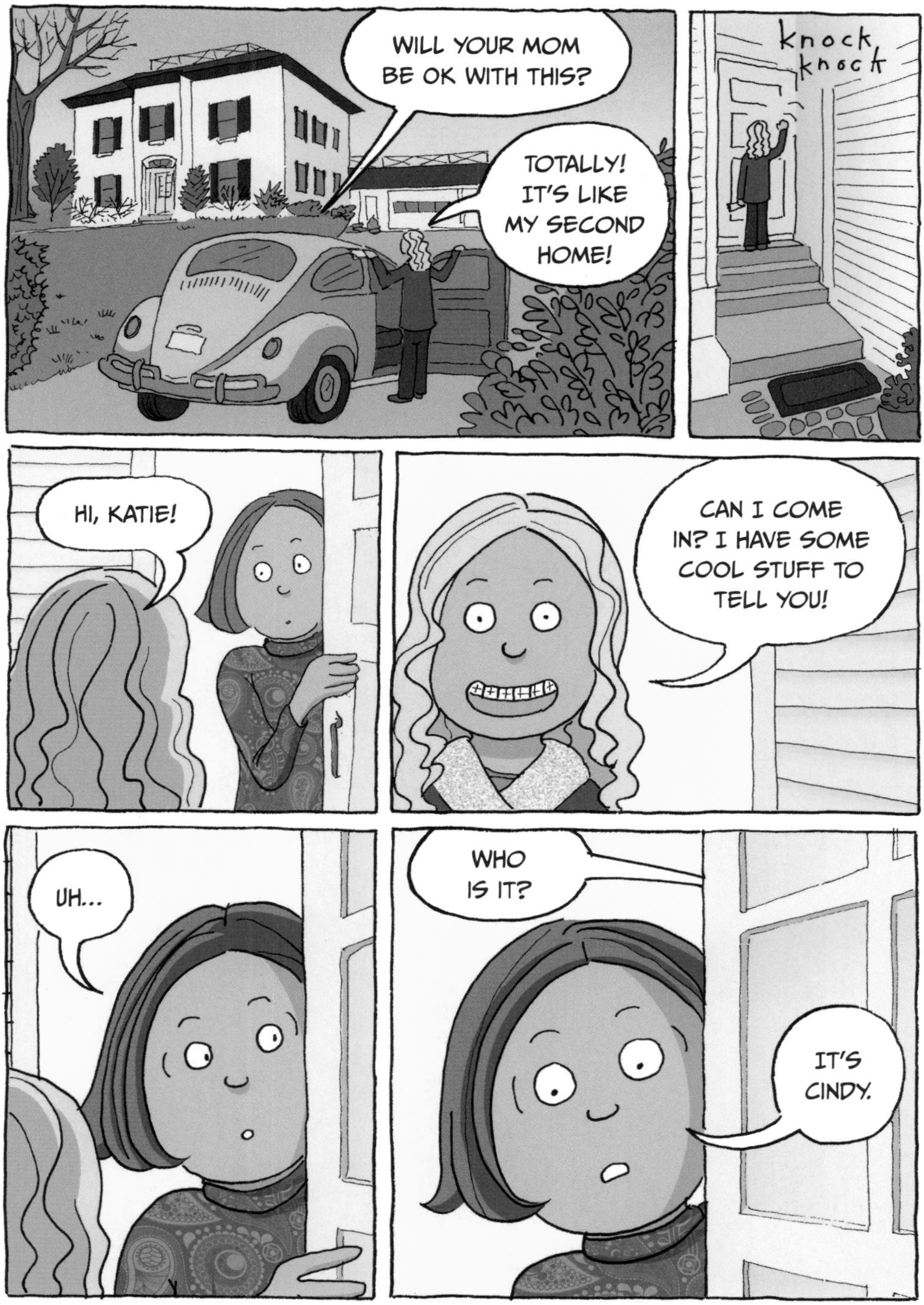
WILL YOUR MOM BE OK WITH THIS?
TOTALLY! IT'S LIKE MY SECOND HOME!
knock knock
HI, KATIE!
CAN I COME IN? I HAVE SOME COOL STUFF TO TELL YOU!
UH...
WHO IS IT?
IT'S CINDY.

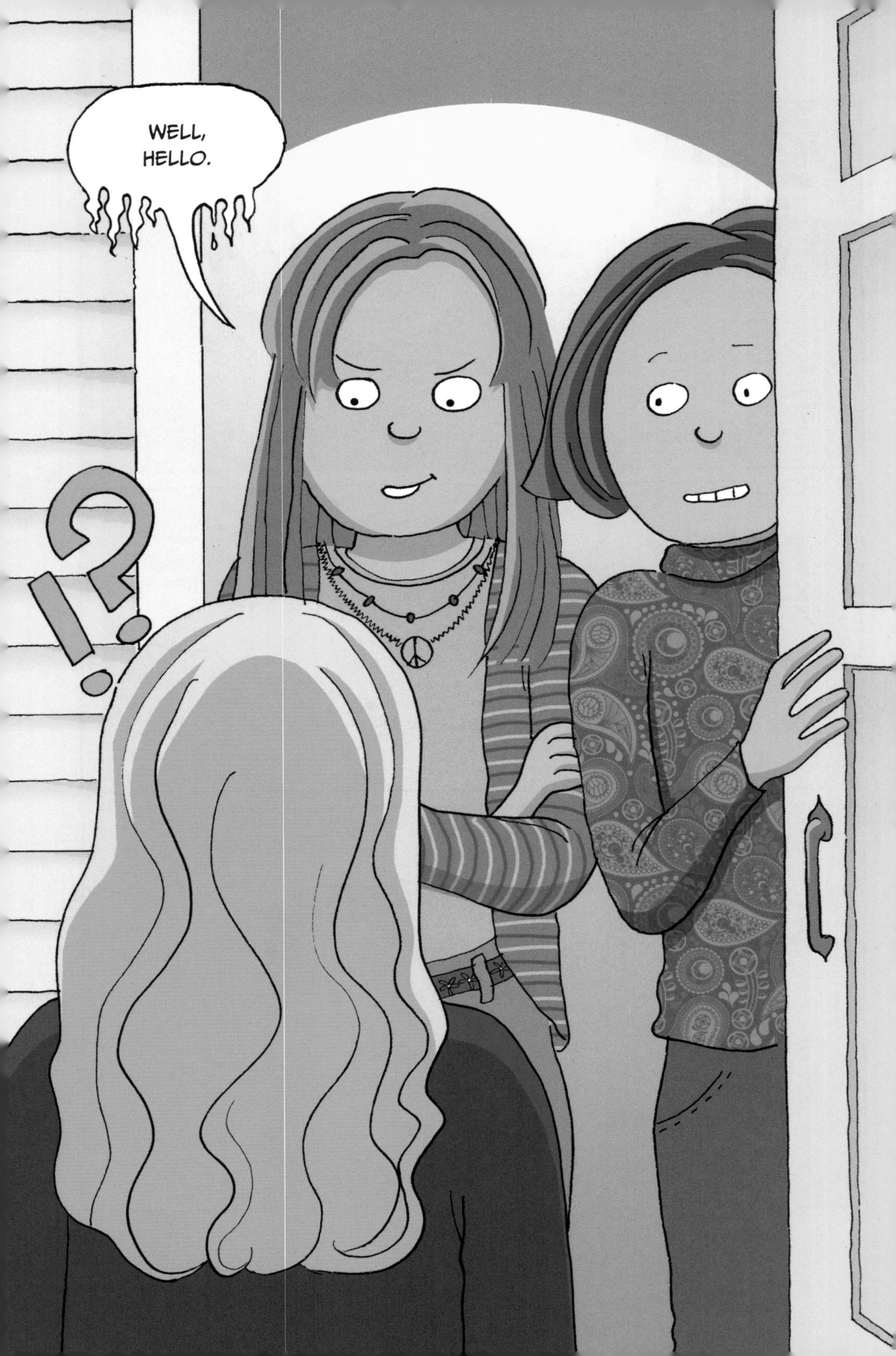
WELL,
HELLO.

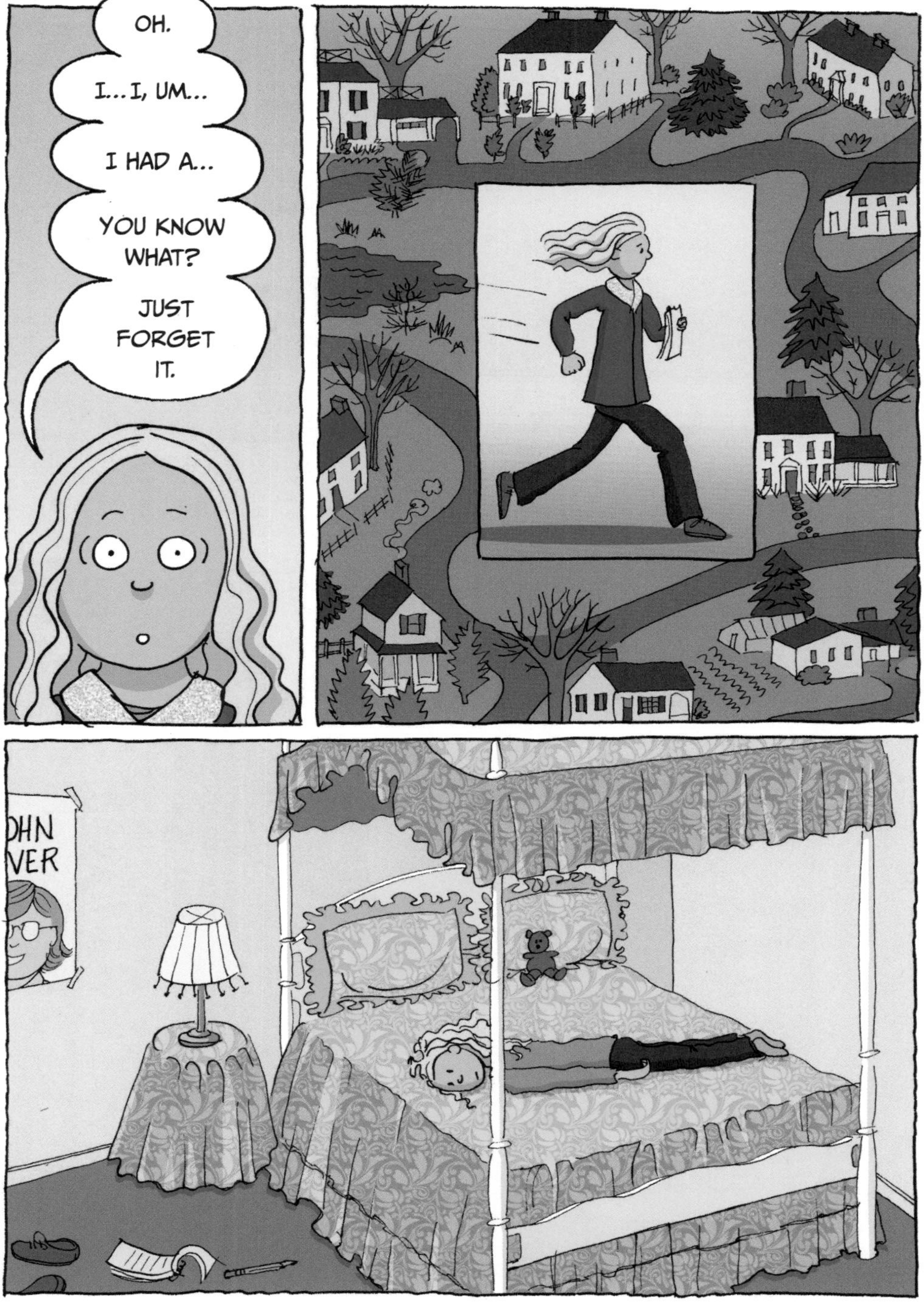
OH.
I... I, UM...
I HAD A...
YOU KNOW WHAT?
JUST FORGET IT.

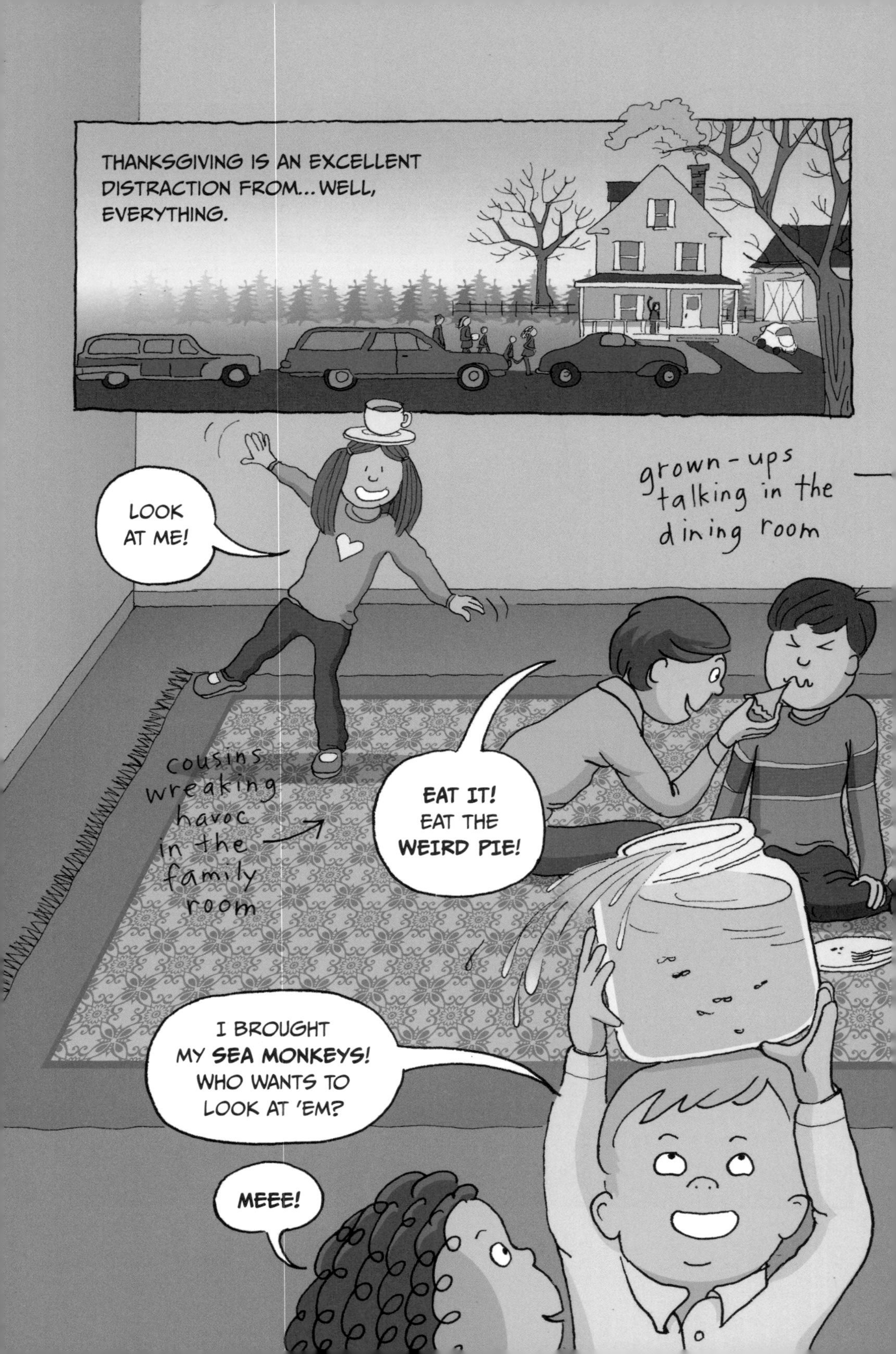

THANKSGIVING IS AN EXCELLENT DISTRACTION FROM...WELL, EVERYTHING.
LOOK AT ME!
grown-ups talking in the dining room
cousins wreaking havoc in the family room
EAT IT! EAT THE WEIRD PIE!
I BROUGHT MY SEA MONKEYS! WHO WANTS TO LOOK AT 'EM?
MEEE!

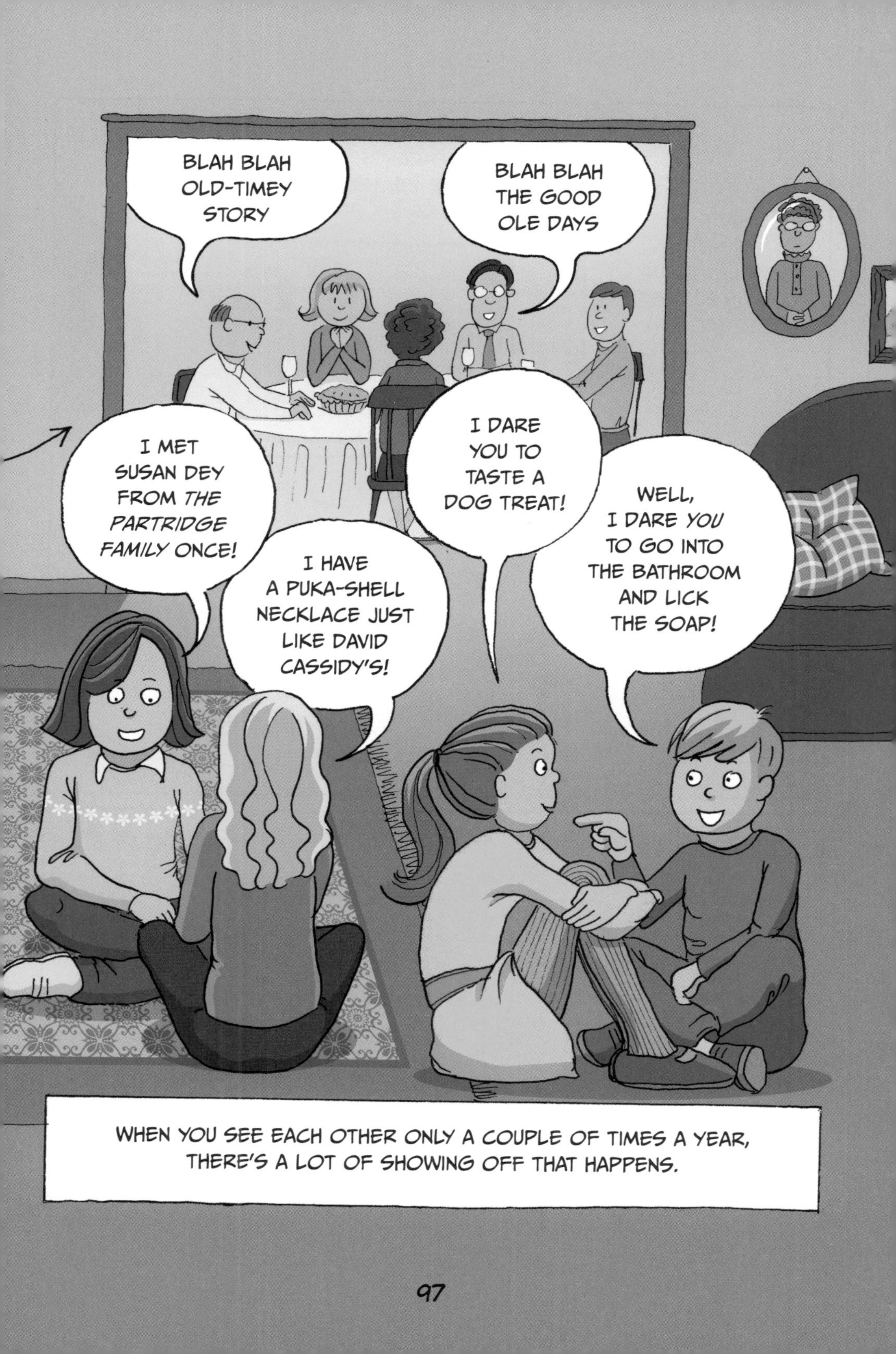
BLAH BLAH OLD-TIMEY STORY
BLAH BLAH THE GOOD OLE DAYS
I MET SUSAN DEY FROM *THE PARTRIDGE FAMILY* ONCE!
I HAVE A PUKA-SHELL NECKLACE JUST LIKE DAVID CASSIDY'S!
I DARE YOU TO TASTE A DOG TREAT!
WELL, I DARE *YOU* TO GO INTO THE BATHROOM AND LICK THE SOAP!
WHEN YOU SEE EACH OTHER ONLY A COUPLE OF TIMES A YEAR, THERE'S A LOT OF SHOWING OFF THAT HAPPENS.

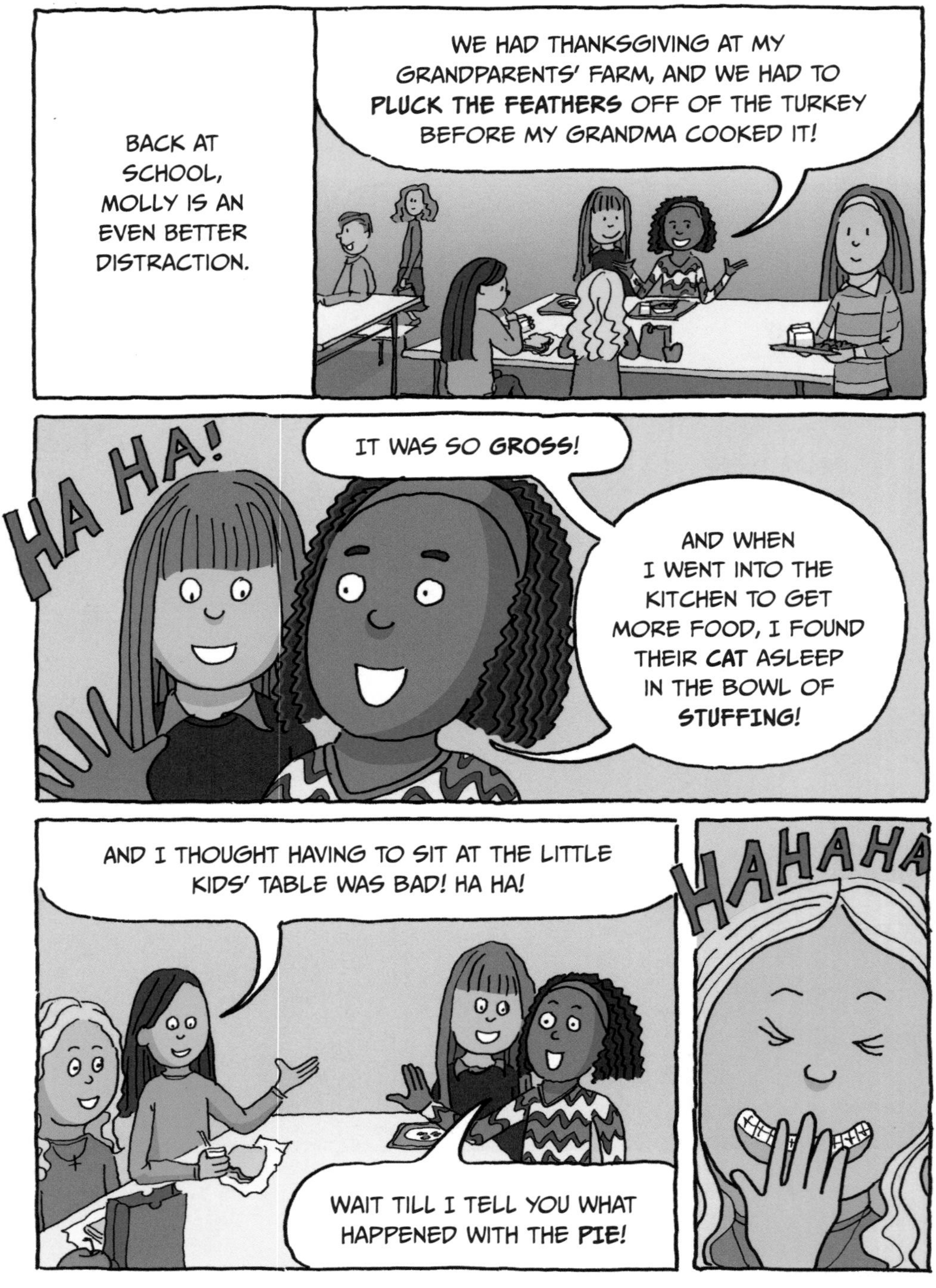
BACK AT SCHOOL, MOLLY IS AN EVEN BETTER DISTRACTION.
WE HAD THANKSGIVING AT MY GRANDPARENTS' FARM, AND WE HAD TO PLUCK THE FEATHERS OFF OF THE TURKEY BEFORE MY GRANDMA COOKED IT!
HA HA!
IT WAS SO GROSS!
AND WHEN I WENT INTO THE KITCHEN TO GET MORE FOOD, I FOUND THEIR CAT ASLEEP IN THE BOWL OF STUFFING!
AND I THOUGHT HAVING TO SIT AT THE LITTLE KIDS' TABLE WAS BAD! HA HA!
WAIT TILL I TELL YOU WHAT HAPPENED WITH THE PIE!
HAHAHA

WE WENT TO MY AUNT'S HOUSE, AND MY COUSIN GAVE ME HER ENTIRE TROLL COLLECTION!

I HAVE TWENTY TROLLS!

I MAKE THE CUTEST CLOTHES FOR MY TROLLS! I HAVE EXTRA OUTFITS IF YOU WANT SOME!

HI, CINDY!

OH, HI, JEAN.

blech

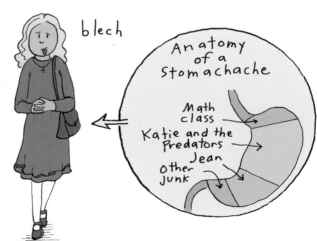

Anatomy of a Stomachache

Math class

Katie and the Predators

Jean

Other Junk

Chapter 9

BECAUSE IT'S THE HOLIDAY SEASON, LESLIE AND I HAVE LOTS OF CHRISTMAS AND HANUKKAH EVENTS TO COVER.

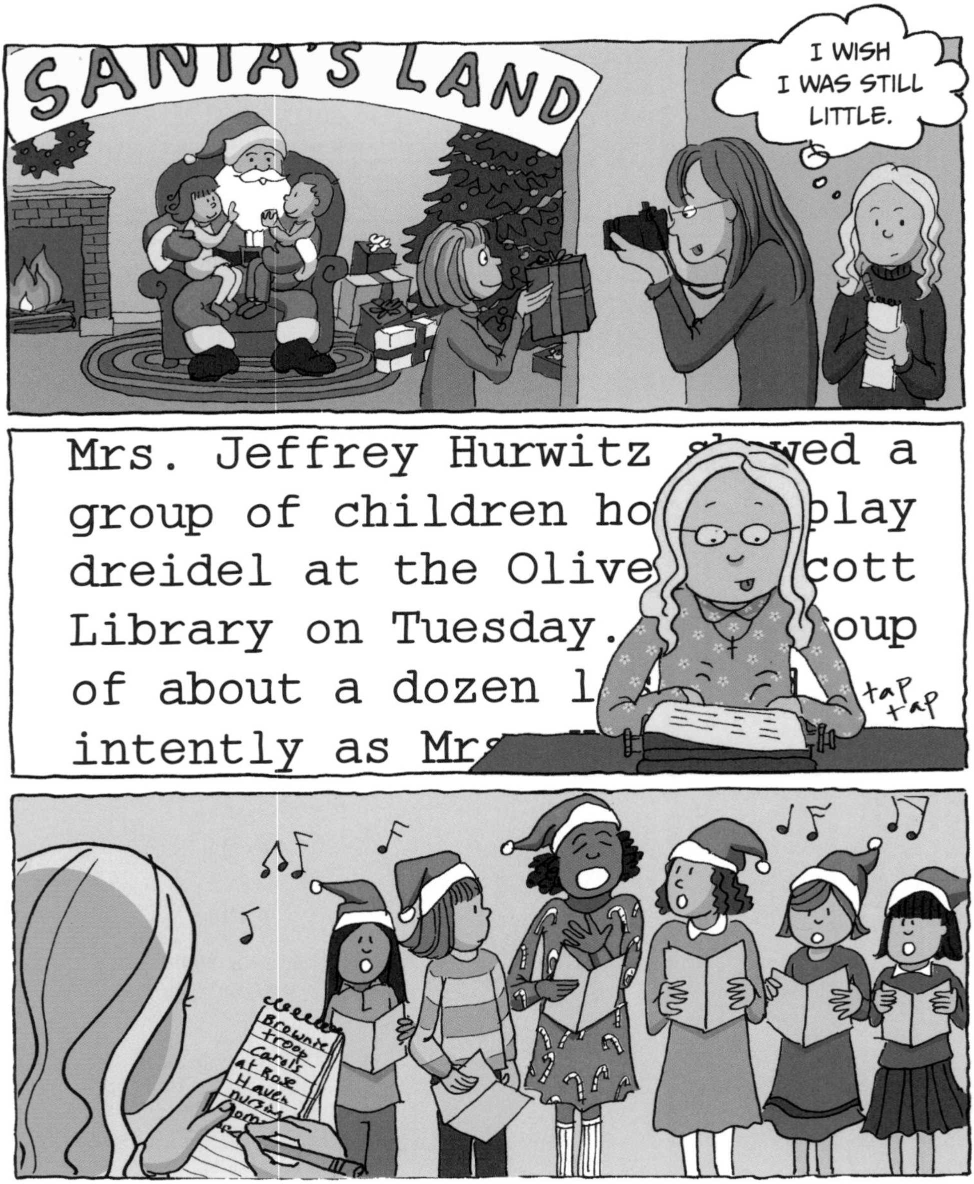
SANTA'S LAND
I WISH I WAS STILL LITTLE.
Mrs. Jeffrey Hurwitz ... wed a
group of children ho ... play
dreidel at the Olive ... cott
Library on Tuesday. ... oup
of about a dozen l ...
intently as Mr ...
tap tap
Brownie troop Carols at Rose Haven

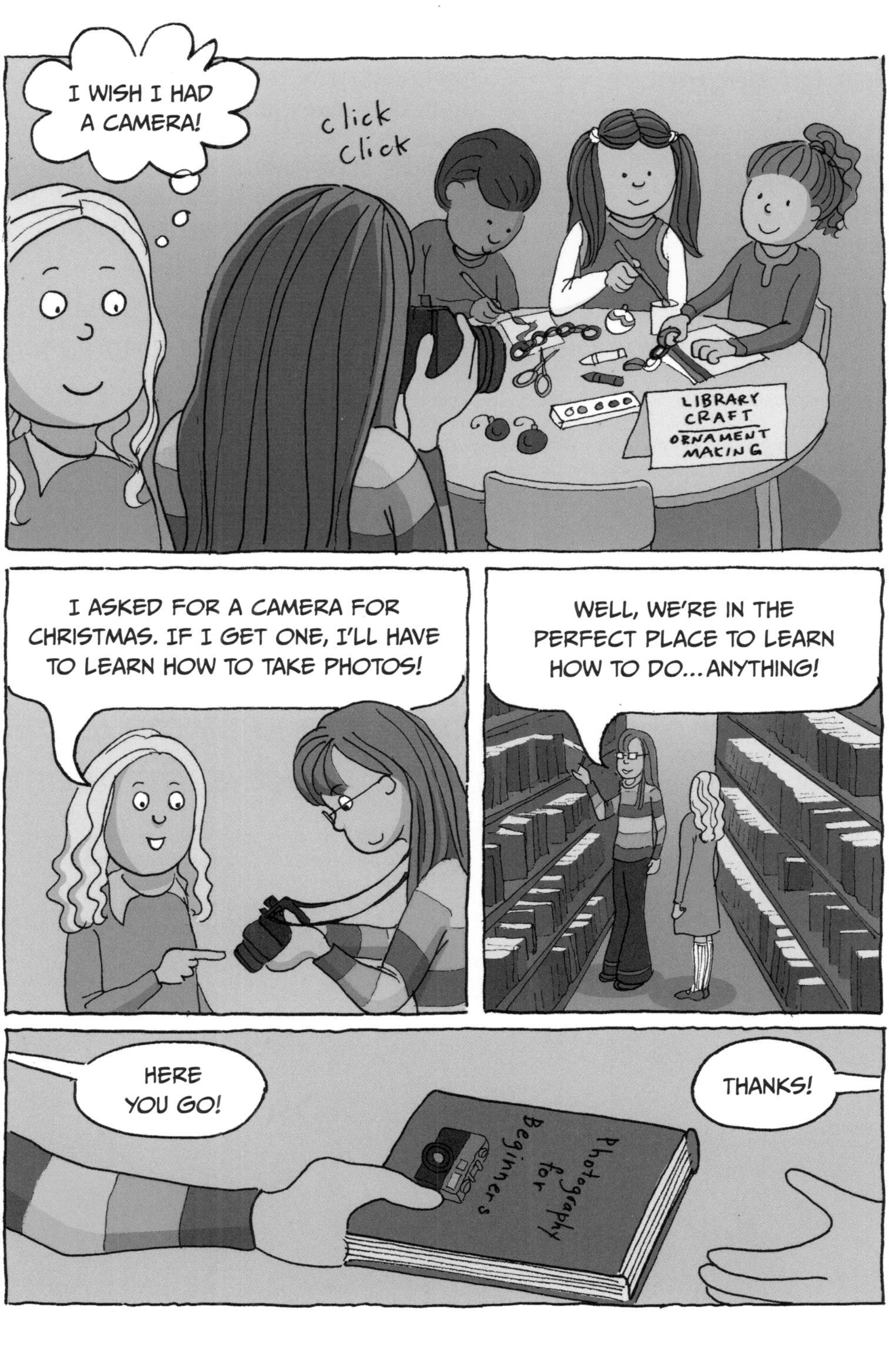
I WISH I HAD A CAMERA!
click click
LIBRARY CRAFT
ORNAMENT MAKING
I ASKED FOR A CAMERA FOR CHRISTMAS. IF I GET ONE, I'LL HAVE TO LEARN HOW TO TAKE PHOTOS!
WELL, WE'RE IN THE PERFECT PLACE TO LEARN HOW TO DO... ANYTHING!
HERE YOU GO!
THANKS!
Photography for Beginners

PHOTOGRAPHY FOR BEGINNERS

Tips for beginners

Interesting light can make a good photograph *great*. Try taking photos one hour *before* sunset or *after* sunrise: photography's "golden hour."

EXPERIMENT WITH DIFFERENT ANGLES! **Don't take every shot at eye level.** Try crouching or standing on a chair or climbing a staircase! Remember to rotate your camera so that some of your shots are vertical. See the world in a different way in order to create exciting images!

Learn the rules of photography so that you can break them intentionally as you become a better photographer!

Strong composition is the **most important** element of a great photo. You want your image to be eye-catching and you don't want viewers to be confused about what they should look at. Imagine your shot as a tic-tac-toe grid and place your subject on one of the spots where the lines intersect.

FOCUS ON YOUR SUBJECT'S EYES We are naturally drawn to a person's—or animal's—eyes in a photograph, so be sure that they are in focus.

Learn how to hold your camera to avoid blurry images: One hand should support the body of the camera; the other should hold the lens. Your elbows should be tight against your body. Just as you press the shutter-release button, hold your breath!

Look at great photographs for inspiration!
Visit an art gallery or look through books of photography. Think about what makes each photograph appealing, and imagine what techniques you can use yourself.

Zoom in and fill the frame! Your subject is important!

Keep both eyes open as you prepare to take a photo! You want to connect with your subject and also see what's happening outside of the frame: you may want to capture a dog that's just about to leap into view!

EVEN THOUGH THE BEST PRESENTS ARE ALWAYS THE ONES YOU DON'T EXPECT...

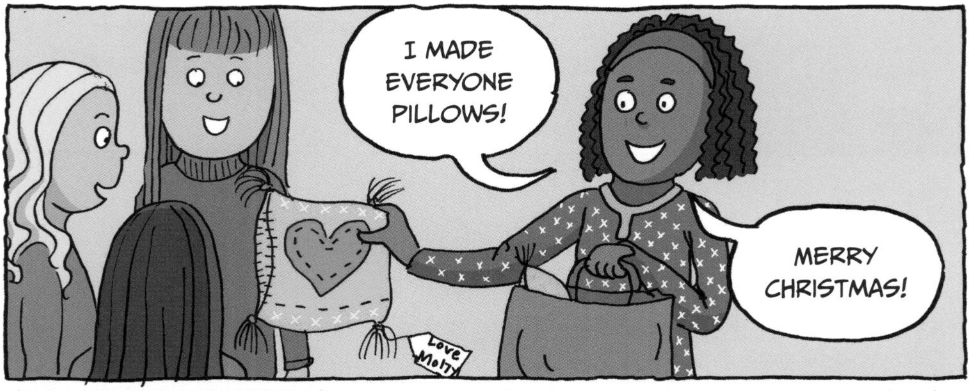
I MADE EVERYONE PILLOWS!
MERRY CHRISTMAS!

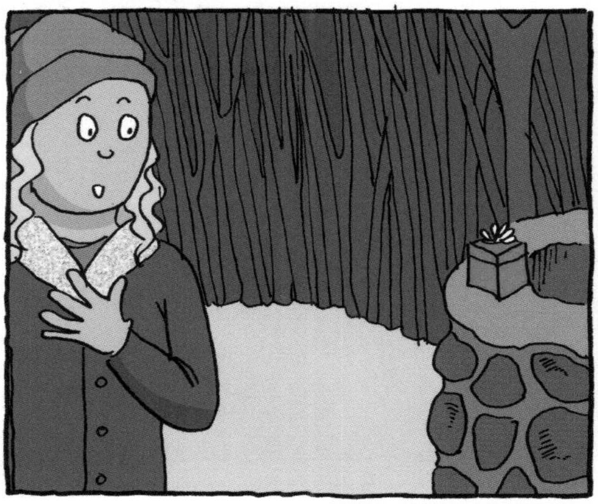

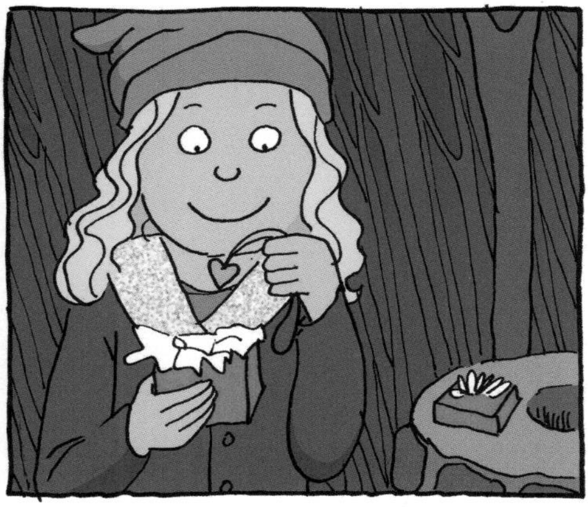

...I DO HOPE I'VE DROPPED ENOUGH HINTS ABOUT A CAMERA. I *NEED* ONE FOR MY *JOB*!

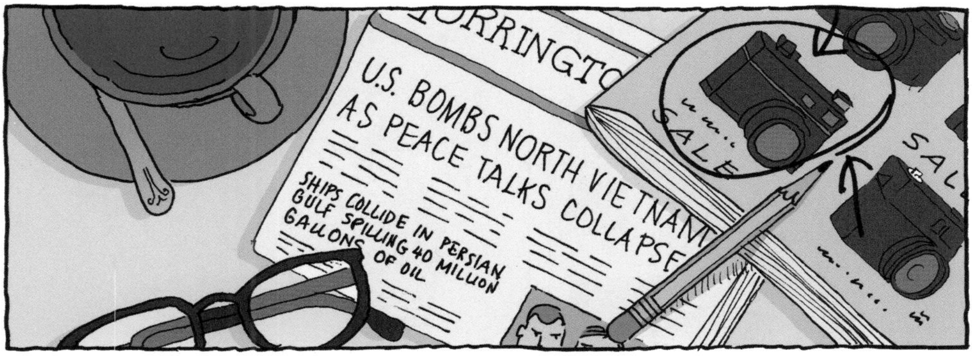
U.S. BOMBS NORTH VIETNAM AS PEACE TALKS COLLAPSE
SHIPS COLLIDE IN PERSIAN GULF SPILLING 40 MILLION GALLONS OF OIL
SALE
SALE

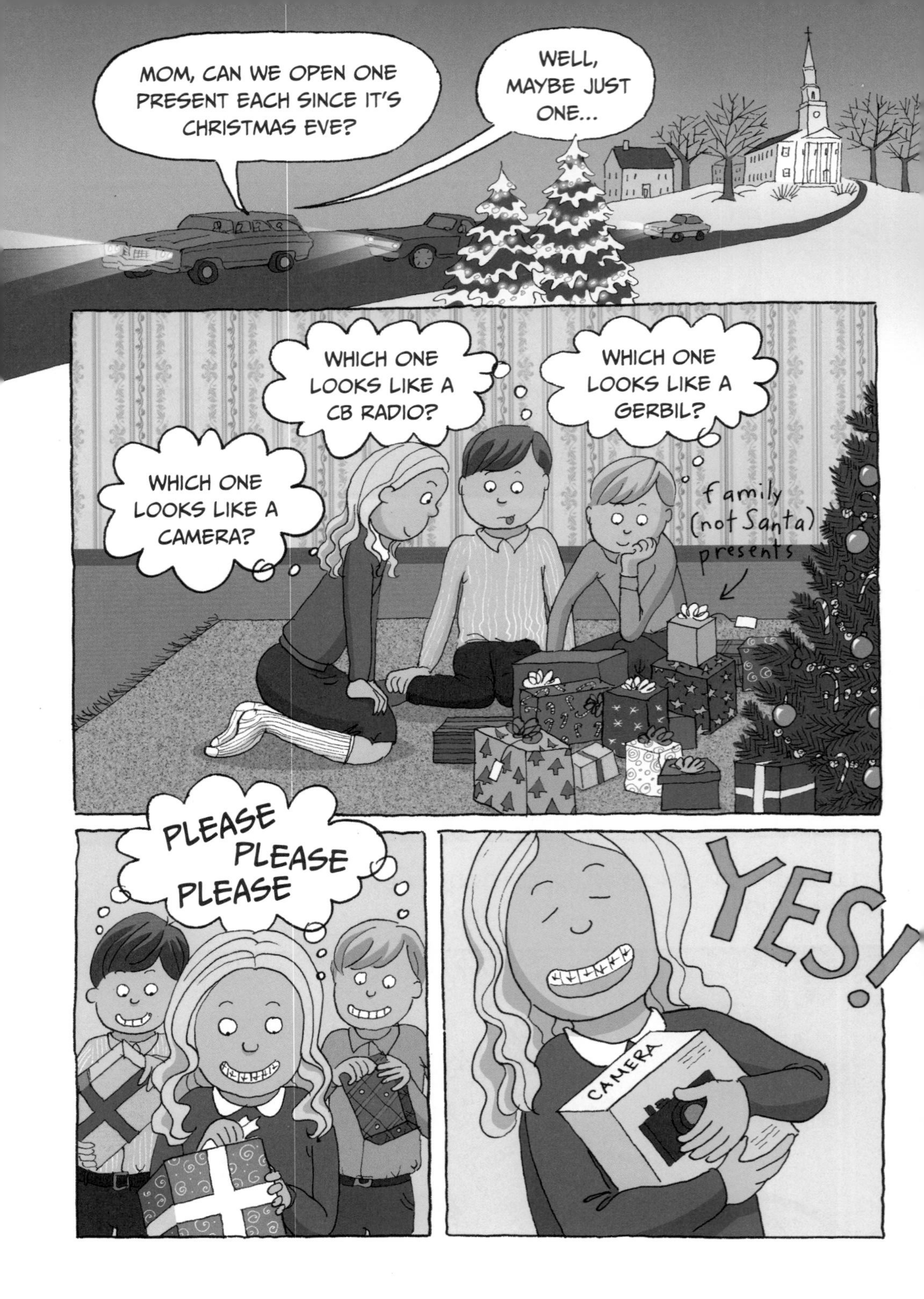
MOM, CAN WE OPEN ONE PRESENT EACH SINCE IT'S CHRISTMAS EVE?
WELL, MAYBE JUST ONE...
WHICH ONE LOOKS LIKE A CAMERA?
WHICH ONE LOOKS LIKE A CB RADIO?
WHICH ONE LOOKS LIKE A GERBIL?
family (not Santa) presents
PLEASE PLEASE PLEASE
YES!
CAMERA

THE NEXT MORNING, SANTA DOES A PRETTY GOOD JOB WITH THE REST OF OUR PRESENTS.

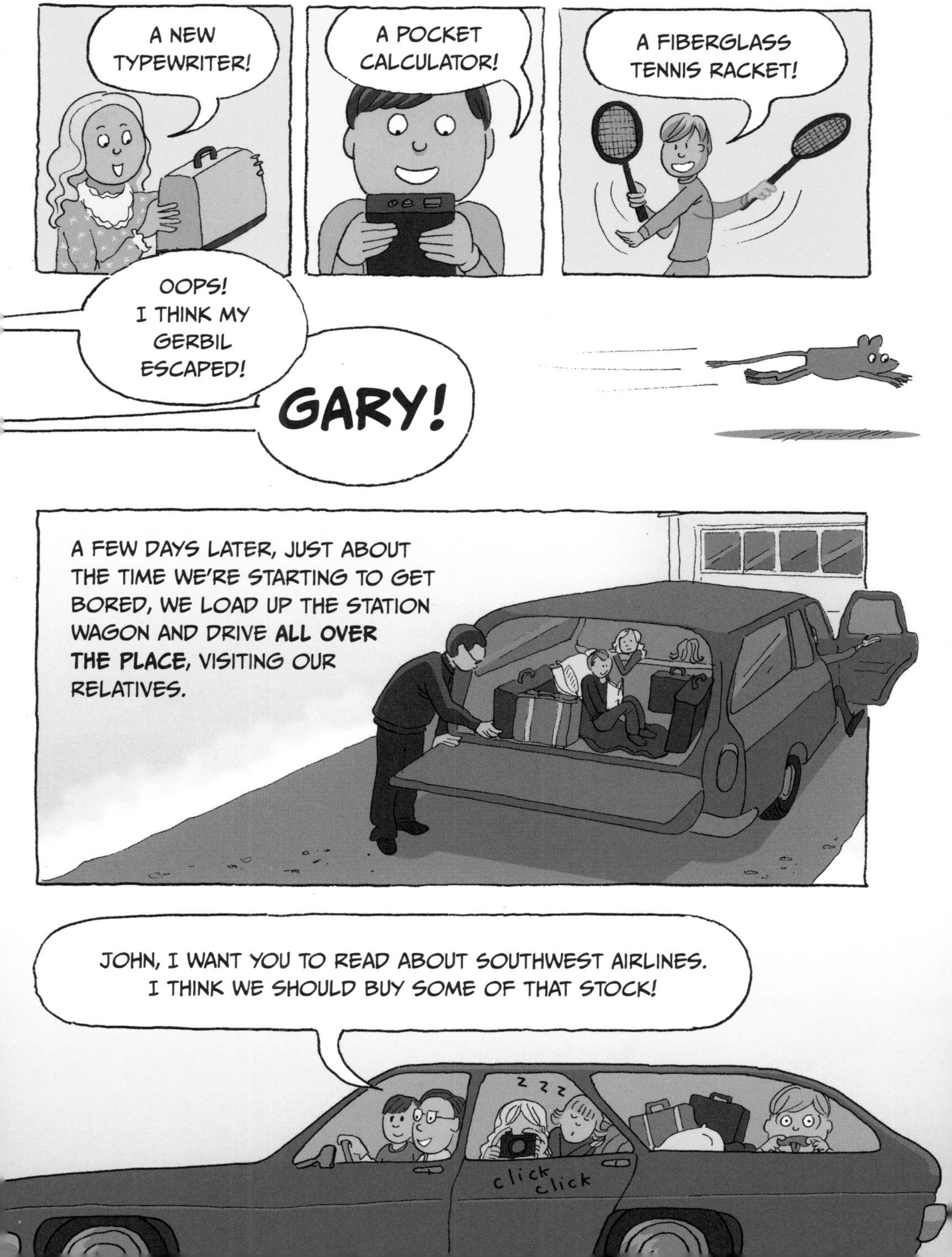
A NEW TYPEWRITER!
A POCKET CALCULATOR!
A FIBERGLASS TENNIS RACKET!
OOPS! I THINK MY GERBIL ESCAPED!
GARY!
A FEW DAYS LATER, JUST ABOUT THE TIME WE'RE STARTING TO GET BORED, WE LOAD UP THE STATION WAGON AND DRIVE **ALL OVER THE PLACE**, VISITING OUR RELATIVES.
JOHN, I WANT YOU TO READ ABOUT SOUTHWEST AIRLINES. I THINK WE SHOULD BUY SOME OF THAT STOCK!
Z Z Z
click click

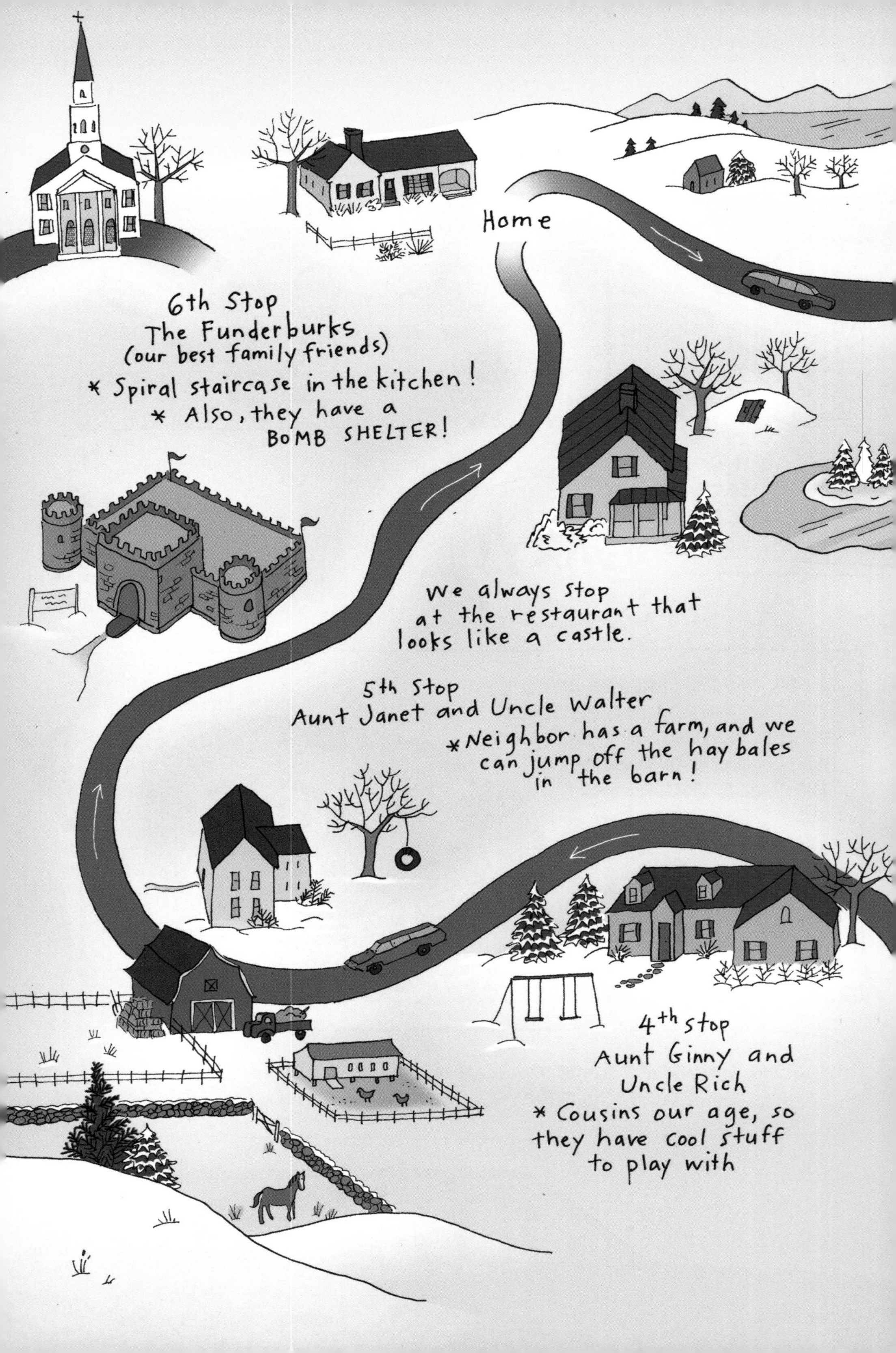
Home
6th Stop
The Funderburks
(our best family friends)
* Spiral staircase in the kitchen!
* Also, they have a BOMB SHELTER!
We always stop at the restaurant that looks like a castle.
5th Stop
Aunt Janet and Uncle Walter
* Neighbor has a farm, and we can jump off the hay bales in the barn!
4th stop
Aunt Ginny and Uncle Rich
* Cousins our age, so they have cool stuff to play with

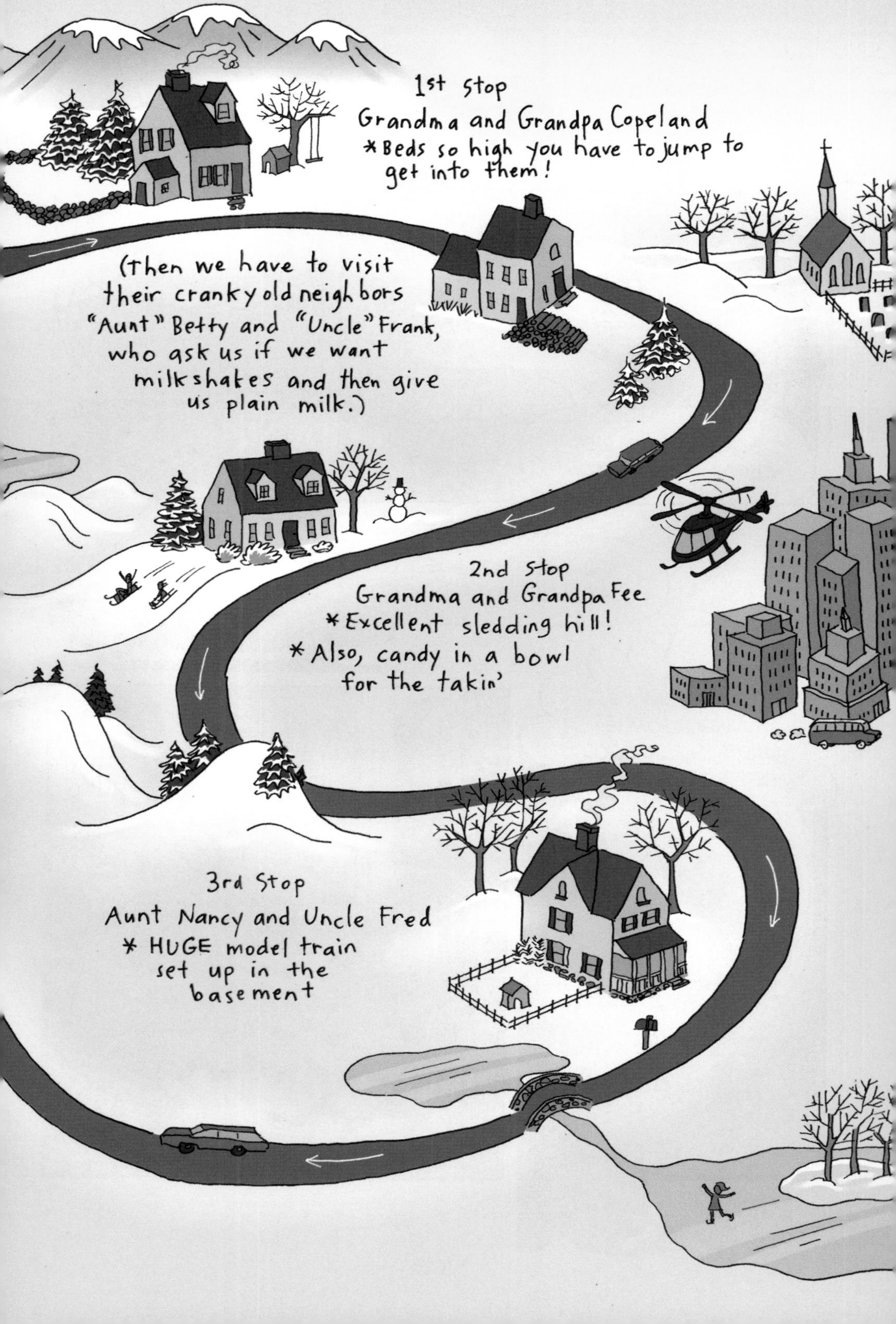
1st Stop
Grandma and Grandpa Copeland
* Beds so high you have to jump to get into them!
(Then we have to visit their cranky old neighbors "Aunt" Betty and "Uncle" Frank, who ask us if we want milkshakes and then give us plain milk.)
2nd Stop
Grandma and Grandpa Fee
* Excellent sledding hill!
* Also, candy in a bowl for the takin'
3rd Stop
Aunt Nancy and Uncle Fred
* HUGE model train set up in the basement

THE VERY SAME DAY WE GET HOME FROM OUR TRIP, PENNY CALLS!

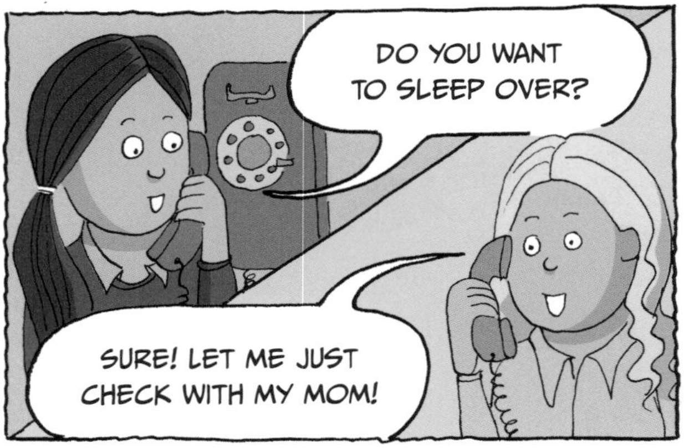
DO YOU WANT TO SLEEP OVER?
SURE! LET ME JUST CHECK WITH MY MOM!

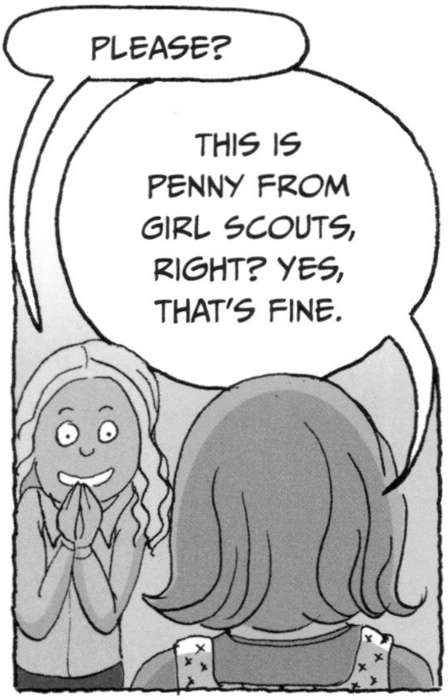
PLEASE?
THIS IS PENNY FROM GIRL SCOUTS, RIGHT? YES, THAT'S FINE.

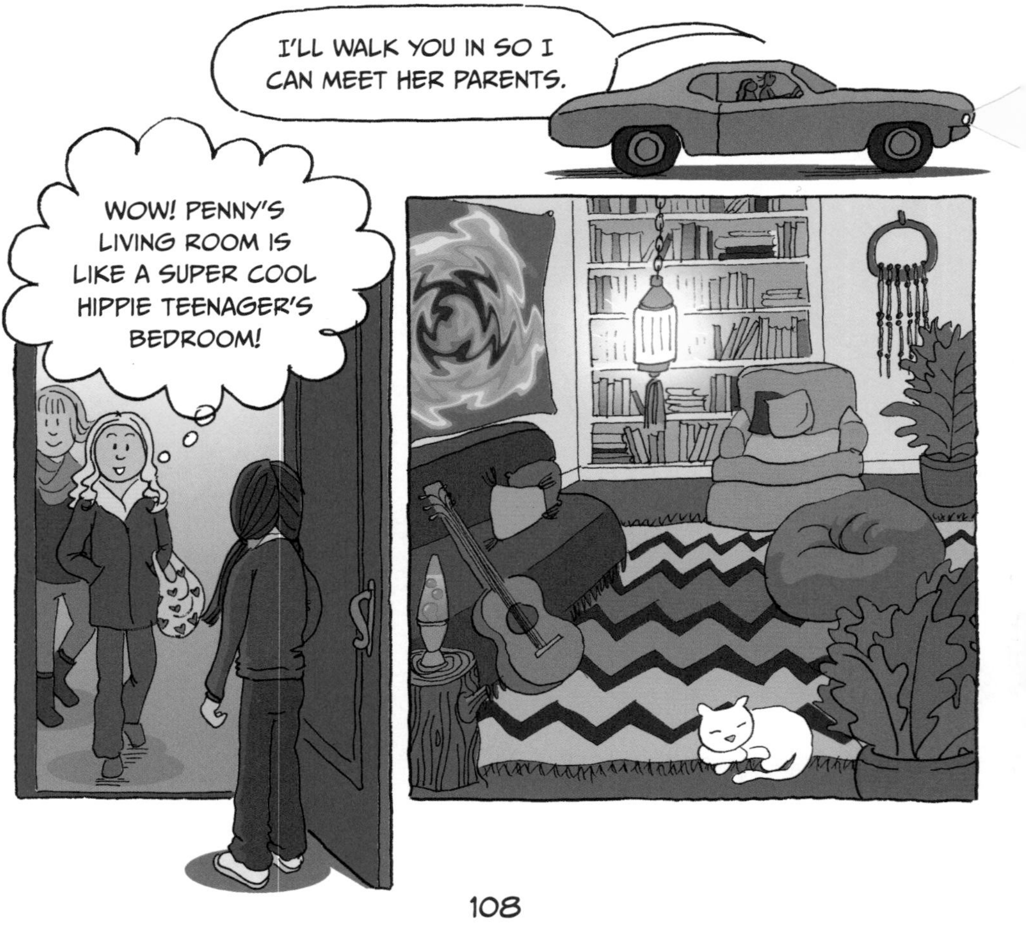
I'LL WALK YOU IN SO I CAN MEET HER PARENTS.
WOW! PENNY'S LIVING ROOM IS LIKE A SUPER COOL HIPPIE TEENAGER'S BEDROOM!

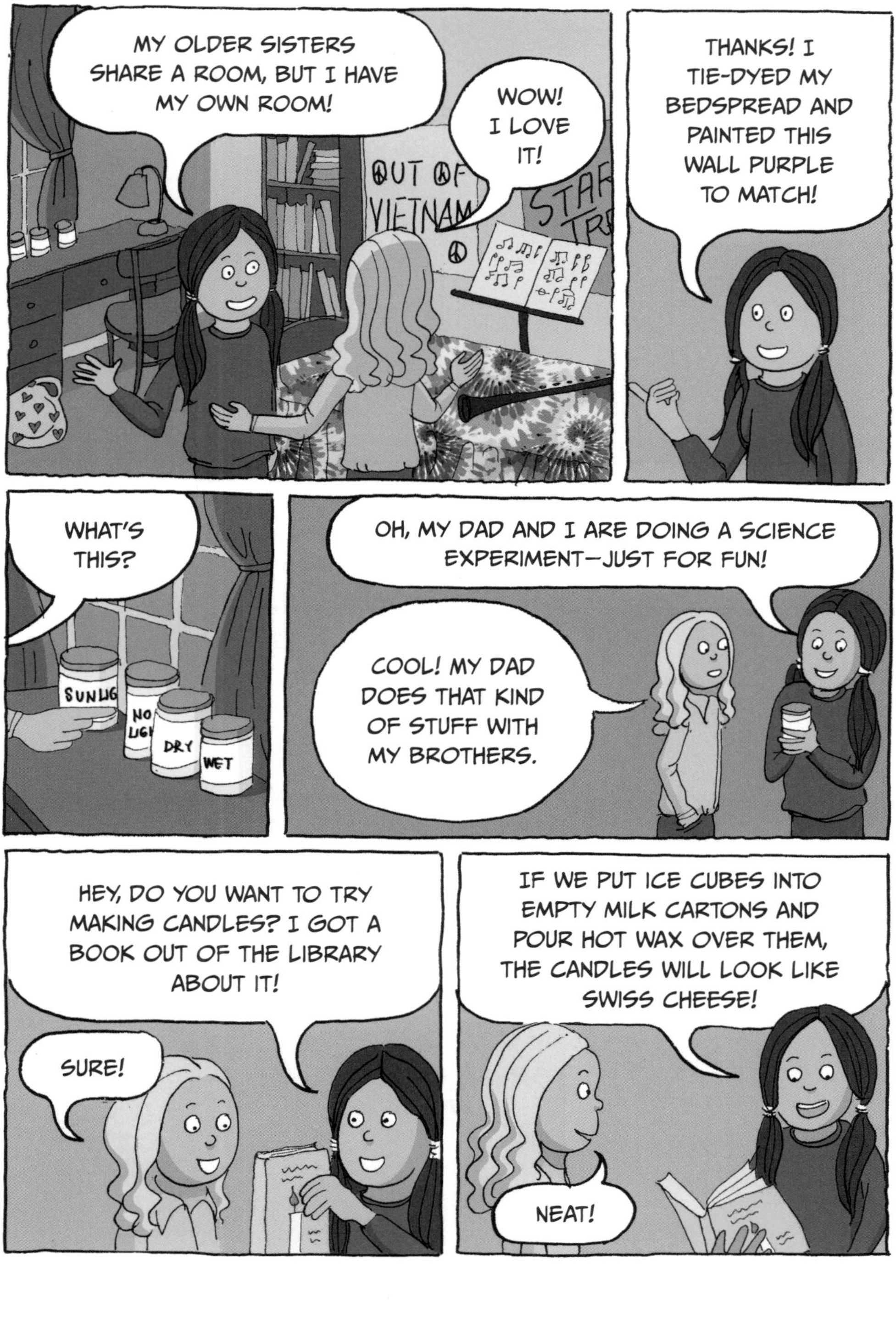

MY OLDER SISTERS SHARE A ROOM, BUT I HAVE MY OWN ROOM!
WOW! I LOVE IT!
OUT OF VIETNAM
THANKS! I TIE-DYED MY BEDSPREAD AND PAINTED THIS WALL PURPLE TO MATCH!
WHAT'S THIS?
DRY
WET
OH, MY DAD AND I ARE DOING A SCIENCE EXPERIMENT—JUST FOR FUN!
COOL! MY DAD DOES THAT KIND OF STUFF WITH MY BROTHERS.
HEY, DO YOU WANT TO TRY MAKING CANDLES? I GOT A BOOK OUT OF THE LIBRARY ABOUT IT!
SURE!
IF WE PUT ICE CUBES INTO EMPTY MILK CARTONS AND POUR HOT WAX OVER THEM, THE CANDLES WILL LOOK LIKE SWISS CHEESE!
NEAT!

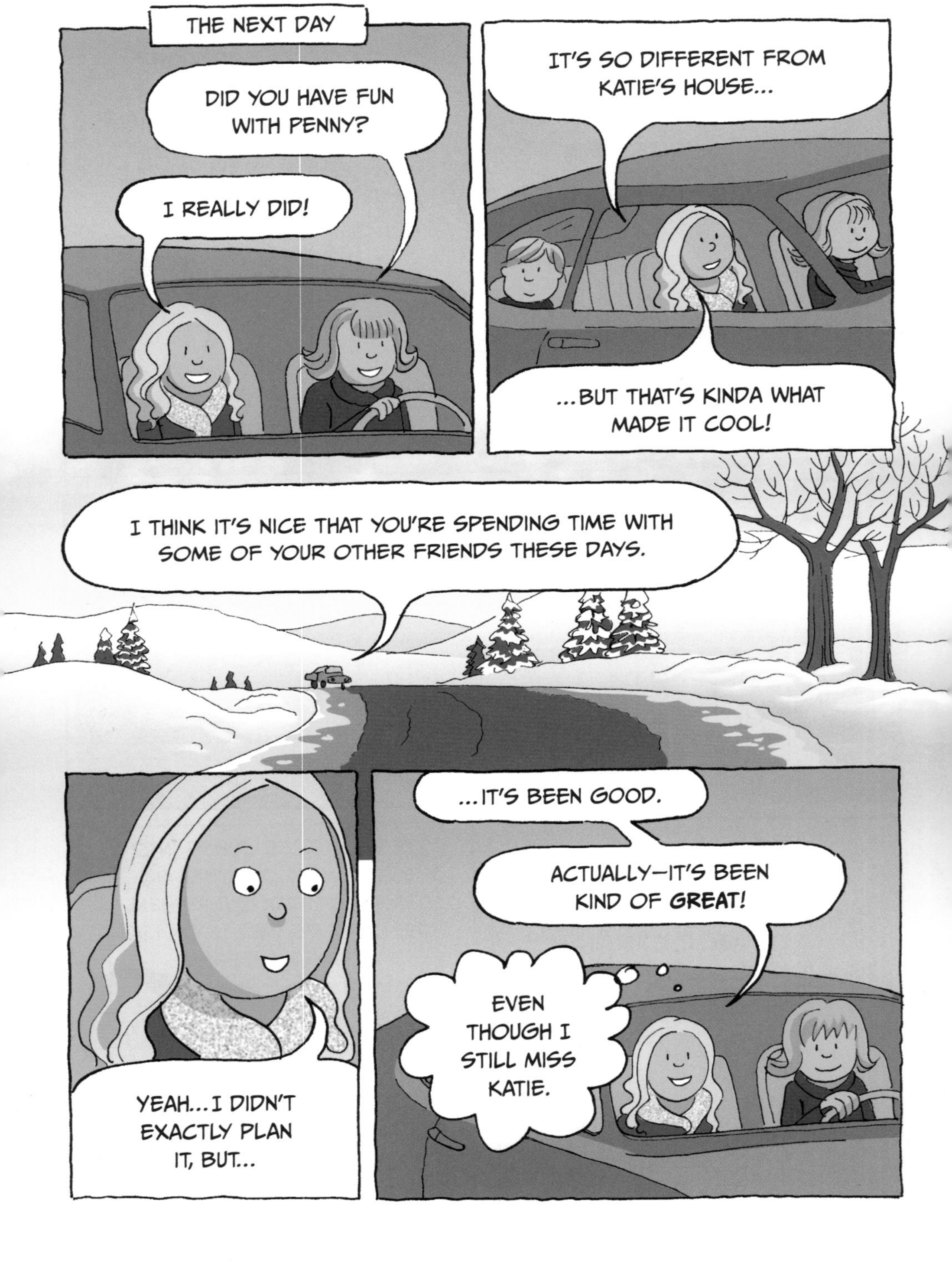
THE NEXT DAY
DID YOU HAVE FUN WITH PENNY?
I REALLY DID!
IT'S SO DIFFERENT FROM KATIE'S HOUSE...
...BUT THAT'S KINDA WHAT MADE IT COOL!
I THINK IT'S NICE THAT YOU'RE SPENDING TIME WITH SOME OF YOUR OTHER FRIENDS THESE DAYS.
YEAH...I DIDN'T EXACTLY PLAN IT, BUT...
...IT'S BEEN GOOD.
ACTUALLY—IT'S BEEN KIND OF **GREAT!**
EVEN THOUGH I STILL MISS KATIE.

Chapter 10

1973

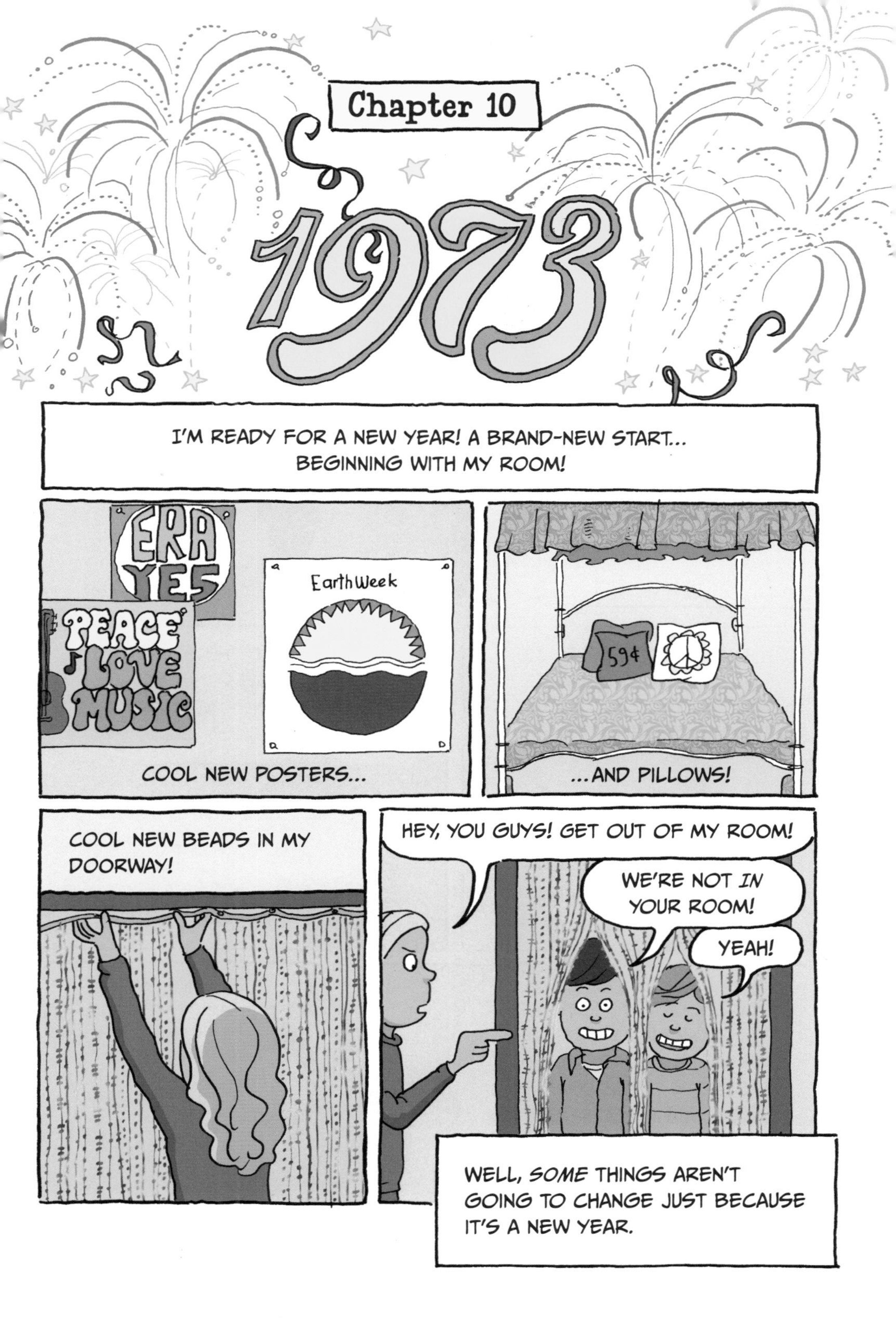

I'M READY FOR A NEW YEAR! A BRAND-NEW START... BEGINNING WITH MY ROOM!
ERA YES
PEACE LOVE MUSIC
Earth Week
COOL NEW POSTERS...
59¢
...AND PILLOWS!
COOL NEW BEADS IN MY DOORWAY!
HEY, YOU GUYS! GET OUT OF MY ROOM!
WE'RE NOT *IN* YOUR ROOM!
YEAH!
WELL, *SOME* THINGS AREN'T GOING TO CHANGE JUST BECAUSE IT'S A NEW YEAR.

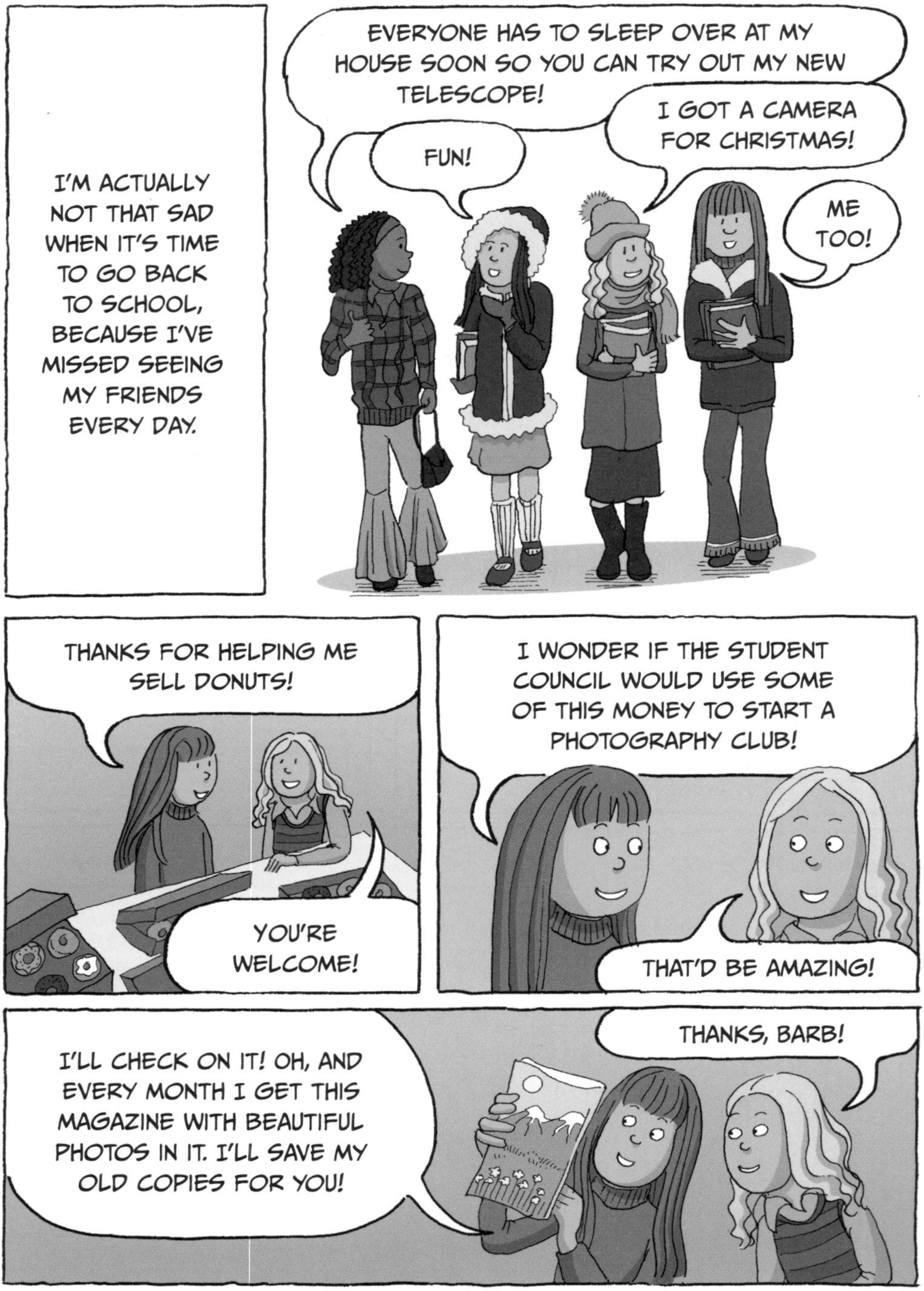

I'M ACTUALLY NOT THAT SAD WHEN IT'S TIME TO GO BACK TO SCHOOL, BECAUSE I'VE MISSED SEEING MY FRIENDS EVERY DAY.
EVERYONE HAS TO SLEEP OVER AT MY HOUSE SOON SO YOU CAN TRY OUT MY NEW TELESCOPE!
FUN!
I GOT A CAMERA FOR CHRISTMAS!
ME TOO!
THANKS FOR HELPING ME SELL DONUTS!
YOU'RE WELCOME!
I WONDER IF THE STUDENT COUNCIL WOULD USE SOME OF THIS MONEY TO START A PHOTOGRAPHY CLUB!
THAT'D BE AMAZING!
I'LL CHECK ON IT! OH, AND EVERY MONTH I GET THIS MAGAZINE WITH BEAUTIFUL PHOTOS IN IT. I'LL SAVE MY OLD COPIES FOR YOU!
THANKS, BARB!

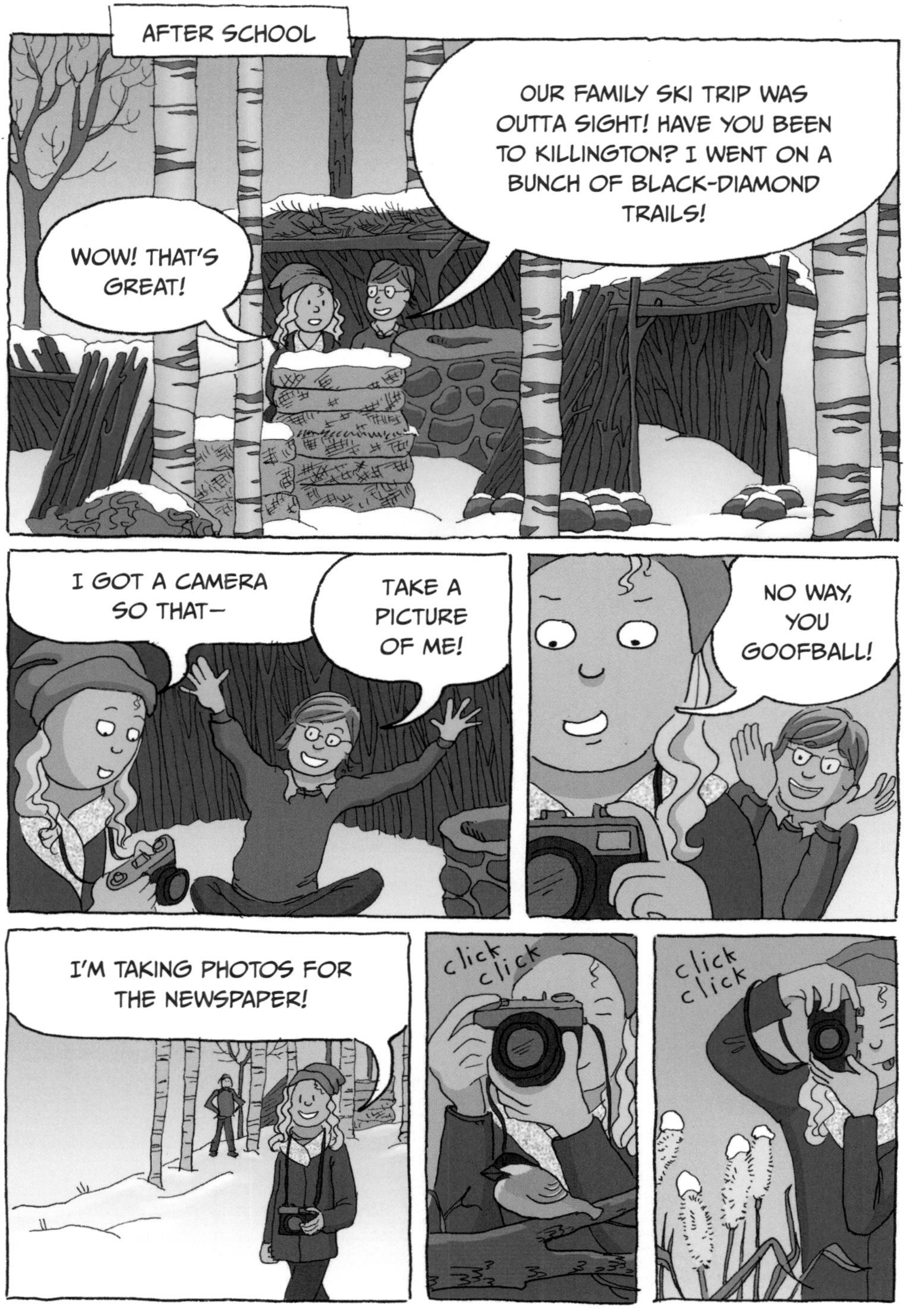
AFTER SCHOOL
OUR FAMILY SKI TRIP WAS OUTTA SIGHT! HAVE YOU BEEN TO KILLINGTON? I WENT ON A BUNCH OF BLACK-DIAMOND TRAILS!
WOW! THAT'S GREAT!
I GOT A CAMERA SO THAT—
TAKE A PICTURE OF ME!
NO WAY, YOU GOOFBALL!
I'M TAKING PHOTOS FOR THE NEWSPAPER!
click click
click click

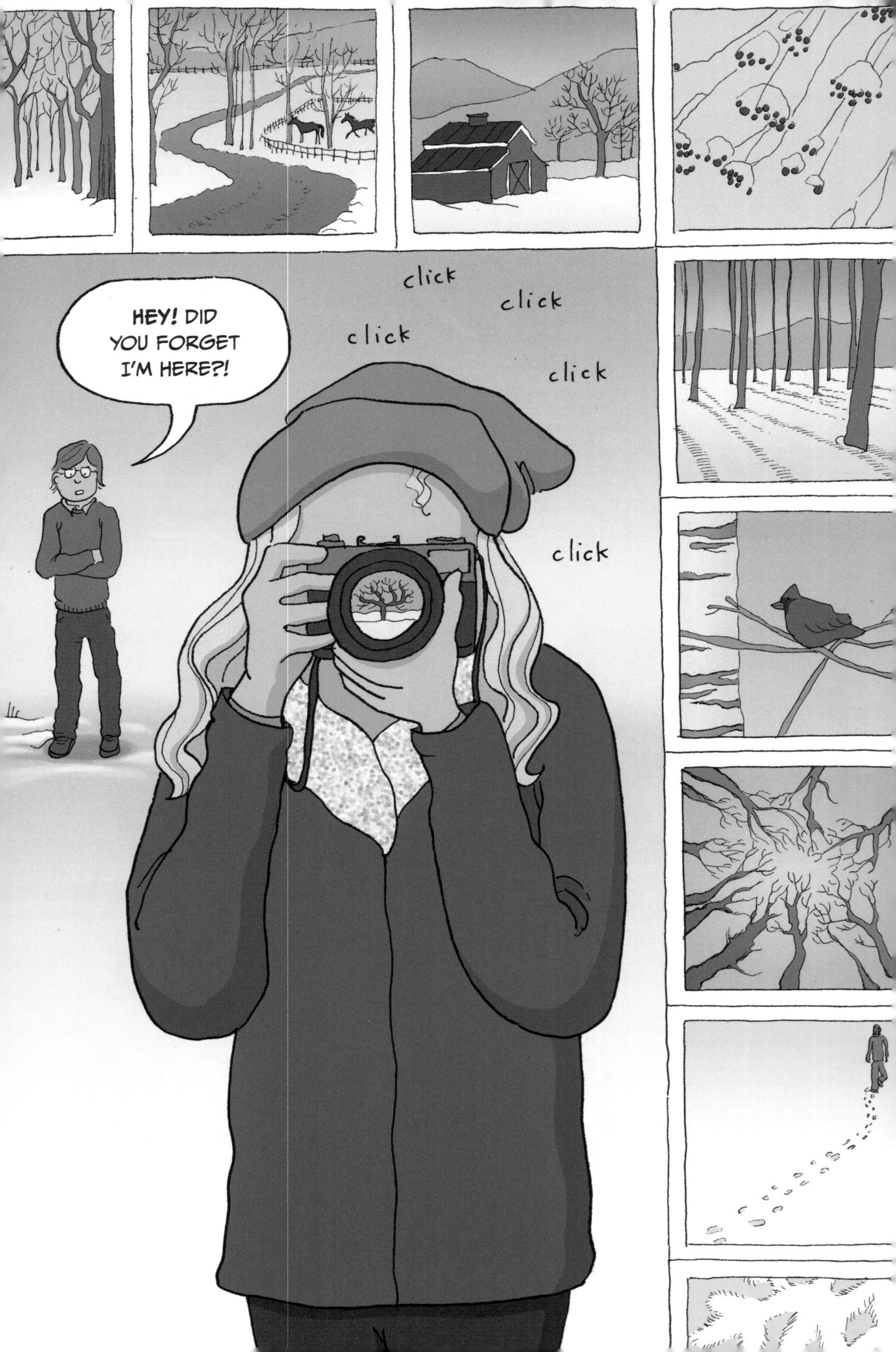

HEY! DID YOU FORGET I'M HERE?!
click
click
click
click
click

HERE'S THE ARTICLE I WROTE ABOUT THE KIDS WHO WENT ON A SCHOOL TRIP TO PARIS.

GREAT! LET ME TAKE A LOOK.

still haven't told Leslie I hate tea

THIS IS VERY GOOD!

AND THE PHOTOS YOU'VE BEEN TAKING ARE EXCELLENT!

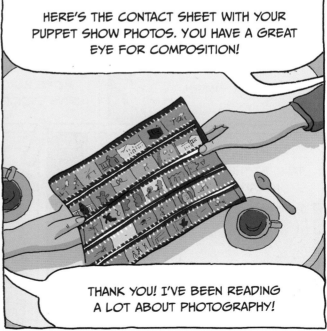

HERE'S THE CONTACT SHEET WITH YOUR PUPPET SHOW PHOTOS. YOU HAVE A GREAT EYE FOR COMPOSITION!

THANK YOU! I'VE BEEN READING A LOT ABOUT PHOTOGRAPHY!

115

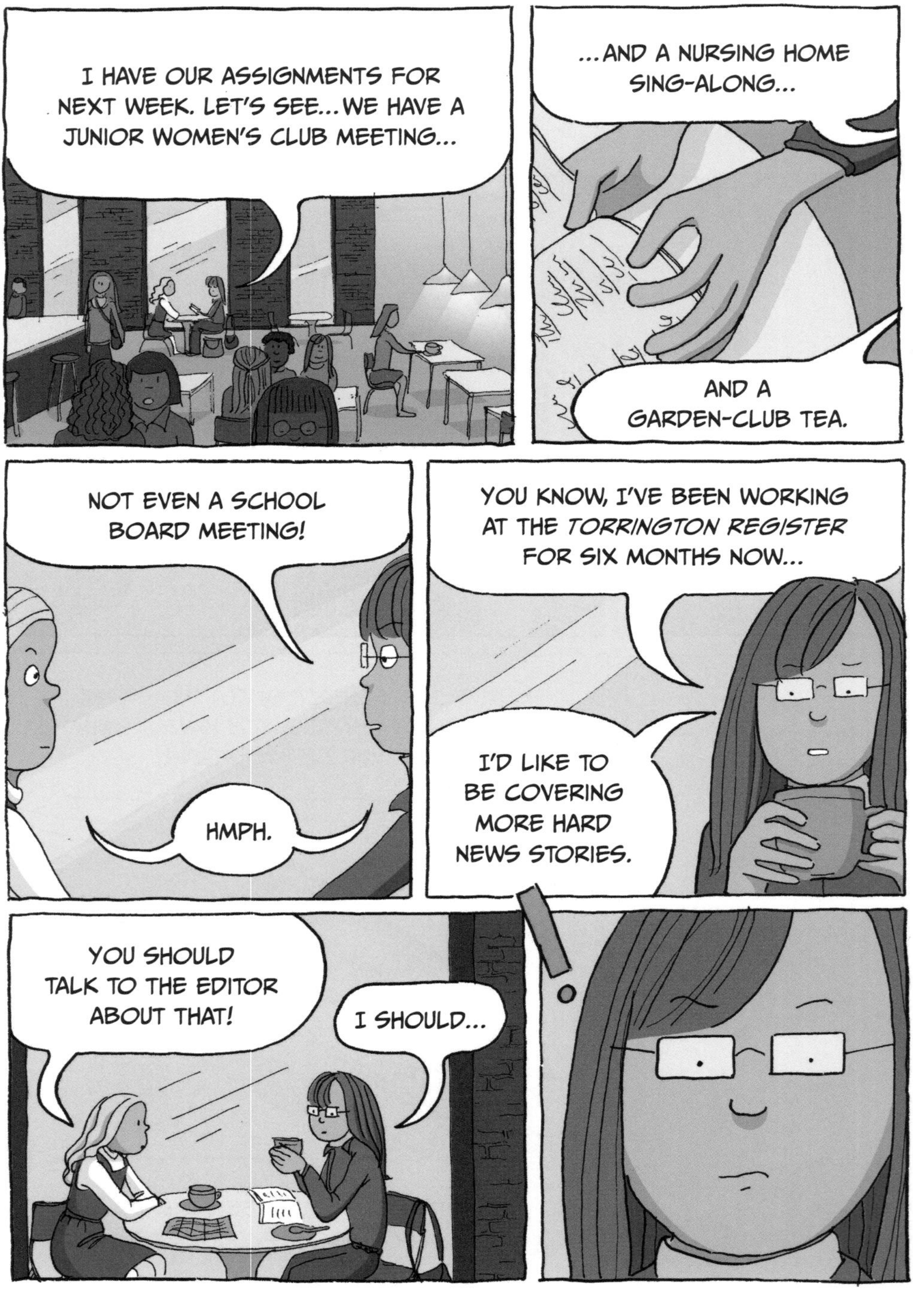
I HAVE OUR ASSIGNMENTS FOR NEXT WEEK. LET'S SEE...WE HAVE A JUNIOR WOMEN'S CLUB MEETING...
...AND A NURSING HOME SING-ALONG...
AND A GARDEN-CLUB TEA.
NOT EVEN A SCHOOL BOARD MEETING!
HMPH.
YOU KNOW, I'VE BEEN WORKING AT THE *TORRINGTON REGISTER* FOR SIX MONTHS NOW...
I'D LIKE TO BE COVERING MORE HARD NEWS STORIES.
YOU SHOULD TALK TO THE EDITOR ABOUT THAT!
I SHOULD...

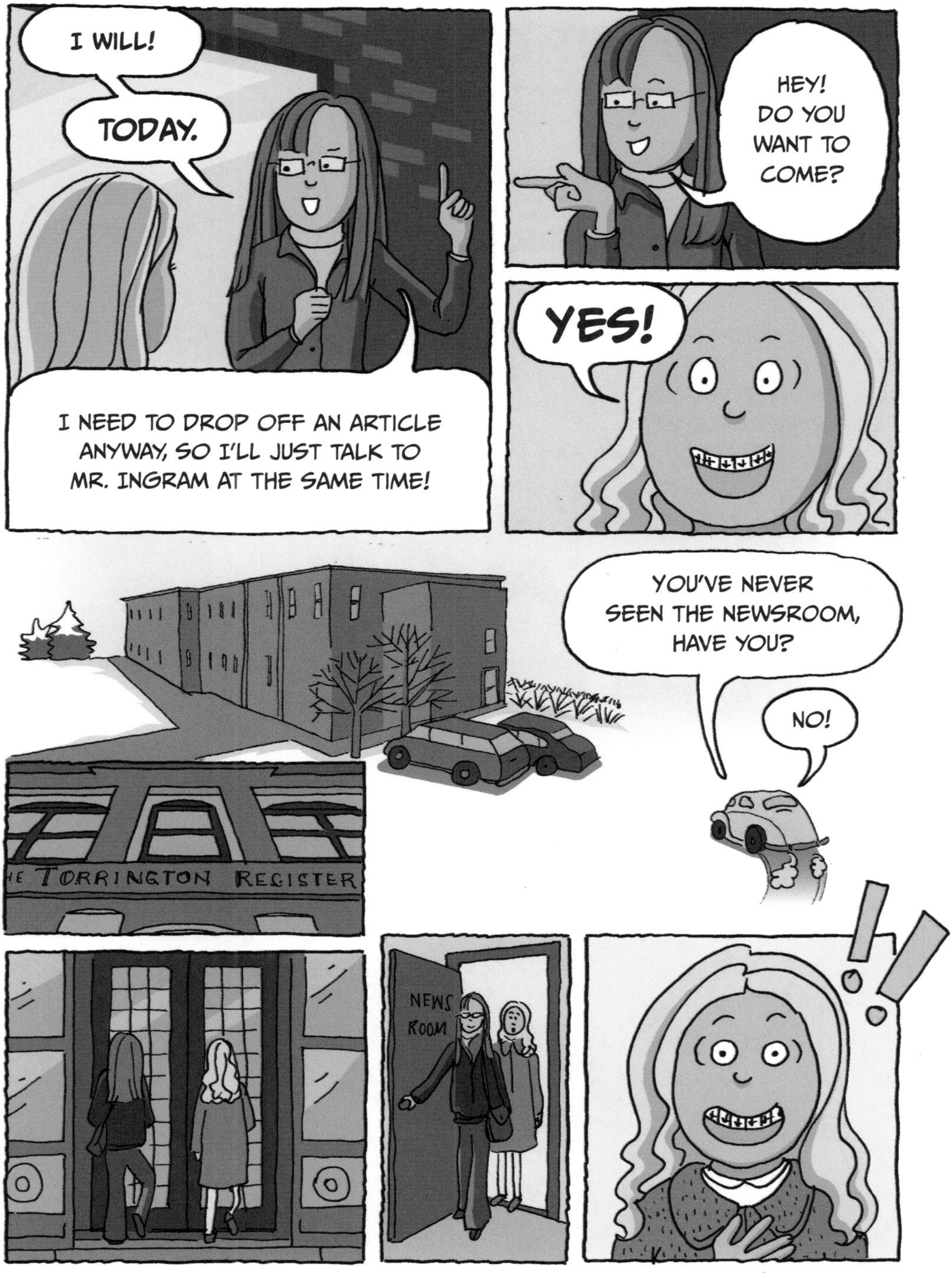
I WILL!
TODAY.
I NEED TO DROP OFF AN ARTICLE ANYWAY, SO I'LL JUST TALK TO MR. INGRAM AT THE SAME TIME!
HEY! DO YOU WANT TO COME?
YES!
YOU'VE NEVER SEEN THE NEWSROOM, HAVE YOU?
NO!
HE TORRINGTON REGISTER
NEWS ROOM

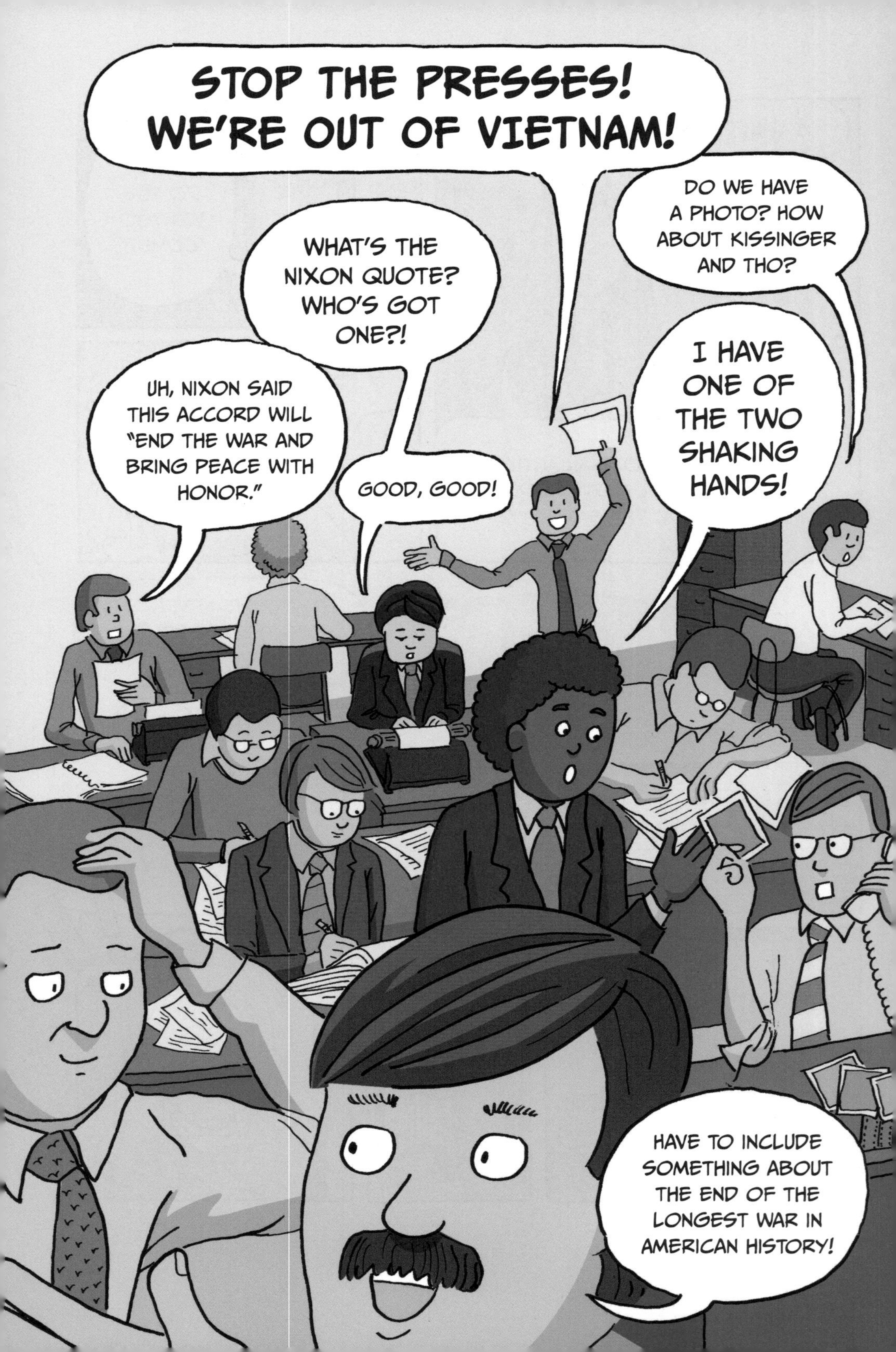
STOP THE PRESSES! WE'RE OUT OF VIETNAM!
WHAT'S THE NIXON QUOTE? WHO'S GOT ONE?!
DO WE HAVE A PHOTO? HOW ABOUT KISSINGER AND THO?
UH, NIXON SAID THIS ACCORD WILL "END THE WAR AND BRING PEACE WITH HONOR."
GOOD, GOOD!
I HAVE ONE OF THE TWO SHAKING HANDS!
HAVE TO INCLUDE SOMETHING ABOUT THE END OF THE LONGEST WAR IN AMERICAN HISTORY!

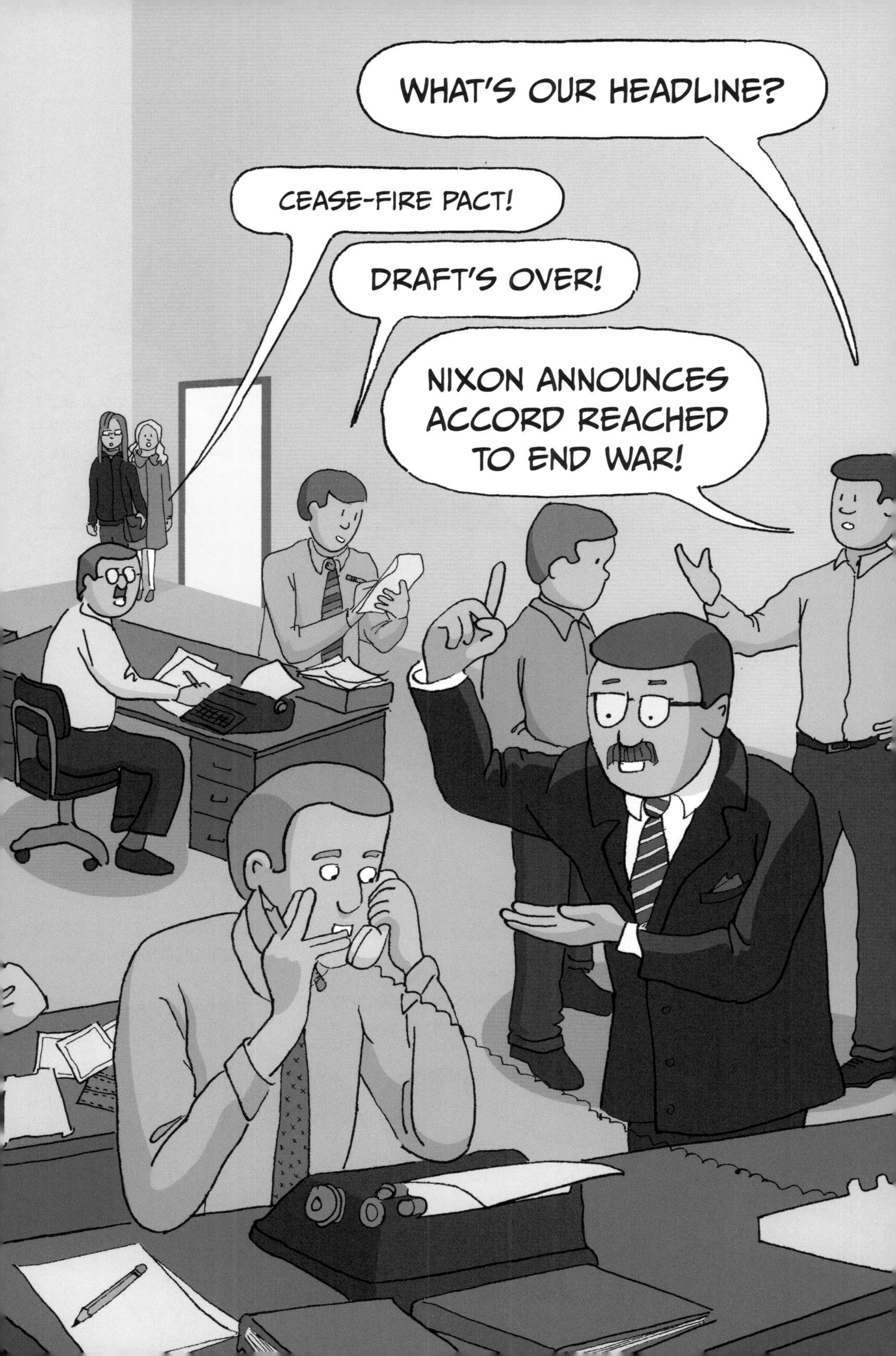
WHAT'S OUR HEADLINE?
CEASE-FIRE PACT!
DRAFT'S OVER!
NIXON ANNOUNCES ACCORD REACHED TO END WAR!

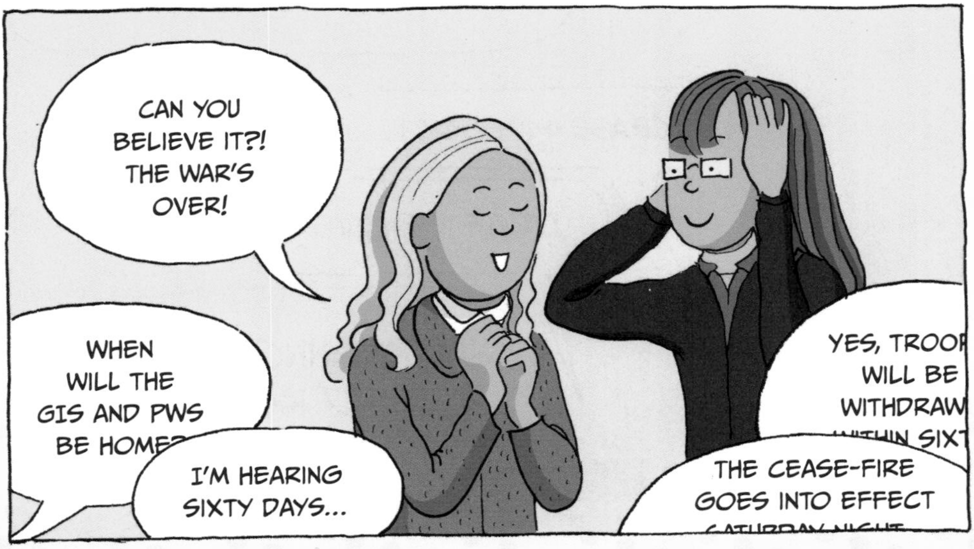
CAN YOU BELIEVE IT?! THE WAR'S OVER!
WHEN WILL THE GIS AND PWS BE HOME
I'M HEARING SIXTY DAYS...
YES, TROO WILL BE WITHDRAW
THE CEASE-FIRE GOES INTO EFFECT

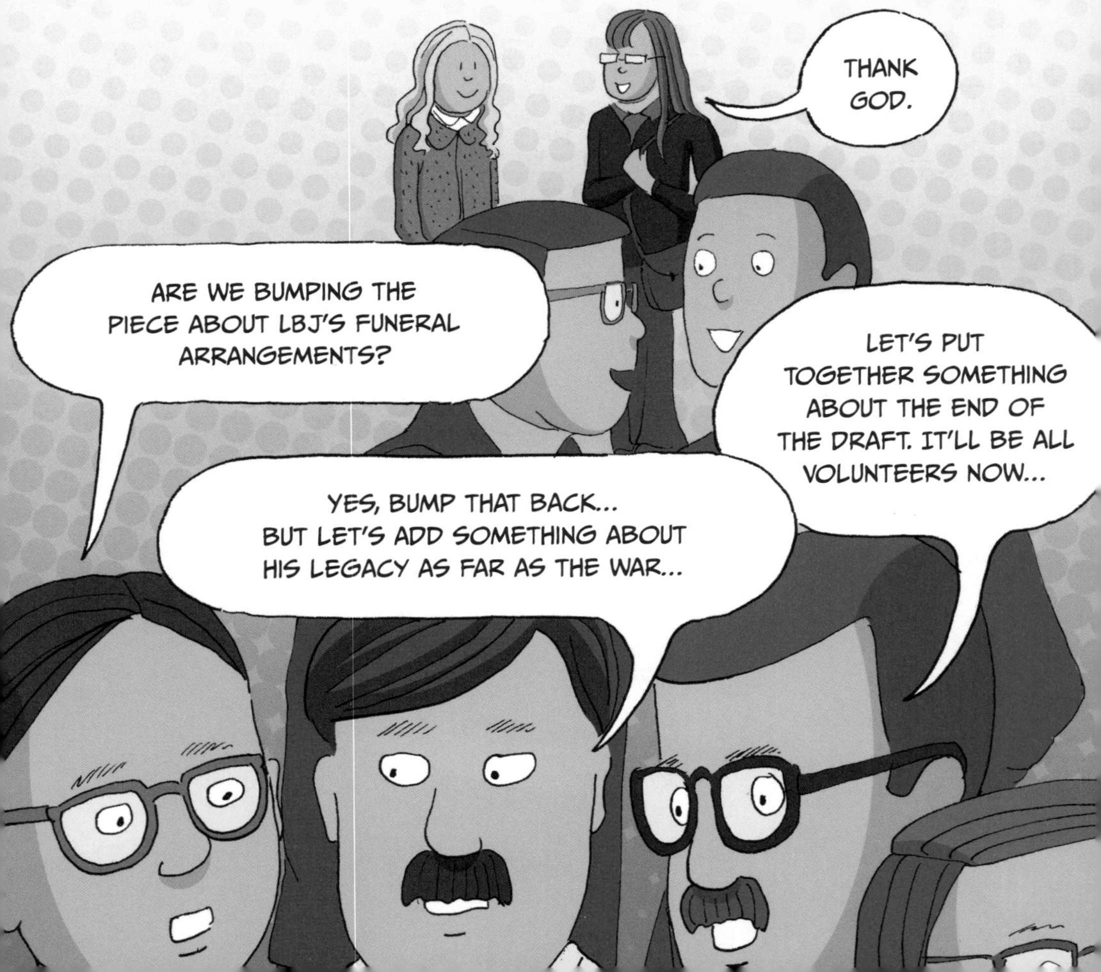
THANK GOD.
ARE WE BUMPING THE PIECE ABOUT LBJ'S FUNERAL ARRANGEMENTS?
LET'S PUT TOGETHER SOMETHING ABOUT THE END OF THE DRAFT. IT'LL BE ALL VOLUNTEERS NOW...
YES, BUMP THAT BACK... BUT LET'S ADD SOMETHING ABOUT HIS LEGACY AS FAR AS THE WAR...

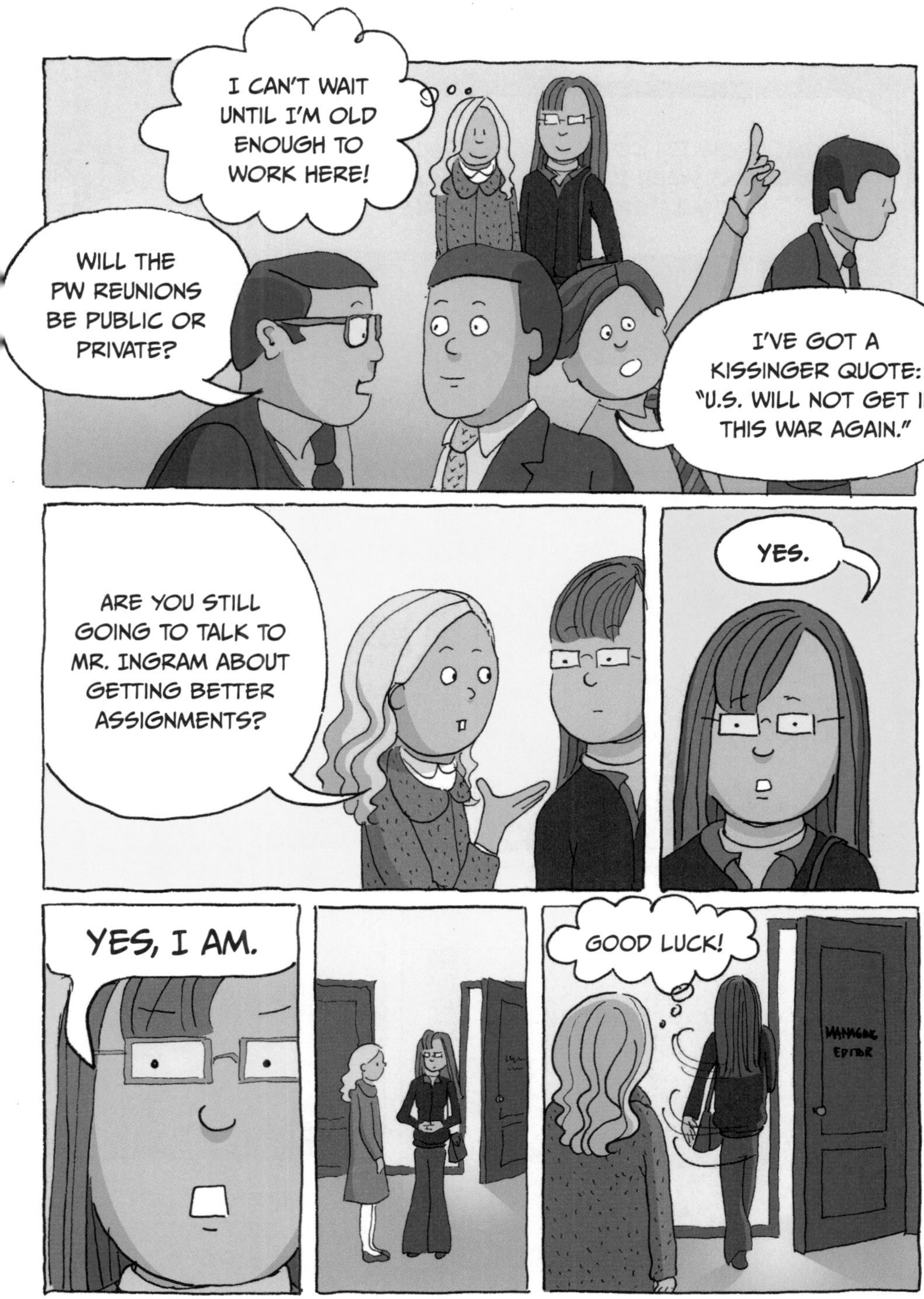
I CAN'T WAIT UNTIL I'M OLD ENOUGH TO WORK HERE!
WILL THE PW REUNIONS BE PUBLIC OR PRIVATE?
I'VE GOT A KISSINGER QUOTE: "U.S. WILL NOT GET IN THIS WAR AGAIN."
ARE YOU STILL GOING TO TALK TO MR. INGRAM ABOUT GETTING BETTER ASSIGNMENTS?
YES.
YES, I AM.
GOOD LUCK!
MANAGING EDITOR

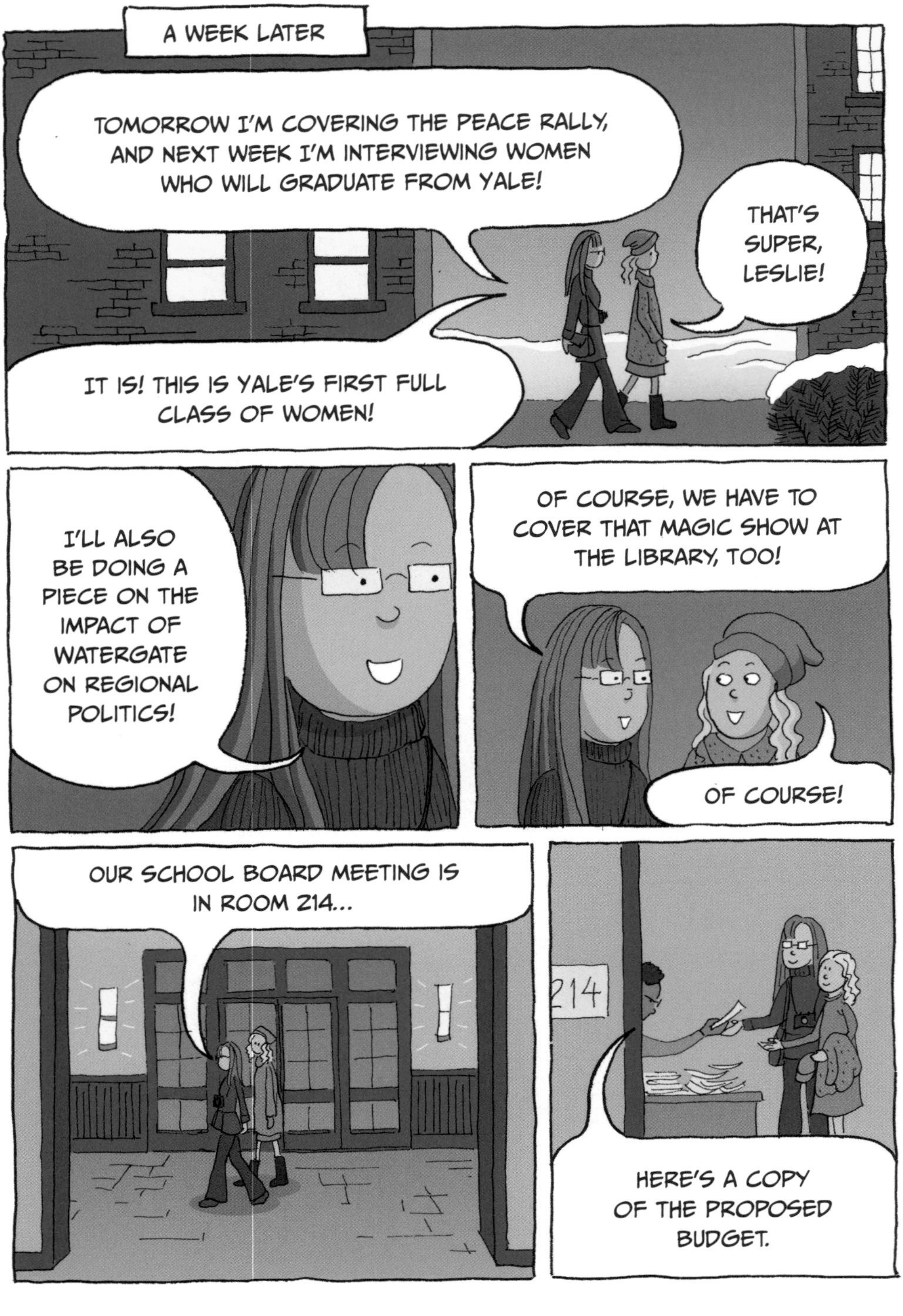
A WEEK LATER
TOMORROW I'M COVERING THE PEACE RALLY, AND NEXT WEEK I'M INTERVIEWING WOMEN WHO WILL GRADUATE FROM YALE!
THAT'S SUPER, LESLIE!
IT IS! THIS IS YALE'S FIRST FULL CLASS OF WOMEN!
I'LL ALSO BE DOING A PIECE ON THE IMPACT OF WATERGATE ON REGIONAL POLITICS!
OF COURSE, WE HAVE TO COVER THAT MAGIC SHOW AT THE LIBRARY, TOO!
OF COURSE!
OUR SCHOOL BOARD MEETING IS IN ROOM 214...
214
HERE'S A COPY OF THE PROPOSED BUDGET.

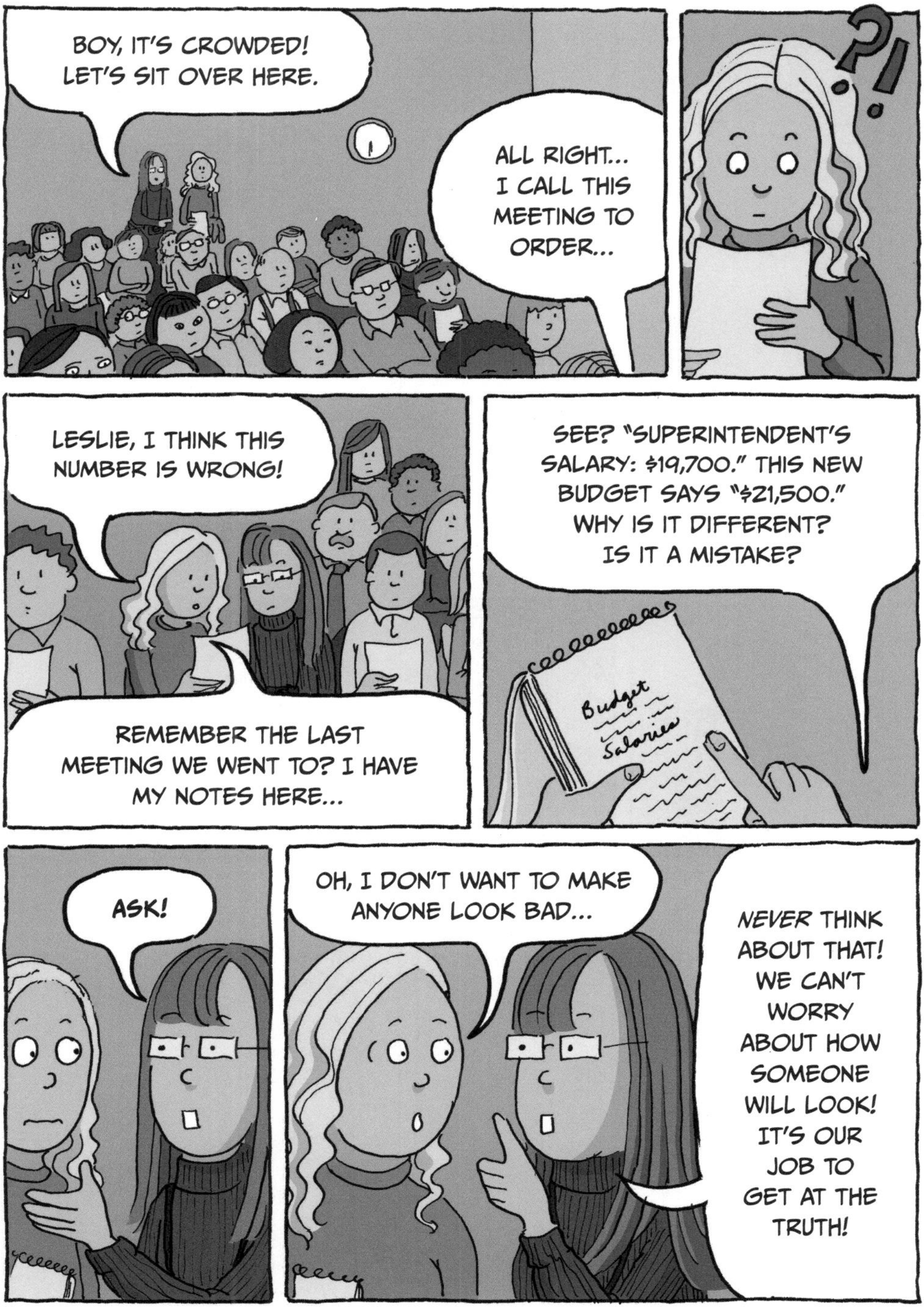
BOY, IT'S CROWDED! LET'S SIT OVER HERE.
ALL RIGHT... I CALL THIS MEETING TO ORDER...
?!
LESLIE, I THINK THIS NUMBER IS WRONG!
REMEMBER THE LAST MEETING WE WENT TO? I HAVE MY NOTES HERE...
SEE? "SUPERINTENDENT'S SALARY: $19,700." THIS NEW BUDGET SAYS "$21,500." WHY IS IT DIFFERENT? IS IT A MISTAKE?
Budget
Salaries
ASK!
OH, I DON'T WANT TO MAKE ANYONE LOOK BAD...
NEVER THINK ABOUT THAT! WE CAN'T WORRY ABOUT HOW SOMEONE WILL LOOK! IT'S OUR JOB TO GET AT THE TRUTH!

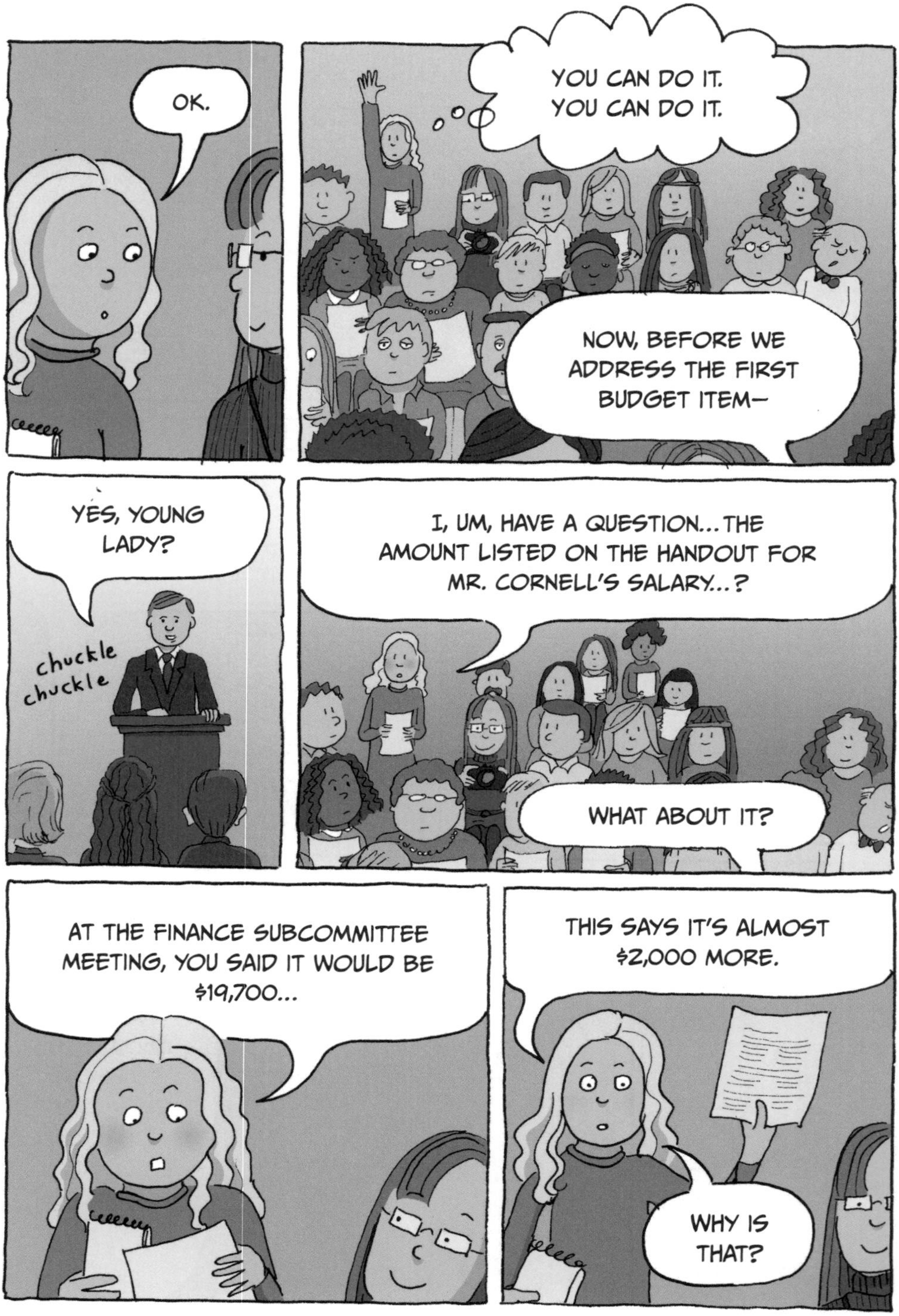
OK.
YOU CAN DO IT. YOU CAN DO IT.
NOW, BEFORE WE ADDRESS THE FIRST BUDGET ITEM—
YES, YOUNG LADY?
chuckle chuckle
I, UM, HAVE A QUESTION... THE AMOUNT LISTED ON THE HANDOUT FOR MR. CORNELL'S SALARY...?
WHAT ABOUT IT?
AT THE FINANCE SUBCOMMITTEE MEETING, YOU SAID IT WOULD BE $19,700...
THIS SAYS IT'S ALMOST $2,000 MORE.
WHY IS THAT?

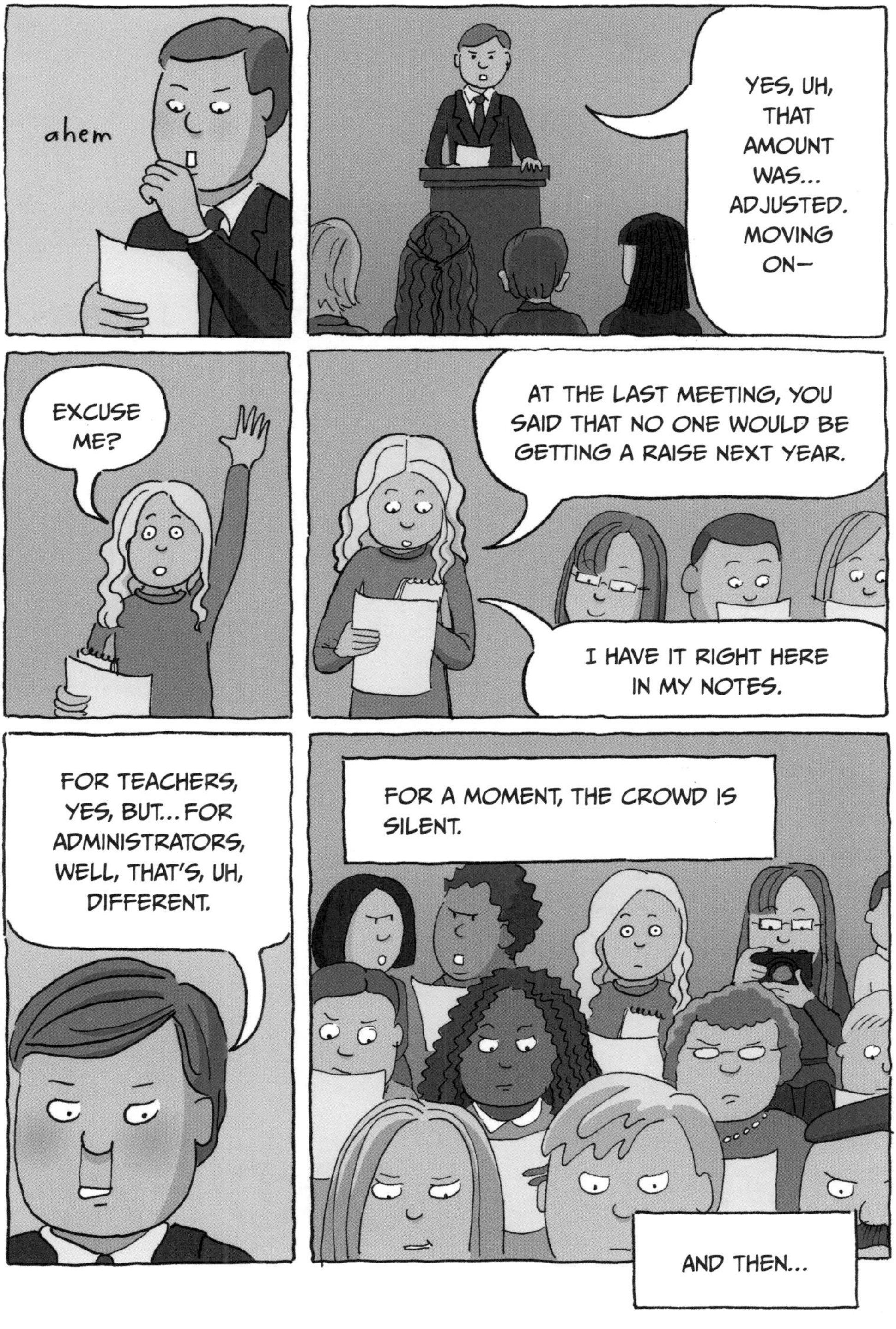
ahem
YES, UH, THAT AMOUNT WAS... ADJUSTED. MOVING ON—
EXCUSE ME?
AT THE LAST MEETING, YOU SAID THAT NO ONE WOULD BE GETTING A RAISE NEXT YEAR.
I HAVE IT RIGHT HERE IN MY NOTES.
FOR TEACHERS, YES, BUT...FOR ADMINISTRATORS, WELL, THAT'S, UH, DIFFERENT.
FOR A MOMENT, THE CROWD IS SILENT.
AND THEN...

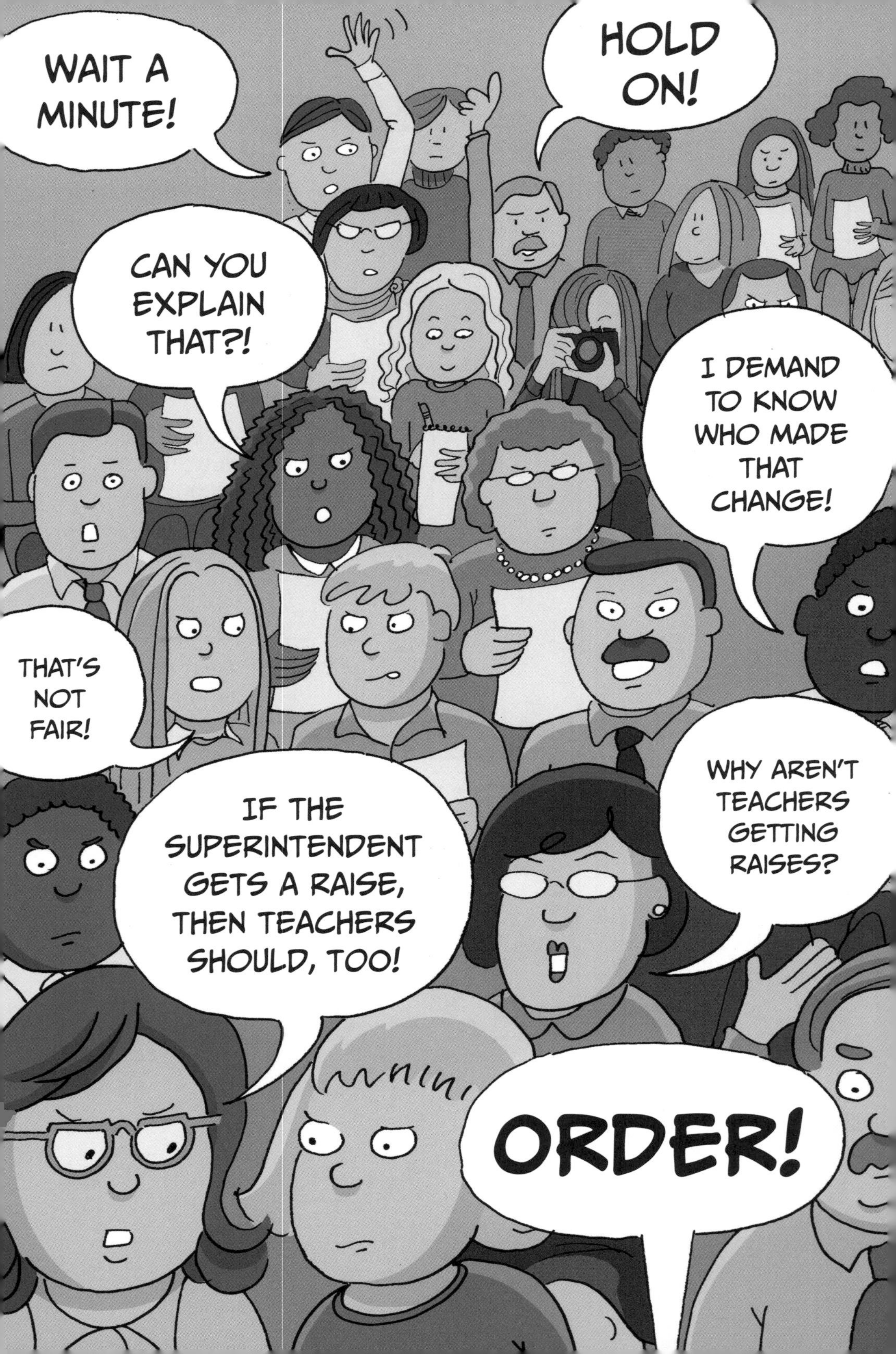
WAIT A MINUTE!
HOLD ON!
CAN YOU EXPLAIN THAT?!
I DEMAND TO KNOW WHO MADE THAT CHANGE!
THAT'S NOT FAIR!
IF THE SUPERINTENDENT GETS A RAISE, THEN TEACHERS SHOULD, TOO!
WHY AREN'T TEACHERS GETTING RAISES?
ORDER!

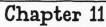

Chapter 11

I'M STILL EXCITED ABOUT FEELING LIKE A **REAL REPORTER** AS I ROUND THE CORNER TO GO TO ENGLISH CLASS THE NEXT DAY.

IS THAT EVIE?!

I'M FROZEN IN PLACE.

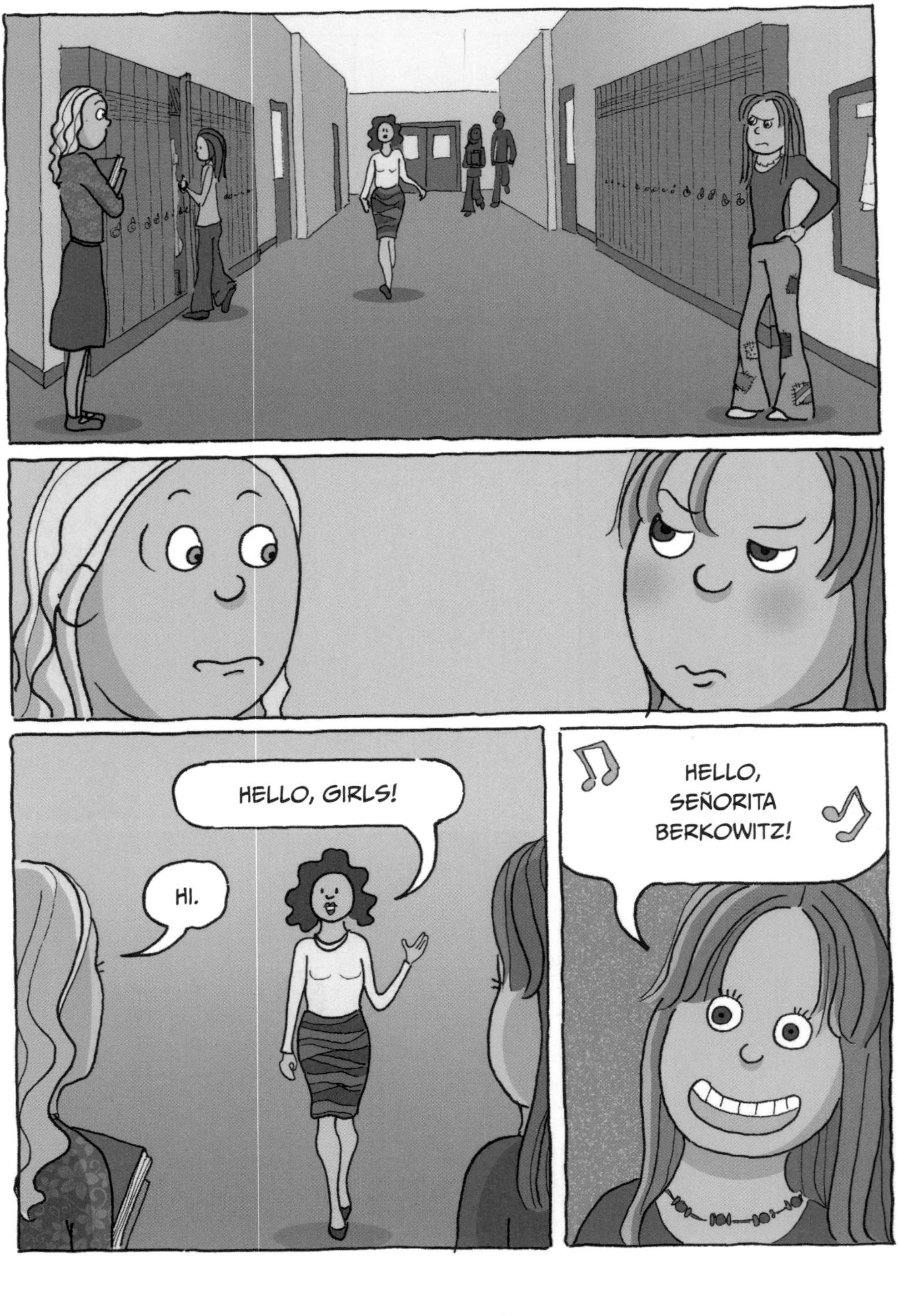

HELLO, GIRLS!
HI.
HELLO, SEÑORITA BERKOWITZ!

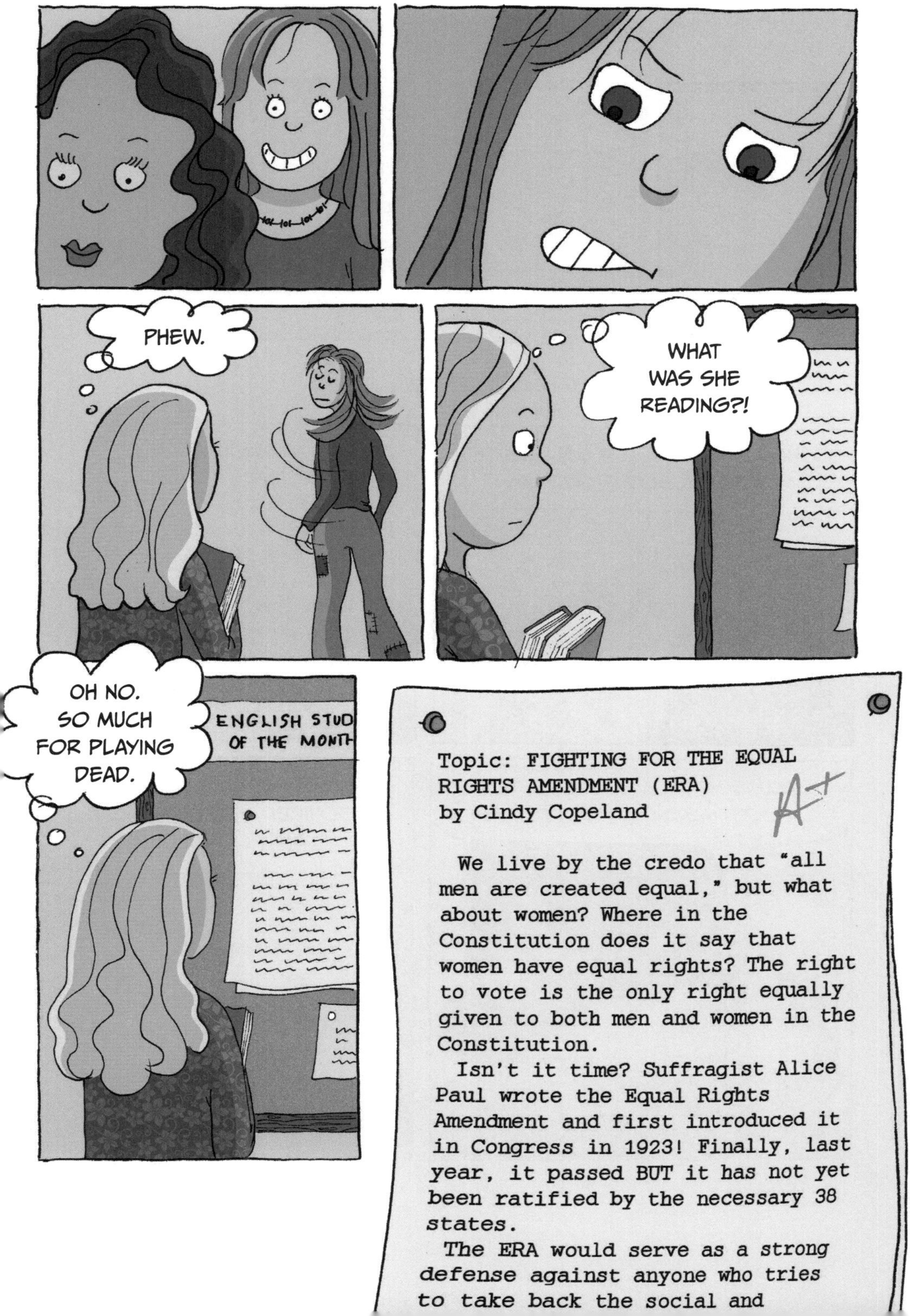
PHEW.
WHAT WAS SHE READING?!
OH NO. SO MUCH FOR PLAYING DEAD.
ENGLISH STUD
OF THE MONTH
Topic: FIGHTING FOR THE EQUAL RIGHTS AMENDMENT (ERA)
by Cindy Copeland
A+
We live by the credo that "all men are created equal," but what about women? Where in the Constitution does it say that women have equal rights? The right to vote is the only right equally given to both men and women in the Constitution.
Isn't it time? Suffragist Alice Paul wrote the Equal Rights Amendment and first introduced it in Congress in 1923! Finally, last year, it passed BUT it has not yet been ratified by the necessary 38 states.
The ERA would serve as a strong defense against anyone who tries to take back the social and

I MAKE A POINT OF LAYING LOW IN SCHOOL...

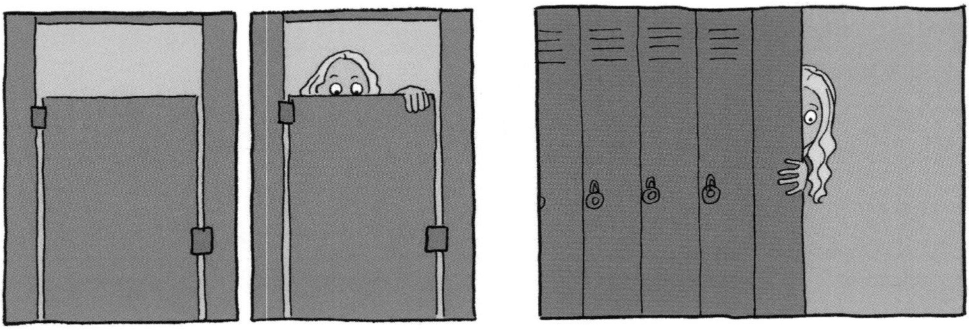

...BUT *AFTER* SCHOOL, I AM *VERY VISIBLE!*

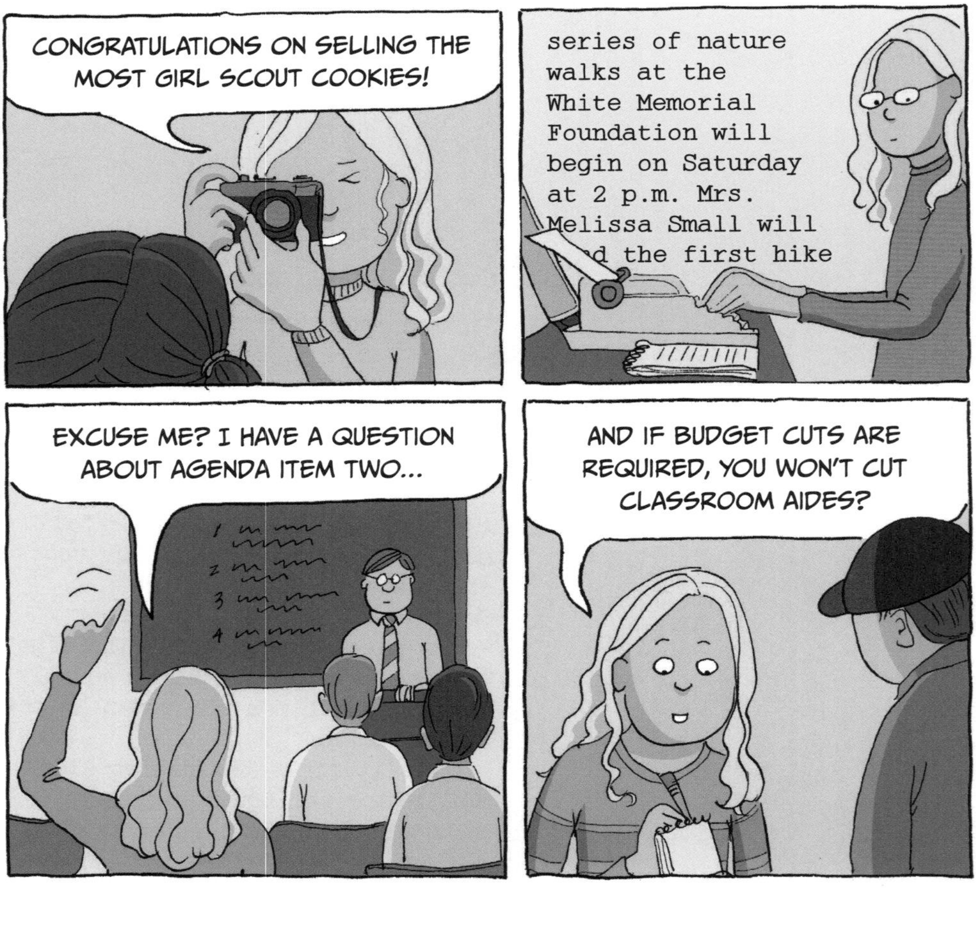
CONGRATULATIONS ON SELLING THE MOST GIRL SCOUT COOKIES!
series of nature walks at the White Memorial Foundation will begin on Saturday at 2 p.m. Mrs. Melissa Small will
the first hike
EXCUSE ME? I HAVE A QUESTION ABOUT AGENDA ITEM TWO...
AND IF BUDGET CUTS ARE REQUIRED, YOU WON'T CUT CLASSROOM AIDES?

WHEN A WEEK GOES BY WITHOUT EVIE DOING ANYTHING MEAN, I BEGIN TO RELAX.

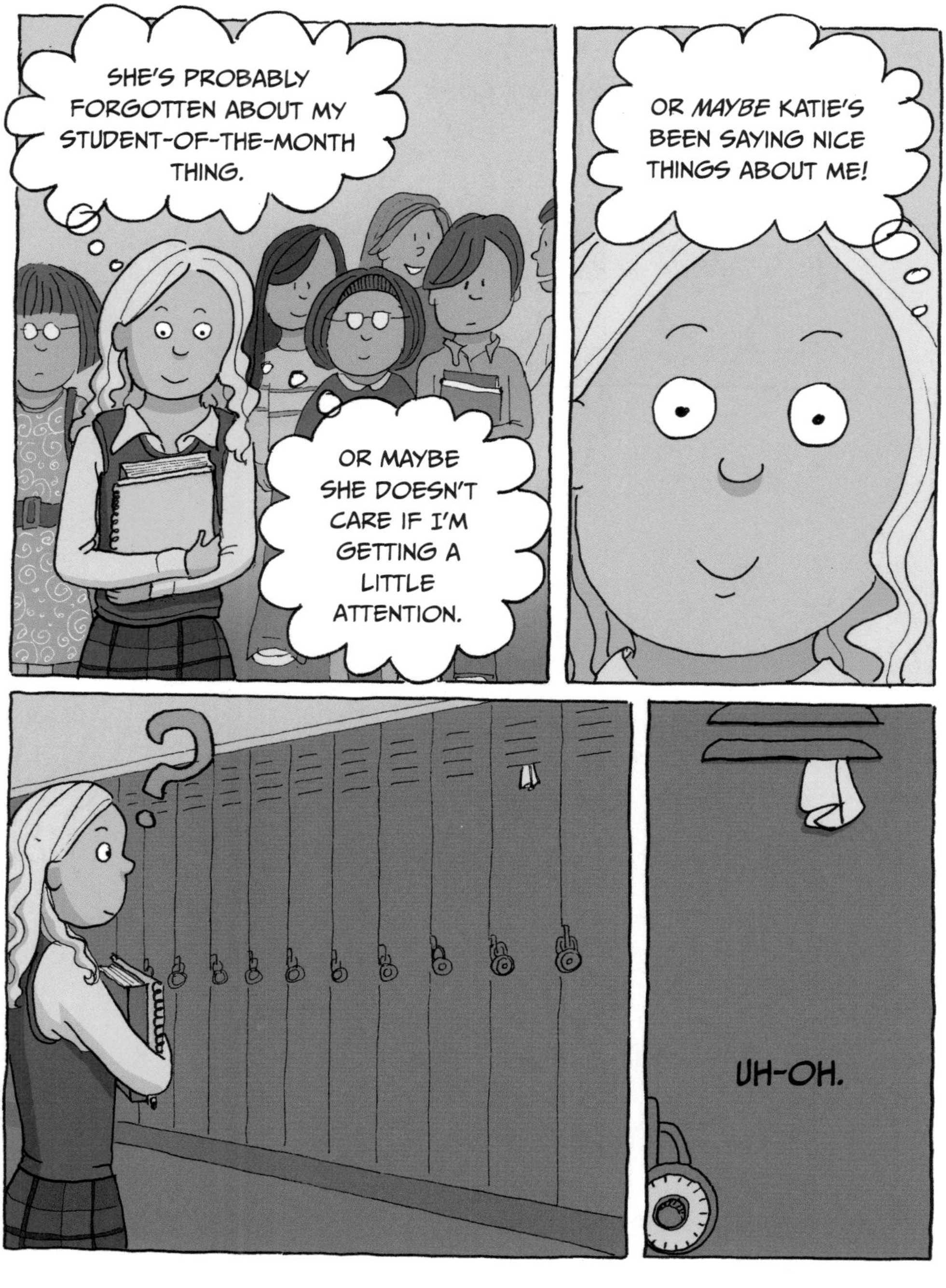
SHE'S PROBABLY FORGOTTEN ABOUT MY STUDENT-OF-THE-MONTH THING.
OR MAYBE SHE DOESN'T CARE IF I'M GETTING A LITTLE ATTENTION.
OR *MAYBE* KATIE'S BEEN SAYING NICE THINGS ABOUT ME!
UH-OH.

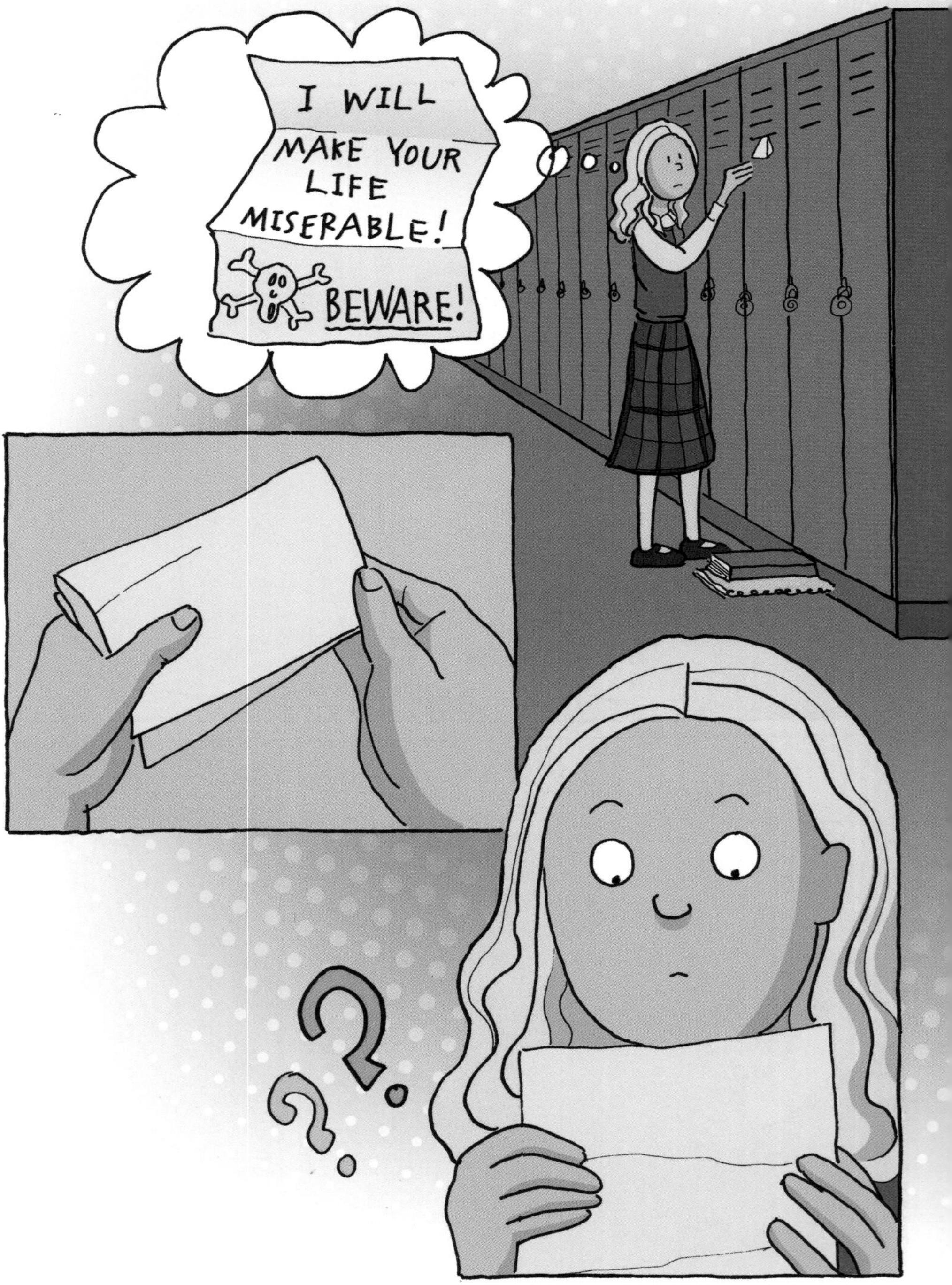
I WILL
MAKE YOUR LIFE MISERABLE!
BEWARE!

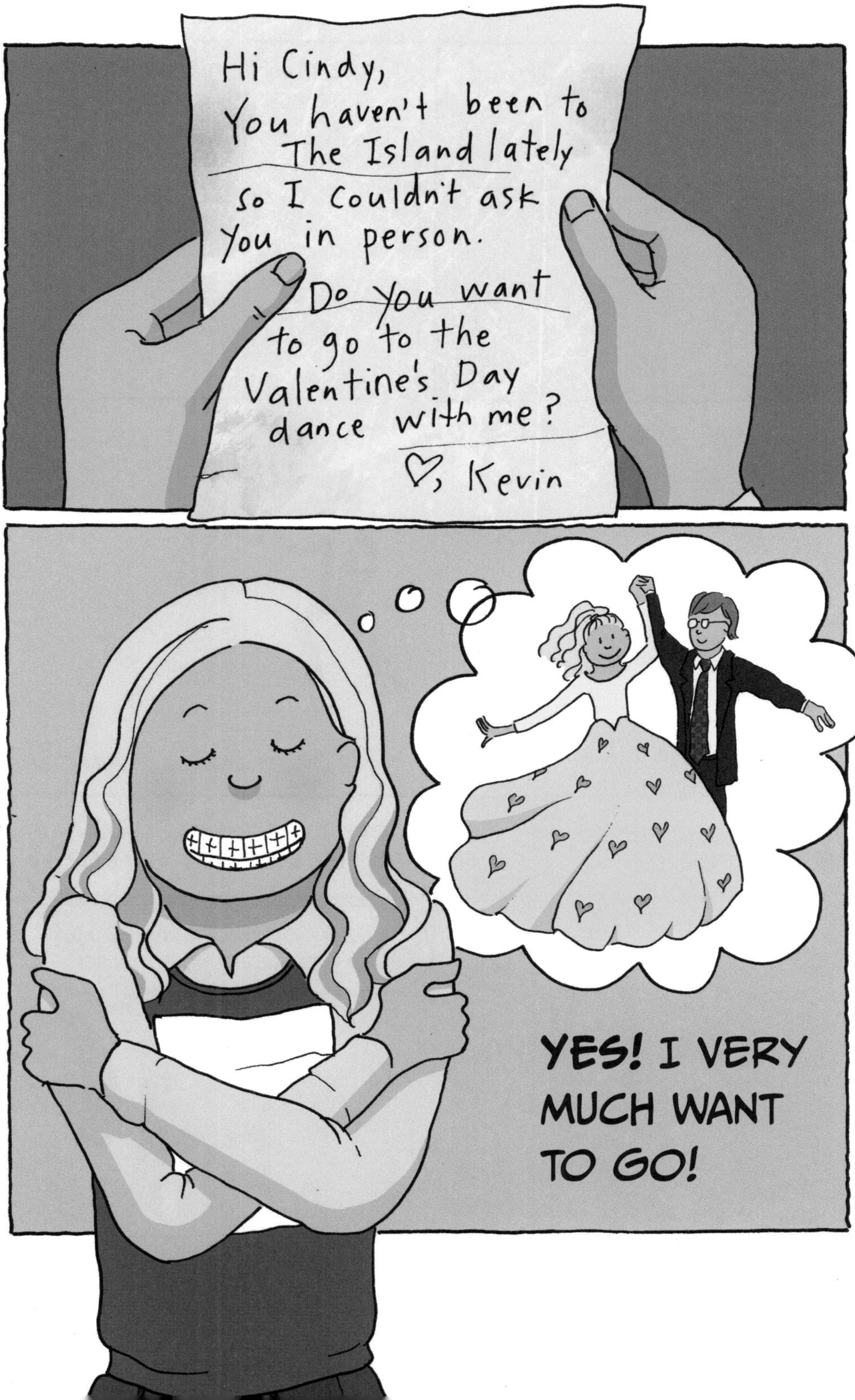
Hi Cindy,
You haven't been to The Island lately so I couldn't ask you in person.
Do you want to go to the Valentine's Day dance with me?
♡, Kevin
YES! I VERY MUCH WANT TO GO!

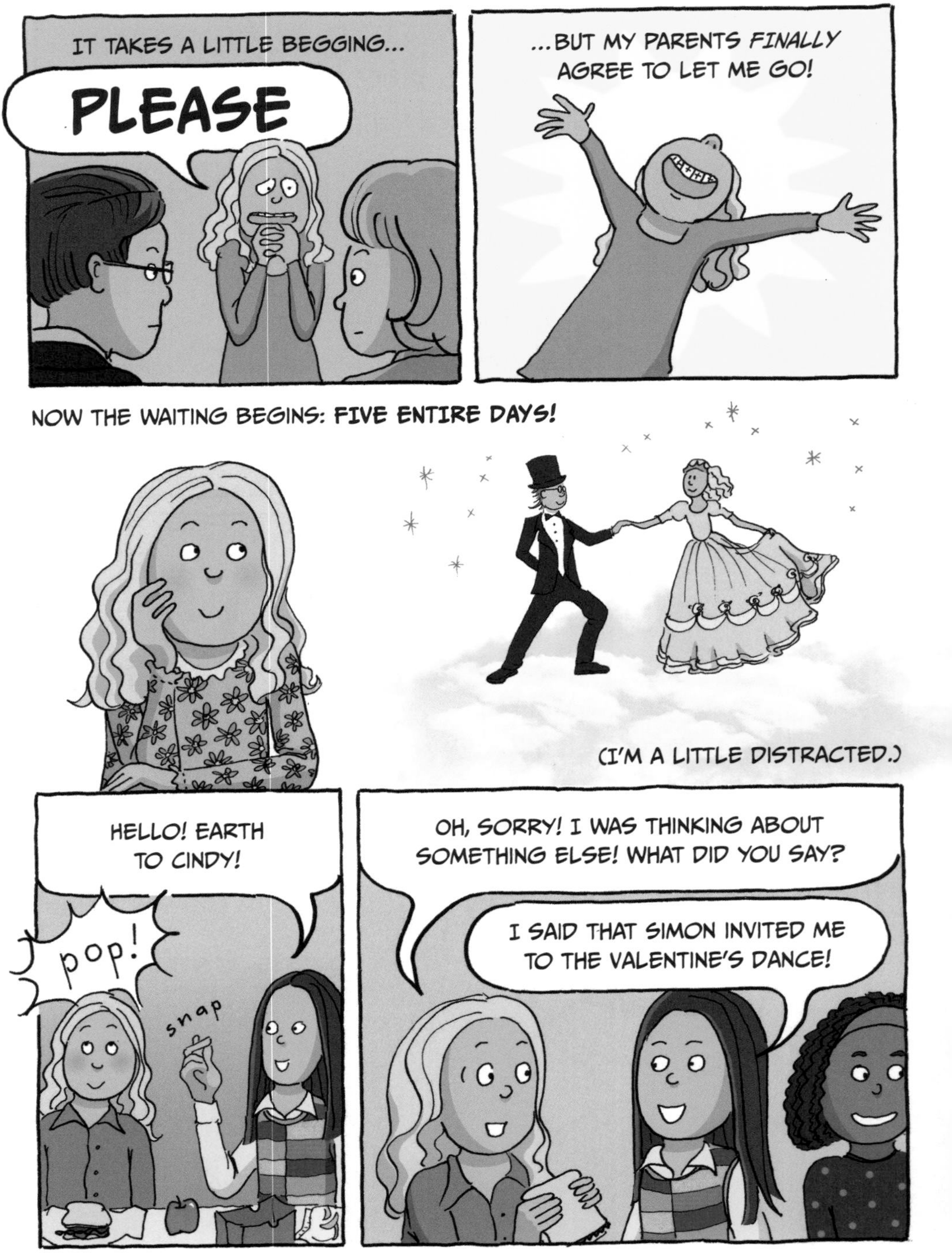
IT TAKES A LITTLE BEGGING...
PLEASE
...BUT MY PARENTS FINALLY AGREE TO LET ME GO!
NOW THE WAITING BEGINS: FIVE ENTIRE DAYS!
(I'M A LITTLE DISTRACTED.)
HELLO! EARTH TO CINDY!
pop!
snap
OH, SORRY! I WAS THINKING ABOUT SOMETHING ELSE! WHAT DID YOU SAY?
I SAID THAT SIMON INVITED ME TO THE VALENTINE'S DANCE!

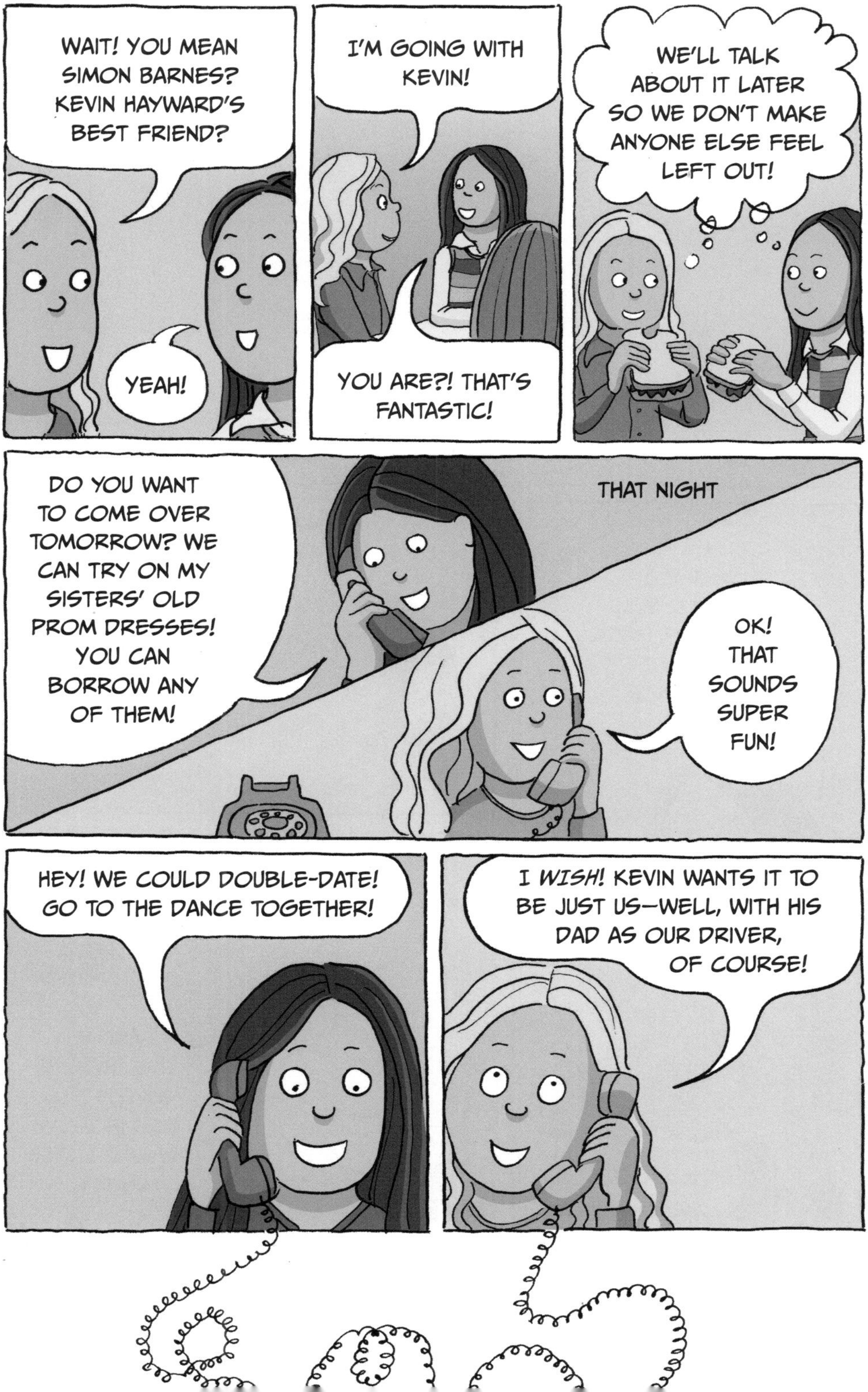
WAIT! YOU MEAN SIMON BARNES? KEVIN HAYWARD'S BEST FRIEND?
YEAH!
I'M GOING WITH KEVIN!
YOU ARE?! THAT'S FANTASTIC!
WE'LL TALK ABOUT IT LATER SO WE DON'T MAKE ANYONE ELSE FEEL LEFT OUT!
THAT NIGHT
DO YOU WANT TO COME OVER TOMORROW? WE CAN TRY ON MY SISTERS' OLD PROM DRESSES! YOU CAN BORROW ANY OF THEM!
OK! THAT SOUNDS SUPER FUN!
HEY! WE COULD DOUBLE-DATE! GO TO THE DANCE TOGETHER!
I *WISH*! KEVIN WANTS IT TO BE JUST US—WELL, WITH HIS DAD AS OUR DRIVER, OF COURSE!

THE NEXT AFTERNOON WE RAID HER SISTERS' CLOSET.

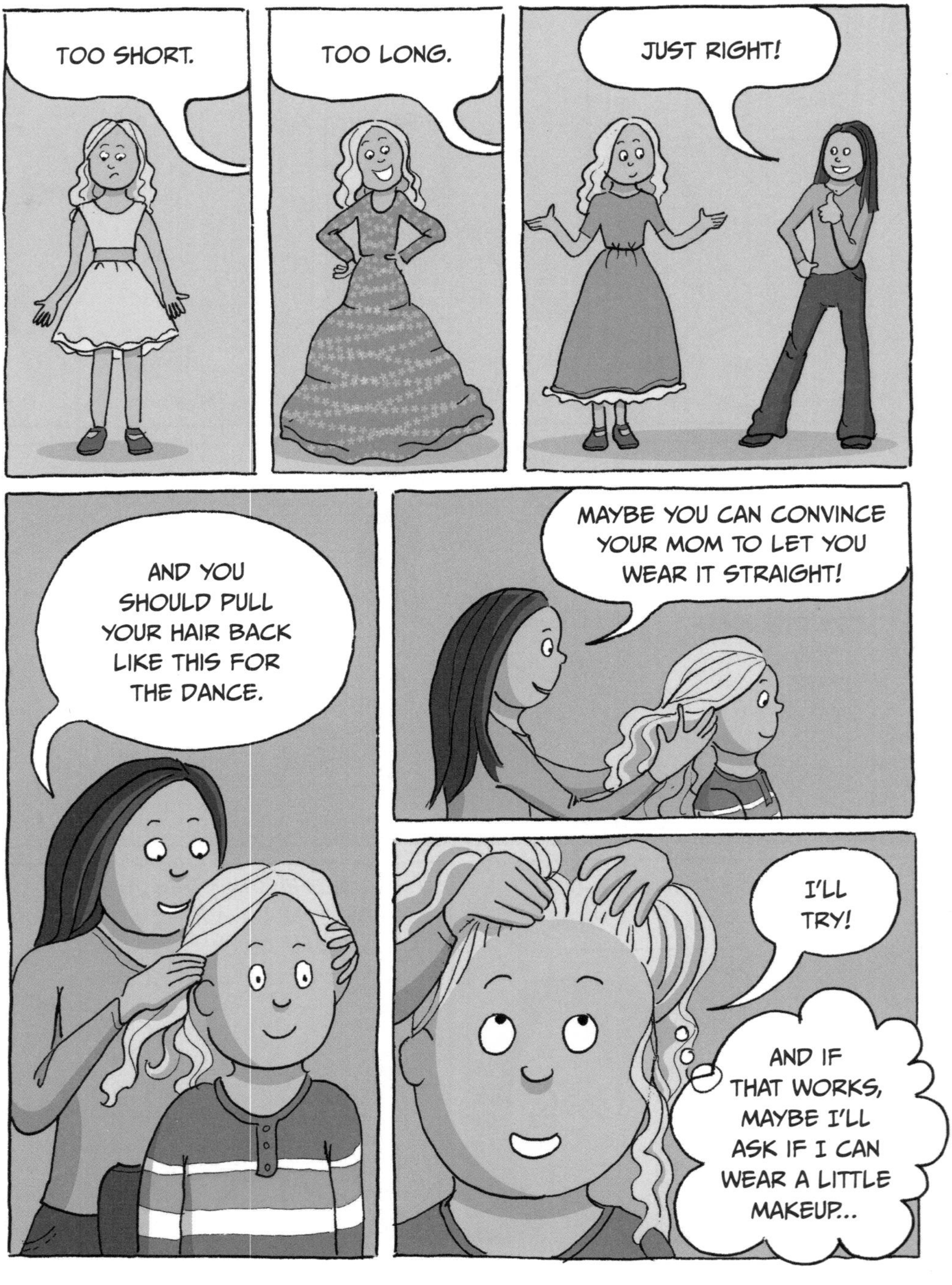
TOO SHORT.
TOO LONG.
JUST RIGHT!
AND YOU SHOULD PULL YOUR HAIR BACK LIKE THIS FOR THE DANCE.
MAYBE YOU CAN CONVINCE YOUR MOM TO LET YOU WEAR IT STRAIGHT!
I'LL TRY!
AND IF THAT WORKS, MAYBE I'LL ASK IF I CAN WEAR A LITTLE MAKEUP...

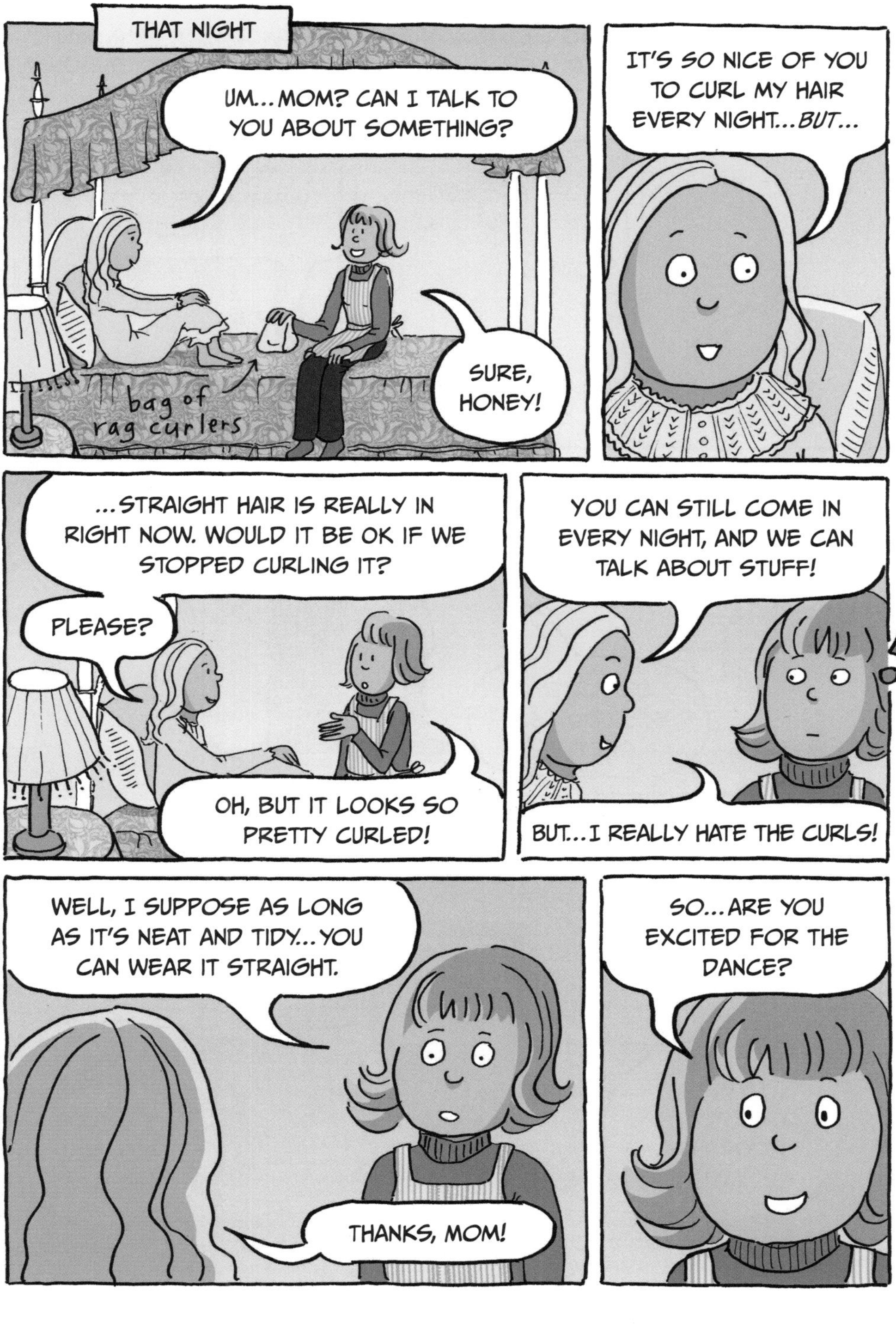

THAT NIGHT
UM...MOM? CAN I TALK TO YOU ABOUT SOMETHING?
SURE, HONEY!
bag of rag curlers
IT'S SO NICE OF YOU TO CURL MY HAIR EVERY NIGHT...*BUT*...
...STRAIGHT HAIR IS REALLY IN RIGHT NOW. WOULD IT BE OK IF WE STOPPED CURLING IT?
PLEASE?
OH, BUT IT LOOKS SO PRETTY CURLED!
YOU CAN STILL COME IN EVERY NIGHT, AND WE CAN TALK ABOUT STUFF!
BUT...I REALLY HATE THE CURLS!
WELL, I SUPPOSE AS LONG AS IT'S NEAT AND TIDY...YOU CAN WEAR IT STRAIGHT.
THANKS, MOM!
SO...ARE YOU EXCITED FOR THE DANCE?

IT WOULD HAVE BEEN FUN TO GET READY FOR THE DANCE WITH PENNY, BUT I'M KIND OF FLATTERED THAT KEVIN WANTS ME ALL TO HIMSELF. (IT'S GONNA BE AMAZING!)

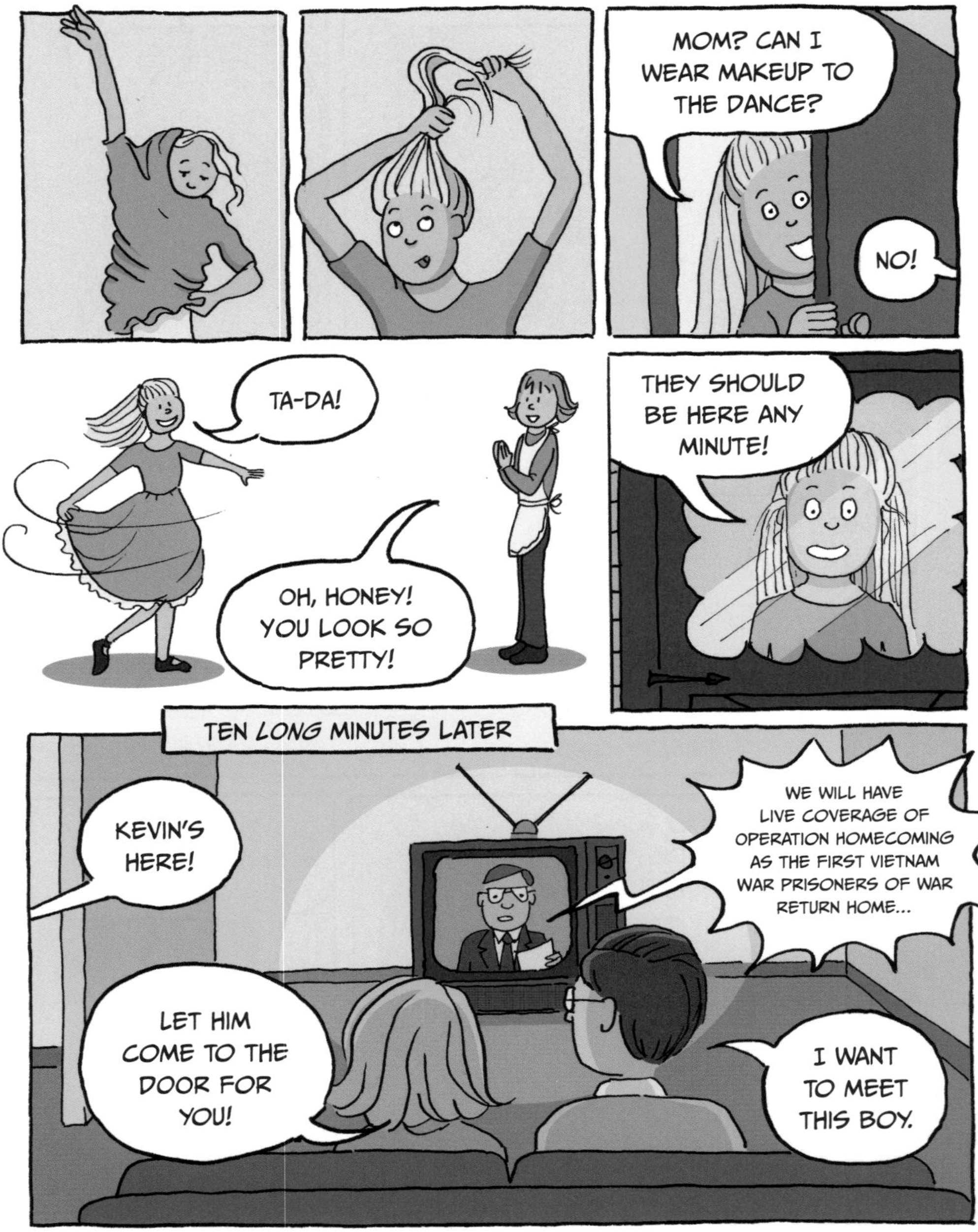
MOM? CAN I WEAR MAKEUP TO THE DANCE?
NO!
TA-DA!
OH, HONEY! YOU LOOK SO PRETTY!
THEY SHOULD BE HERE ANY MINUTE!
TEN *LONG* MINUTES LATER
KEVIN'S HERE!
WE WILL HAVE LIVE COVERAGE OF OPERATION HOMECOMING AS THE FIRST VIETNAM WAR PRISONERS OF WAR RETURN HOME...
LET HIM COME TO THE DOOR FOR YOU!
I WANT TO MEET THIS BOY.

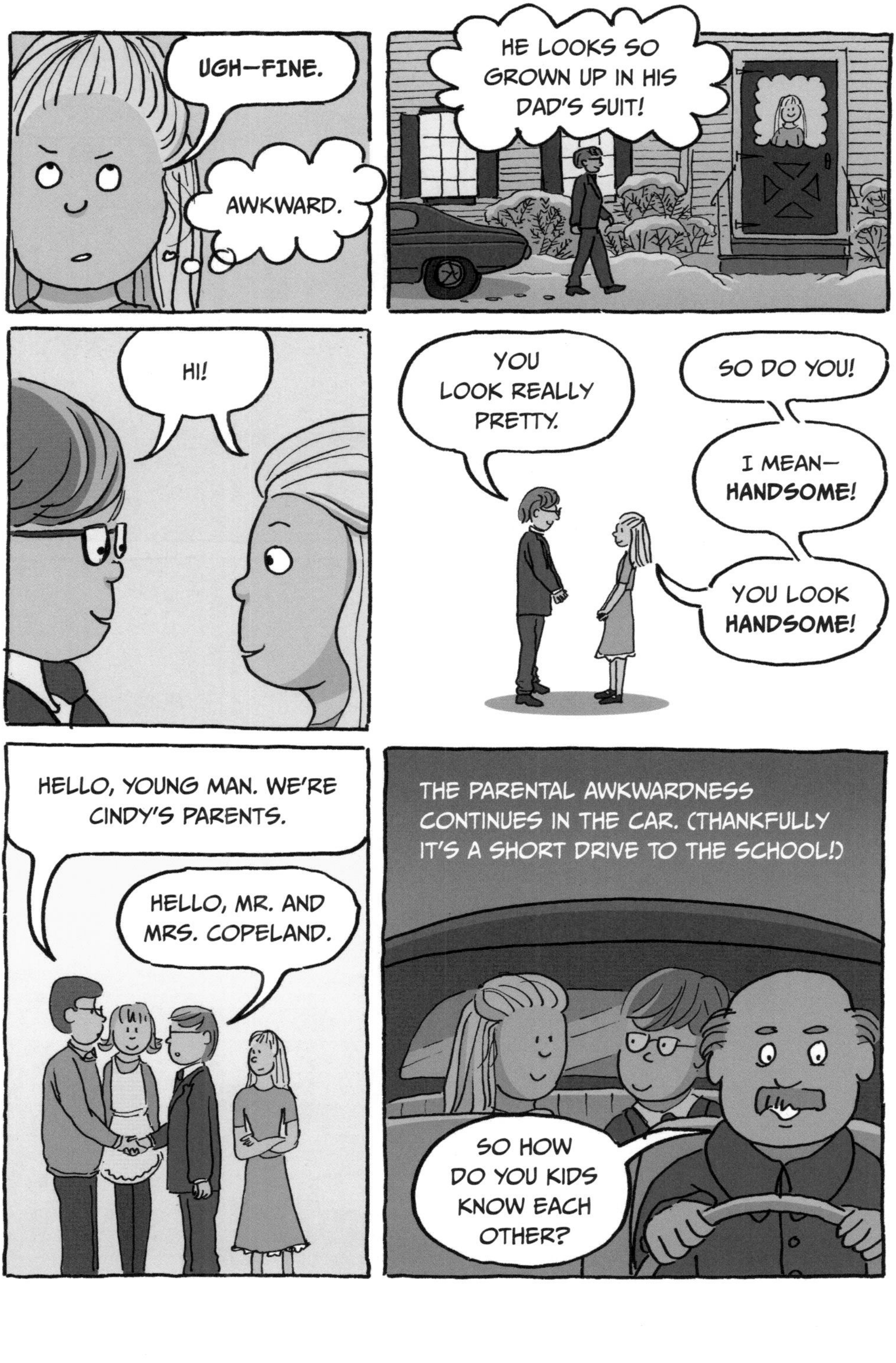
UGH—FINE.
AWKWARD.
HE LOOKS SO GROWN UP IN HIS DAD'S SUIT!
HI!
YOU LOOK REALLY PRETTY.
SO DO YOU!
I MEAN— HANDSOME!
YOU LOOK HANDSOME!
HELLO, YOUNG MAN. WE'RE CINDY'S PARENTS.
HELLO, MR. AND MRS. COPELAND.
THE PARENTAL AWKWARDNESS CONTINUES IN THE CAR. (THANKFULLY IT'S A SHORT DRIVE TO THE SCHOOL!)
SO HOW DO YOU KIDS KNOW EACH OTHER?

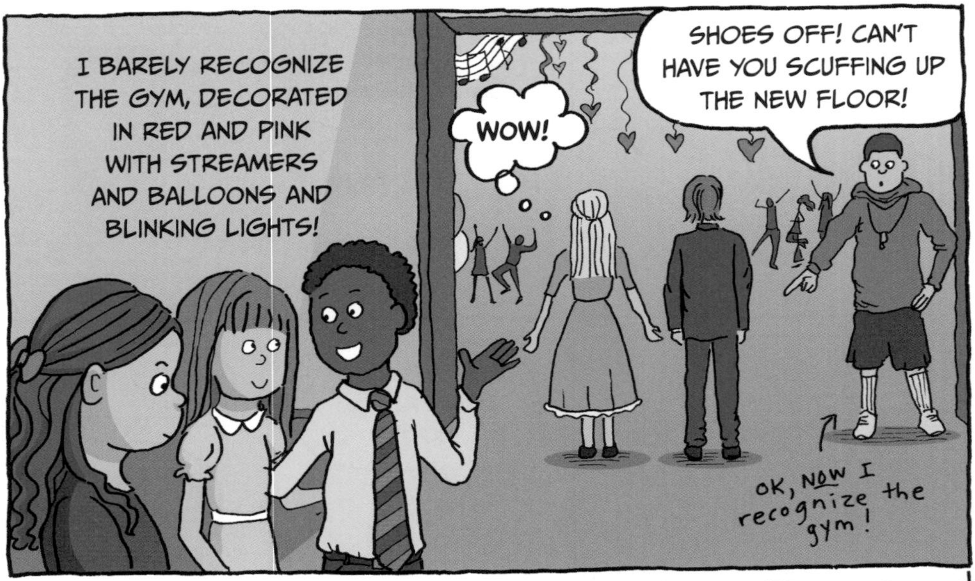
I BARELY RECOGNIZE THE GYM, DECORATED IN RED AND PINK WITH STREAMERS AND BALLOONS AND BLINKING LIGHTS!
WOW!
SHOES OFF! CAN'T HAVE YOU SCUFFING UP THE NEW FLOOR!
ok, NOW I recognize the gym!

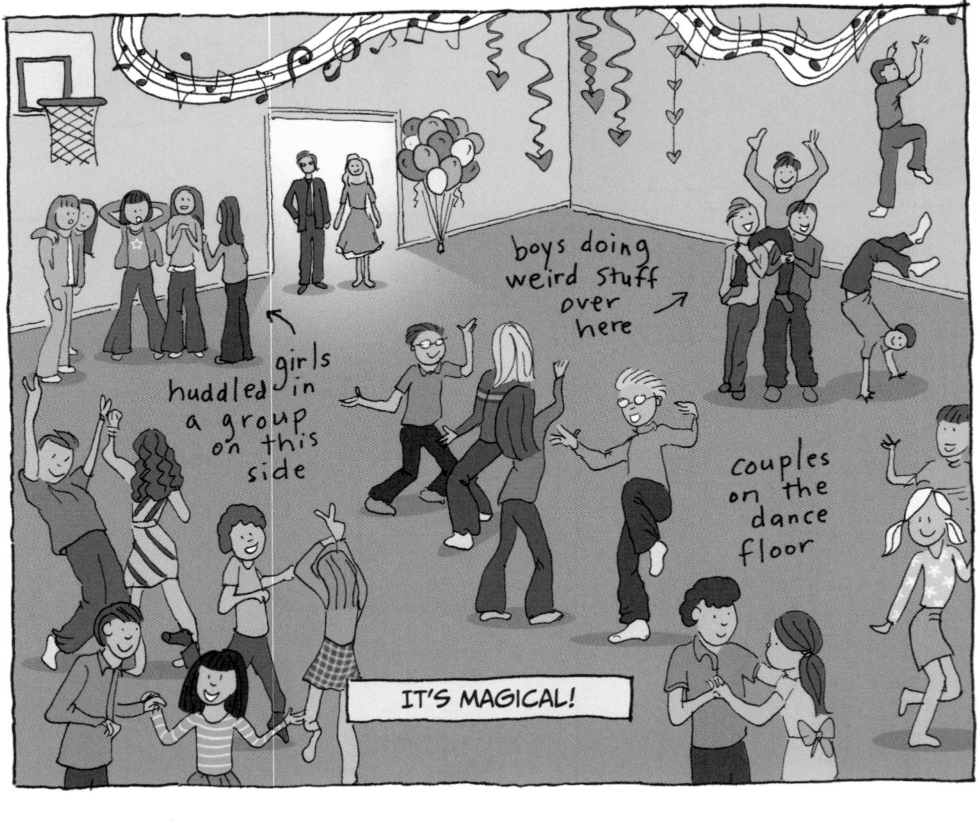
girls huddled in a group on this side
boys doing weird stuff over here
couples on the dance floor
IT'S MAGICAL!

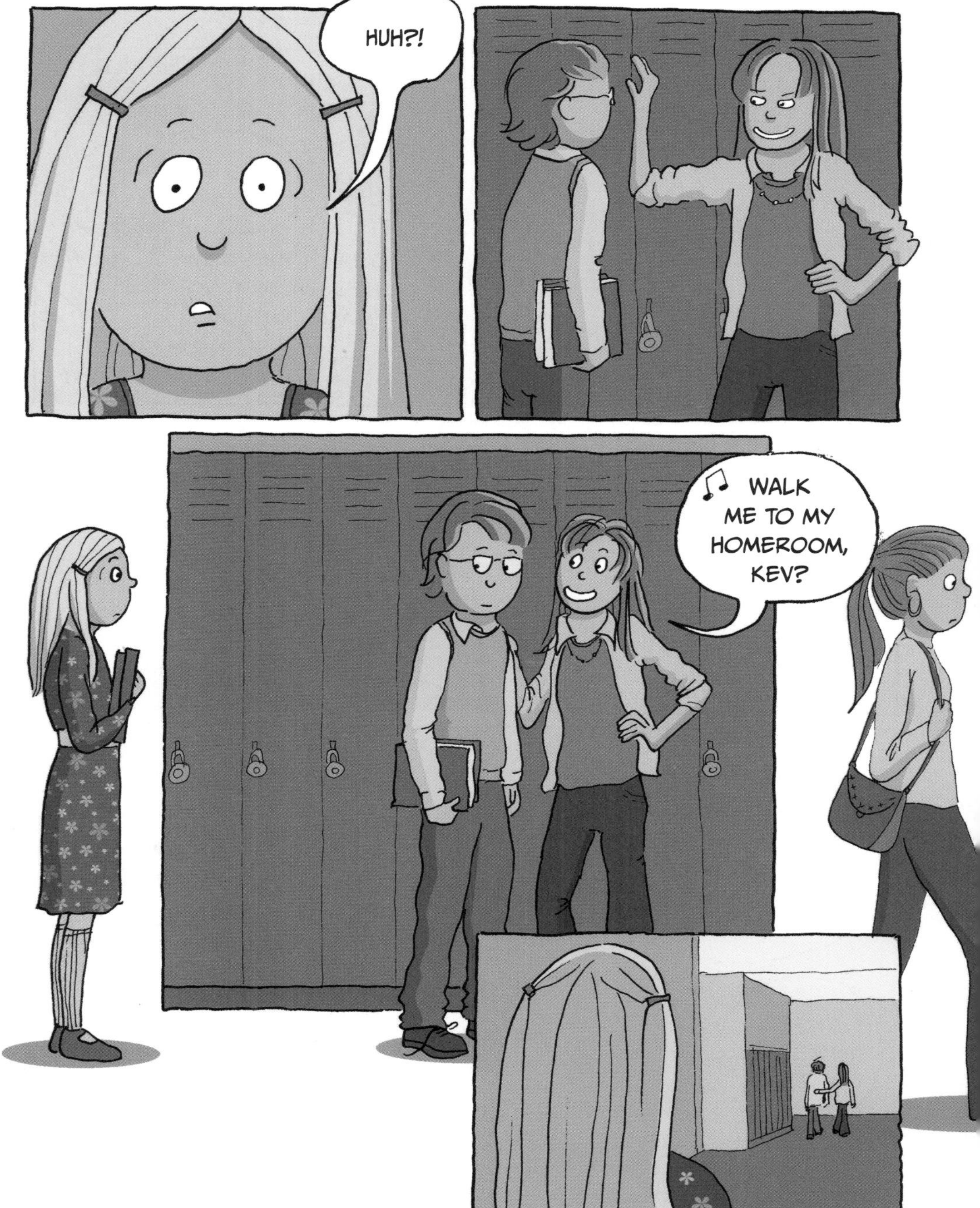
HUH?!
WALK ME TO MY HOMEROOM, KEV?

LUNCH PERIOD IS EVEN WORSE THAN I IMAGINED IT WOULD BE.

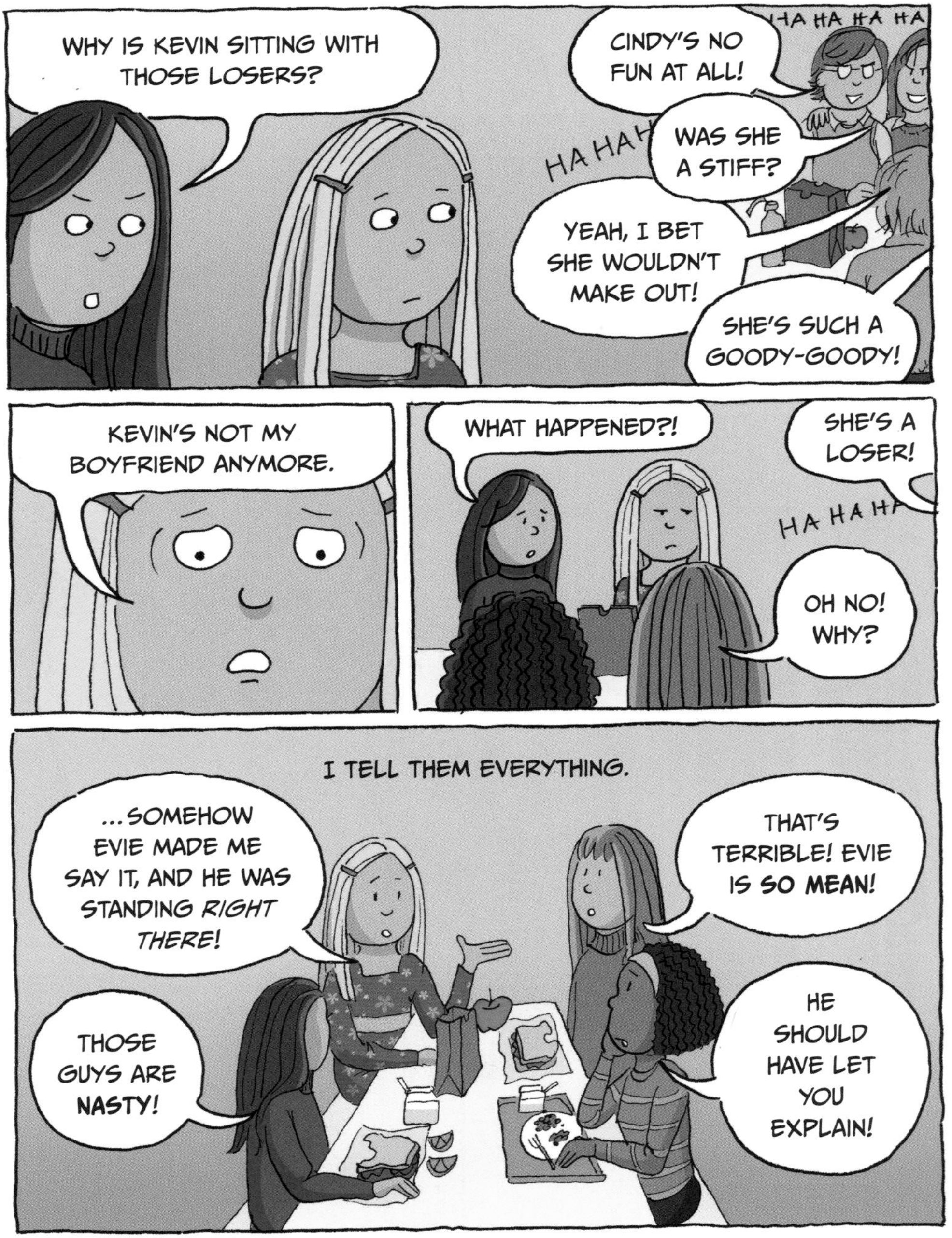
WHY IS KEVIN SITTING WITH THOSE LOSERS?
CINDY'S NO FUN AT ALL!
HA HA HA HA
HA HAH
WAS SHE A STIFF?
YEAH, I BET SHE WOULDN'T MAKE OUT!
SHE'S SUCH A GOODY-GOODY!
KEVIN'S NOT MY BOYFRIEND ANYMORE.
WHAT HAPPENED?!
SHE'S A LOSER!
HA HA HA
OH NO! WHY?
I TELL THEM EVERYTHING.
...SOMEHOW EVIE MADE ME SAY IT, AND HE WAS STANDING *RIGHT THERE!*
THAT'S TERRIBLE! EVIE IS **SO MEAN!**
THOSE GUYS ARE **NASTY!**
HE SHOULD HAVE LET YOU EXPLAIN!

SAYING IT OUT LOUD MAKES ME FEEL A LITTLE BETTER.

AT LUNCH THE NEXT DAY, MY FRIENDS AREN'T SITTING AT OUR REGULAR TABLE.

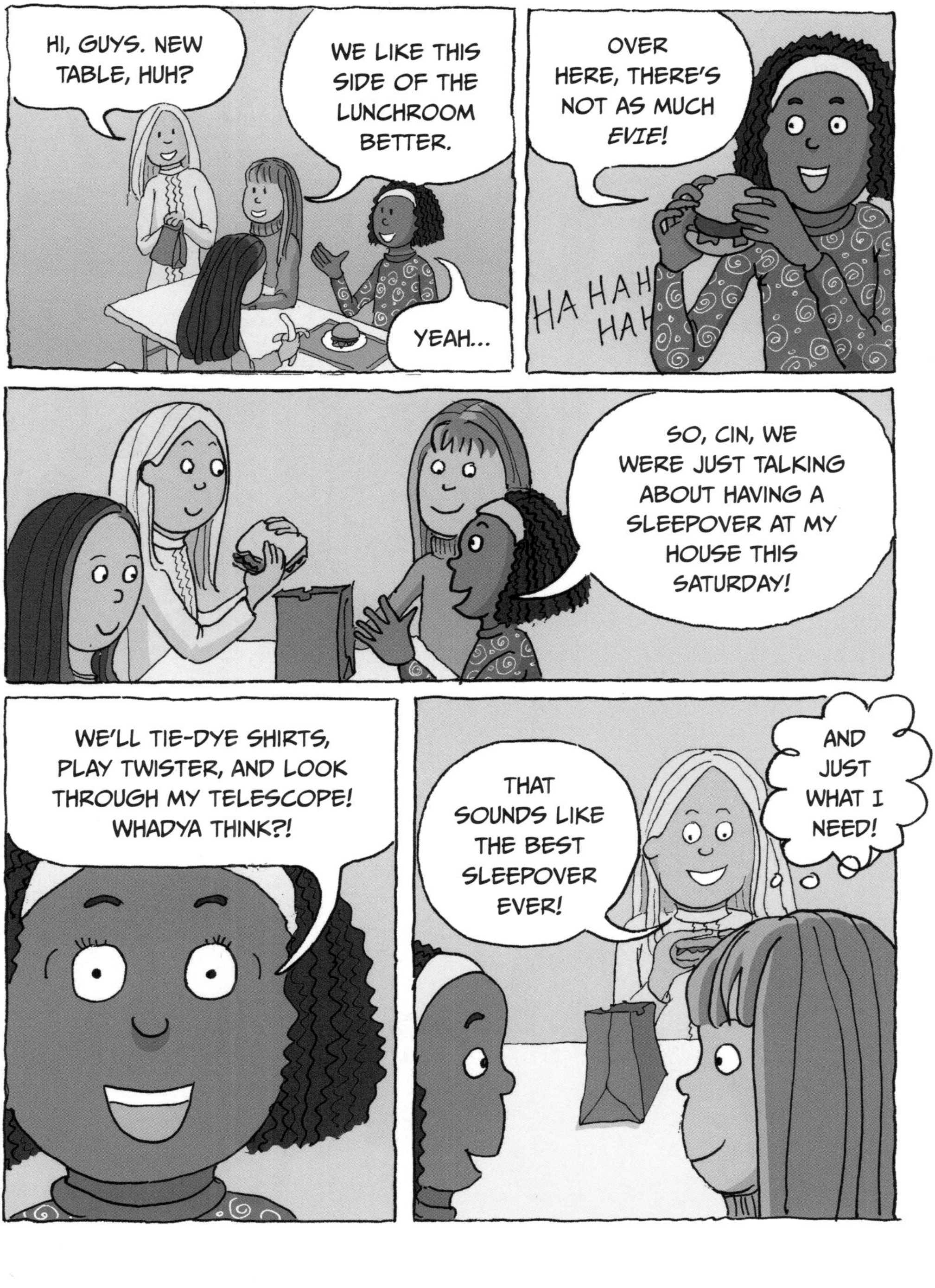
HI, GUYS. NEW TABLE, HUH?
WE LIKE THIS SIDE OF THE LUNCHROOM BETTER.
YEAH...
OVER HERE, THERE'S NOT AS MUCH *EVIE*!
HA HAH HAH
SO, CIN, WE WERE JUST TALKING ABOUT HAVING A SLEEPOVER AT MY HOUSE THIS SATURDAY!
WE'LL TIE-DYE SHIRTS, PLAY TWISTER, AND LOOK THROUGH MY TELESCOPE! WHADYA THINK?!
THAT SOUNDS LIKE THE BEST SLEEPOVER EVER!
AND JUST WHAT I NEED!

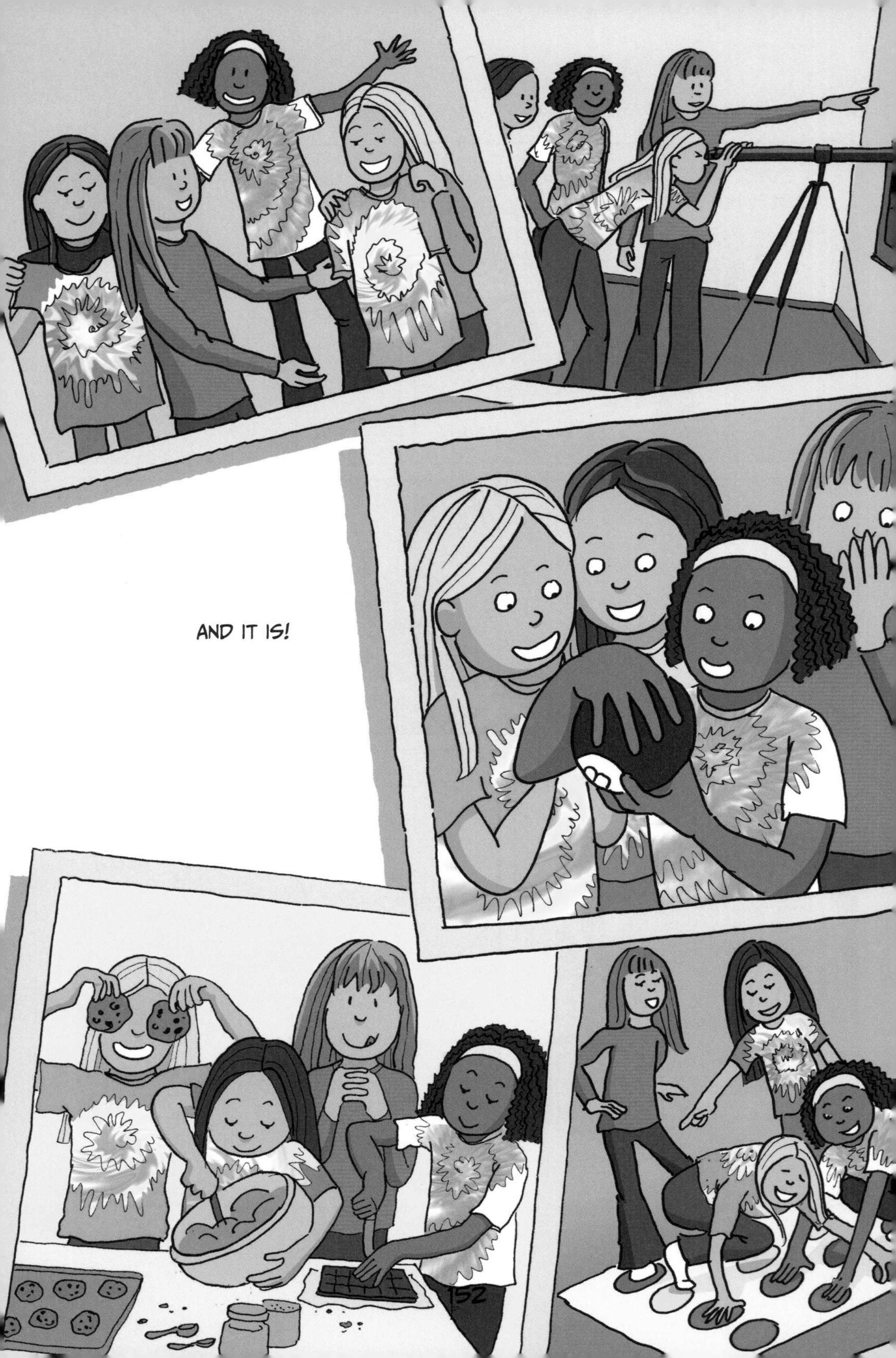
AND IT IS!

NO ONE TALKS ABOUT BOYS *AT ALL* UNTIL JUST BEFORE MIDNIGHT. PENNY PULLS A OUIJA BOARD FROM HER DUFFEL BAG AND SETS IT UP ON MOLLY'S BED.

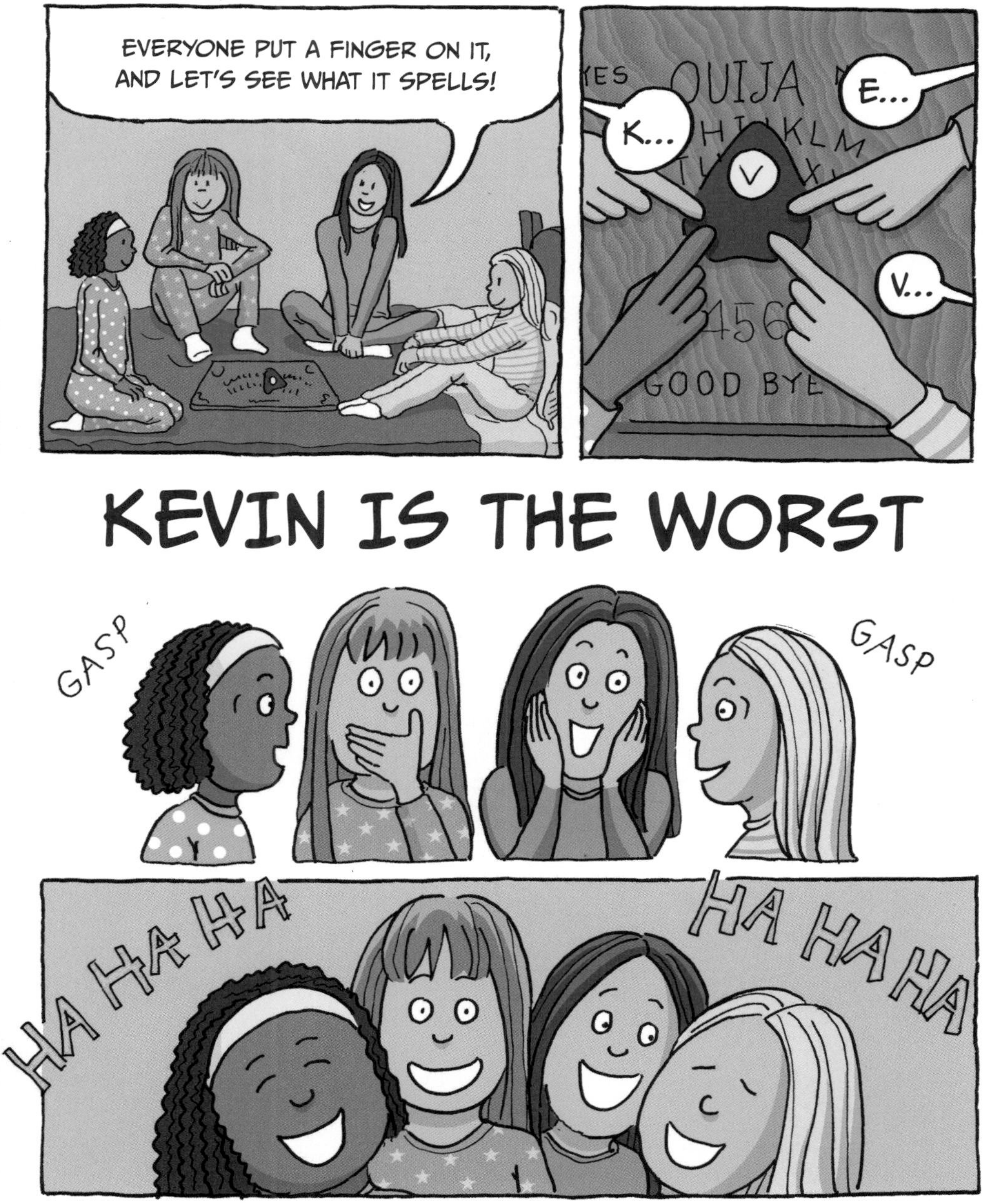
EVERYONE PUT A FINGER ON IT, AND LET'S SEE WHAT IT SPELLS!
YES
OUIJA
K...
E...
V...
GOOD BYE
KEVIN IS THE WORST
GASP
GASP
HA HA HA HA
HA HA HA HA

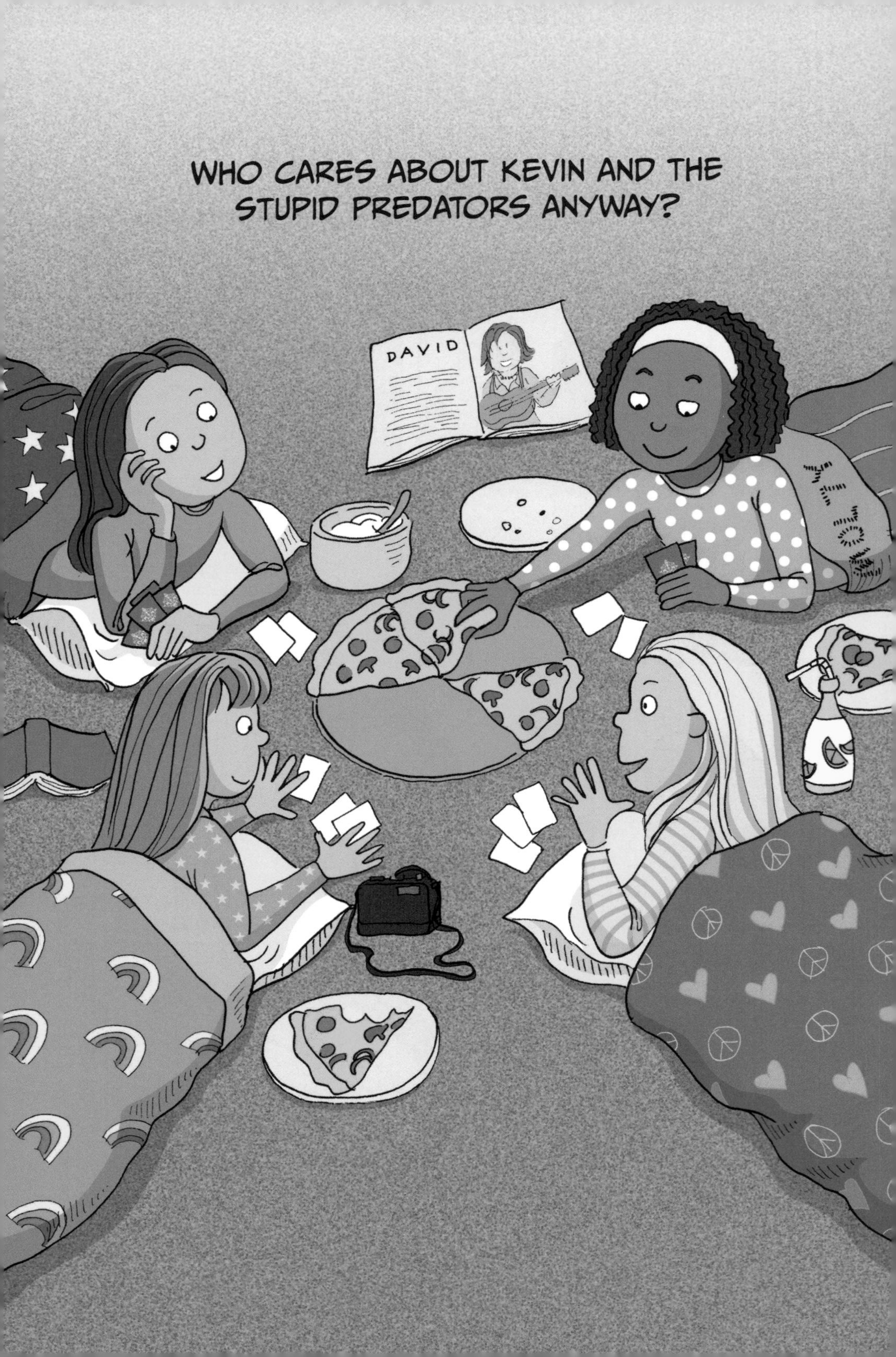
WHO CARES ABOUT KEVIN AND THE
STUPID PREDATORS ANYWAY?
DAVID

Chapter 13

THERE'S *ONE* GOOD THING ABOUT WHAT HAPPENED WITH KEVIN: I DON'T HAVE TO WORRY ABOUT HIM BEING ANNOYED WHEN I HAVE A PLAN WITH LESLIE. AND RIGHT NOW, WE HAVE A **FULL SCHEDULE!**

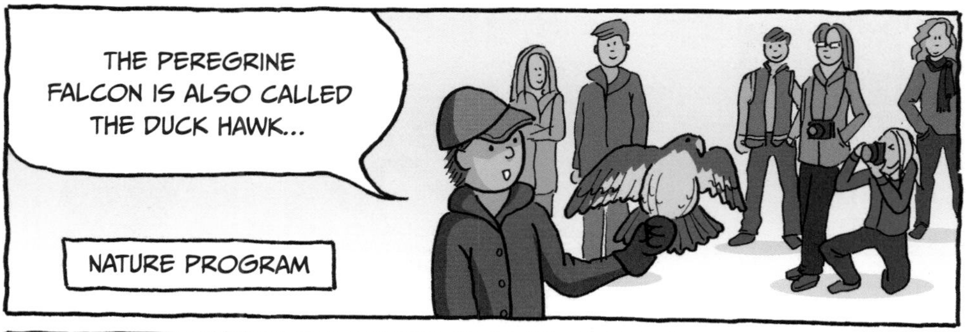
THE PEREGRINE FALCON IS ALSO CALLED THE DUCK HAWK...
NATURE PROGRAM

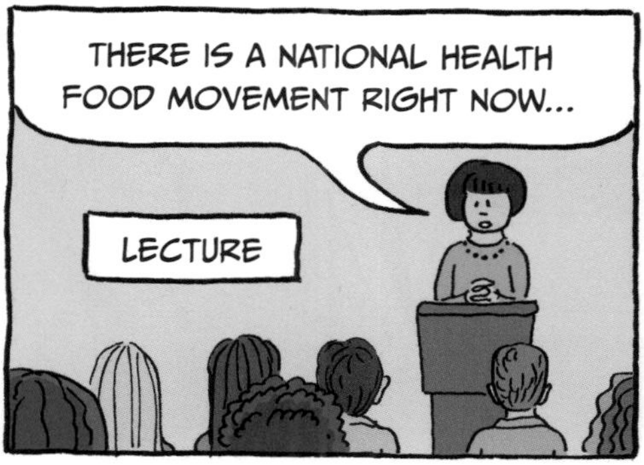
THERE IS A NATIONAL HEALTH FOOD MOVEMENT RIGHT NOW...
LECTURE

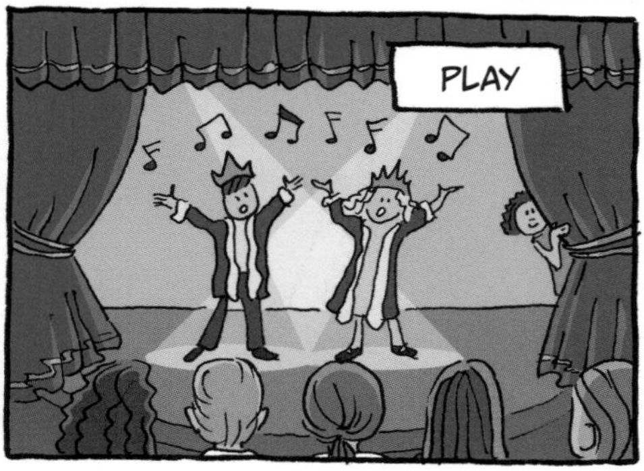
PLAY

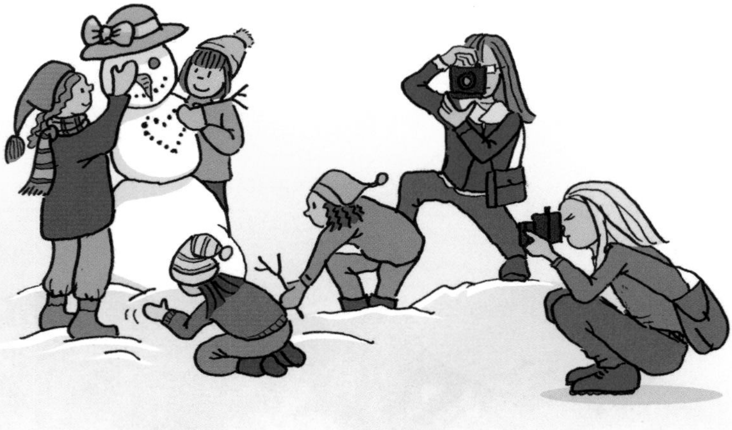

WHEN WE DON'T HAVE AN EVENT TO ATTEND, WE DRIVE AROUND TOWN, LOOKING FOR GREAT PHOTOS.

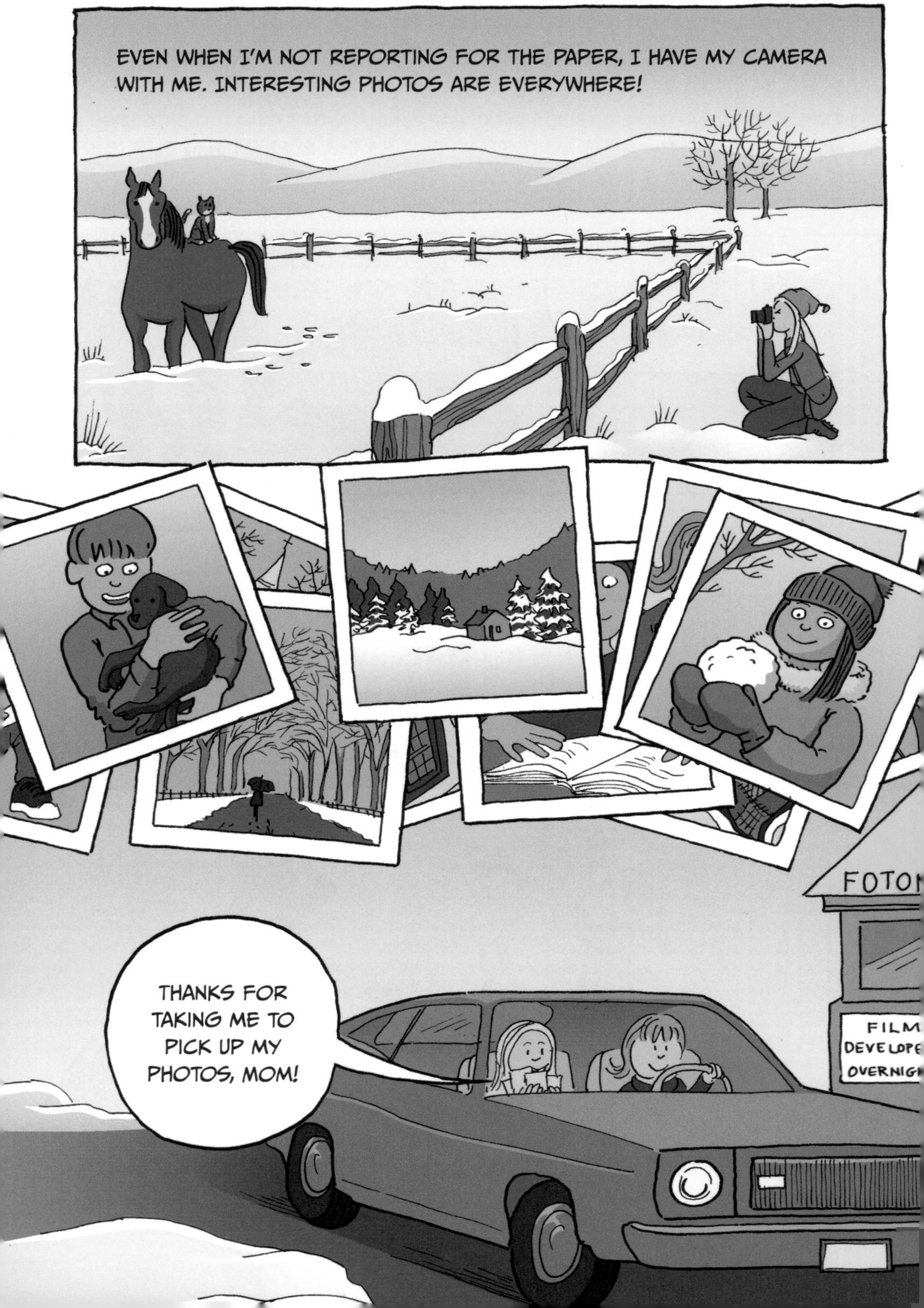
EVEN WHEN I'M NOT REPORTING FOR THE PAPER, I HAVE MY CAMERA WITH ME. INTERESTING PHOTOS ARE EVERYWHERE!
FILM
THANKS FOR TAKING ME TO PICK UP MY PHOTOS, MOM!

BARB, CHECK OUT THESE PHOTOS I TOOK OF THE OLD BARN ON MEADOW STREET!

THOSE ARE GREAT! LOOK AT THE ONES I TOOK AFTER THAT BIG SNOWSTORM!

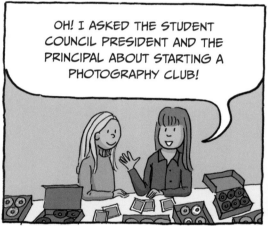

OH! I ASKED THE STUDENT COUNCIL PRESIDENT AND THE PRINCIPAL ABOUT STARTING A PHOTOGRAPHY CLUB!

WHAT DID THEY SAY?

THEY SAID IT LOOKS GOOD FOR NEXT YEAR!

FAR OUT!

HERE'S TEN CENTS FOR ONE DONUT

THANKS!

UH-OH! HERE COMES KEVIN!

RATS!

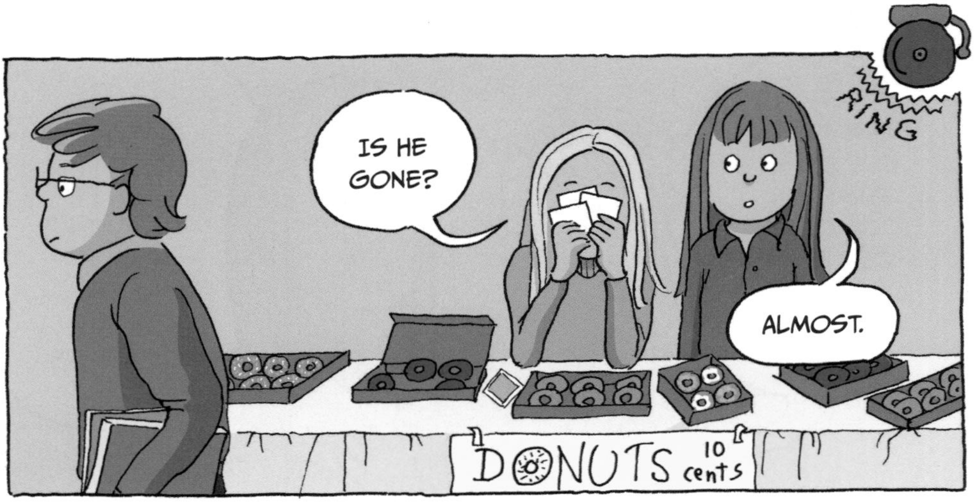
RING
IS HE GONE?
ALMOST.
DONUTS 10 cents

IT'S FINE. I'M ~~TOTALLY~~ MOSTLY OVER HIM.

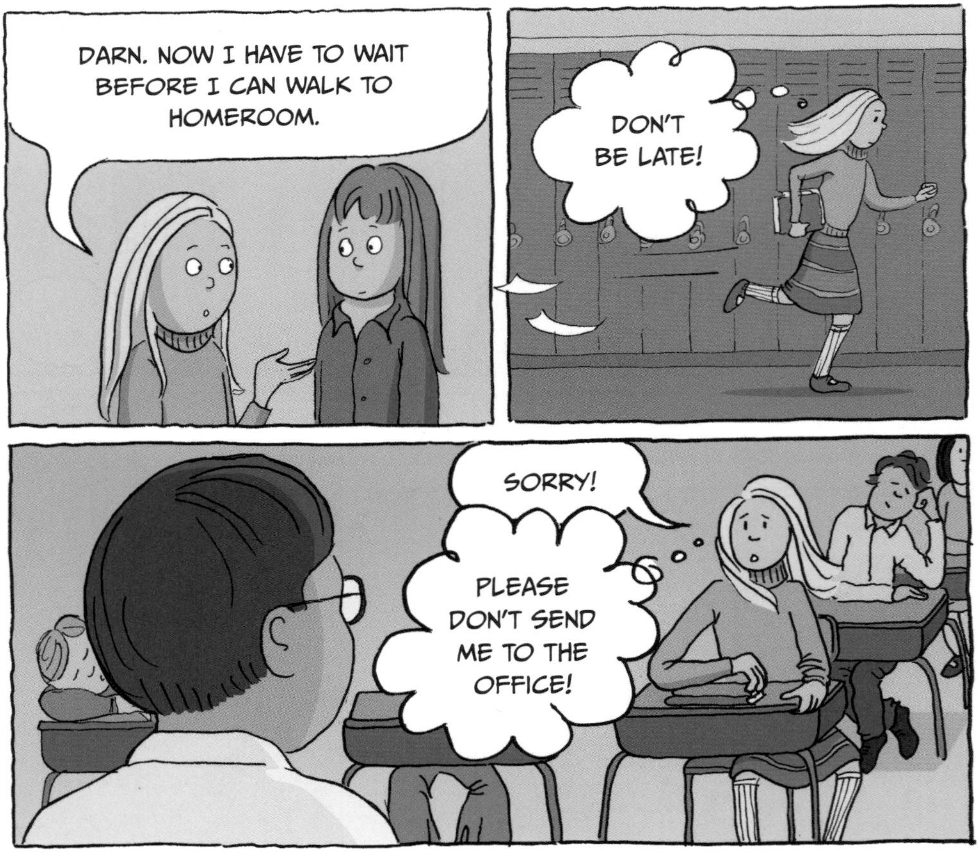
DARN. NOW I HAVE TO WAIT BEFORE I CAN WALK TO HOMEROOM.
DON'T BE LATE!
SORRY!
PLEASE DON'T SEND ME TO THE OFFICE!

JUST AS MR. KRAMER TURNS TOWARD ME, A GIRL WE'VE NEVER SEEN BEFORE WALKS INTO THE ROOM. (NO ONE REALLY MOVES IN OR OUT OF LITCHFIELD, SO NEW KIDS ARE PRETTY RARE.)

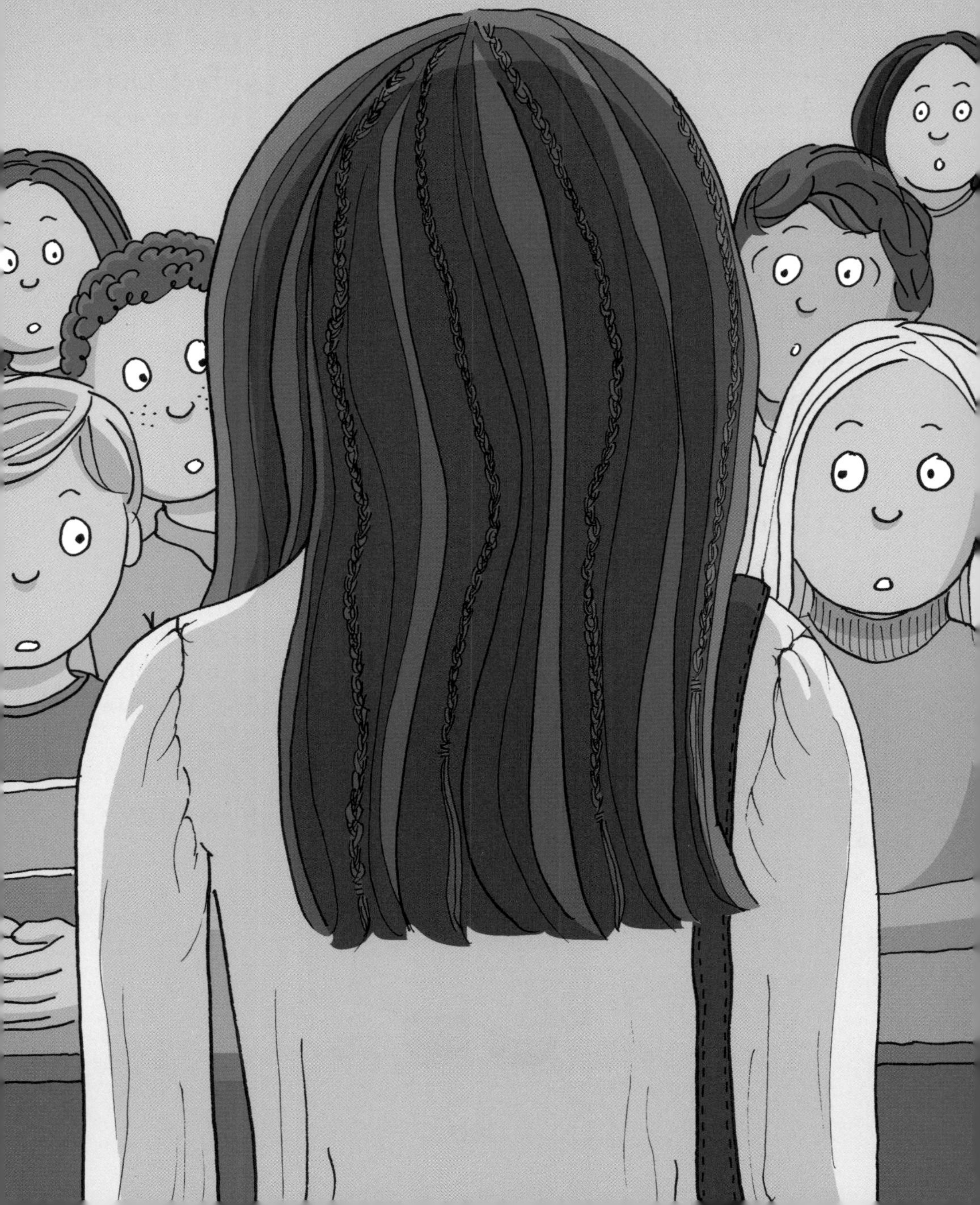

The New Girl

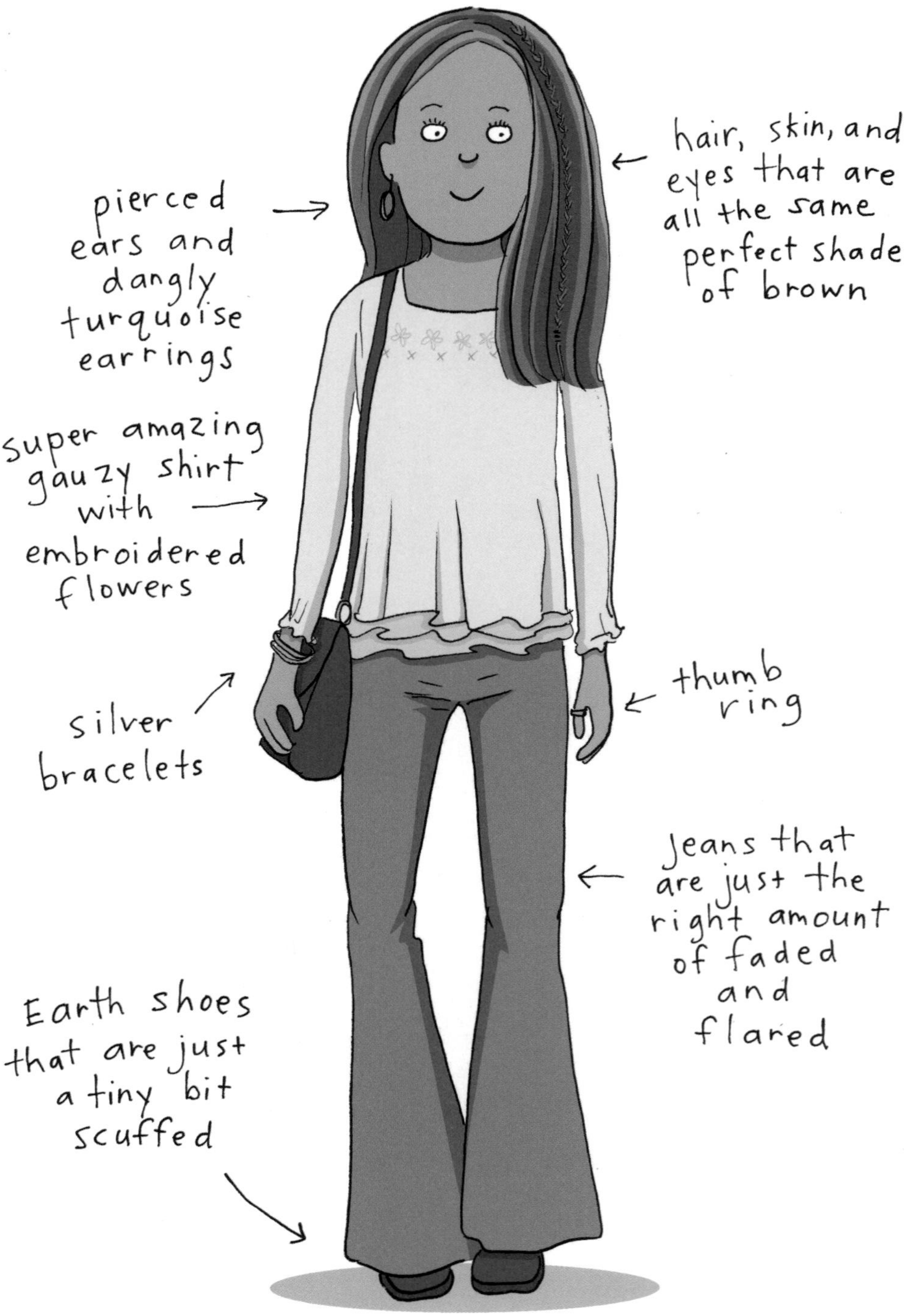
pierced ears and dangly turquoise earrings
hair, skin, and eyes that are all the same perfect shade of brown
super amazing gauzy shirt with embroidered flowers
silver bracelets
thumb ring
jeans that are just the right amount of faded and flared
Earth shoes that are just a tiny bit scuffed

CAN I SIT HERE?

MR. KRAMER BLINKS AND STAMMERS BECAUSE HE IS VERY SHY AND ONLY LIKES TO DO MATH OR READ THE ANNOUNCEMENTS.

YOUNG, UH, YOUNG LADY, ARE YOU, UM, NEW TO LJHS?

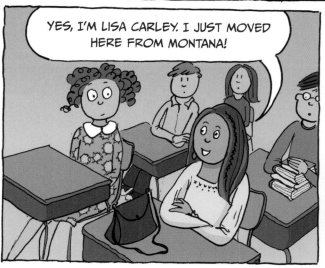

YES, I'M LISA CARLEY. I JUST MOVED HERE FROM MONTANA!

UH-HUH, UH-HUH.

LISA SEEMS TO UNDERSTAND THAT SHE NEEDS TO HELP HIM OUT.

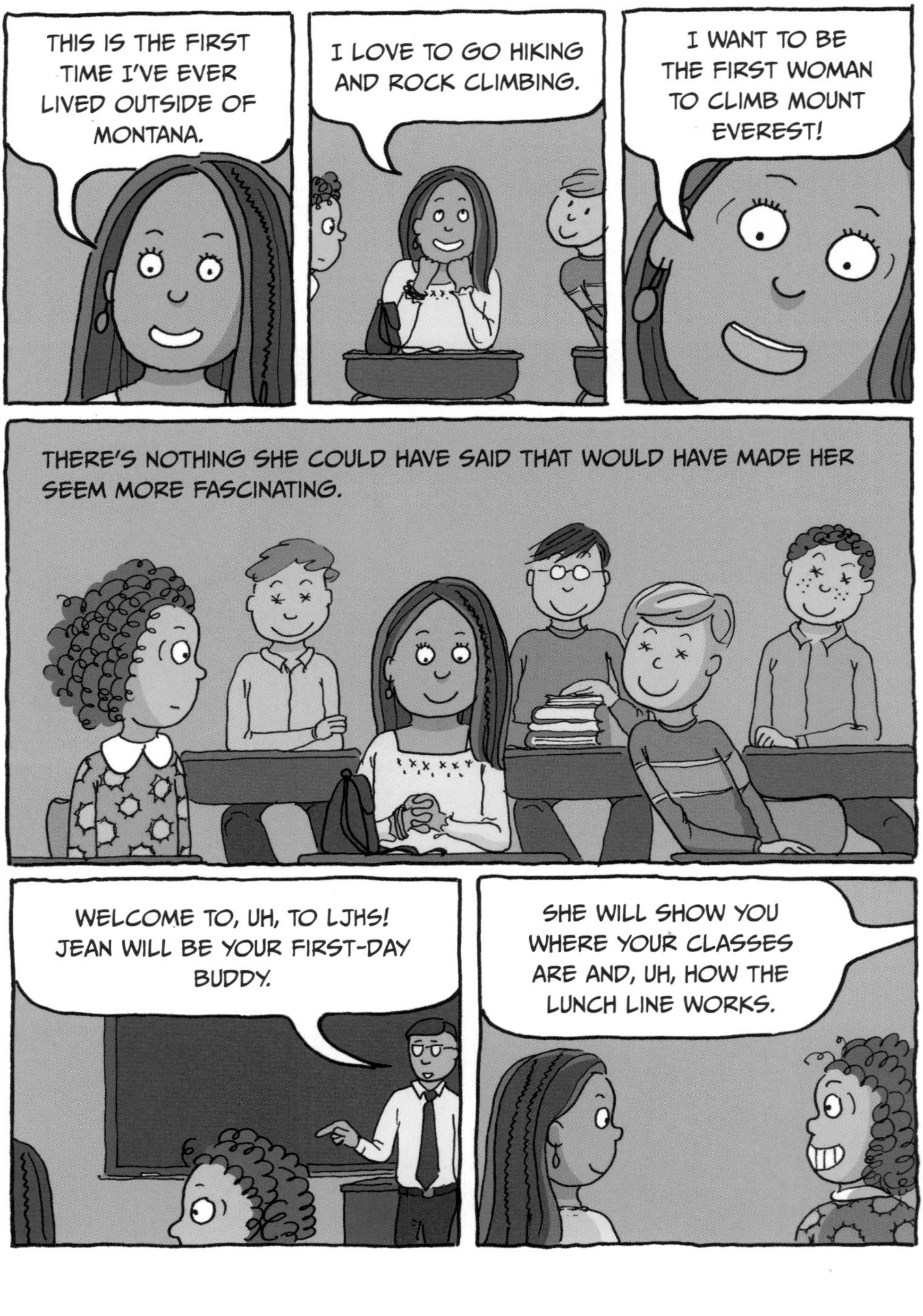
THIS IS THE FIRST TIME I'VE EVER LIVED OUTSIDE OF MONTANA.
I LOVE TO GO HIKING AND ROCK CLIMBING.
I WANT TO BE THE FIRST WOMAN TO CLIMB MOUNT EVEREST!
THERE'S NOTHING SHE COULD HAVE SAID THAT WOULD HAVE MADE HER SEEM MORE FASCINATING.
WELCOME TO, UH, TO LJHS! JEAN WILL BE YOUR FIRST-DAY BUDDY.
SHE WILL SHOW YOU WHERE YOUR CLASSES ARE AND, UH, HOW THE LUNCH LINE WORKS.

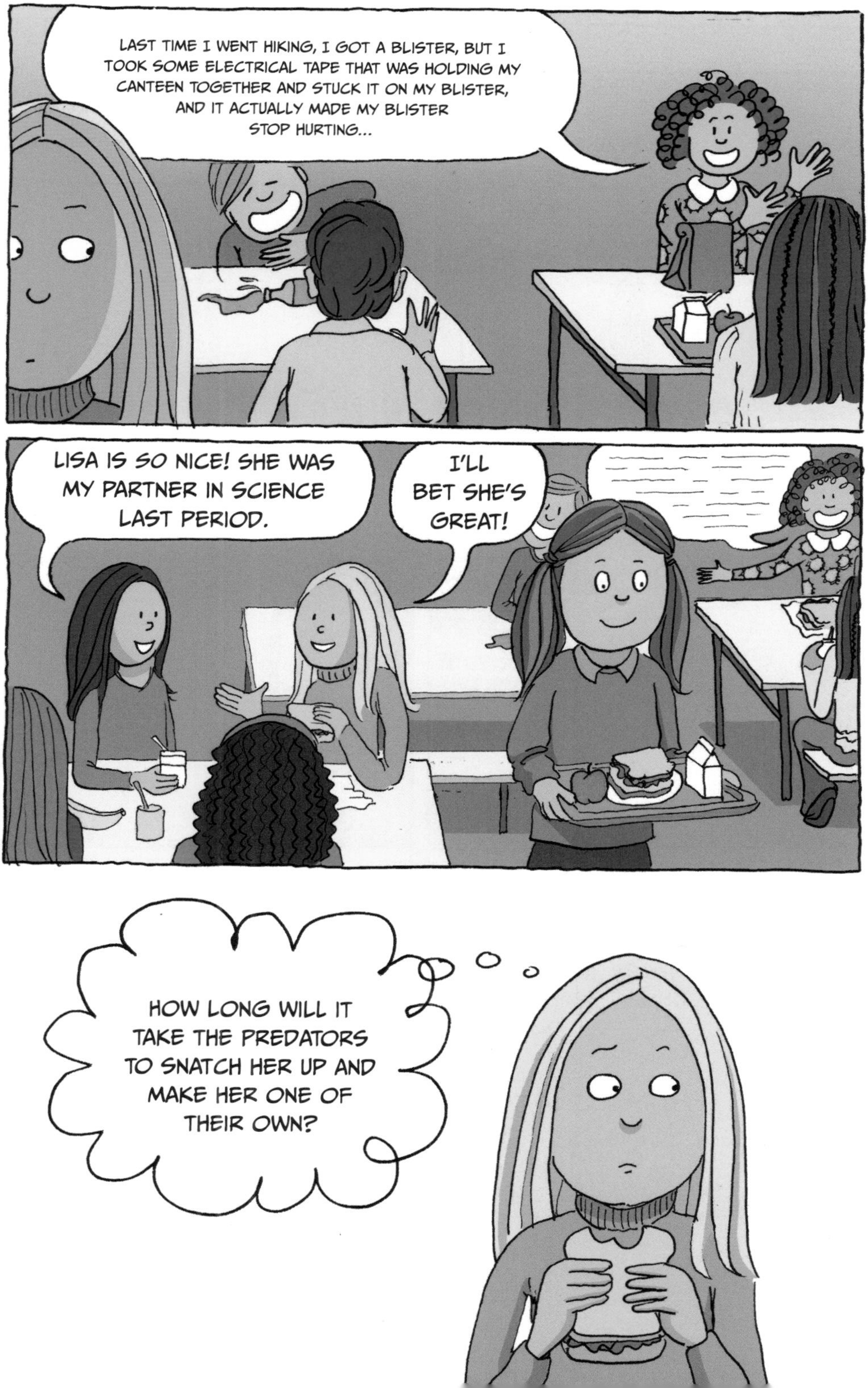
LAST TIME I WENT HIKING, I GOT A BLISTER, BUT I TOOK SOME ELECTRICAL TAPE THAT WAS HOLDING MY CANTEEN TOGETHER AND STUCK IT ON MY BLISTER, AND IT ACTUALLY MADE MY BLISTER STOP HURTING...
LISA IS SO NICE! SHE WAS MY PARTNER IN SCIENCE LAST PERIOD.
I'LL BET SHE'S GREAT!
HOW LONG WILL IT TAKE THE PREDATORS TO SNATCH HER UP AND MAKE HER ONE OF THEIR OWN?

THE NEXT DAY, LISA WALKS INTO THE LUNCHROOM ALONE AND PAUSES.

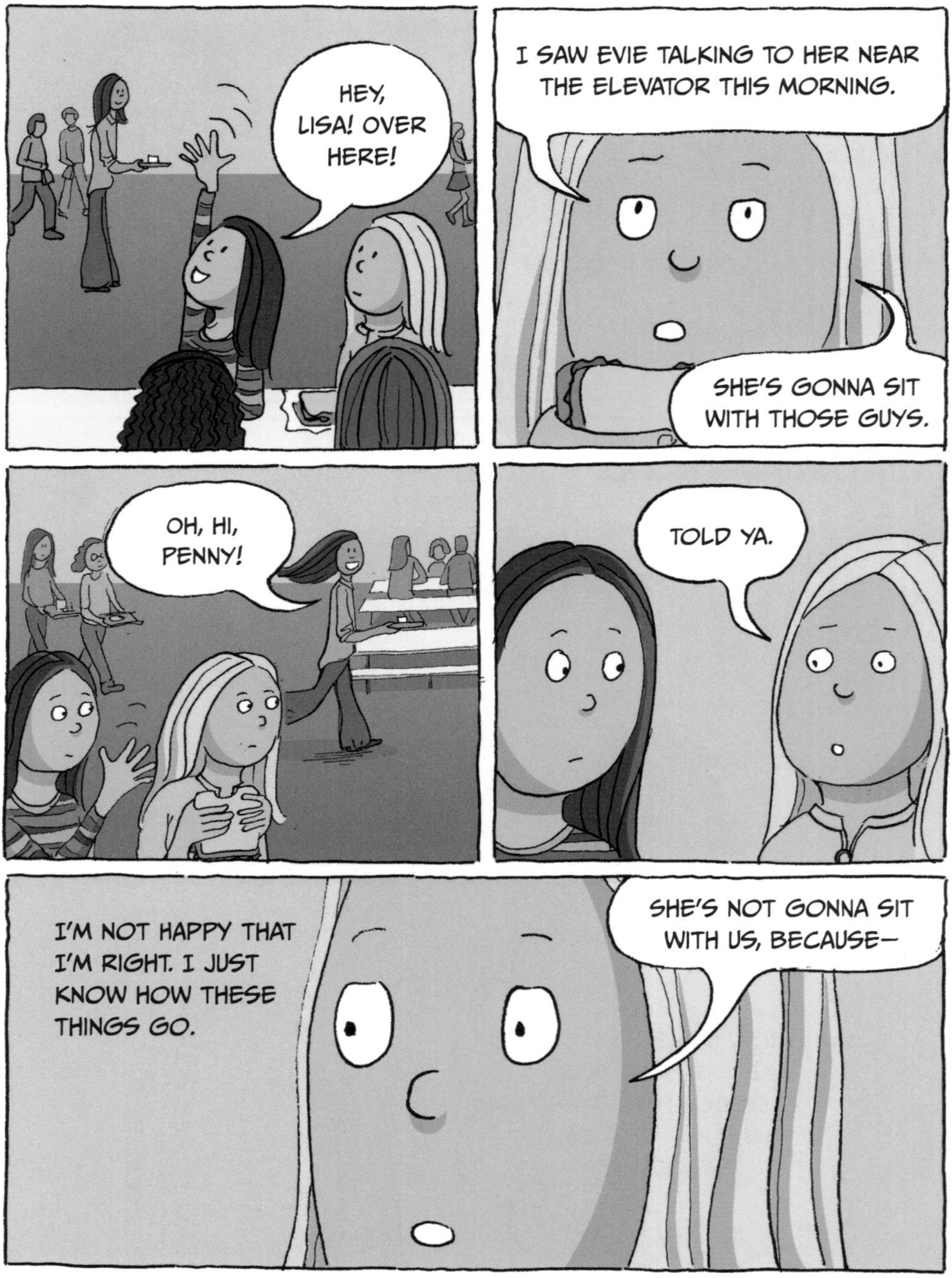
HEY, LISA! OVER HERE!
I SAW EVIE TALKING TO HER NEAR THE ELEVATOR THIS MORNING.
SHE'S GONNA SIT WITH THOSE GUYS.
OH, HI, PENNY!
TOLD YA.
I'M NOT HAPPY THAT I'M RIGHT. I JUST KNOW HOW THESE THINGS GO.
SHE'S NOT GONNA SIT WITH US, BECAUSE—

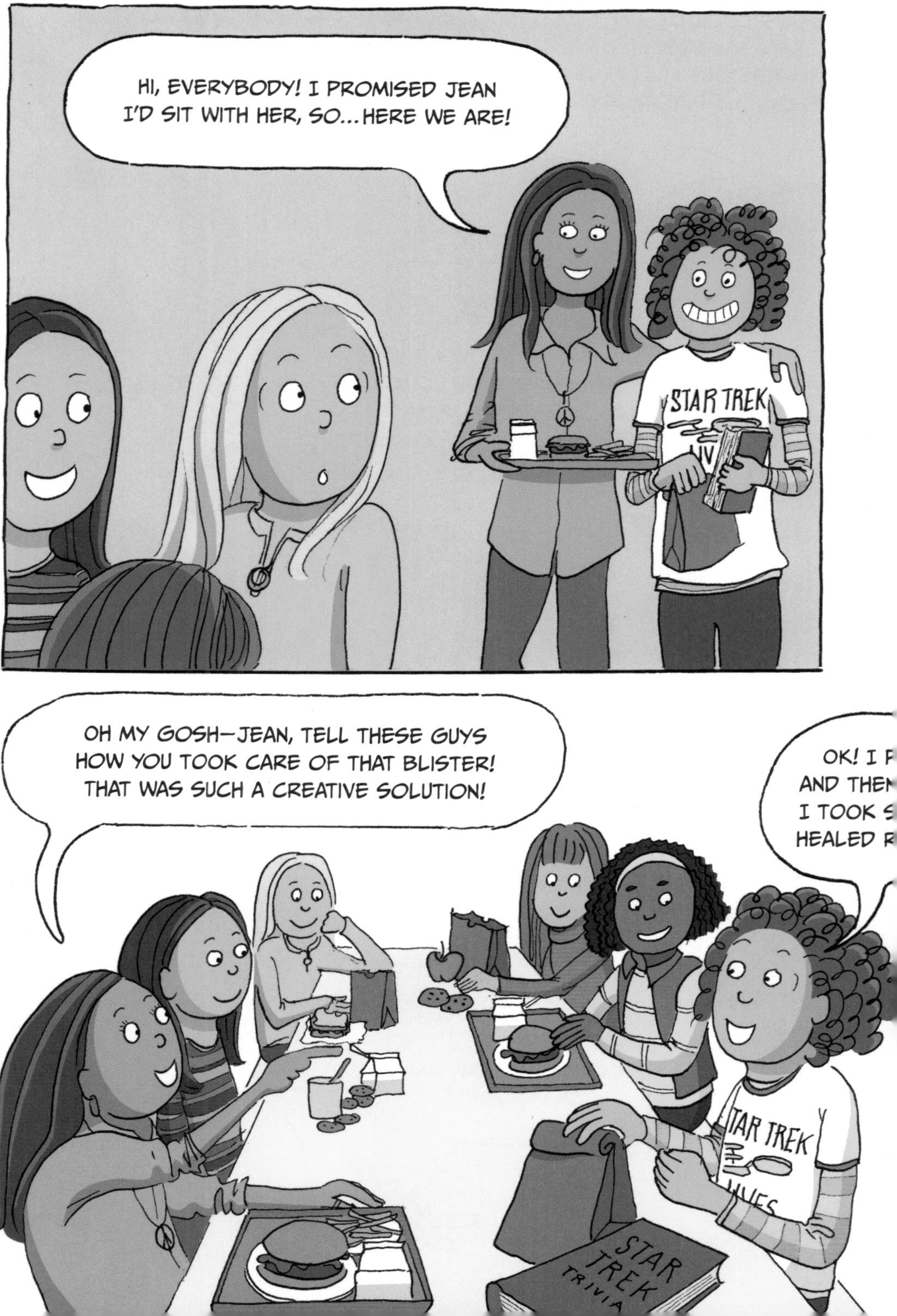
HI, EVERYBODY! I PROMISED JEAN I'D SIT WITH HER, SO...HERE WE ARE!
STAR TREK
OH MY GOSH—JEAN, TELL THESE GUYS HOW YOU TOOK CARE OF THAT BLISTER! THAT WAS SUCH A CREATIVE SOLUTION!
OK! I
AND THEN
I TOOK
HEALED
STAR TREK
STAR TREK TRIVIA

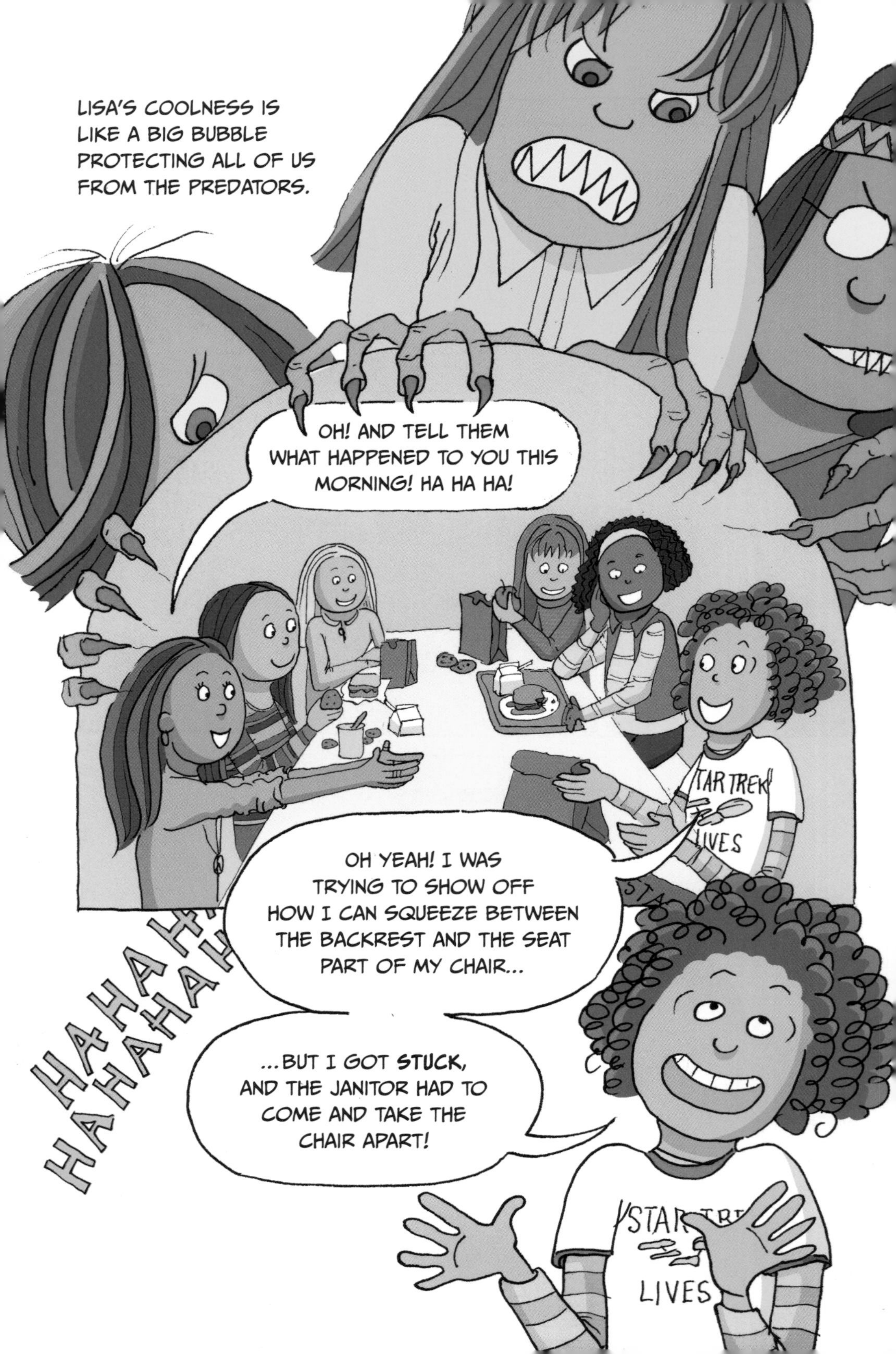
LISA'S COOLNESS IS LIKE A BIG BUBBLE PROTECTING ALL OF US FROM THE PREDATORS.
OH! AND TELL THEM WHAT HAPPENED TO YOU THIS MORNING! HA HA HA!
OH YEAH! I WAS TRYING TO SHOW OFF HOW I CAN SQUEEZE BETWEEN THE BACKREST AND THE SEAT PART OF MY CHAIR...
...BUT I GOT **STUCK**, AND THE JANITOR HAD TO COME AND TAKE THE CHAIR APART!
HAHAHA
HAHAHAHA
STAR TREK LIVES
STAR TREK LIVES

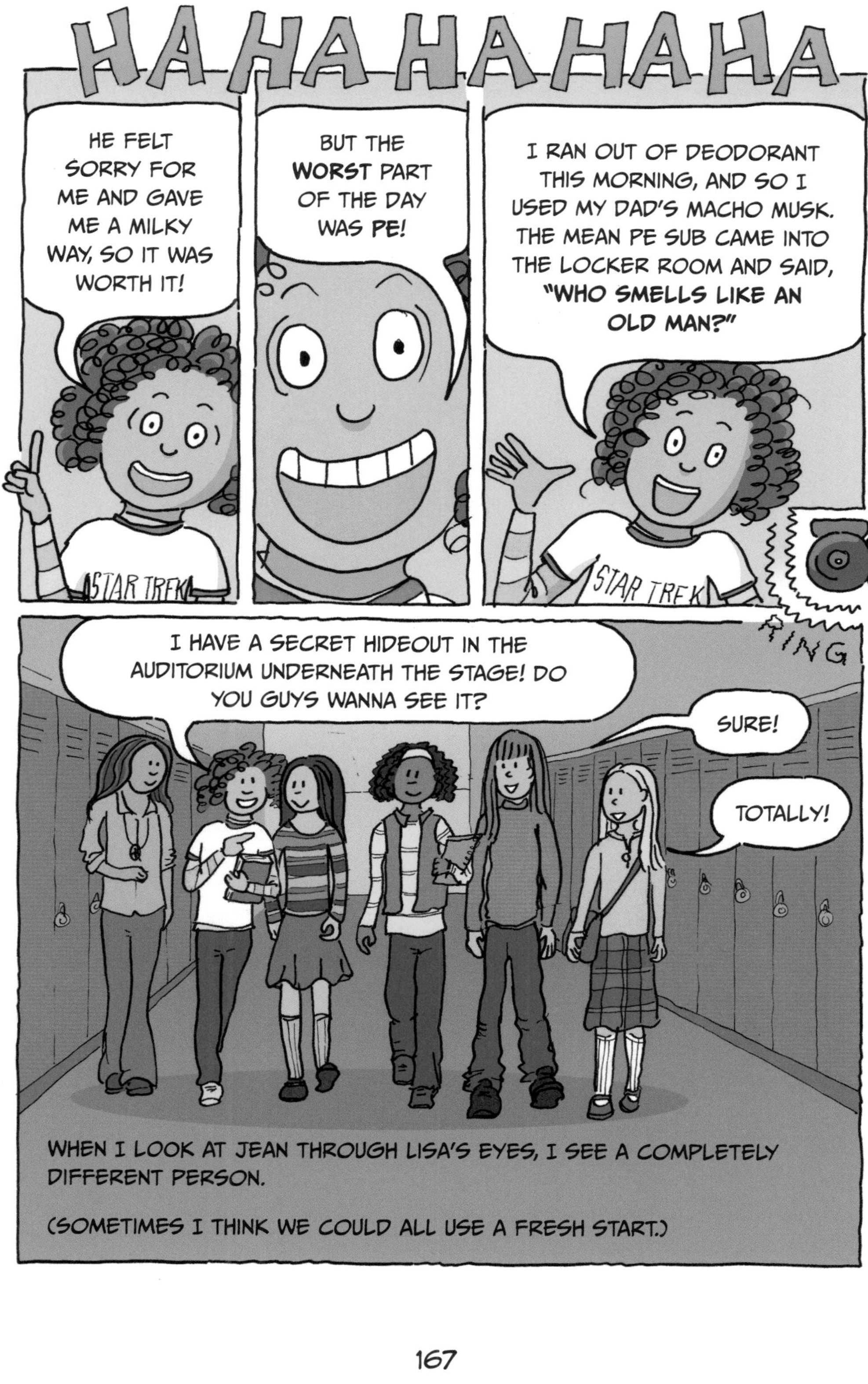
HA HA HA HA HA HA HA
HE FELT SORRY FOR ME AND GAVE ME A MILKY WAY, SO IT WAS WORTH IT!
STAR TREK
BUT THE **WORST** PART OF THE DAY WAS **PE!**
I RAN OUT OF DEODORANT THIS MORNING, AND SO I USED MY DAD'S MACHO MUSK. THE MEAN PE SUB CAME INTO THE LOCKER ROOM AND SAID, **"WHO SMELLS LIKE AN OLD MAN?"**
STAR TREK
RING
I HAVE A SECRET HIDEOUT IN THE AUDITORIUM UNDERNEATH THE STAGE! DO YOU GUYS WANNA SEE IT?
SURE!
TOTALLY!
WHEN I LOOK AT JEAN THROUGH LISA'S EYES, I SEE A COMPLETELY DIFFERENT PERSON.
(SOMETIMES I THINK WE COULD ALL USE A FRESH START.)

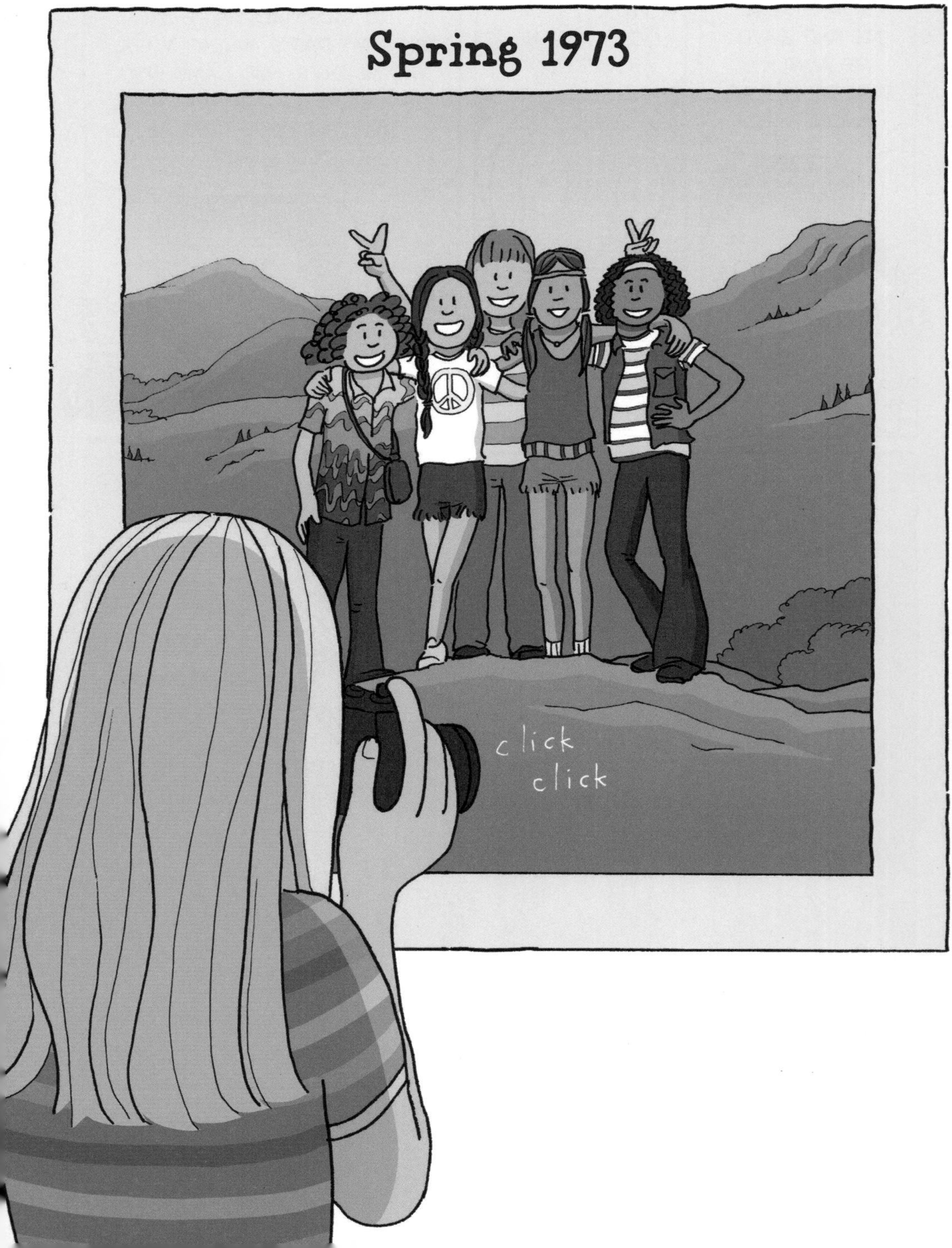
Spring 1973
click
click

Chapter 14

WHOA.
HOPEFULLY, YOU'LL BE EVEN MORE IMPRESSED BY WHAT HAPPENS *INSIDE* THE STATEHOUSE!

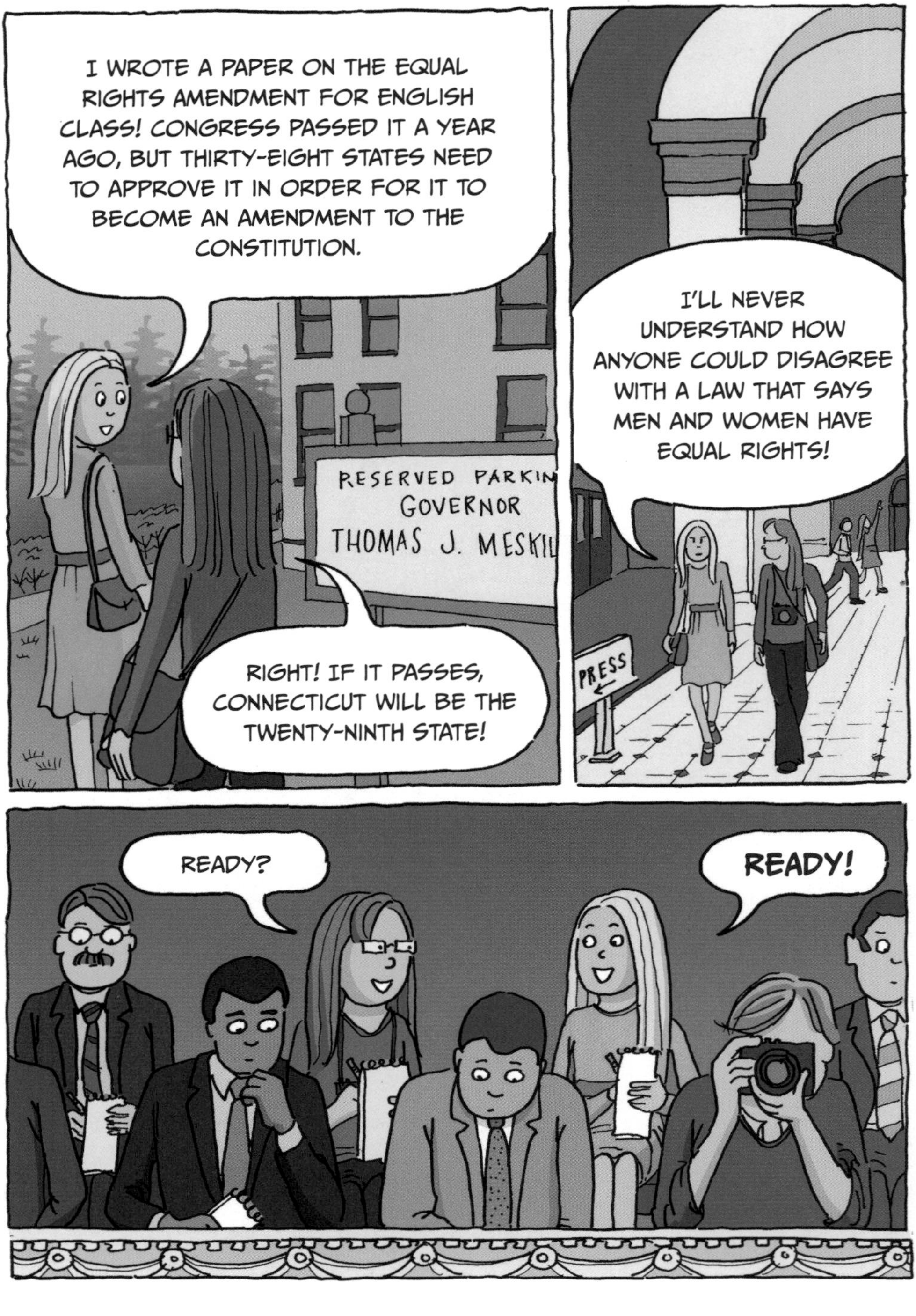
I WROTE A PAPER ON THE EQUAL RIGHTS AMENDMENT FOR ENGLISH CLASS! CONGRESS PASSED IT A YEAR AGO, BUT THIRTY-EIGHT STATES NEED TO APPROVE IT IN ORDER FOR IT TO BECOME AN AMENDMENT TO THE CONSTITUTION.
RESERVED PARKIN
GOVERNOR
THOMAS J. MESKIL
RIGHT! IF IT PASSES, CONNECTICUT WILL BE THE TWENTY-NINTH STATE!
I'LL NEVER UNDERSTAND HOW ANYONE COULD DISAGREE WITH A LAW THAT SAYS MEN AND WOMEN HAVE EQUAL RIGHTS!
PRESS
READY?
READY!

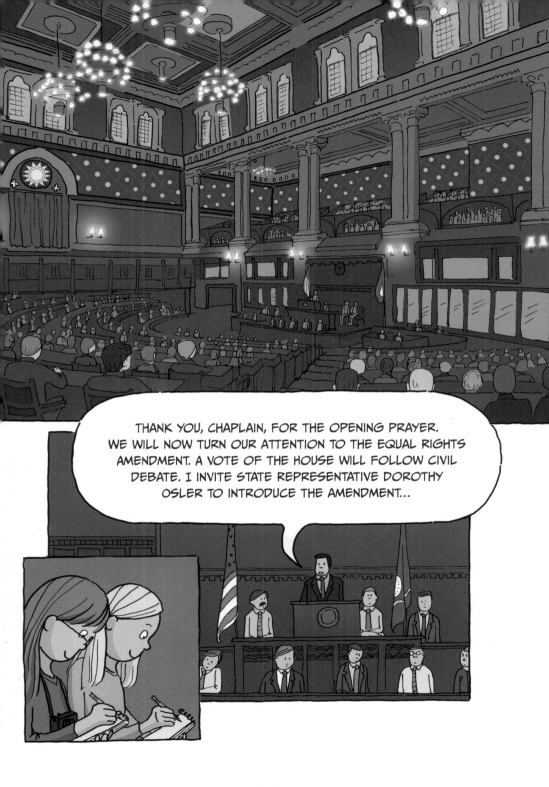

THANK YOU, CHAPLAIN, FOR THE OPENING PRAYER. WE WILL NOW TURN OUR ATTENTION TO THE EQUAL RIGHTS AMENDMENT. A VOTE OF THE HOUSE WILL FOLLOW CIVIL DEBATE. I INVITE STATE REPRESENTATIVE DOROTHY OSLER TO INTRODUCE THE AMENDMENT...

Torrington Register

TORRINGTON, CONNECTICUT FRIDAY, MARCH 9, 1973 VOL 99 NO 58 10 CENTS

State House passes ERA after heated debate

Senate approval still needed

by Leslie Jacobs

Following a lengthy, emotional debate, the State House of Representatives voted 99–47 in favor of ratifying the Equal Rights Amendment to the US Constitution.

Cheers rang out from the ...lic gallery, crowded to capacity by women who had come to witness the historic vote.

According to State Rep. Dorothy Osler (R-Greenwich), the amendment will simply prohibit discrimination on the basis of a person'... equa...

Osler insisted that men will also reap benefits if the amendment is adopted.

The amendment does not mean that housewives will be discriminated against or that men's rights will be weakened, Osler stated.

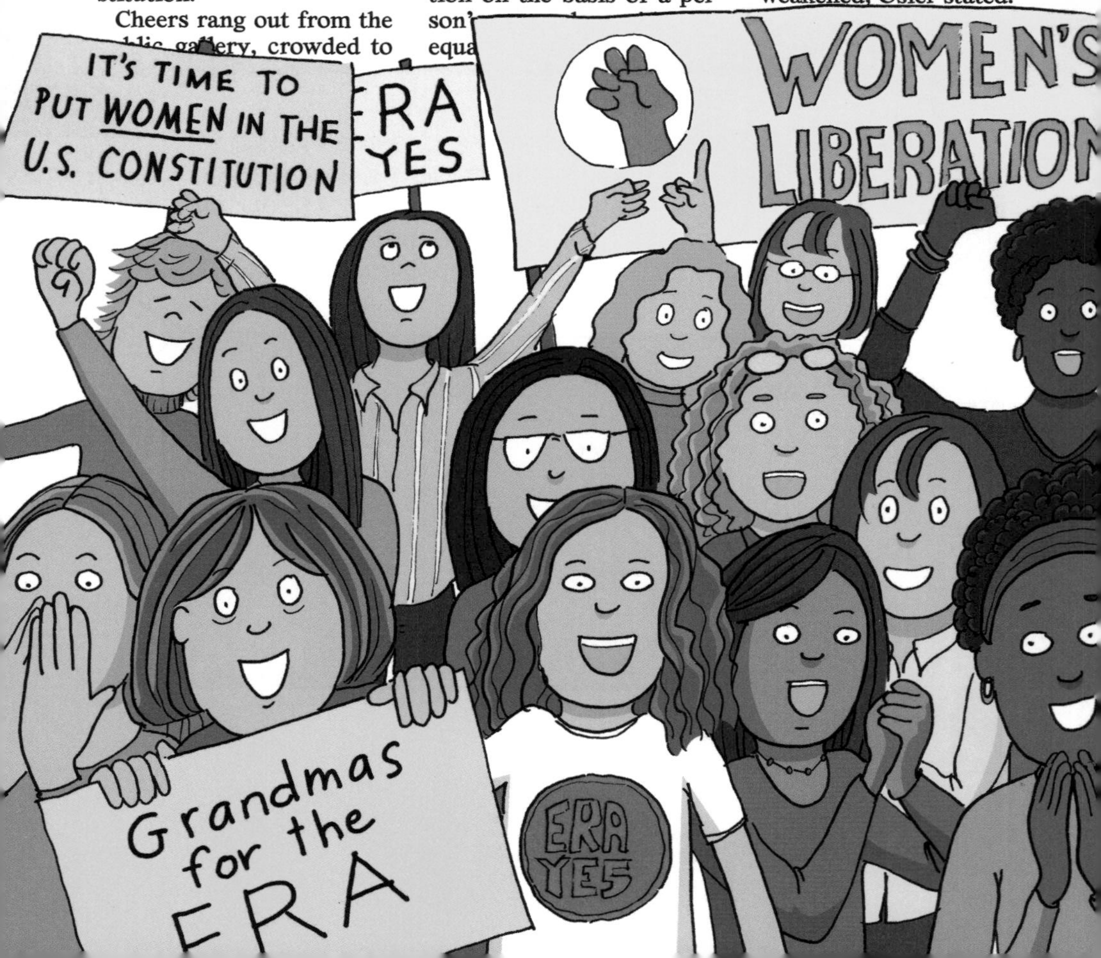
IT'S TIME TO PUT WOMEN IN THE U.S. CONSTITUTION
ERA YES
WOMEN'S LIBERATION
Grandmas for the ERA
ERA YES

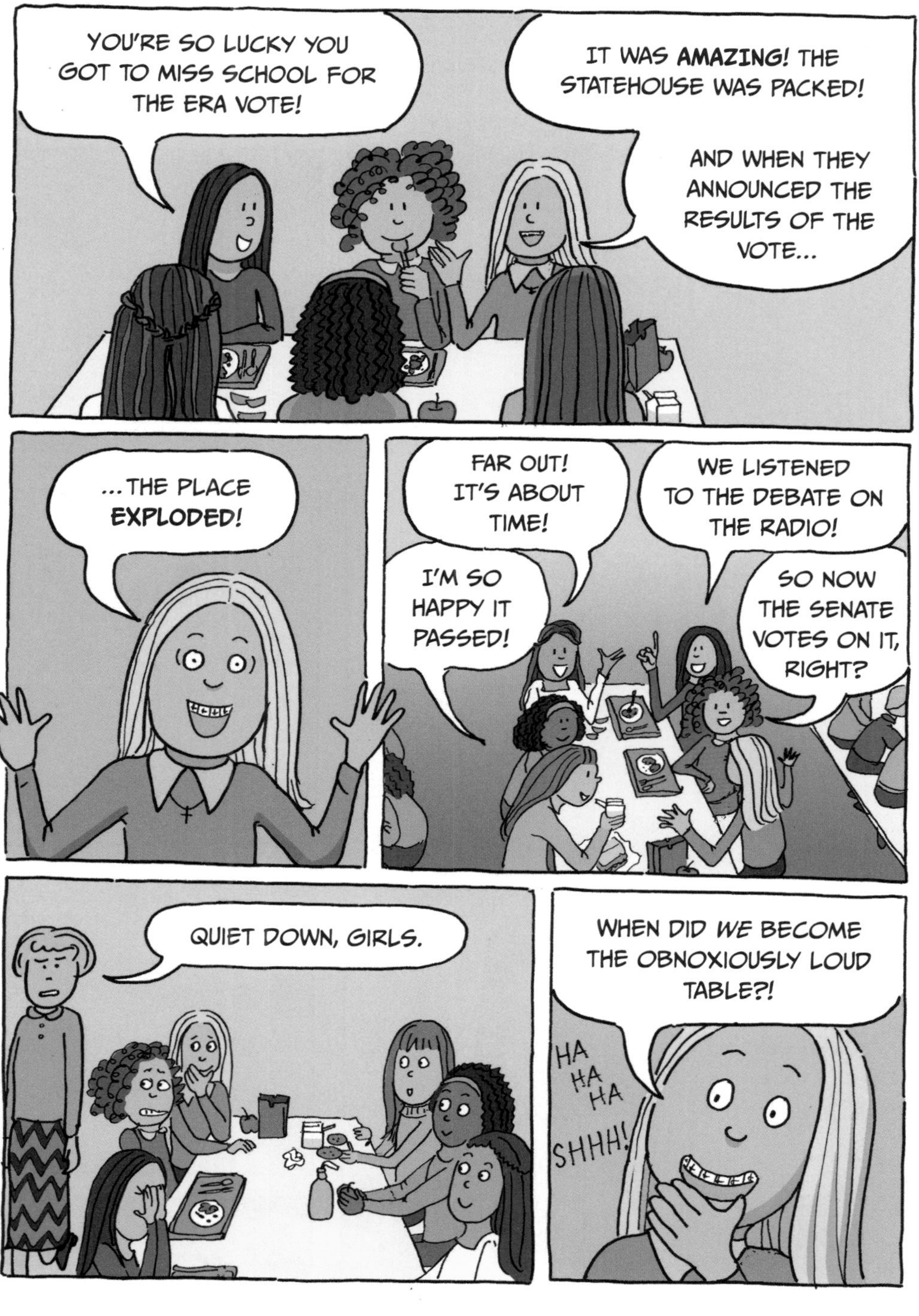
YOU'RE SO LUCKY YOU GOT TO MISS SCHOOL FOR THE ERA VOTE!
IT WAS **AMAZING!** THE STATEHOUSE WAS PACKED!
AND WHEN THEY ANNOUNCED THE RESULTS OF THE VOTE...
...THE PLACE **EXPLODED!**
FAR OUT! IT'S ABOUT TIME!
WE LISTENED TO THE DEBATE ON THE RADIO!
I'M SO HAPPY IT PASSED!
SO NOW THE SENATE VOTES ON IT, RIGHT?
QUIET DOWN, GIRLS.
WHEN DID *WE* BECOME THE OBNOXIOUSLY LOUD TABLE?!
HA HA HA
SHHH!

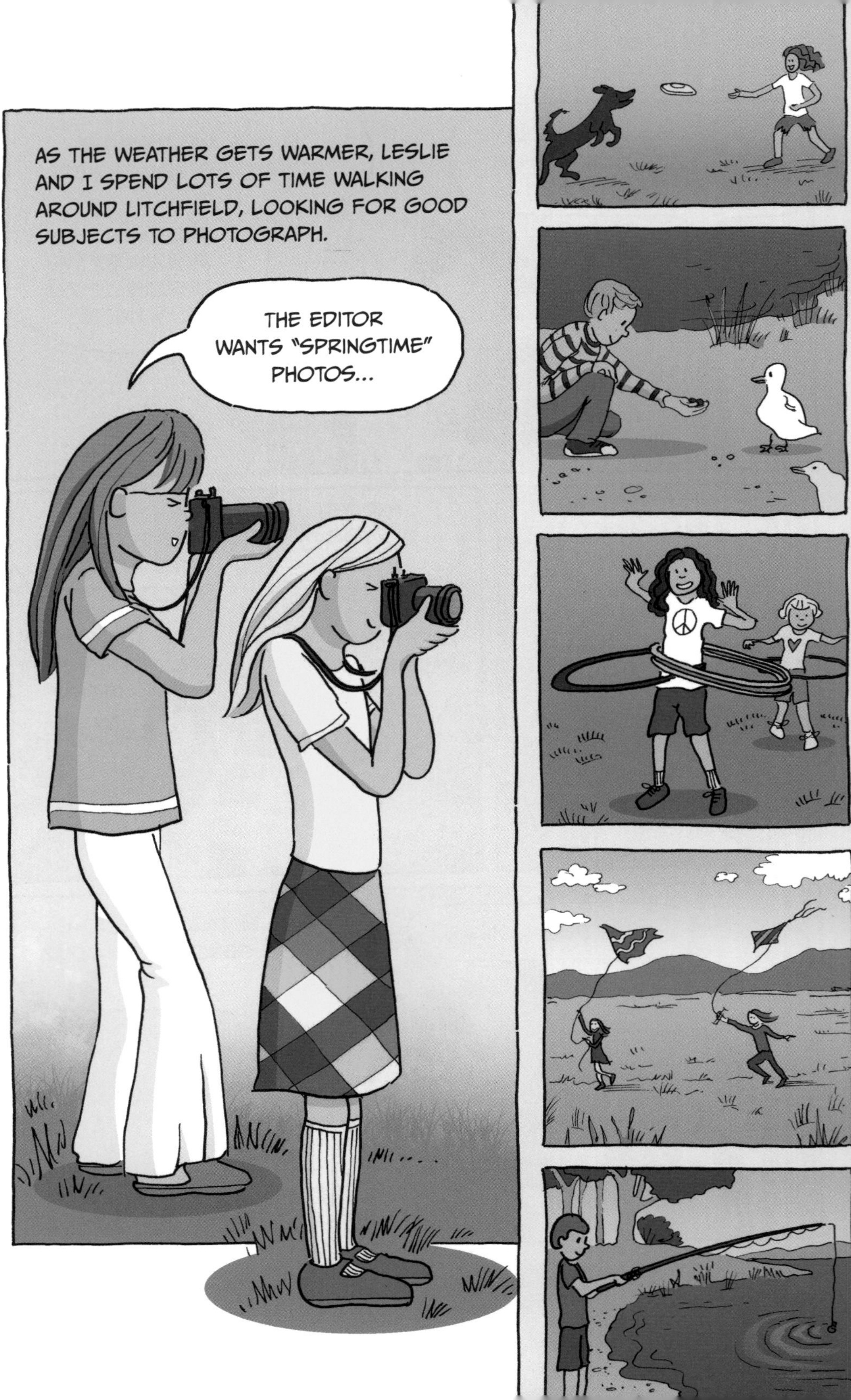
AS THE WEATHER GETS WARMER, LESLIE AND I SPEND LOTS OF TIME WALKING AROUND LITCHFIELD, LOOKING FOR GOOD SUBJECTS TO PHOTOGRAPH.
THE EDITOR WANTS "SPRINGTIME" PHOTOS...

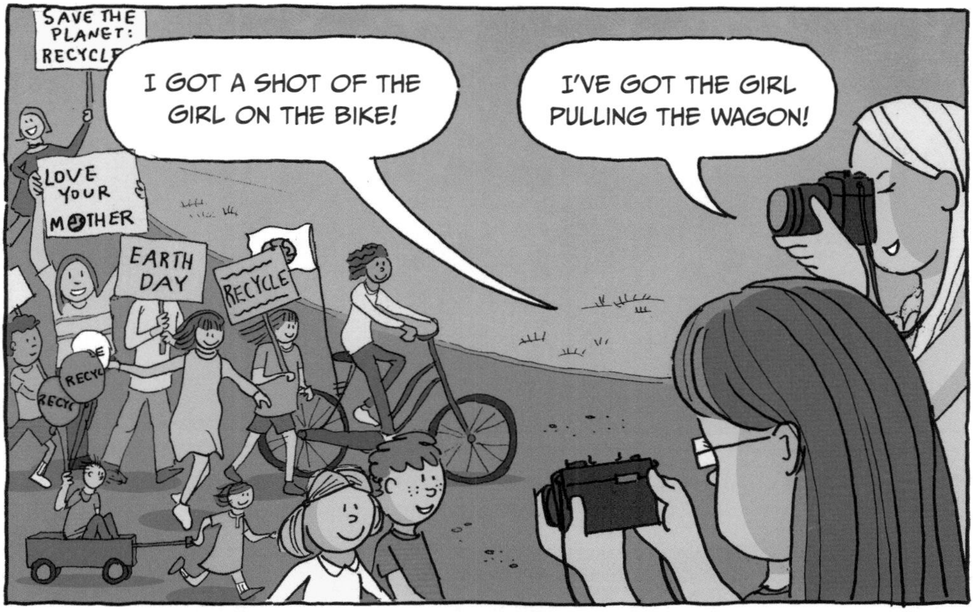
SAVE THE PLANET: RECYCLE
I GOT A SHOT OF THE GIRL ON THE BIKE!
I'VE GOT THE GIRL PULLING THE WAGON!
LOVE YOUR MOTHER
EARTH DAY
RECYCLE

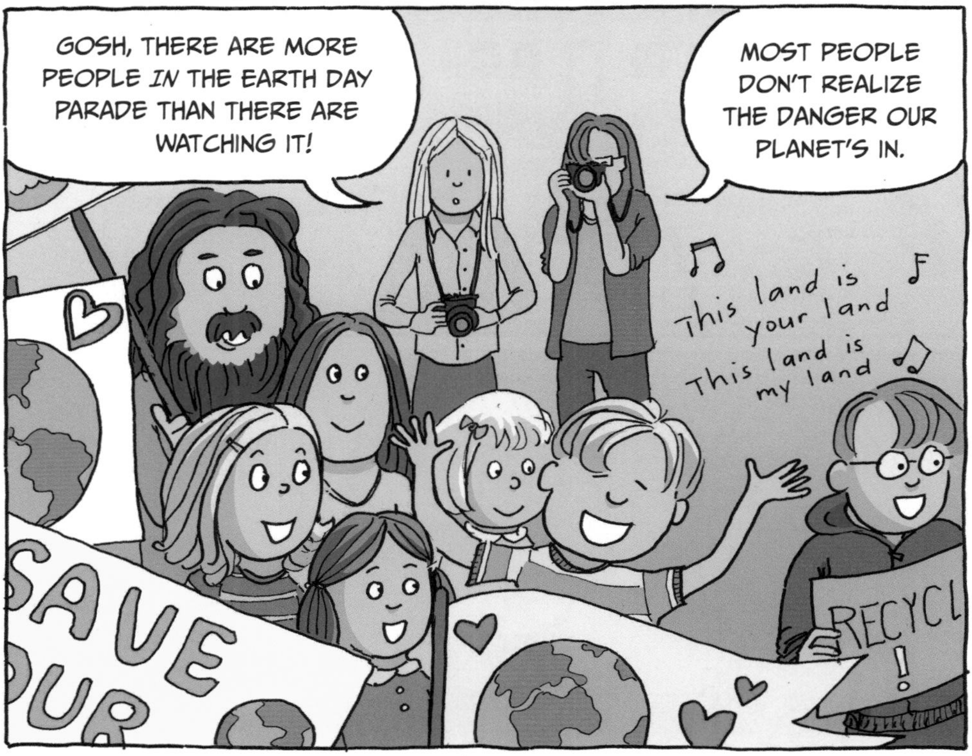
GOSH, THERE ARE MORE PEOPLE *IN* THE EARTH DAY PARADE THAN THERE ARE WATCHING IT!
MOST PEOPLE DON'T REALIZE THE DANGER OUR PLANET'S IN.
This land is your land
This land is my land
SAVE OUR
RECYCL !

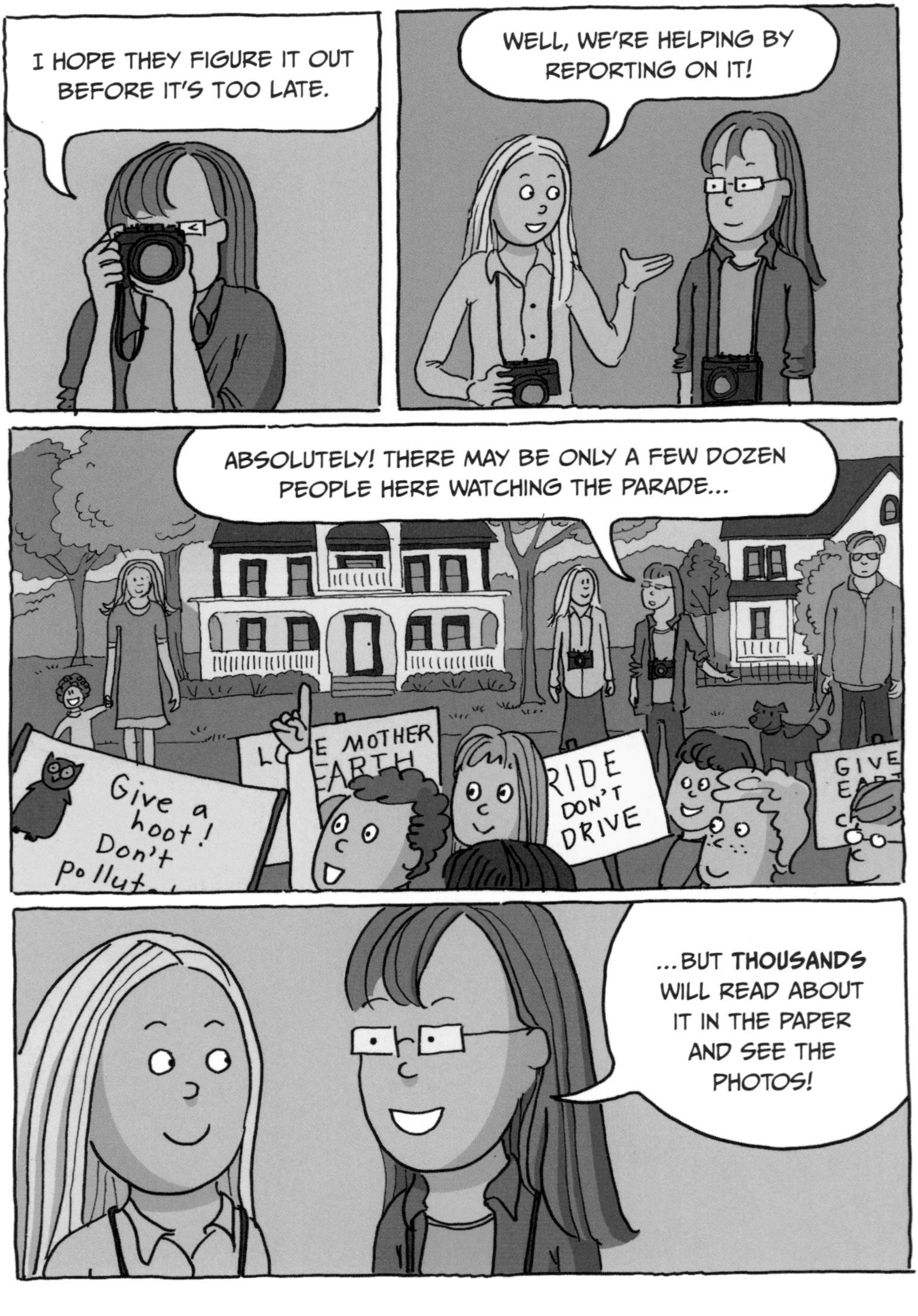
I HOPE THEY FIGURE IT OUT BEFORE IT'S TOO LATE.
WELL, WE'RE HELPING BY REPORTING ON IT!
ABSOLUTELY! THERE MAY BE ONLY A FEW DOZEN PEOPLE HERE WATCHING THE PARADE...
Give a hoot! Don't
RIDE DON'T DRIVE
...BUT **THOUSANDS** WILL READ ABOUT IT IN THE PAPER AND SEE THE PHOTOS!

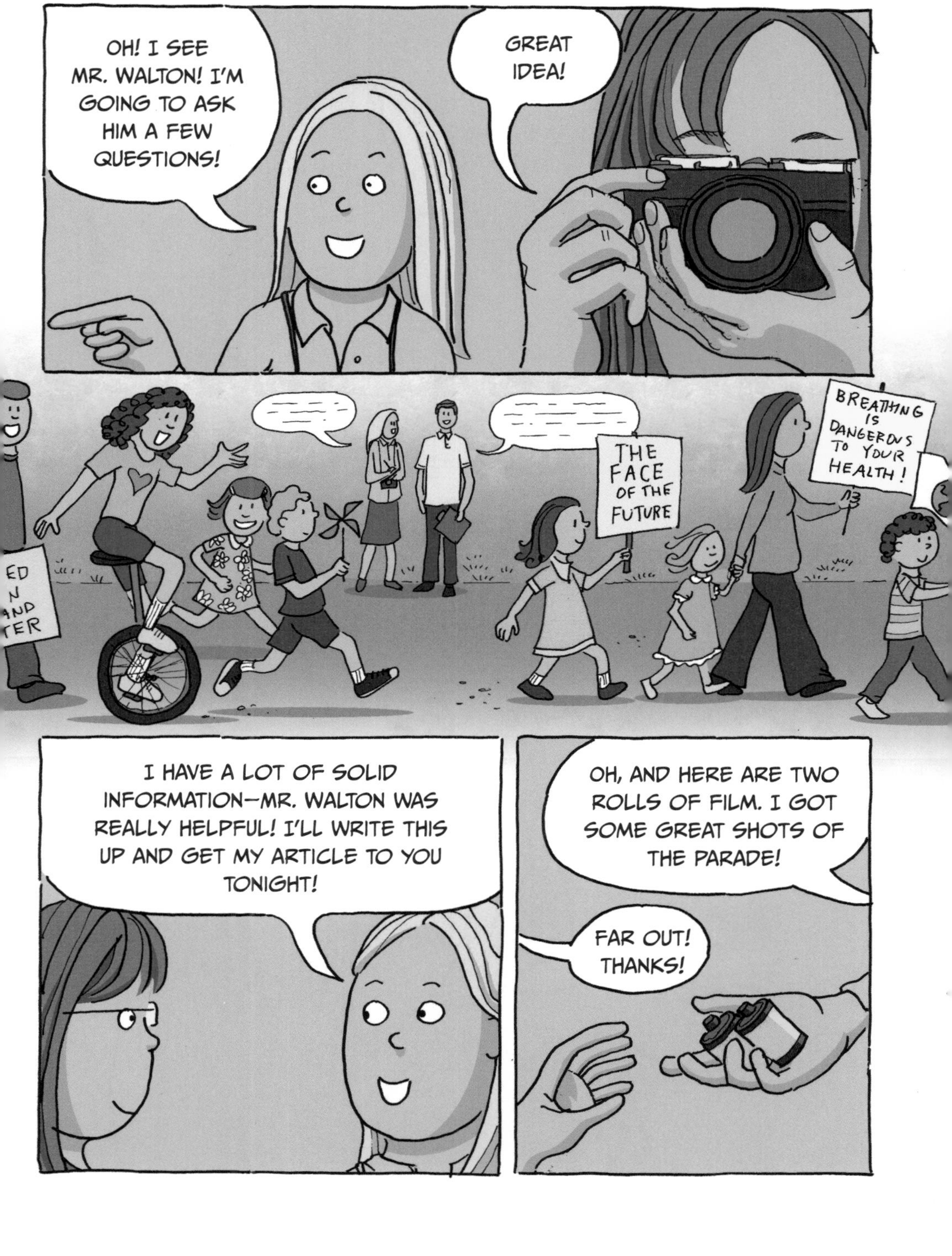
OH! I SEE MR. WALTON! I'M GOING TO ASK HIM A FEW QUESTIONS!
GREAT IDEA!
THE FACE OF THE FUTURE
BREATHING IS DANGEROUS TO YOUR HEALTH!
I HAVE A LOT OF SOLID INFORMATION—MR. WALTON WAS REALLY HELPFUL! I'LL WRITE THIS UP AND GET MY ARTICLE TO YOU TONIGHT!
OH, AND HERE ARE TWO ROLLS OF FILM. I GOT SOME GREAT SHOTS OF THE PARADE!
FAR OUT! THANKS!

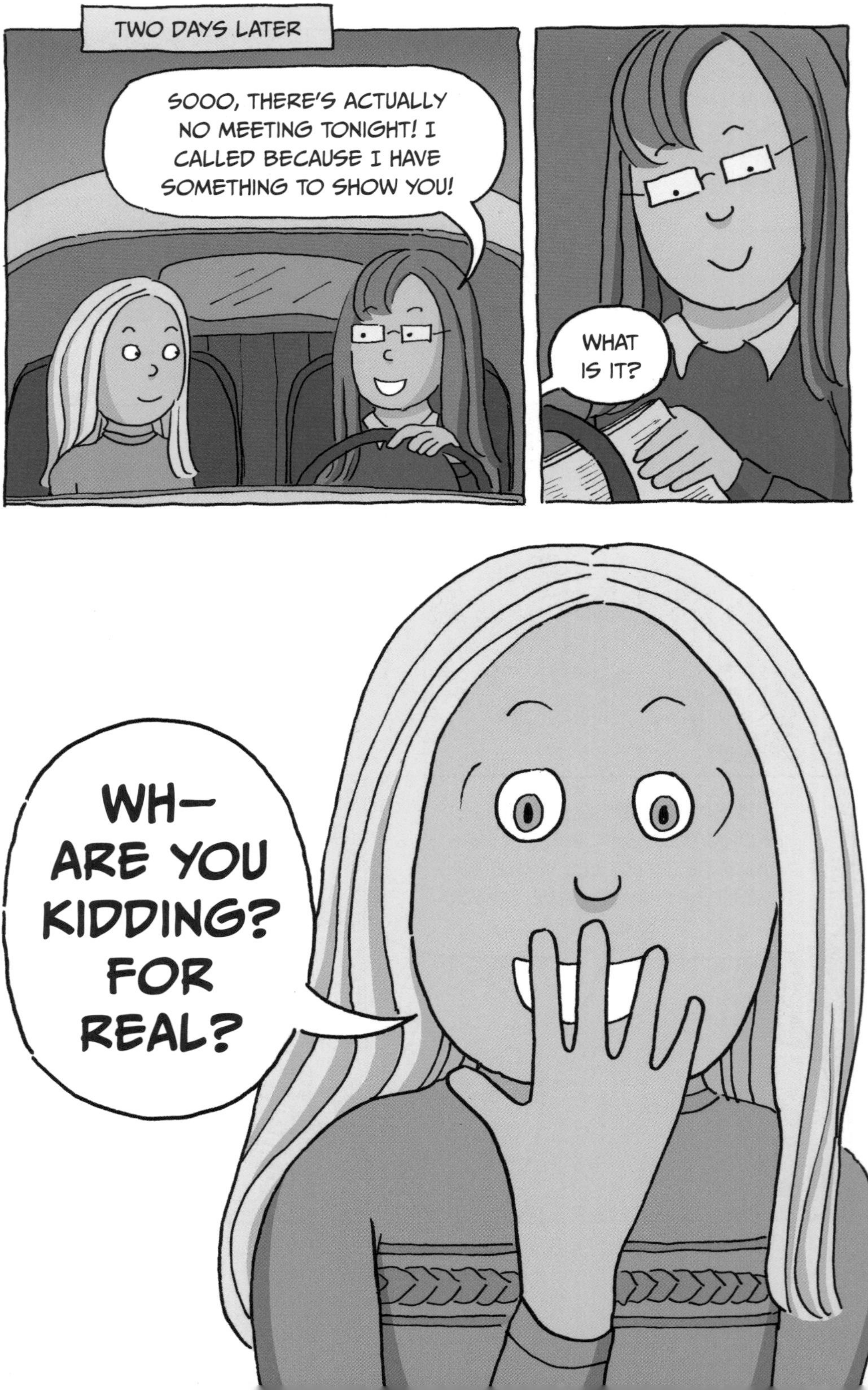
TWO DAYS LATER
SOOO, THERE'S ACTUALLY NO MEETING TONIGHT! I CALLED BECAUSE I HAVE SOMETHING TO SHOW YOU!
WHAT IS IT?
WH— ARE YOU KIDDING? FOR REAL?

CONGRATULATIONS!

Be the pollution solution!

Earth Day Marchers Put the Focus on Recycling

by Cindy Copeland

Enthusiastic participants outnumbered spectators at Litchfield's "Earth Day: We Care" parade. Bicyclists, horse-back riders, and walkers traveled from Old South Road to the recycling [center] on Goshen Road, modeling modes of transportation that don't add to the pollution problem. Two horse-drawn wagons carried town officials as well as representatives from the Sierra Club [and] the Litchfield Hills Audubon Society. The local Fife and Drum Marching [band] added a festive air. According to [?] Walton, whose group Eco-Action [organ]ized the recycling movement in [?], the parade's theme was "Don't trash our future: Recycle!" Walton hopes the parade will inspire more people to become involved in Litchfield's recycling effort.

This event marks the third year that people in Litchfield as well as across the country have gathered to celebrate Earth Day. The Earth Day movement was founded by Wisconsin Senator Gaylord Nelson, who wanted to bring national attention to environmental issues like air and water pollution. Inspired by student anti-war protests, Senator Nelson decided to channel that youthful energy into a movement focused on promoting a healthy, sustainable environment.

Occupation of Wounded Knee Ends

After 70 days, the Second Battle of Wounded Knee ended today as members of the American Indian Movement (AIM) surrendered the occupied reservation in South Dakota to leery government officials. More than 200 of the militants had seized control of the town on the Pine Ridge Reservation on February 27, in an effort to call attention to injustices such as broken treaties, inadequate compensation for lost lands, and fading tribal identity. Late last week, White House representatives guaranteed a meeting with tribal elders to discuss their concerns, leading to today's surrender.

Washington Post Awarded Pulitzer Prize for Watergate

The Washington Post [was awarded a] Pulitzer Prize for public service on Monday for its investigative report[ing] of the Watergate scandal. It was one of 11 prizes awarded this year for jour[nalism].

Proxmire: Press "Grossly Unfair" to Nixon

Senator William Proxmire criticized the press from the Senate floor for being "grossly unfair" to President Nixon. The Democratic Senator from Wisconsin claimed that the press has been engaging in a "McCarthyistic destruction" of the President that showed the "press at its worst." Just a day earlier, Proxmire, known as a Nixon critic, confided to a newspaper editor that he believed the President was "involved in Watergate up to his ears."

Chapter 15

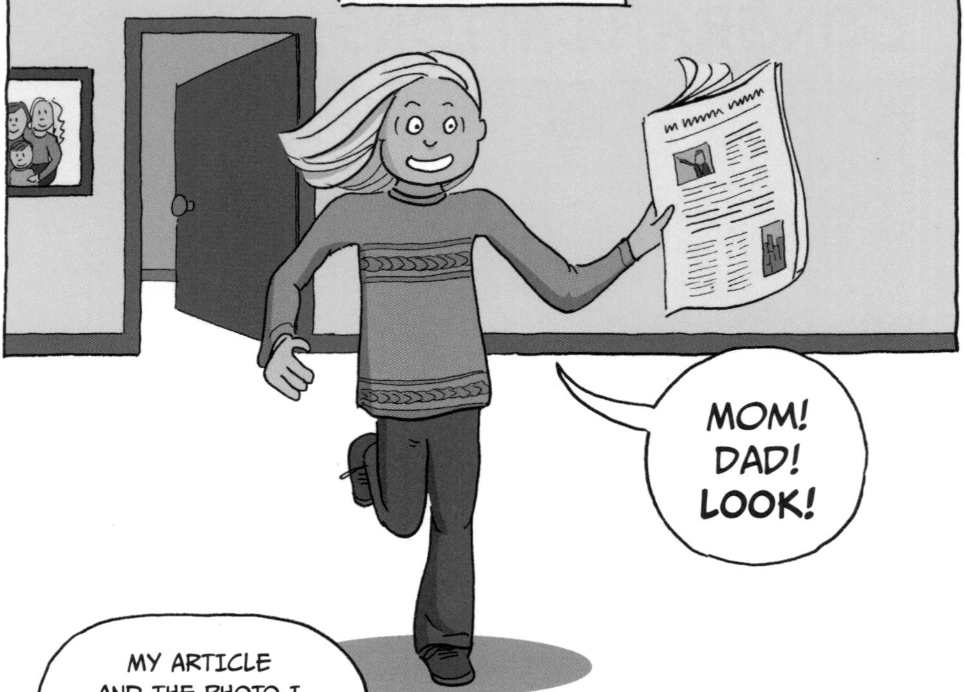
MOM! DAD! LOOK!

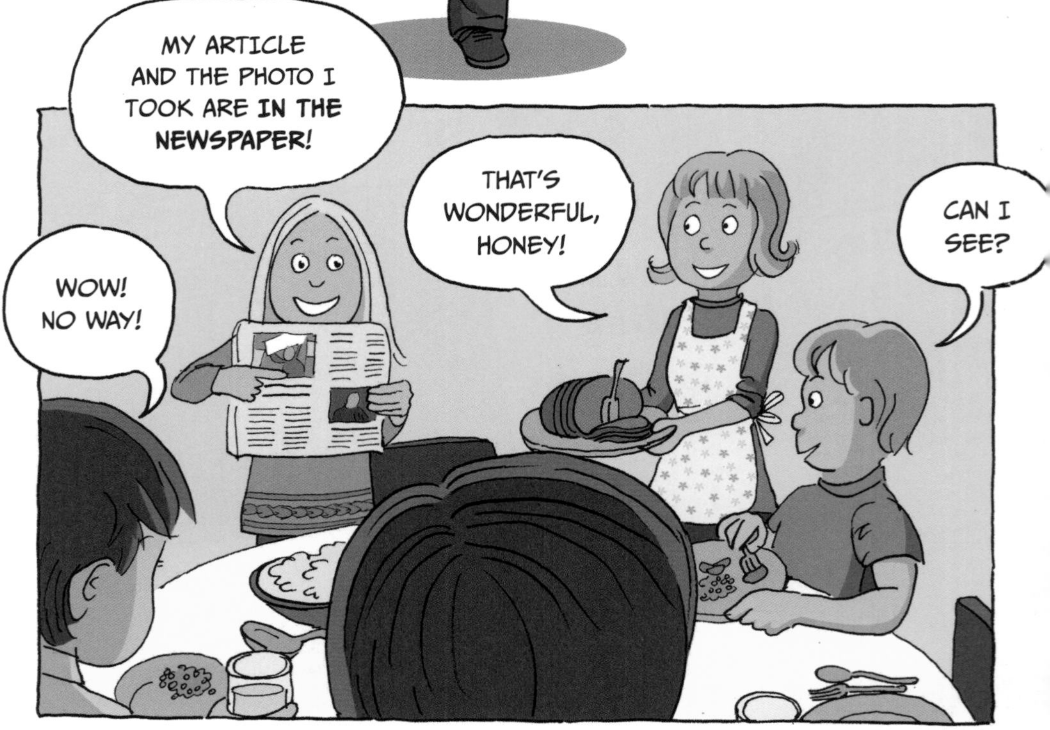
MY ARTICLE AND THE PHOTO I TOOK ARE IN THE NEWSPAPER!
WOW! NO WAY!
THAT'S WONDERFUL, HONEY!
CAN I SEE?

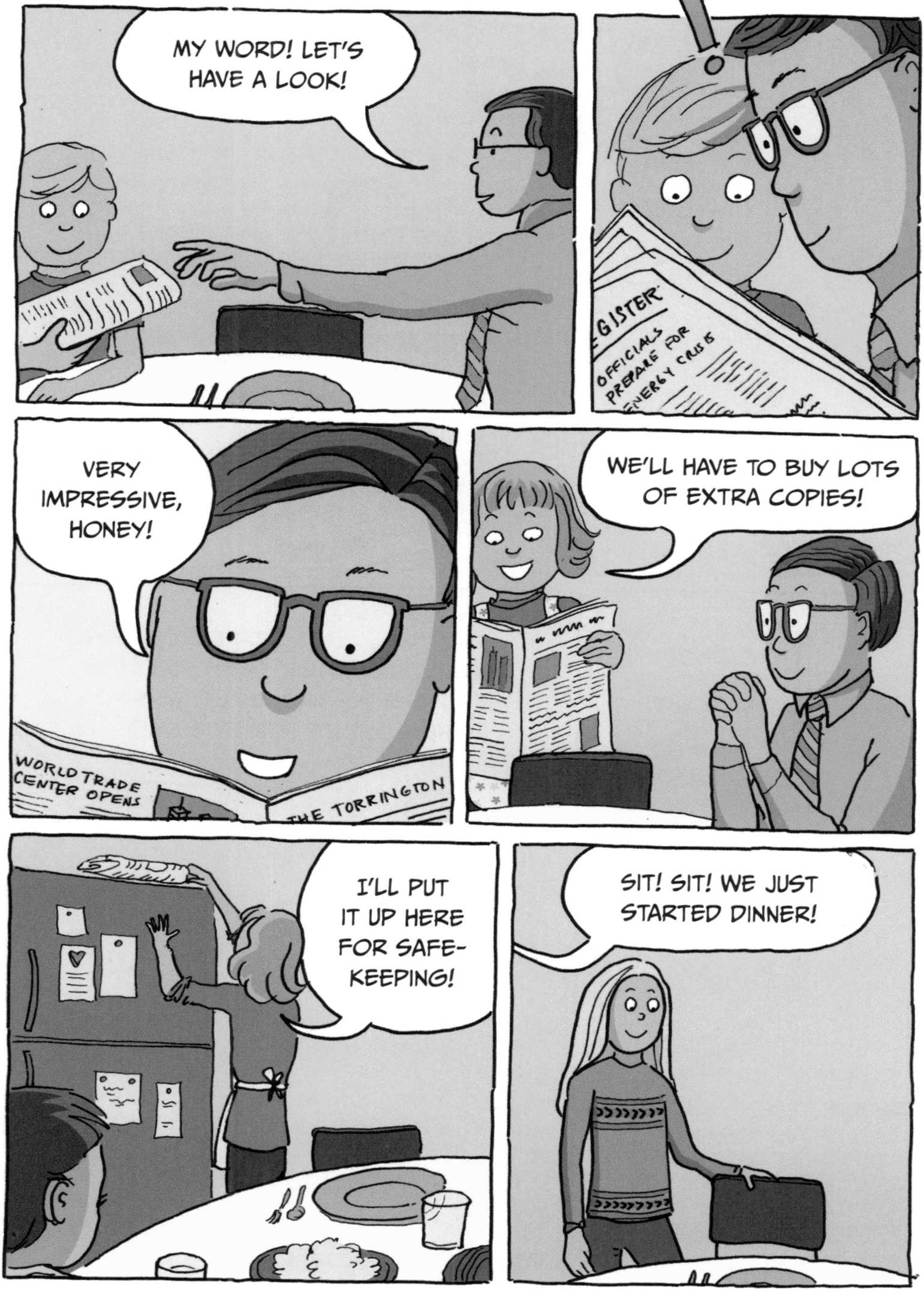
MY WORD! LET'S HAVE A LOOK!
EGISTER
OFFICIALS PREPARE FOR ENERGY CRISIS
VERY IMPRESSIVE, HONEY!
WORLD TRADE CENTER OPENS
THE TORRINGTON
WE'LL HAVE TO BUY LOTS OF EXTRA COPIES!
I'LL PUT IT UP HERE FOR SAFE-KEEPING!
SIT! SIT! WE JUST STARTED DINNER!

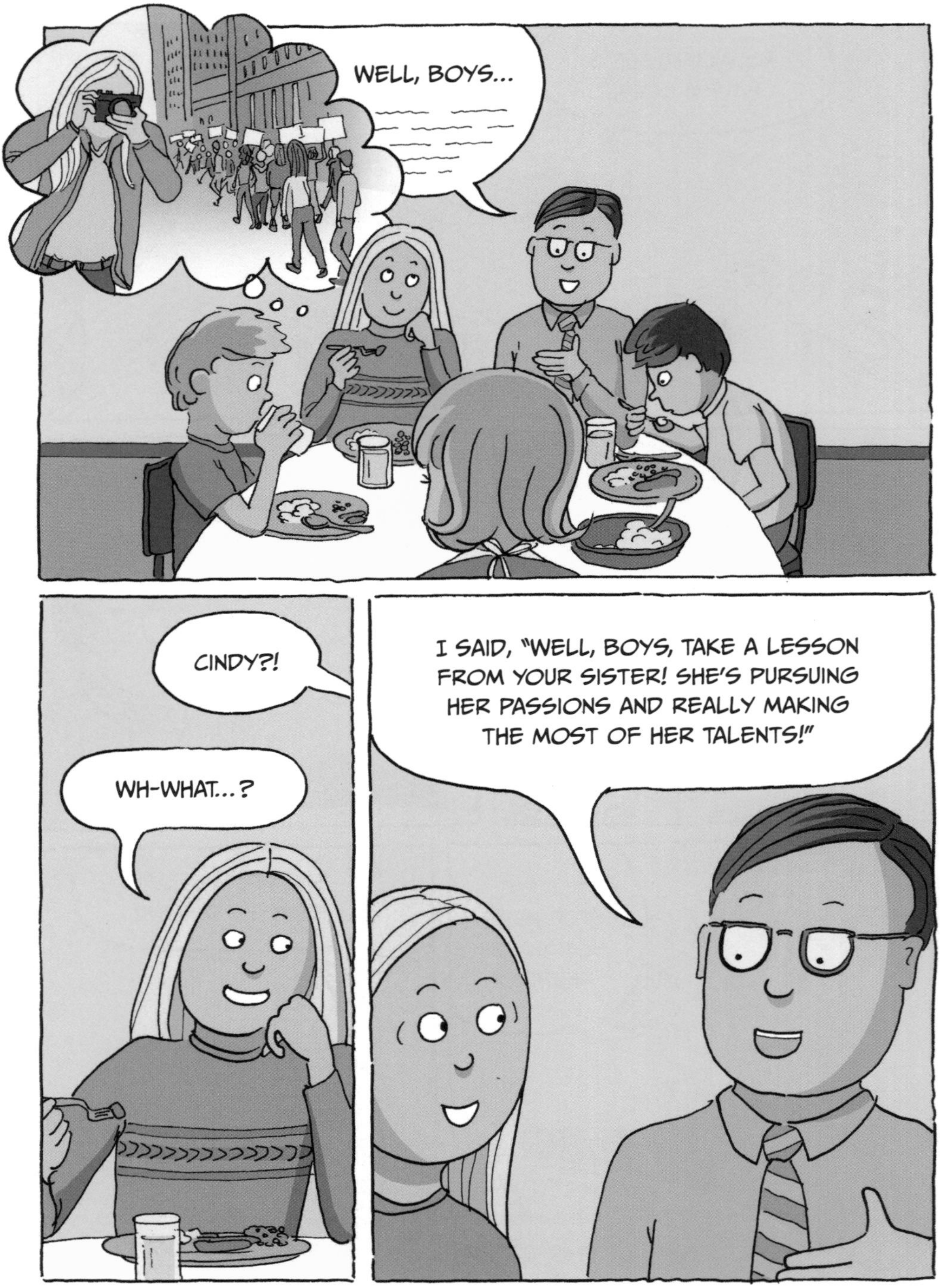

WELL, BOYS...
CINDY?!
WH-WHAT...?
I SAID, "WELL, BOYS, TAKE A LESSON FROM YOUR SISTER! SHE'S PURSUING HER PASSIONS AND REALLY MAKING THE MOST OF HER TALENTS!"

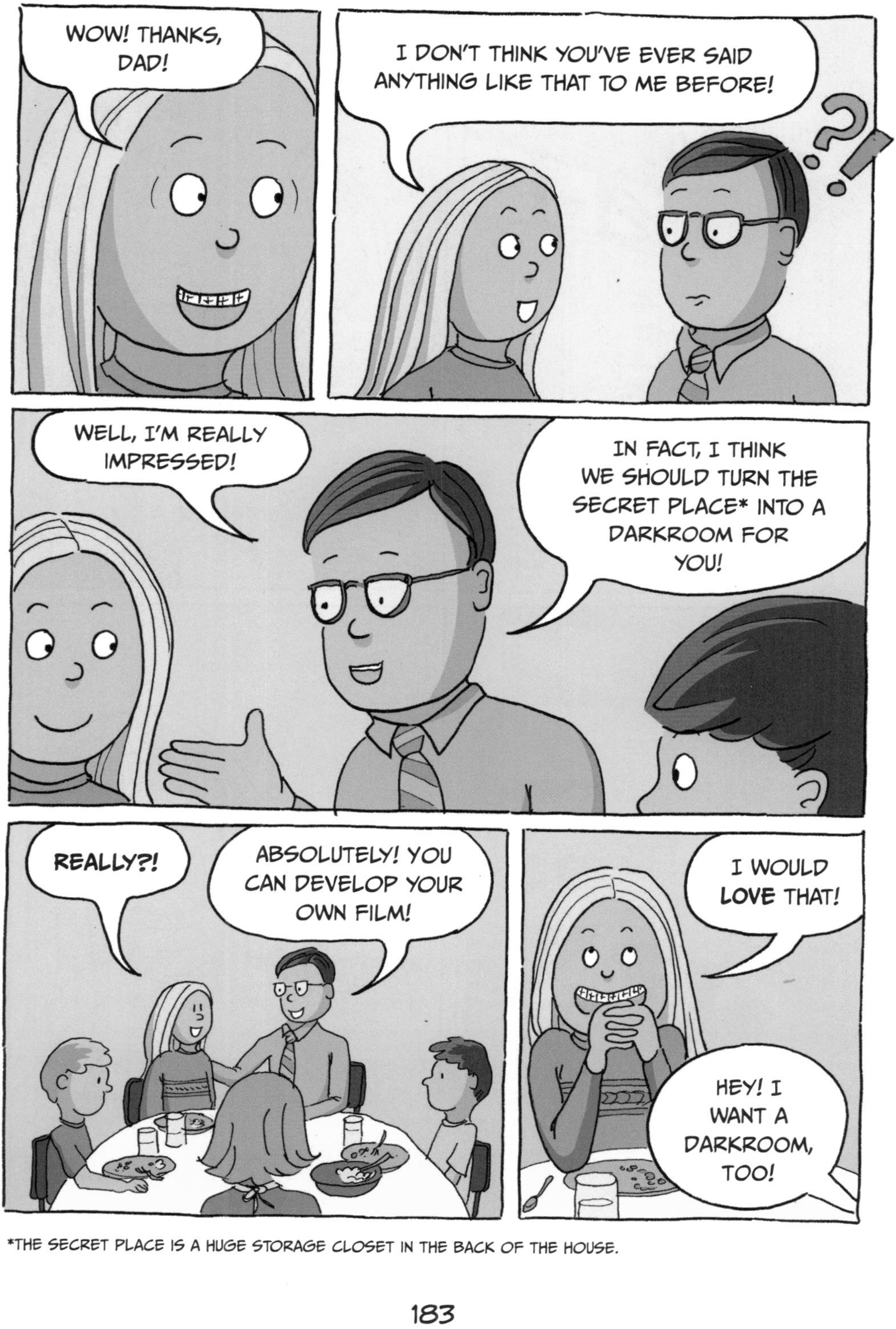
WOW! THANKS, DAD!
I DON'T THINK YOU'VE EVER SAID ANYTHING LIKE THAT TO ME BEFORE!
?!
WELL, I'M REALLY IMPRESSED!
IN FACT, I THINK WE SHOULD TURN THE SECRET PLACE* INTO A DARKROOM FOR YOU!
REALLY?!
ABSOLUTELY! YOU CAN DEVELOP YOUR OWN FILM!
I WOULD **LOVE** THAT!
HEY! I WANT A DARKROOM, TOO!

*THE SECRET PLACE IS A HUGE STORAGE CLOSET IN THE BACK OF THE HOUSE.

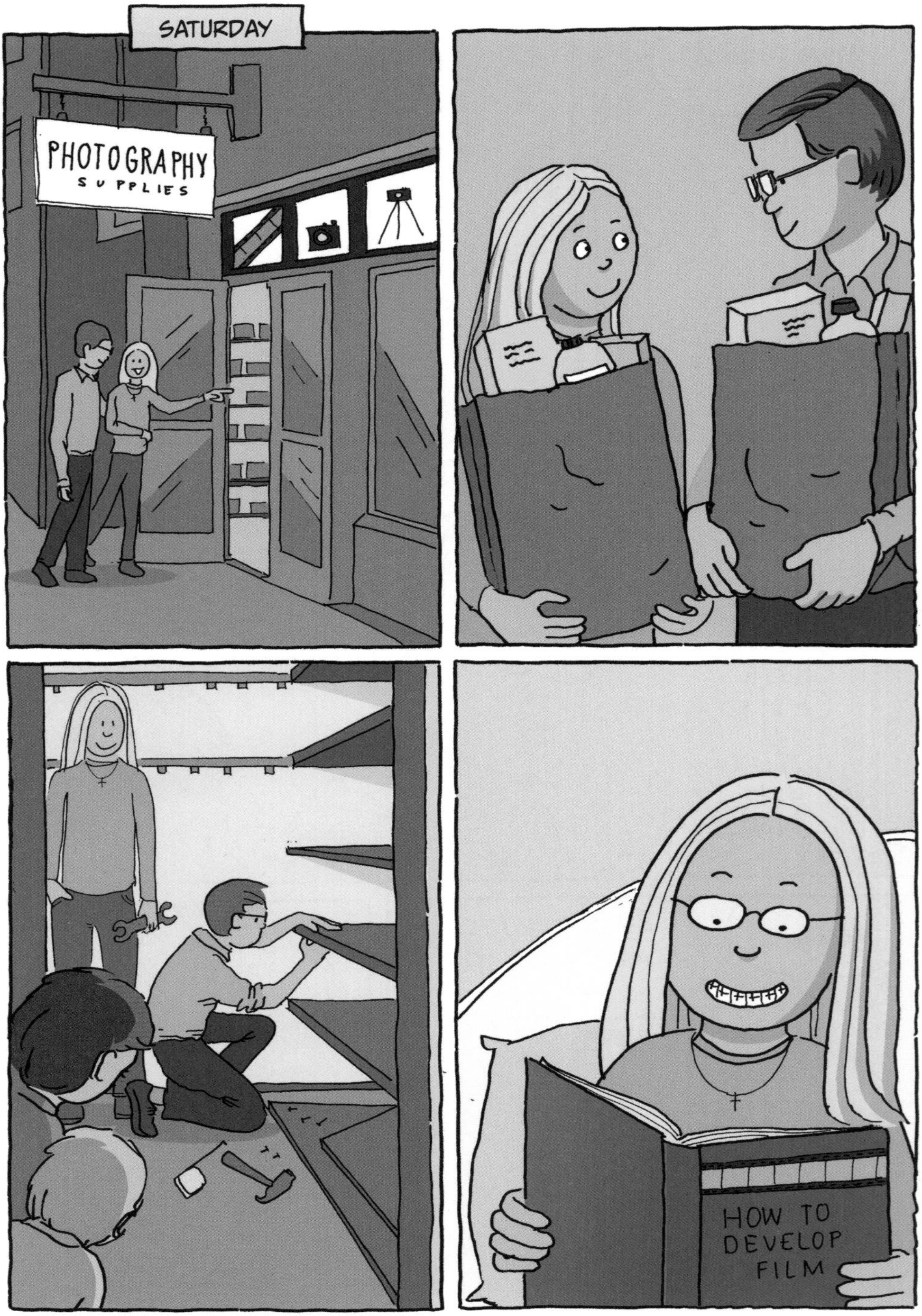
SATURDAY
PHOTOGRAPHY
SUPPLIES
HOW TO
DEVELOP
FILM

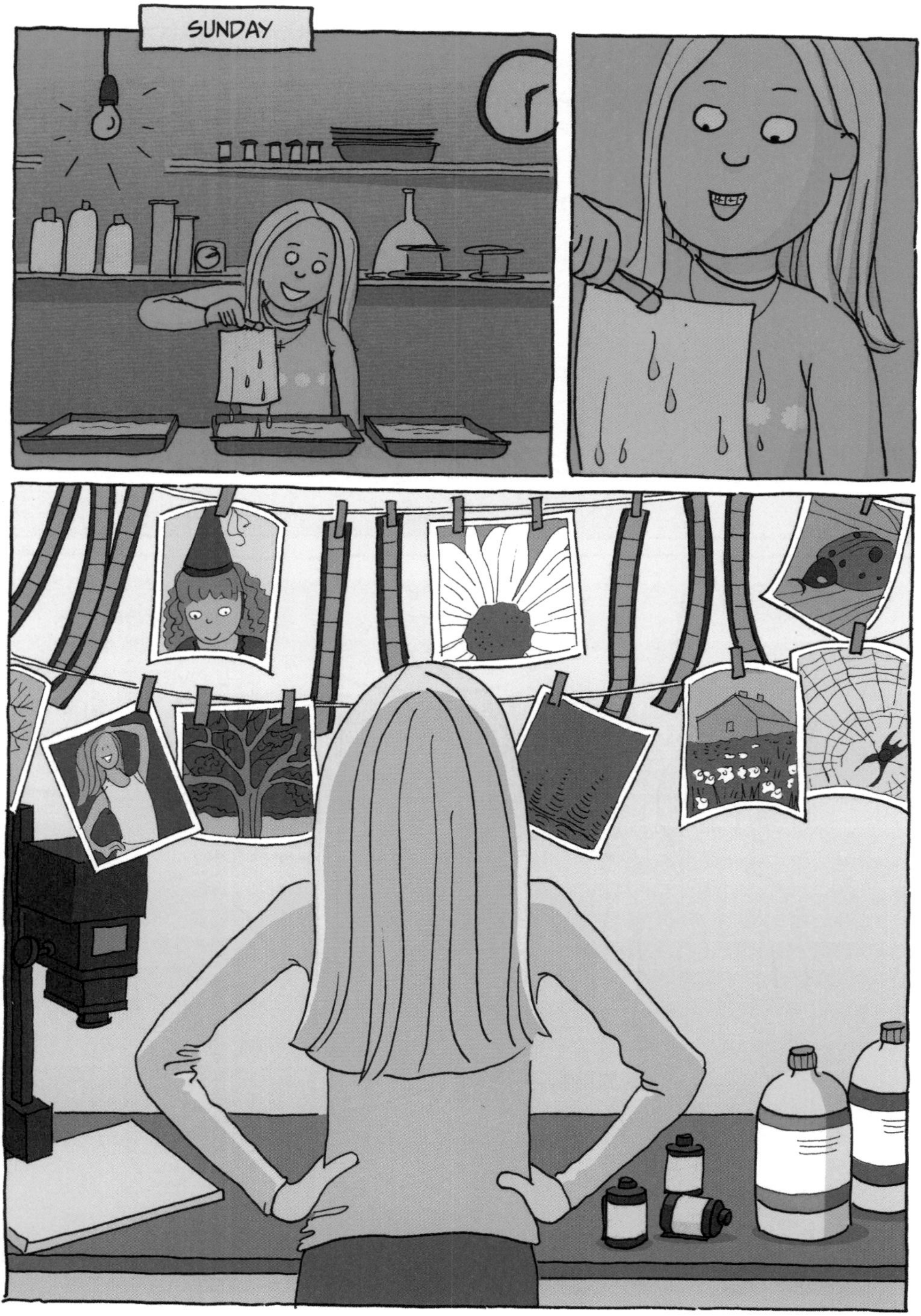
SUNDAY

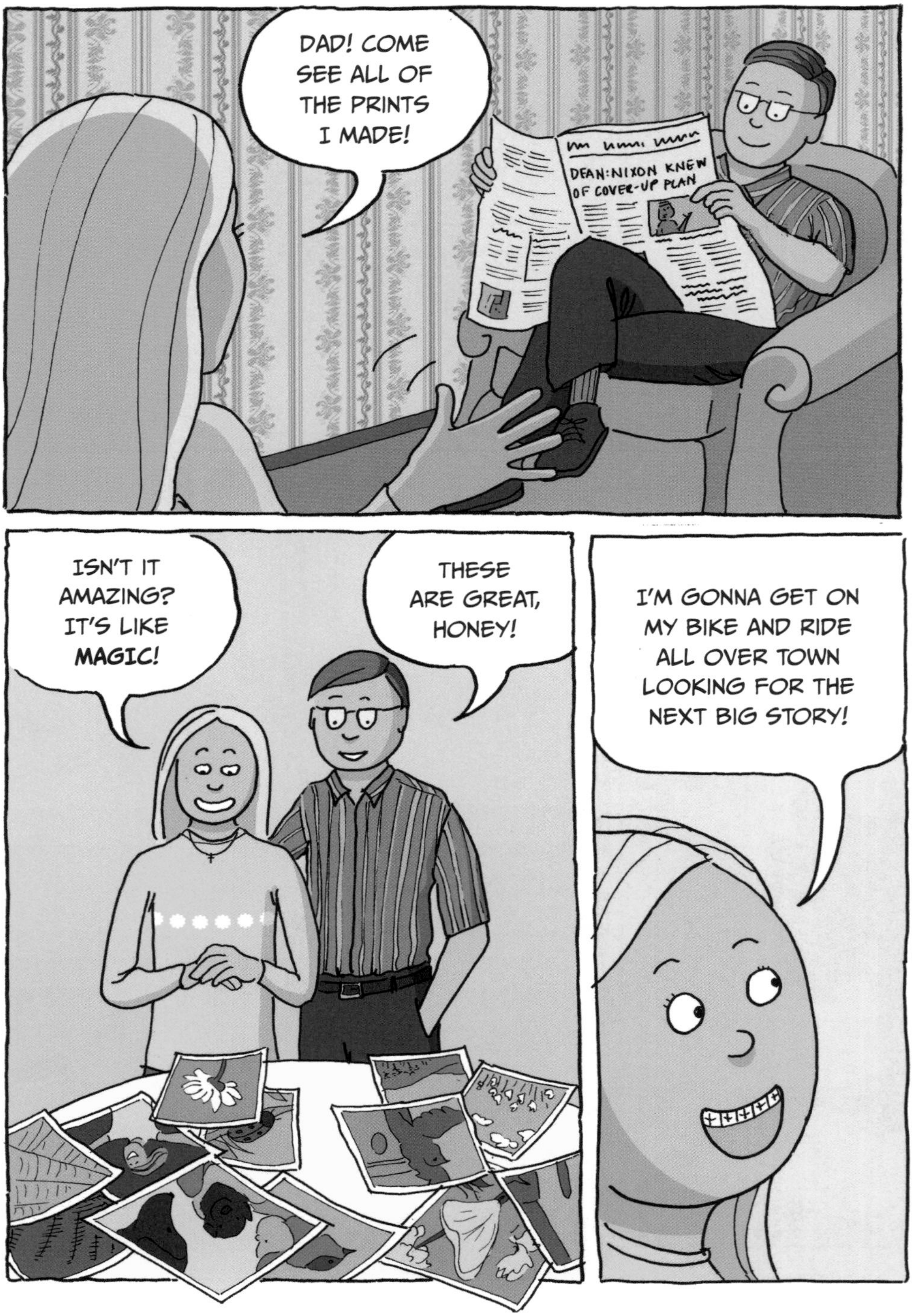
DAD! COME SEE ALL OF THE PRINTS I MADE!
DEAN: NIXON KNEW OF COVER-UP PLAN
ISN'T IT AMAZING? IT'S LIKE **MAGIC**!
THESE ARE GREAT, HONEY!
I'M GONNA GET ON MY BIKE AND RIDE ALL OVER TOWN LOOKING FOR THE NEXT BIG STORY!

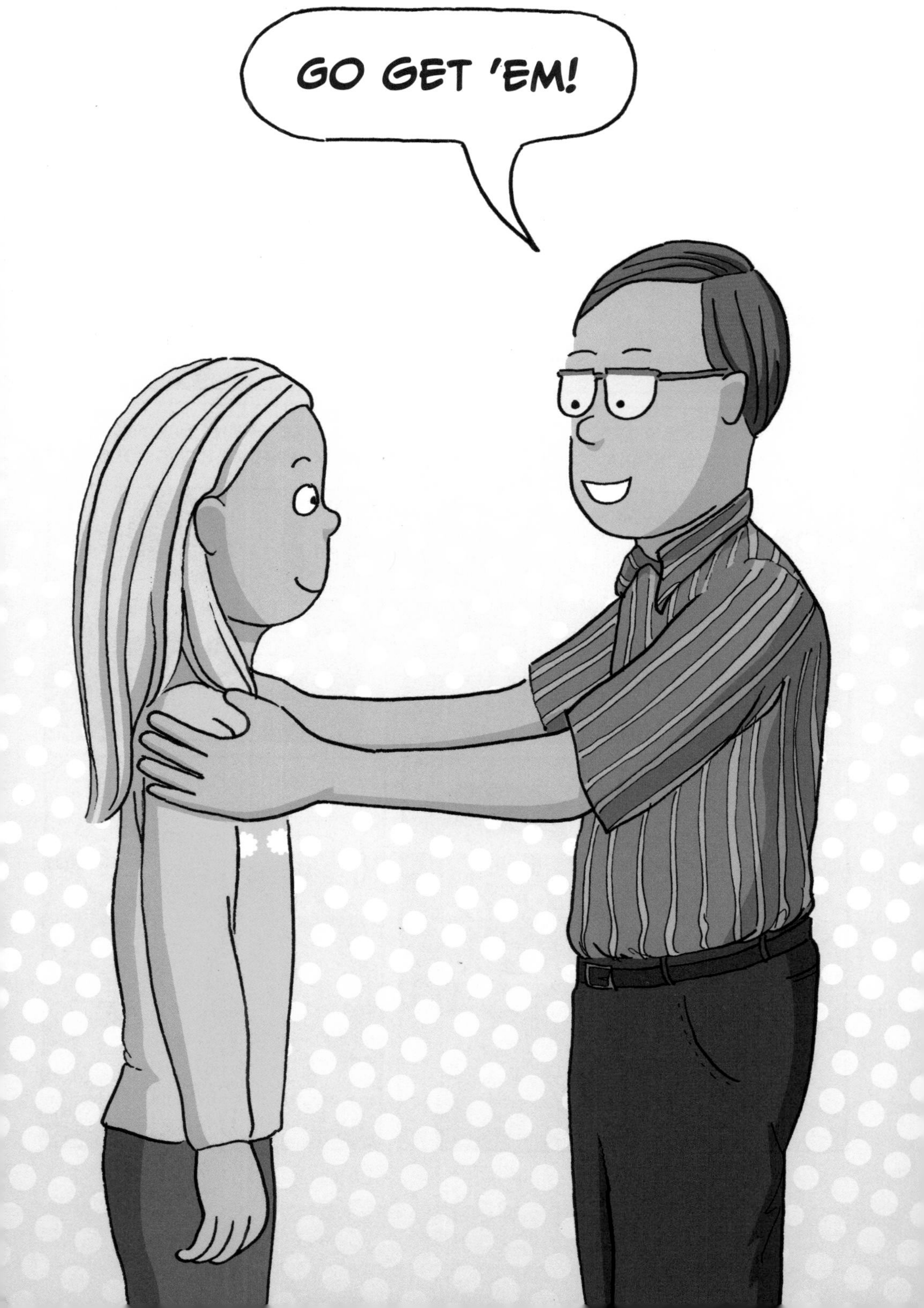
GO GET 'EM!

Chapter 16

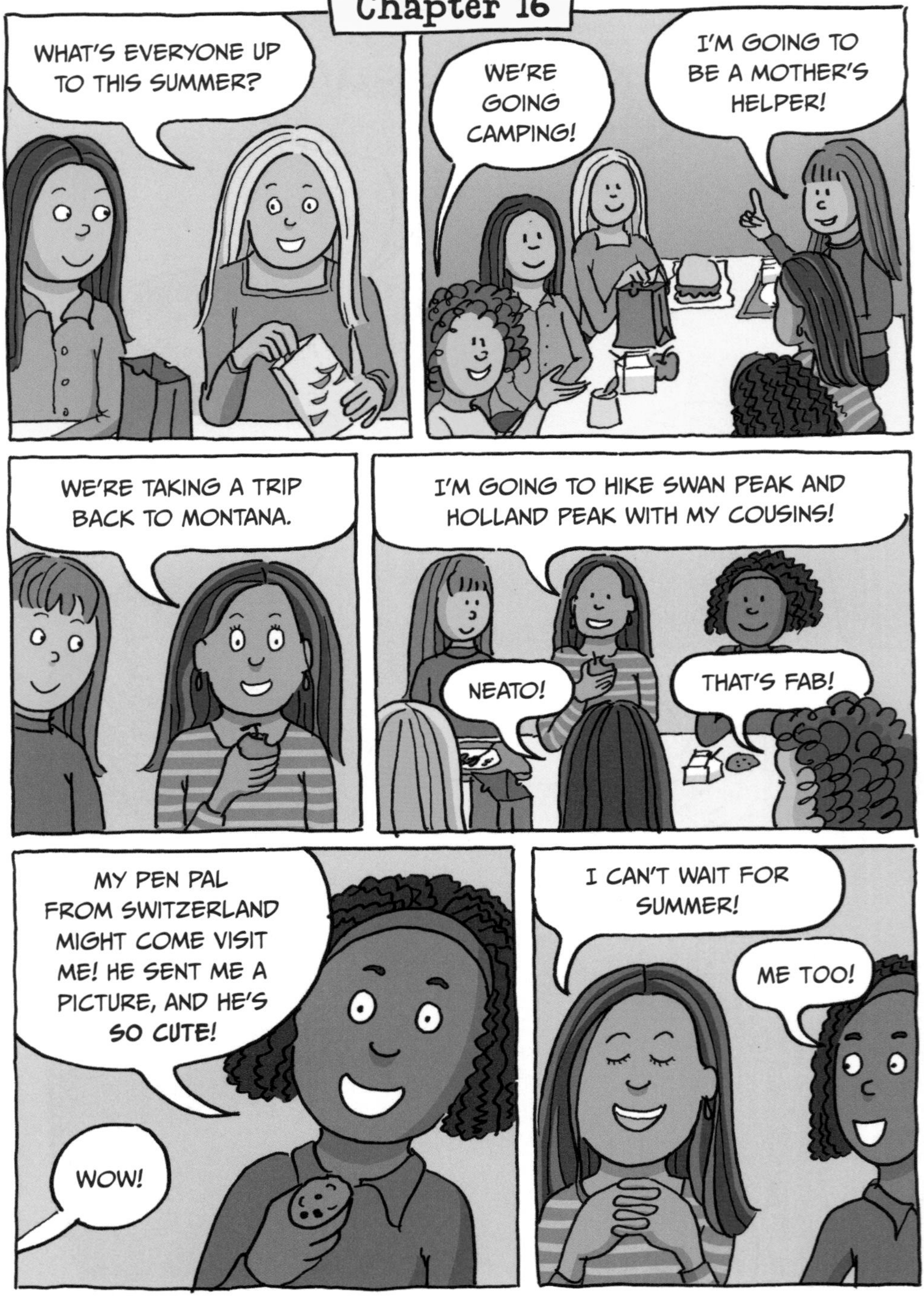
WHAT'S EVERYONE UP TO THIS SUMMER?
WE'RE GOING CAMPING!
I'M GOING TO BE A MOTHER'S HELPER!
WE'RE TAKING A TRIP BACK TO MONTANA.
I'M GOING TO HIKE SWAN PEAK AND HOLLAND PEAK WITH MY COUSINS!
NEATO!
THAT'S FAB!
MY PEN PAL FROM SWITZERLAND MIGHT COME VISIT ME! HE SENT ME A PICTURE, AND HE'S SO CUTE!
WOW!
I CAN'T WAIT FOR SUMMER!
ME TOO!

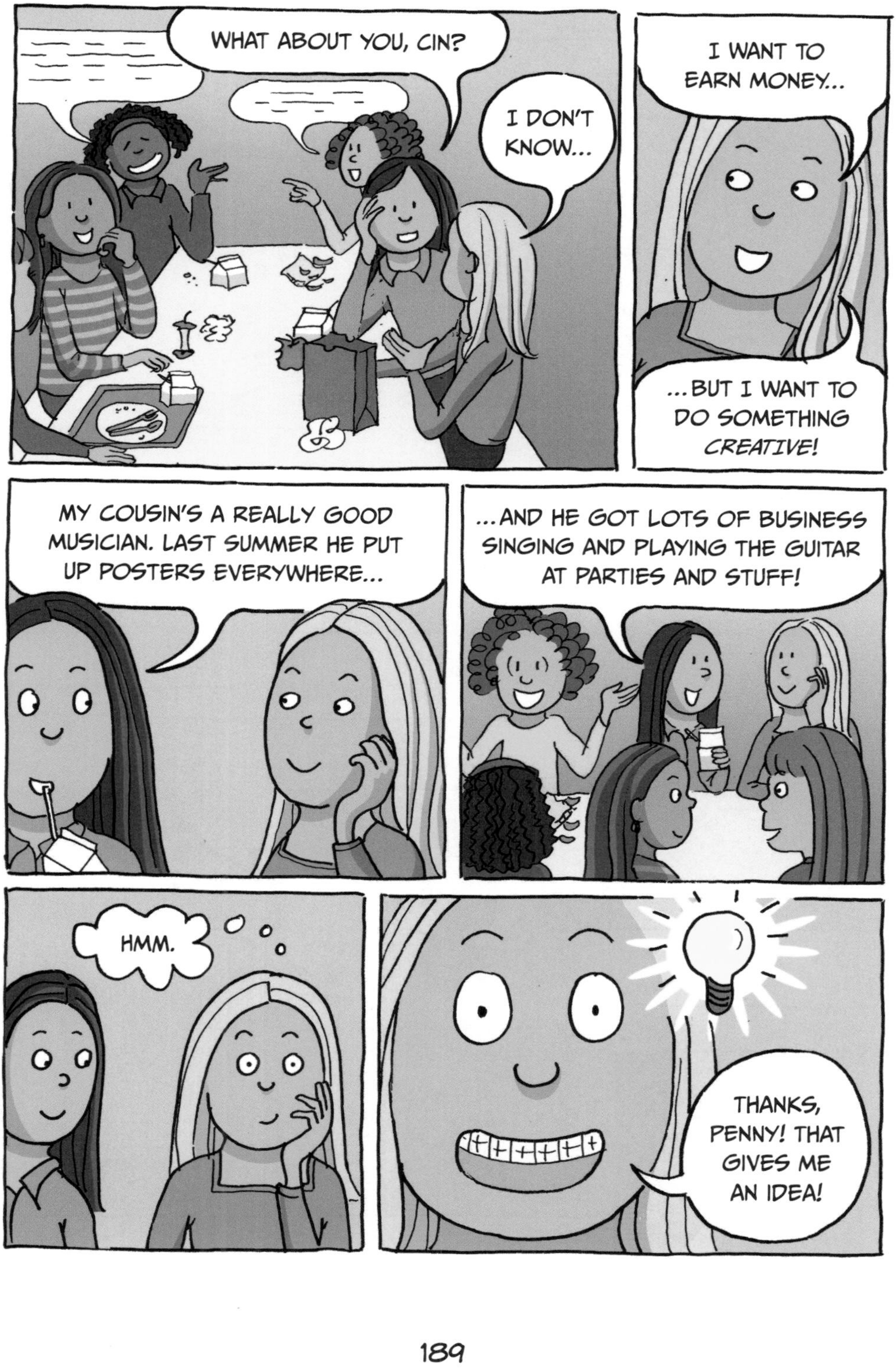
WHAT ABOUT YOU, CIN?
I DON'T KNOW...
I WANT TO EARN MONEY...
...BUT I WANT TO DO SOMETHING *CREATIVE!*
MY COUSIN'S A REALLY GOOD MUSICIAN. LAST SUMMER HE PUT UP POSTERS EVERYWHERE...
...AND HE GOT LOTS OF BUSINESS SINGING AND PLAYING THE GUITAR AT PARTIES AND STUFF!
HMM.
THANKS, PENNY! THAT GIVES ME AN IDEA!

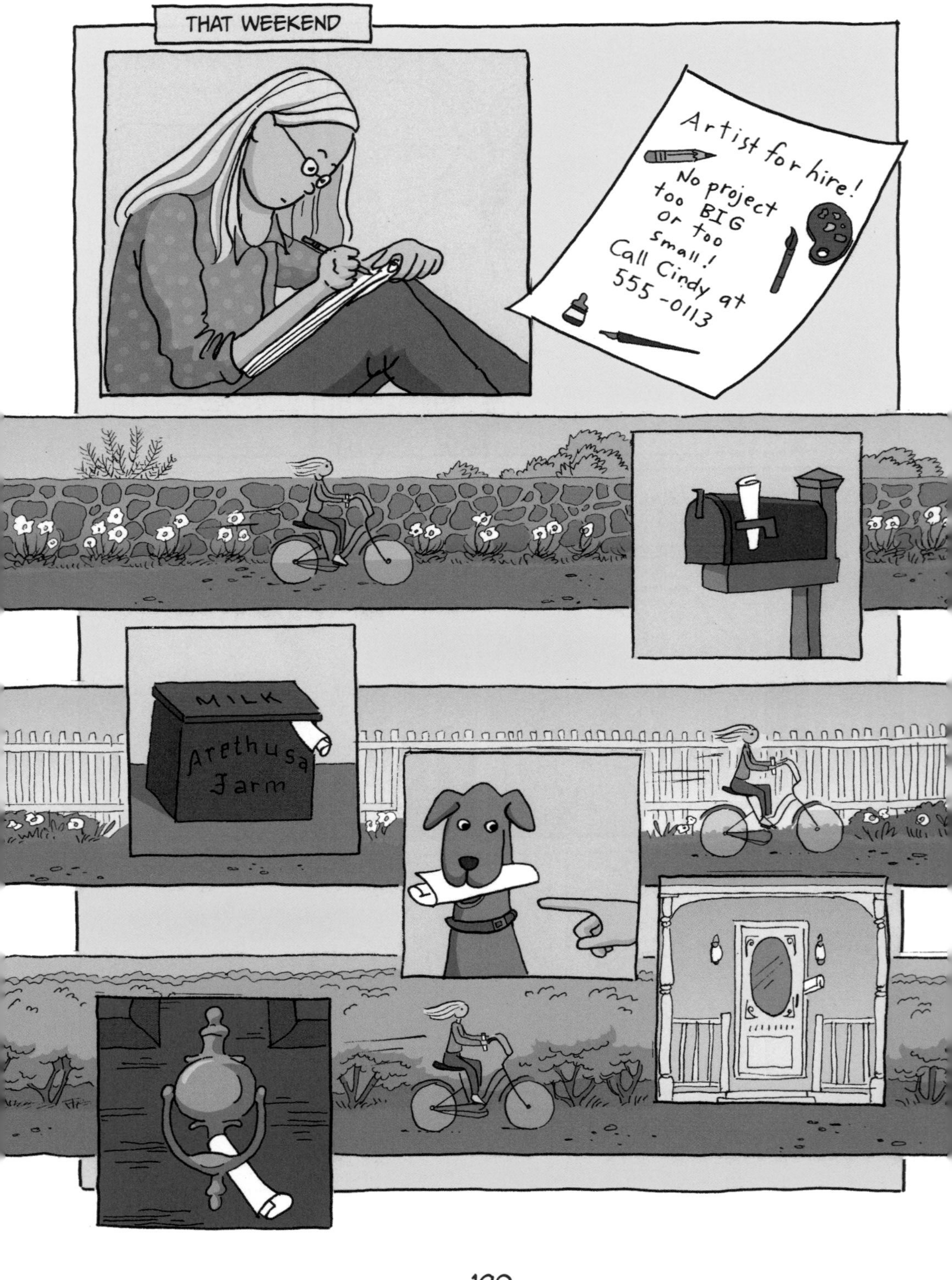
THAT WEEKEND
Artist for hire!
No project too BIG or too small!
Call Cindy at 555-0113
MILK
Arethusa Farm

AFTER I DELIVER THE FLYERS, I STAY NEAR THE PHONE. I DON'T WANT TO MISS A CALL!

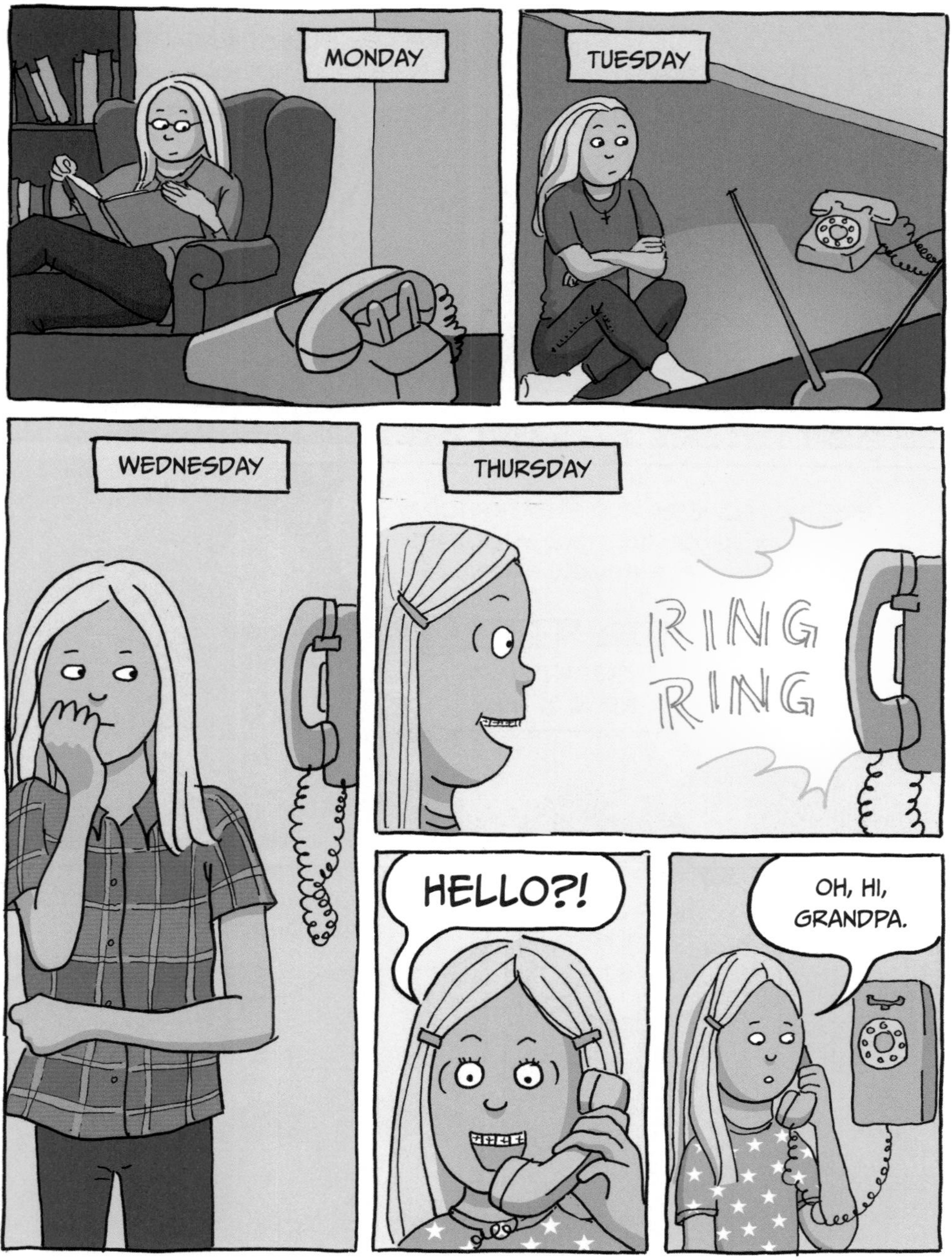
MONDAY
TUESDAY
WEDNESDAY
THURSDAY
RING
RING
HELLO?!
OH, HI, GRANDPA.

EVERYONE'S DISTRACTED BY SUMMER PLANS. THE TEACHERS TRY ALL SORTS OF TRICKS TO KEEP US "ENGAGED."

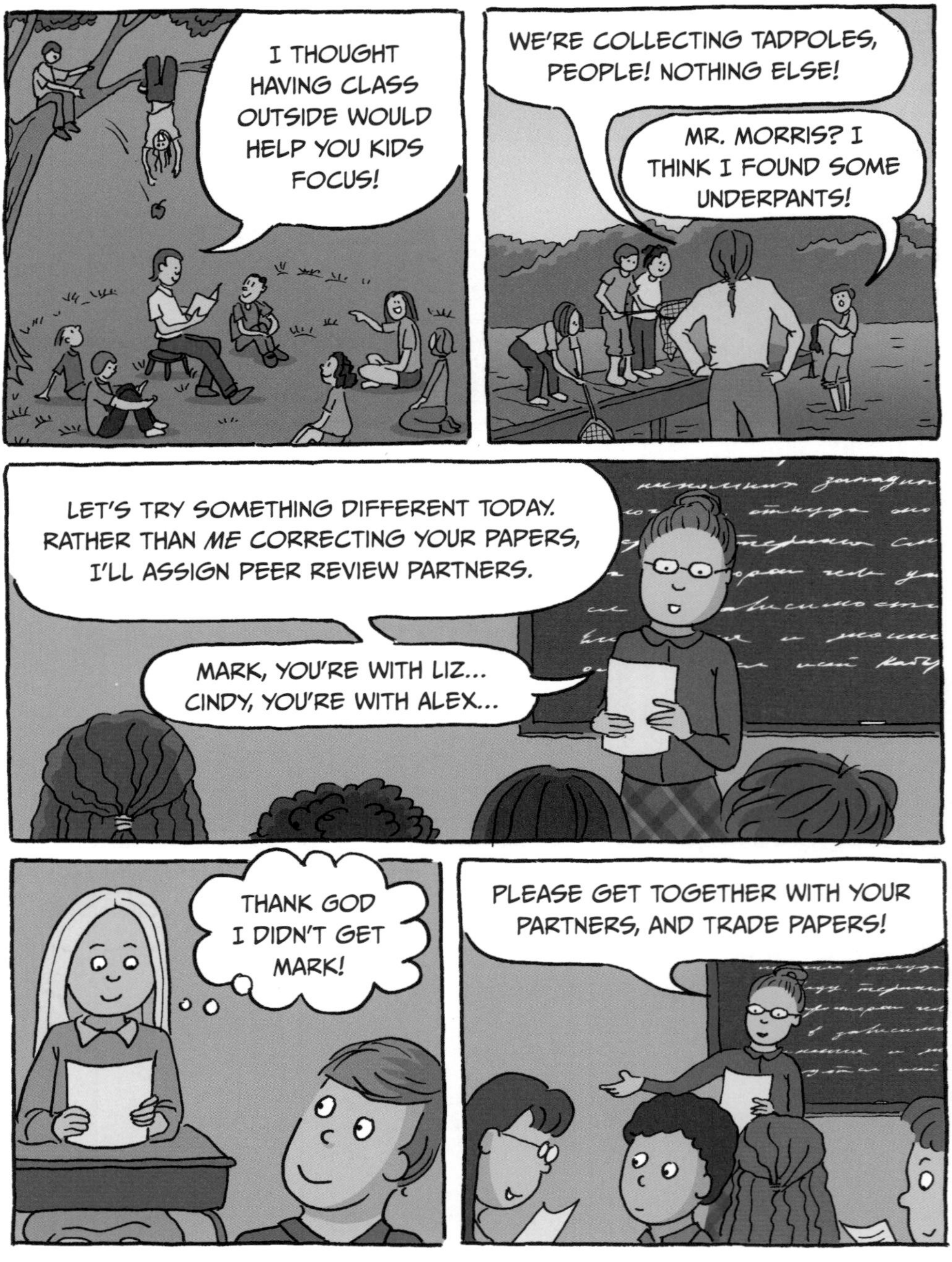
I THOUGHT HAVING CLASS OUTSIDE WOULD HELP YOU KIDS FOCUS!
WE'RE COLLECTING TADPOLES, PEOPLE! NOTHING ELSE!
MR. MORRIS? I THINK I FOUND SOME UNDERPANTS!
LET'S TRY SOMETHING DIFFERENT TODAY. RATHER THAN *ME* CORRECTING YOUR PAPERS, I'LL ASSIGN PEER REVIEW PARTNERS.
MARK, YOU'RE WITH LIZ... CINDY, YOU'RE WITH ALEX...
THANK GOD I DIDN'T GET MARK!
PLEASE GET TOGETHER WITH YOUR PARTNERS, AND TRADE PAPERS!

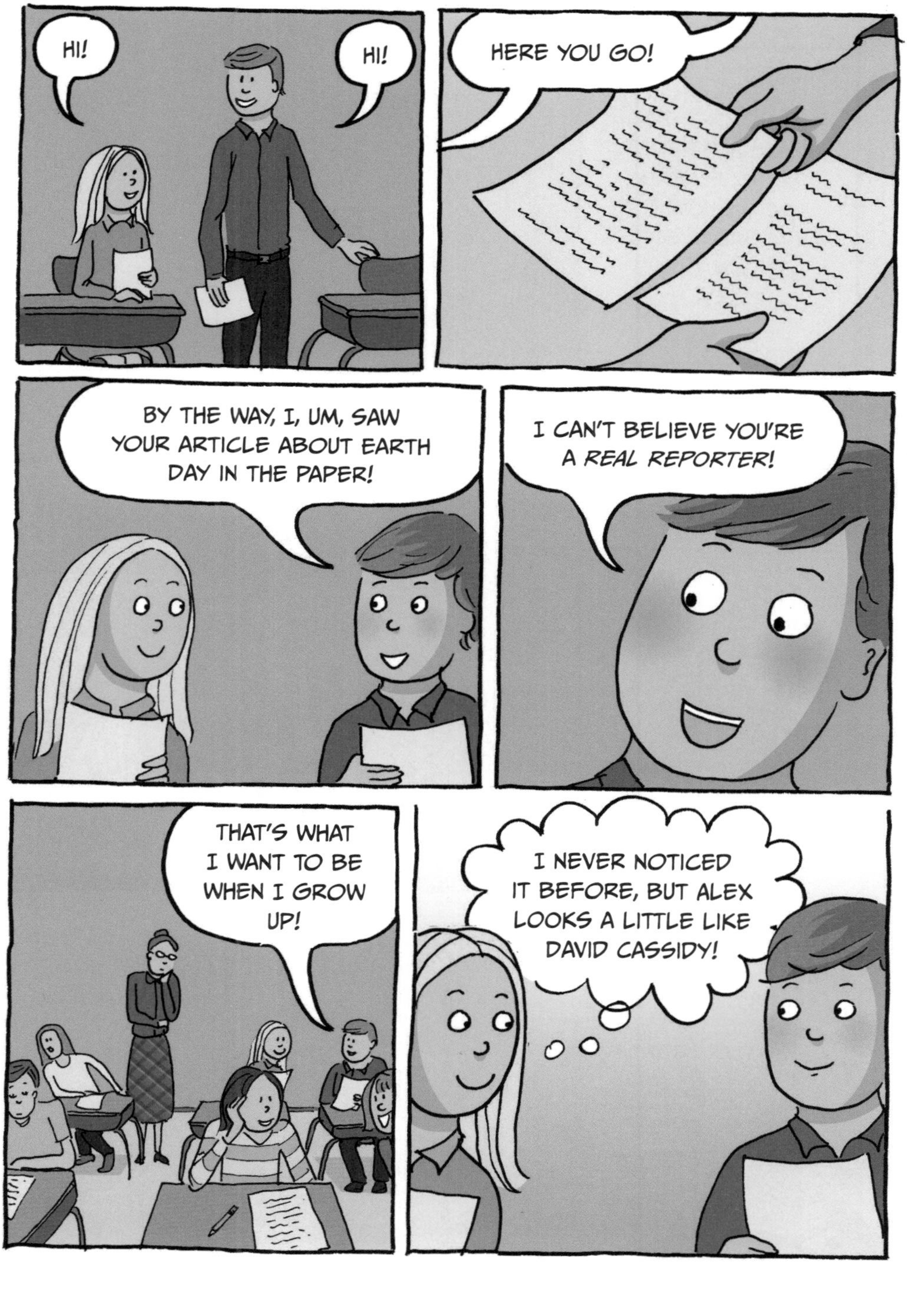
HI!
HI!
HERE YOU GO!
BY THE WAY, I, UM, SAW YOUR ARTICLE ABOUT EARTH DAY IN THE PAPER!
I CAN'T BELIEVE YOU'RE A *REAL REPORTER!*
THAT'S WHAT I WANT TO BE WHEN I GROW UP!
I NEVER NOTICED IT BEFORE, BUT ALEX LOOKS A LITTLE LIKE DAVID CASSIDY!

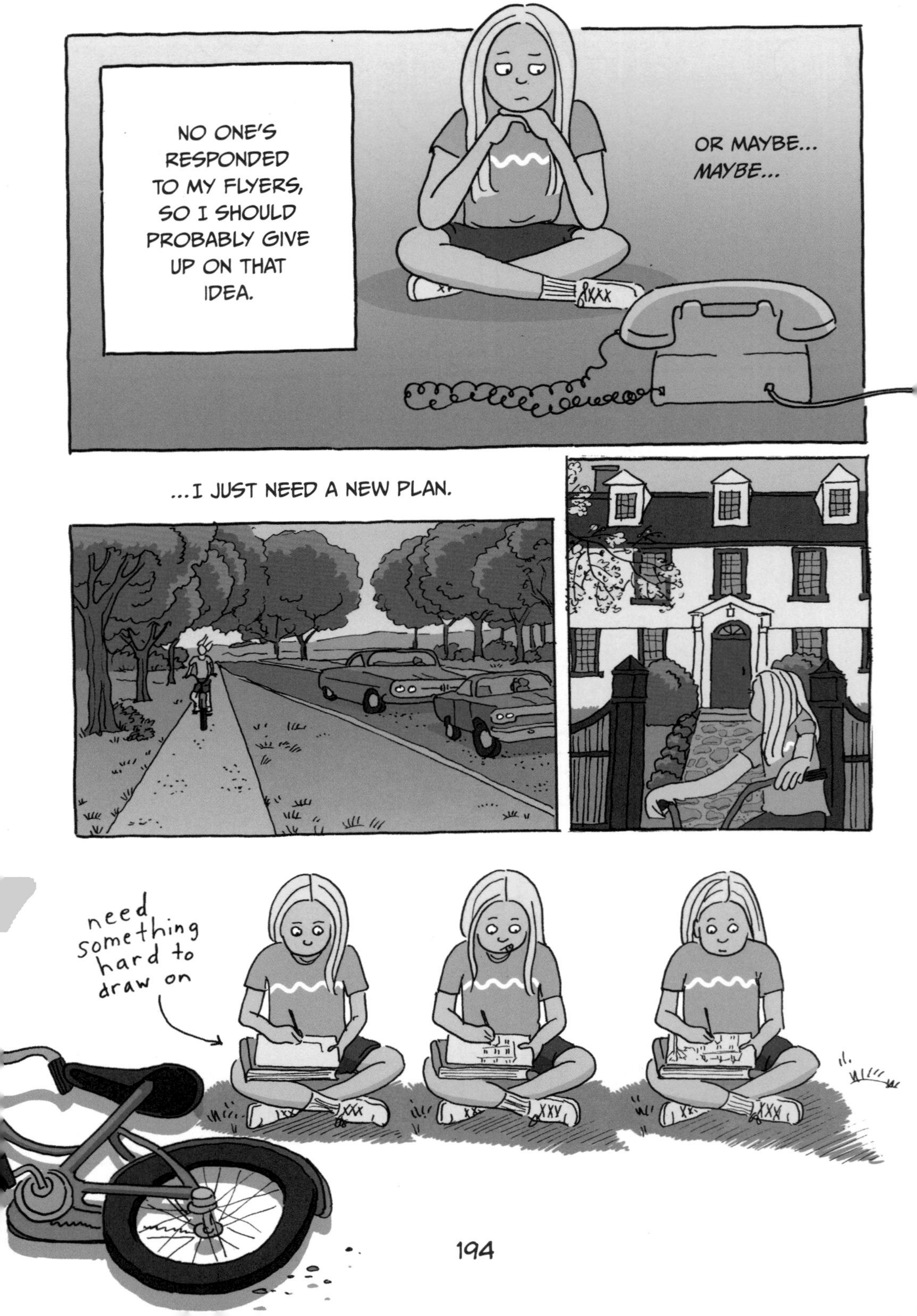
NO ONE'S RESPONDED TO MY FLYERS, SO I SHOULD PROBABLY GIVE UP ON THAT IDEA.
OR MAYBE... MAYBE...
...I JUST NEED A NEW PLAN.
need something hard to draw on

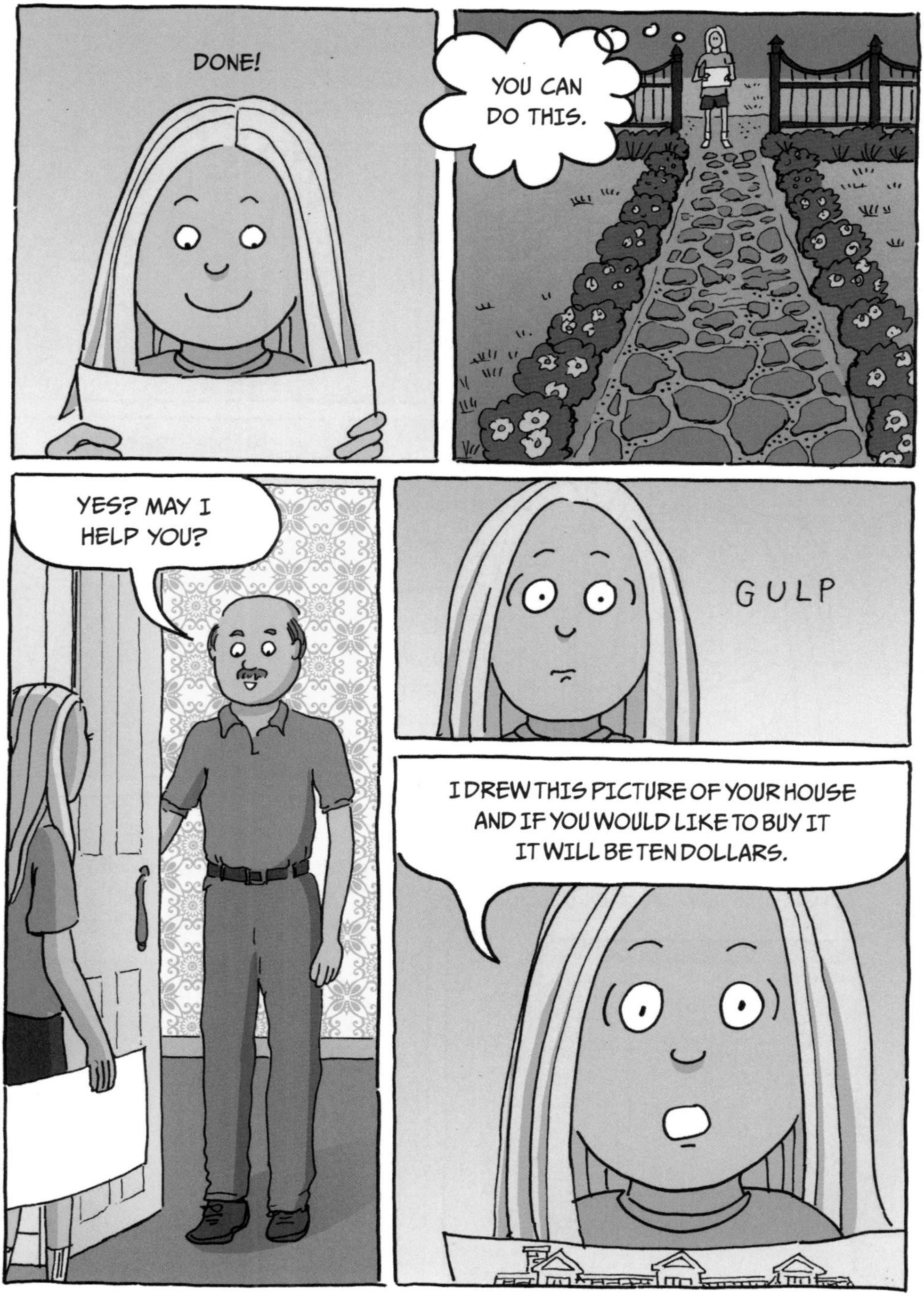
DONE!
YOU CAN DO THIS.
YES? MAY I HELP YOU?
GULP
I DREW THIS PICTURE OF YOUR HOUSE AND IF YOU WOULD LIKE TO BUY IT IT WILL BE TEN DOLLARS.

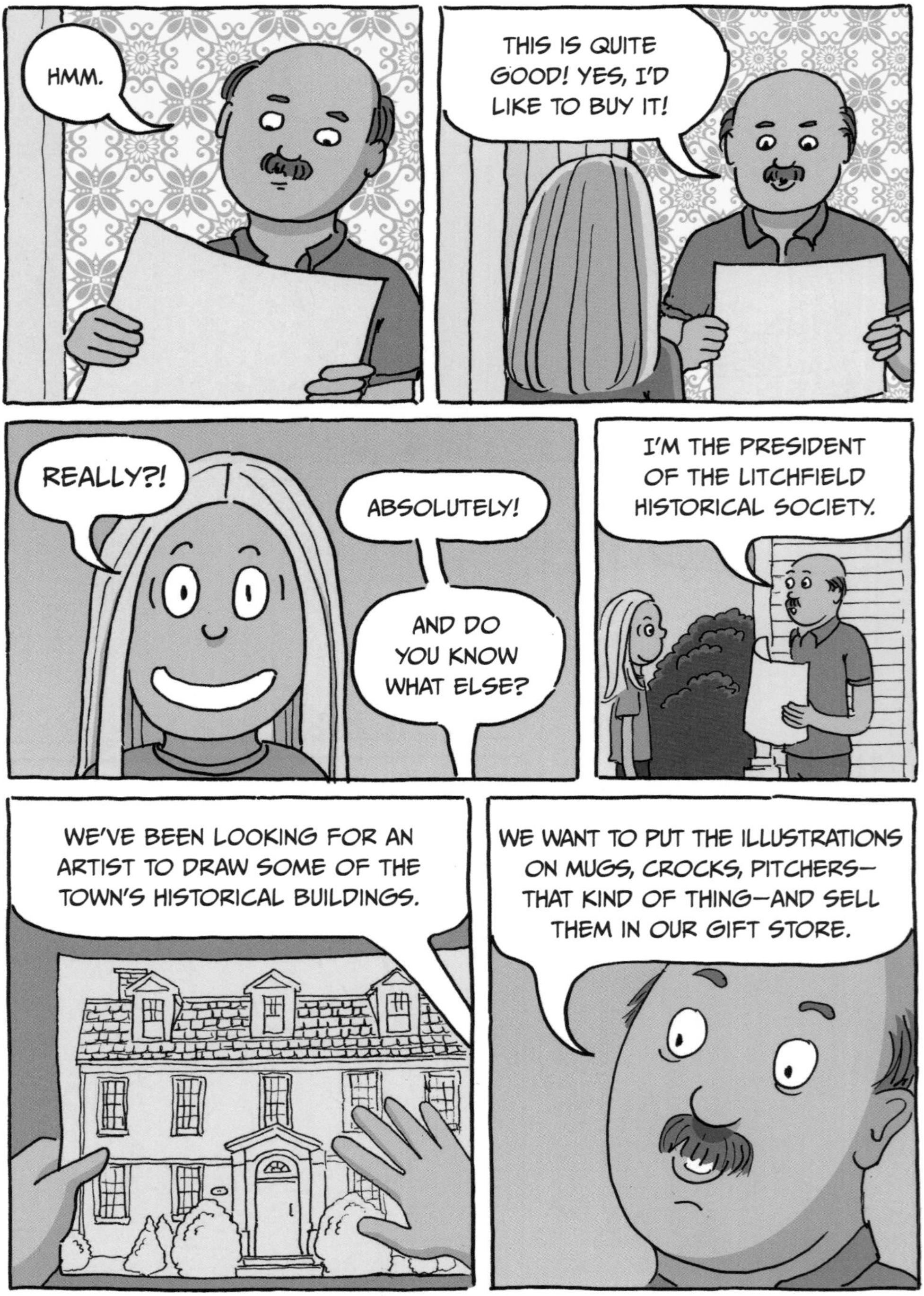
HMM.
THIS IS QUITE GOOD! YES, I'D LIKE TO BUY IT!
REALLY?!
ABSOLUTELY!
AND DO YOU KNOW WHAT ELSE?
I'M THE PRESIDENT OF THE LITCHFIELD HISTORICAL SOCIETY.
WE'VE BEEN LOOKING FOR AN ARTIST TO DRAW SOME OF THE TOWN'S HISTORICAL BUILDINGS.
WE WANT TO PUT THE ILLUSTRATIONS ON MUGS, CROCKS, PITCHERS—THAT KIND OF THING—AND SELL THEM IN OUR GIFT STORE.

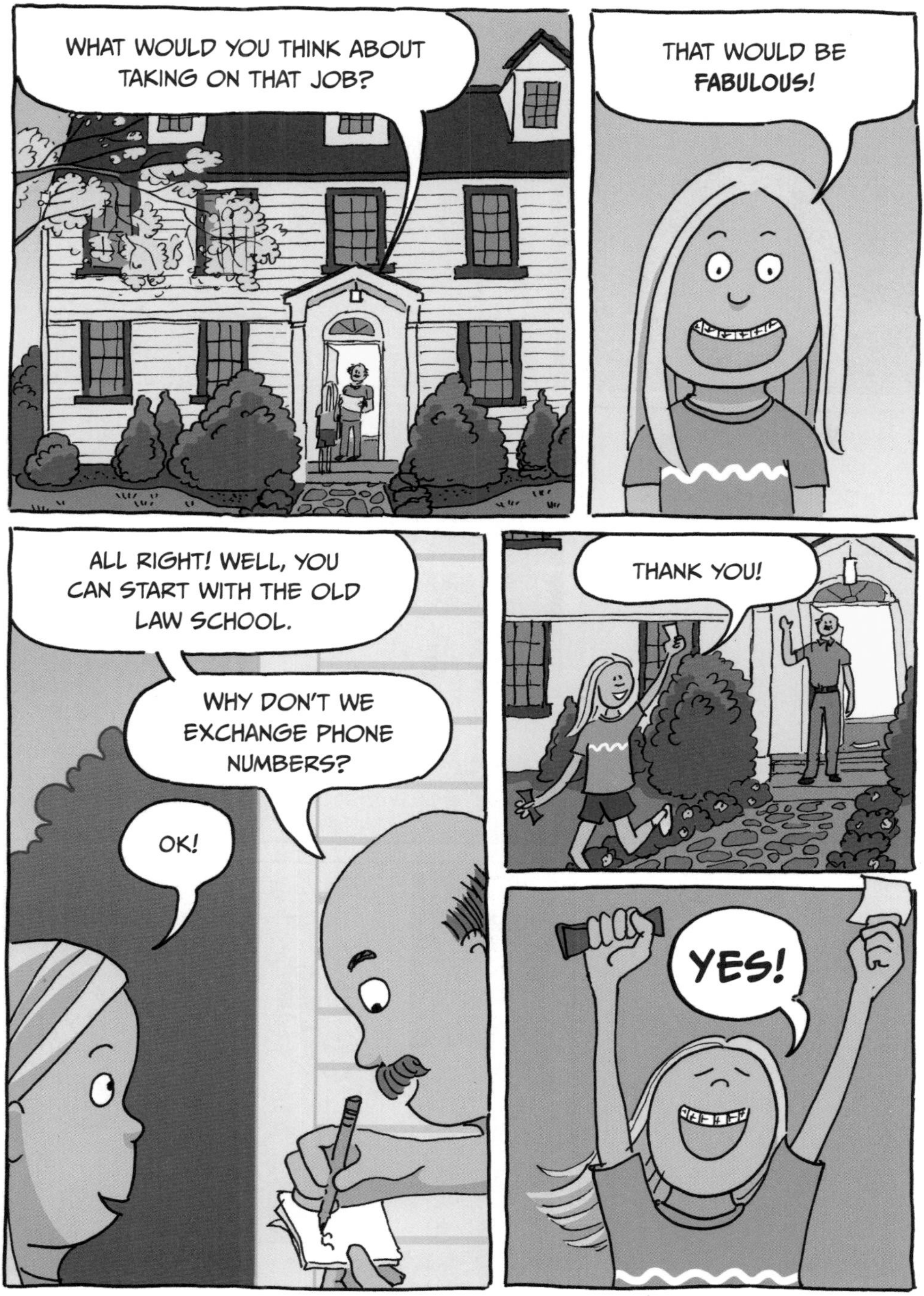
WHAT WOULD YOU THINK ABOUT TAKING ON THAT JOB?
THAT WOULD BE **FABULOUS!**
ALL RIGHT! WELL, YOU CAN START WITH THE OLD LAW SCHOOL.
WHY DON'T WE EXCHANGE PHONE NUMBERS?
OK!
THANK YOU!
YES!

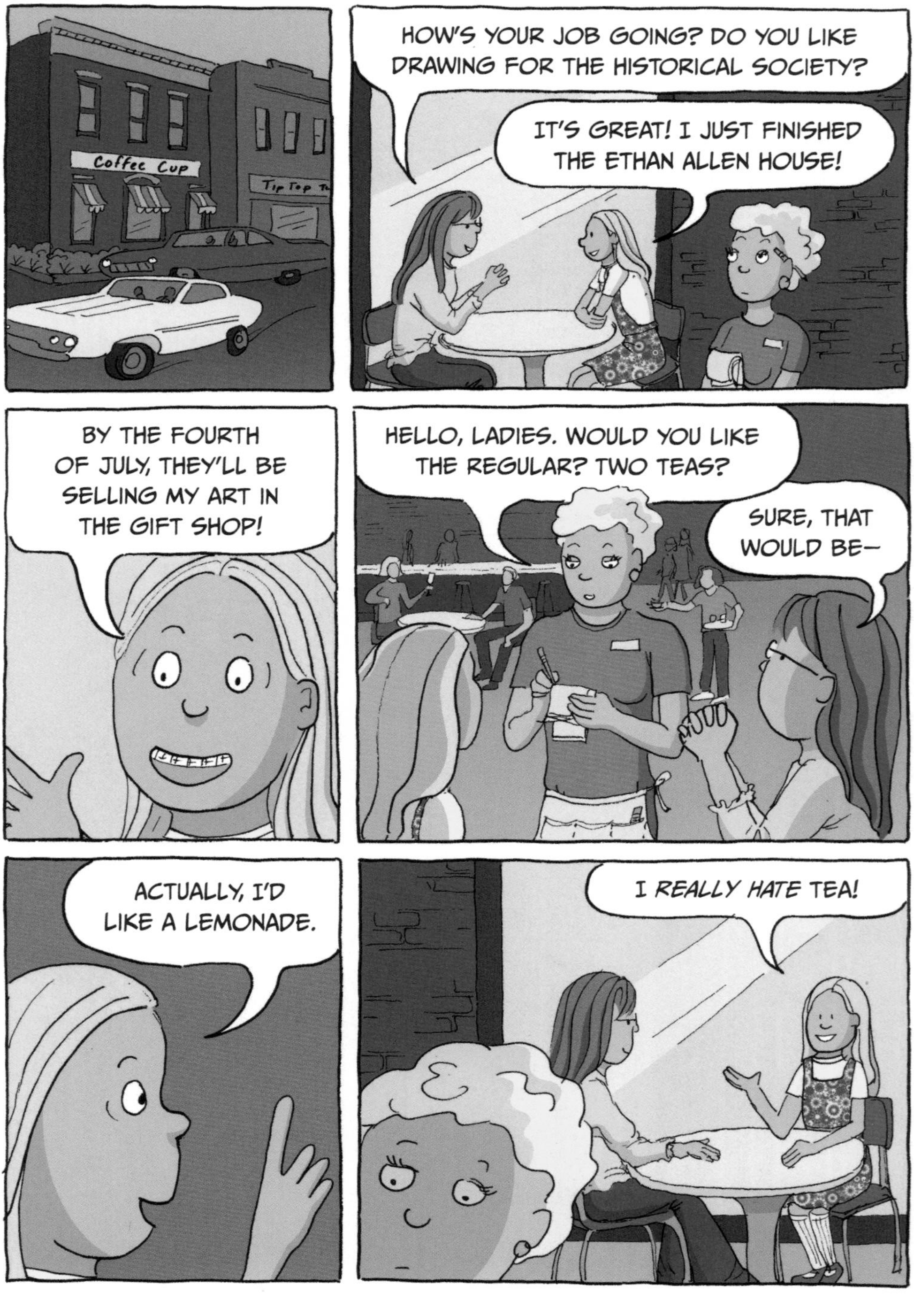
Coffee Cup
Tip Top
HOW'S YOUR JOB GOING? DO YOU LIKE DRAWING FOR THE HISTORICAL SOCIETY?
IT'S GREAT! I JUST FINISHED THE ETHAN ALLEN HOUSE!
BY THE FOURTH OF JULY, THEY'LL BE SELLING MY ART IN THE GIFT SHOP!
HELLO, LADIES. WOULD YOU LIKE THE REGULAR? TWO TEAS?
SURE, THAT WOULD BE—
ACTUALLY, I'D LIKE A LEMONADE.
I *REALLY HATE* TEA!

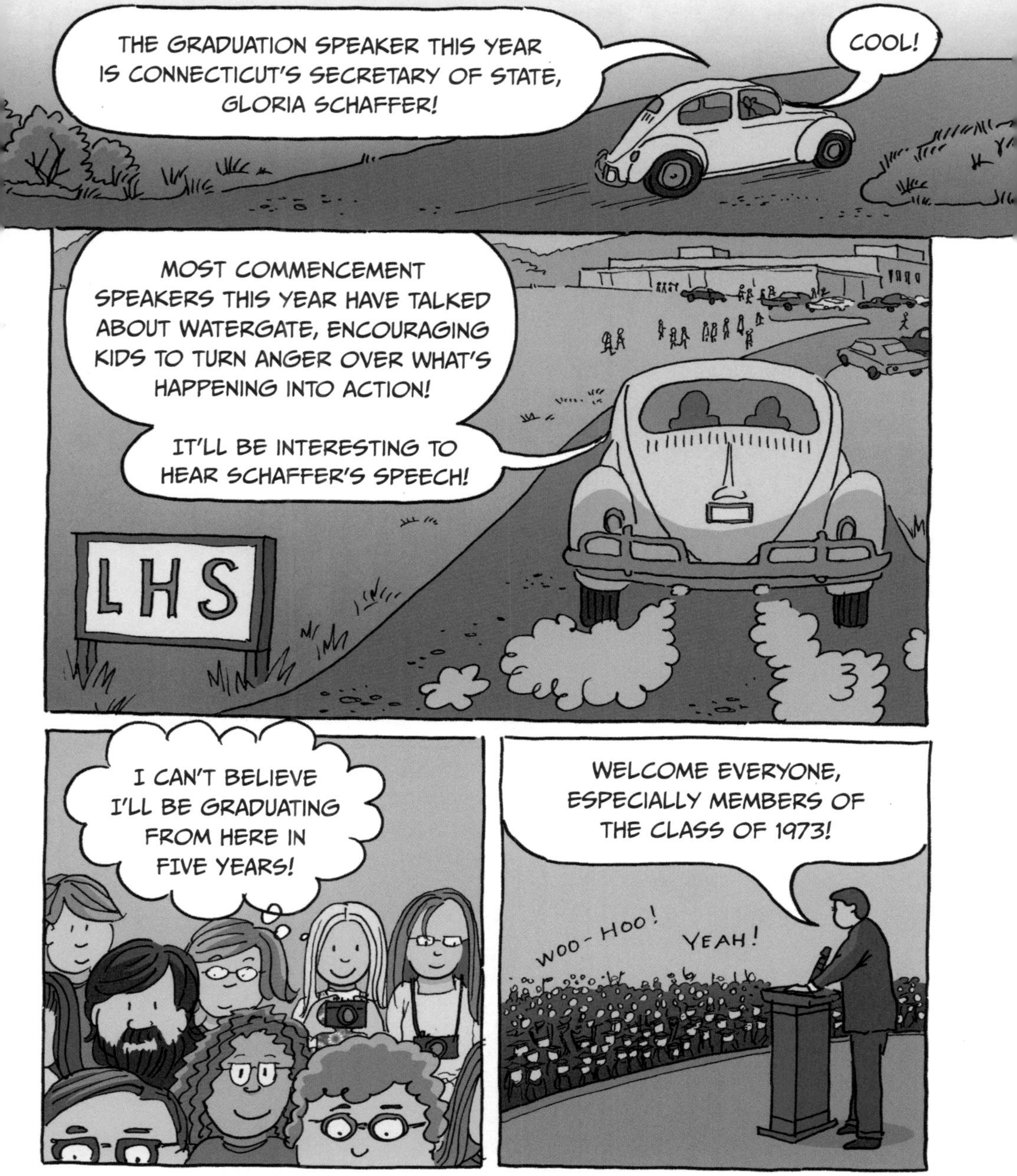
THE GRADUATION SPEAKER THIS YEAR IS CONNECTICUT'S SECRETARY OF STATE, GLORIA SCHAFFER!
COOL!
MOST COMMENCEMENT SPEAKERS THIS YEAR HAVE TALKED ABOUT WATERGATE, ENCOURAGING KIDS TO TURN ANGER OVER WHAT'S HAPPENING INTO ACTION!
IT'LL BE INTERESTING TO HEAR SCHAFFER'S SPEECH!
LHS
I CAN'T BELIEVE I'LL BE GRADUATING FROM HERE IN FIVE YEARS!
WELCOME EVERYONE, ESPECIALLY MEMBERS OF THE CLASS OF 1973!
WOO-HOO!
YEAH!

SUDDENLY, SEVENTH-GRADE PROBLEMS SEEM VERY FAR AWAY...AND VERY INSIGNIFICANT.

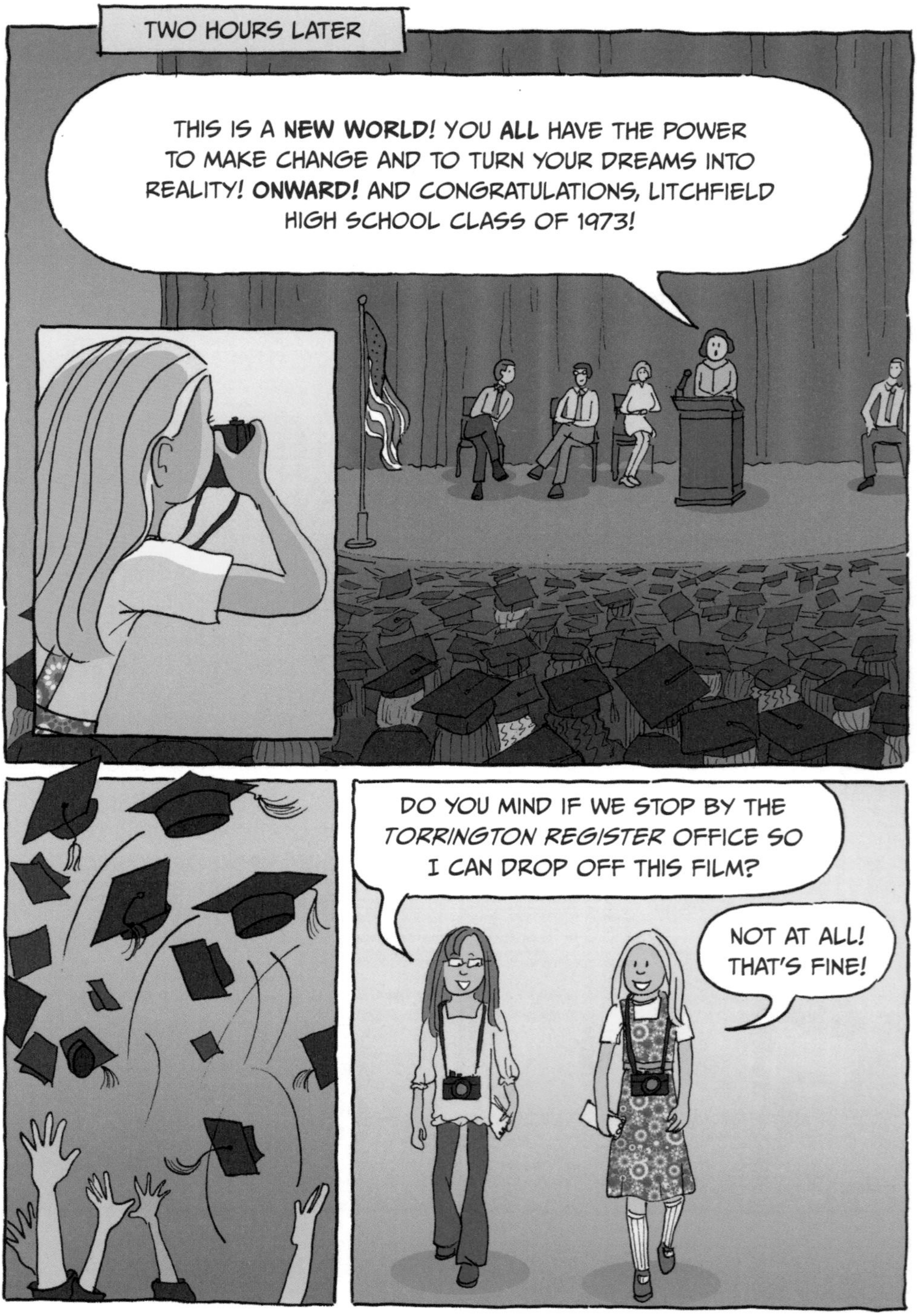
TWO HOURS LATER
THIS IS A **NEW WORLD!** YOU **ALL** HAVE THE POWER TO MAKE CHANGE AND TO TURN YOUR DREAMS INTO REALITY! **ONWARD!** AND CONGRATULATIONS, LITCHFIELD HIGH SCHOOL CLASS OF 1973!
DO YOU MIND IF WE STOP BY THE *TORRINGTON REGISTER* OFFICE SO I CAN DROP OFF THIS FILM?
NOT AT ALL! THAT'S FINE!

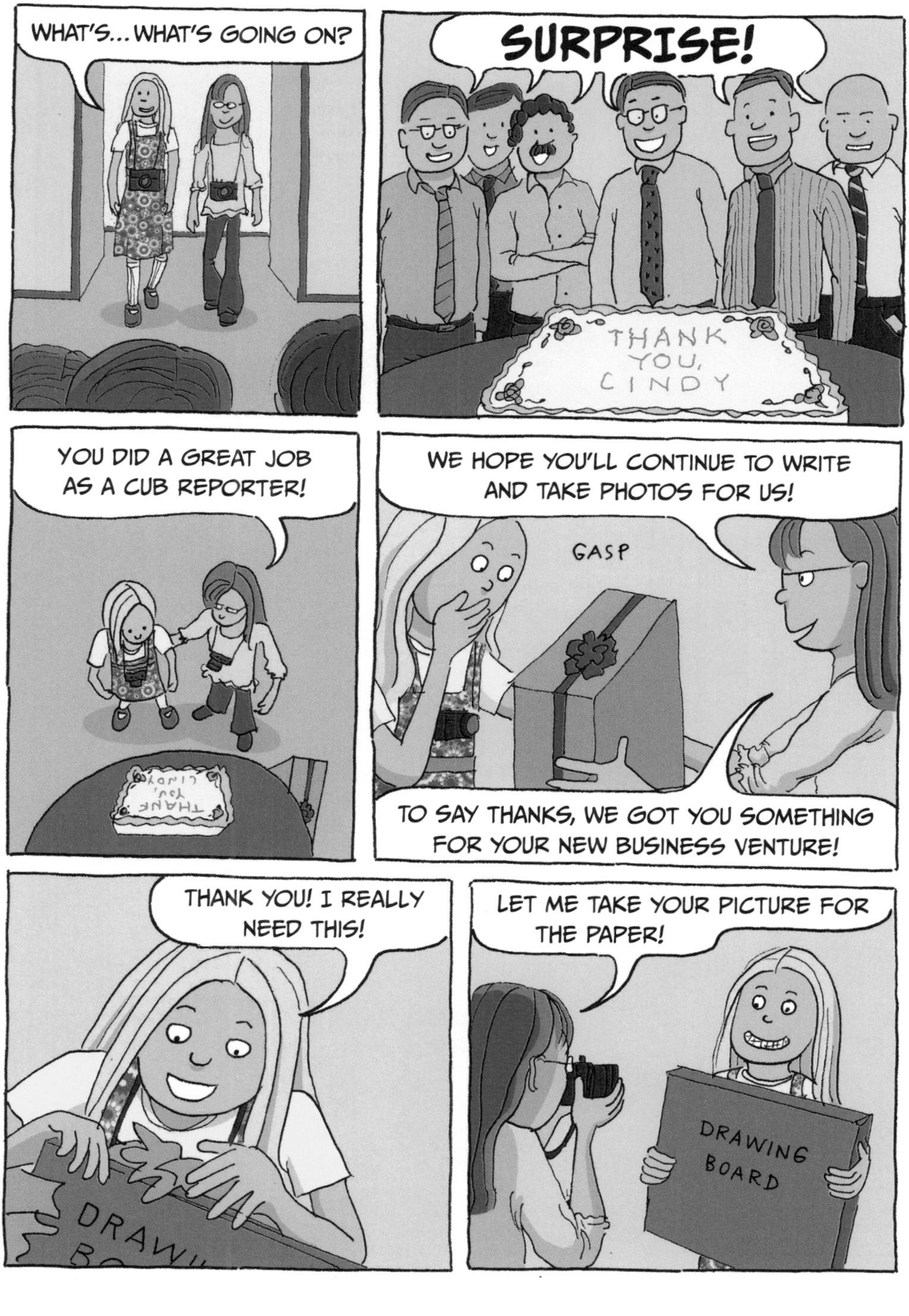
WHAT'S... WHAT'S GOING ON?
SURPRISE!
THANK YOU, CINDY
YOU DID A GREAT JOB AS A CUB REPORTER!
WE HOPE YOU'LL CONTINUE TO WRITE AND TAKE PHOTOS FOR US!
GASP
TO SAY THANKS, WE GOT YOU SOMETHING FOR YOUR NEW BUSINESS VENTURE!
THANK YOU! I REALLY NEED THIS!
LET ME TAKE YOUR PICTURE FOR THE PAPER!
DRAWING BOARD

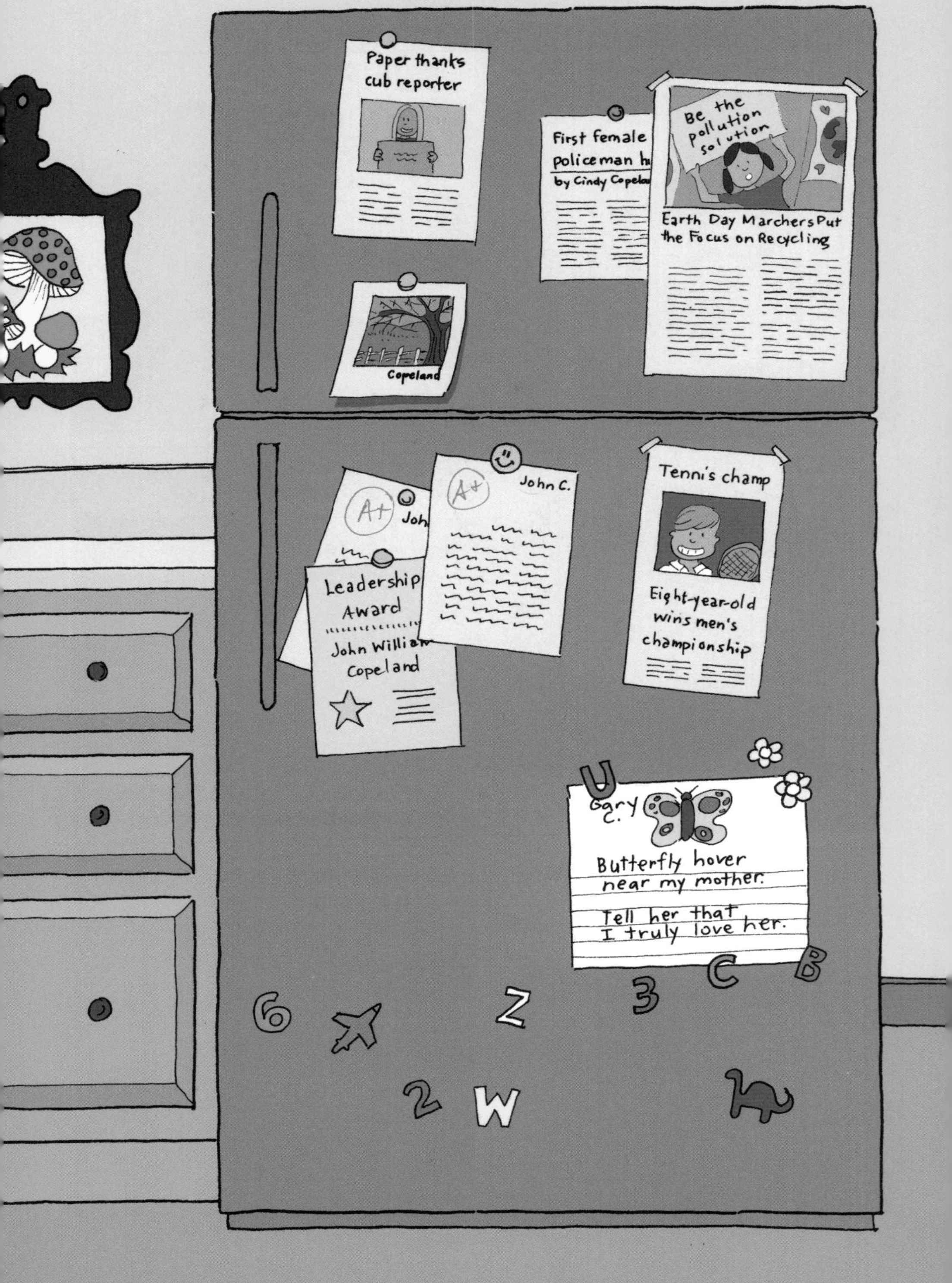

Paper thanks cub reporter
First female policeman h
by Cindy Copela
Be the pollution solution
Earth Day Marchers Put the Focus on Recycling
Copeland
John C.
Leadership Award
John William Copeland
Tennis champ
Eight-year-old wins men's championship
Gary C.
Butterfly hover near my mother.
Tell her that I truly love her.

Chapter 17

WOO-HOO! LAST DAY OF SCHOOL!
YES! WE'RE DONE!
YIPPEE!
NO MORE MATH HOMEWORK!
FINALLY! SUMMER VACATION!
WOOOOO!

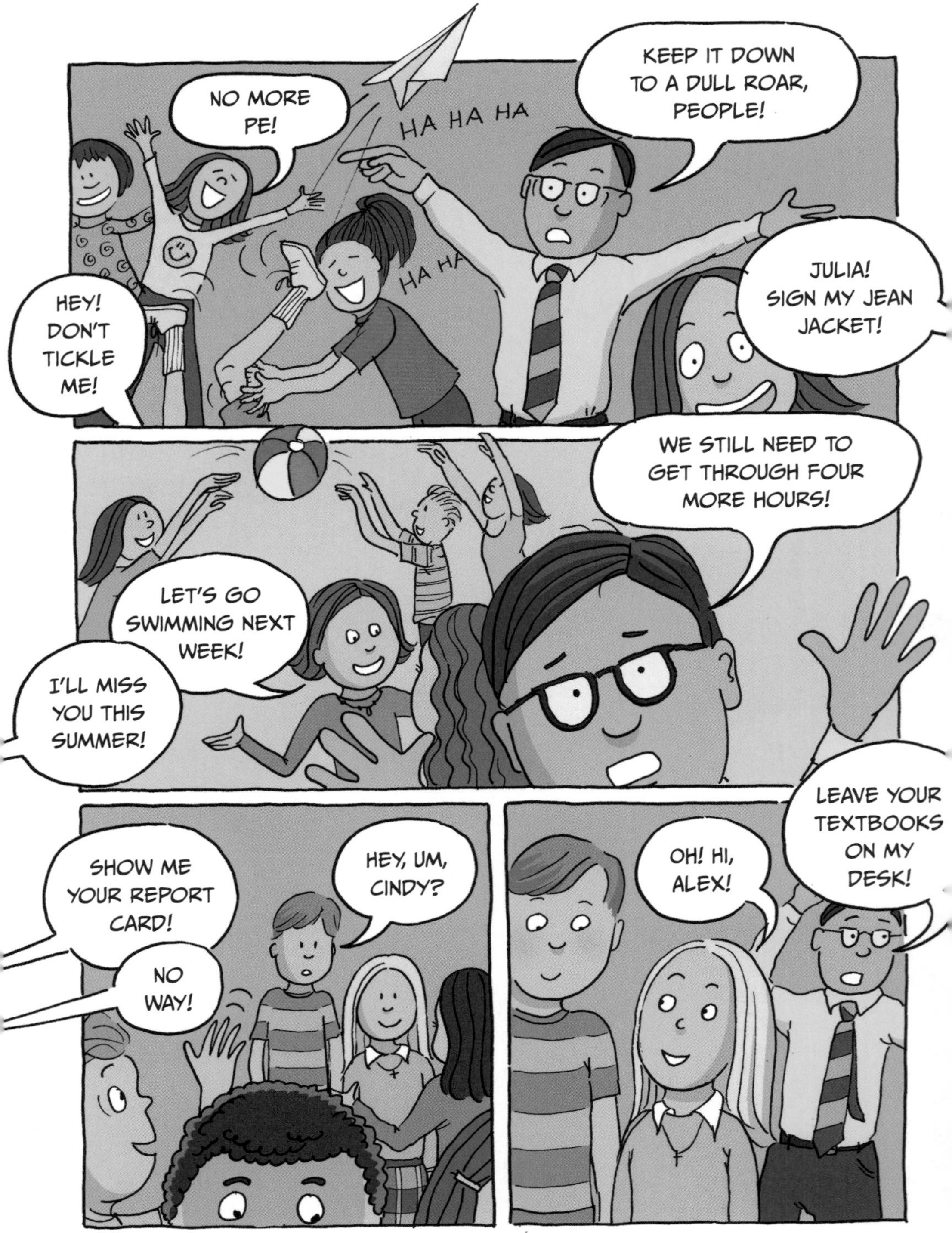
NO MORE PE!
HA HA HA
KEEP IT DOWN TO A DULL ROAR, PEOPLE!
HA HA
HEY! DON'T TICKLE ME!
JULIA! SIGN MY JEAN JACKET!
WE STILL NEED TO GET THROUGH FOUR MORE HOURS!
LET'S GO SWIMMING NEXT WEEK!
I'LL MISS YOU THIS SUMMER!
SHOW ME YOUR REPORT CARD!
HEY, UM, CINDY?
NO WAY!
OH! HI, ALEX!
LEAVE YOUR TEXTBOOKS ON MY DESK!

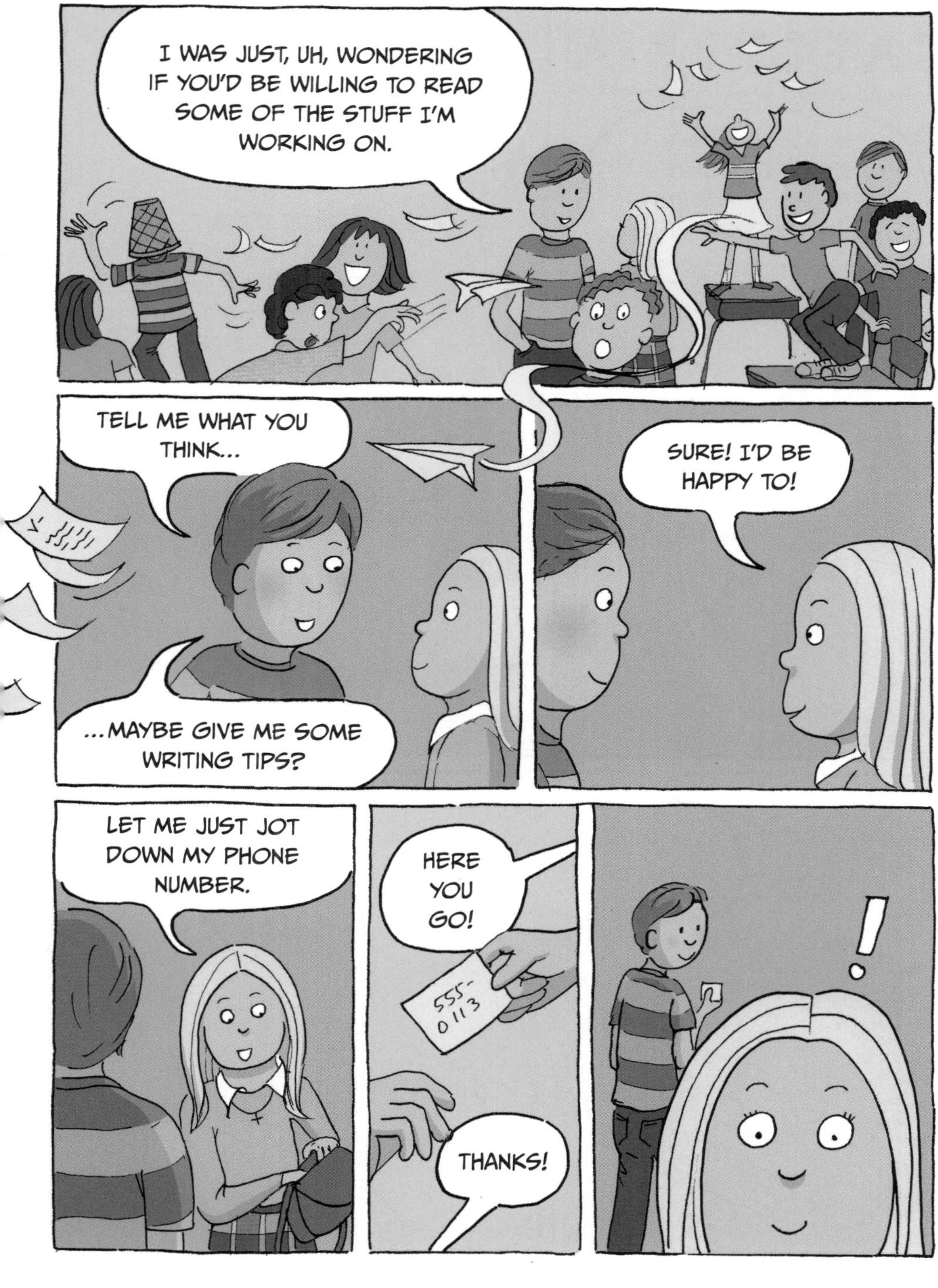
I WAS JUST, UH, WONDERING IF YOU'D BE WILLING TO READ SOME OF THE STUFF I'M WORKING ON.
TELL ME WHAT YOU THINK...
...MAYBE GIVE ME SOME WRITING TIPS?
SURE! I'D BE HAPPY TO!
LET ME JUST JOT DOWN MY PHONE NUMBER.
HERE YOU GO!
555-0113
THANKS!
!

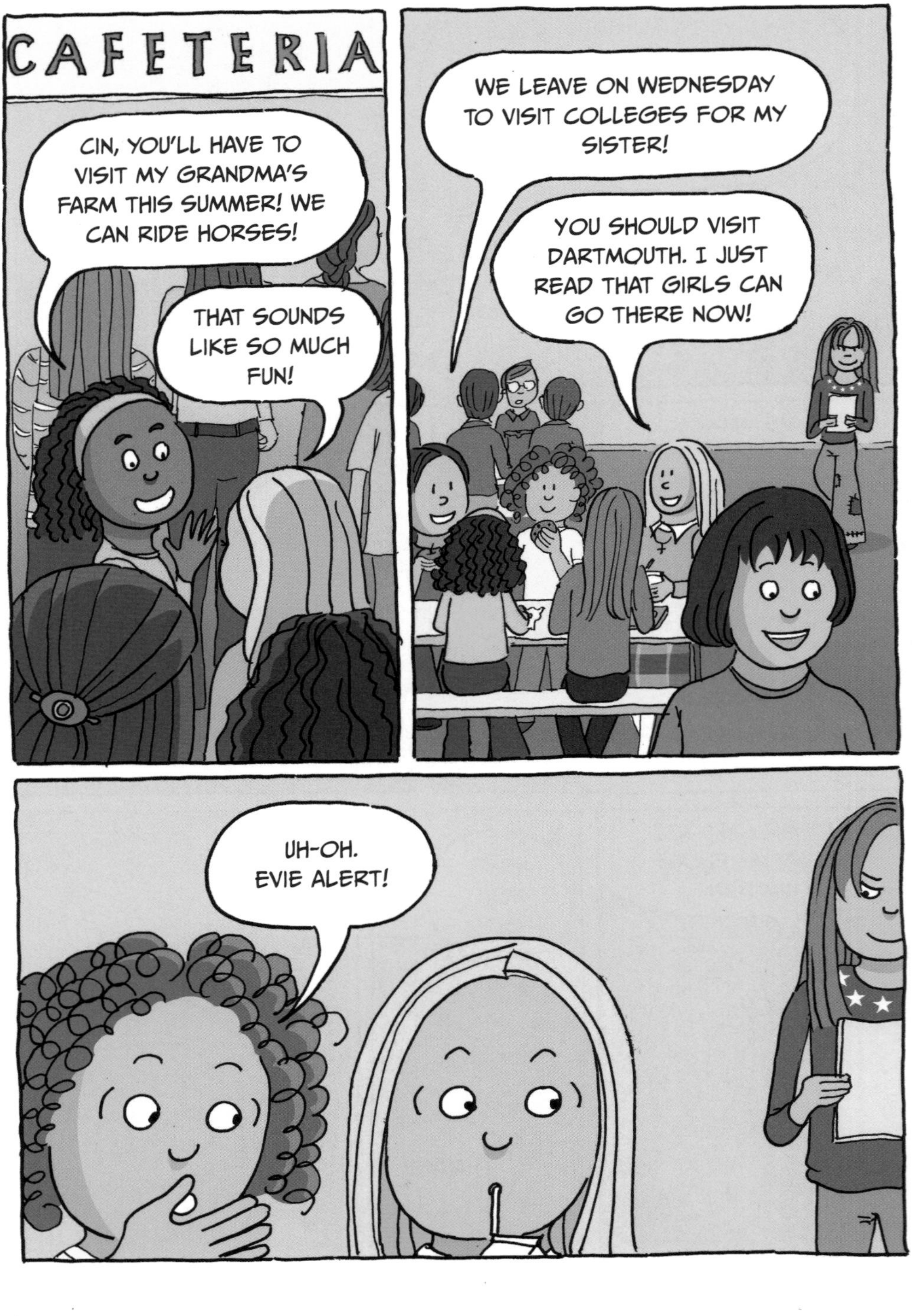
CAFETERIA
CIN, YOU'LL HAVE TO VISIT MY GRANDMA'S FARM THIS SUMMER! WE CAN RIDE HORSES!
THAT SOUNDS LIKE SO MUCH FUN!
WE LEAVE ON WEDNESDAY TO VISIT COLLEGES FOR MY SISTER!
YOU SHOULD VISIT DARTMOUTH. I JUST READ THAT GIRLS CAN GO THERE NOW!
UH-OH. EVIE ALERT!

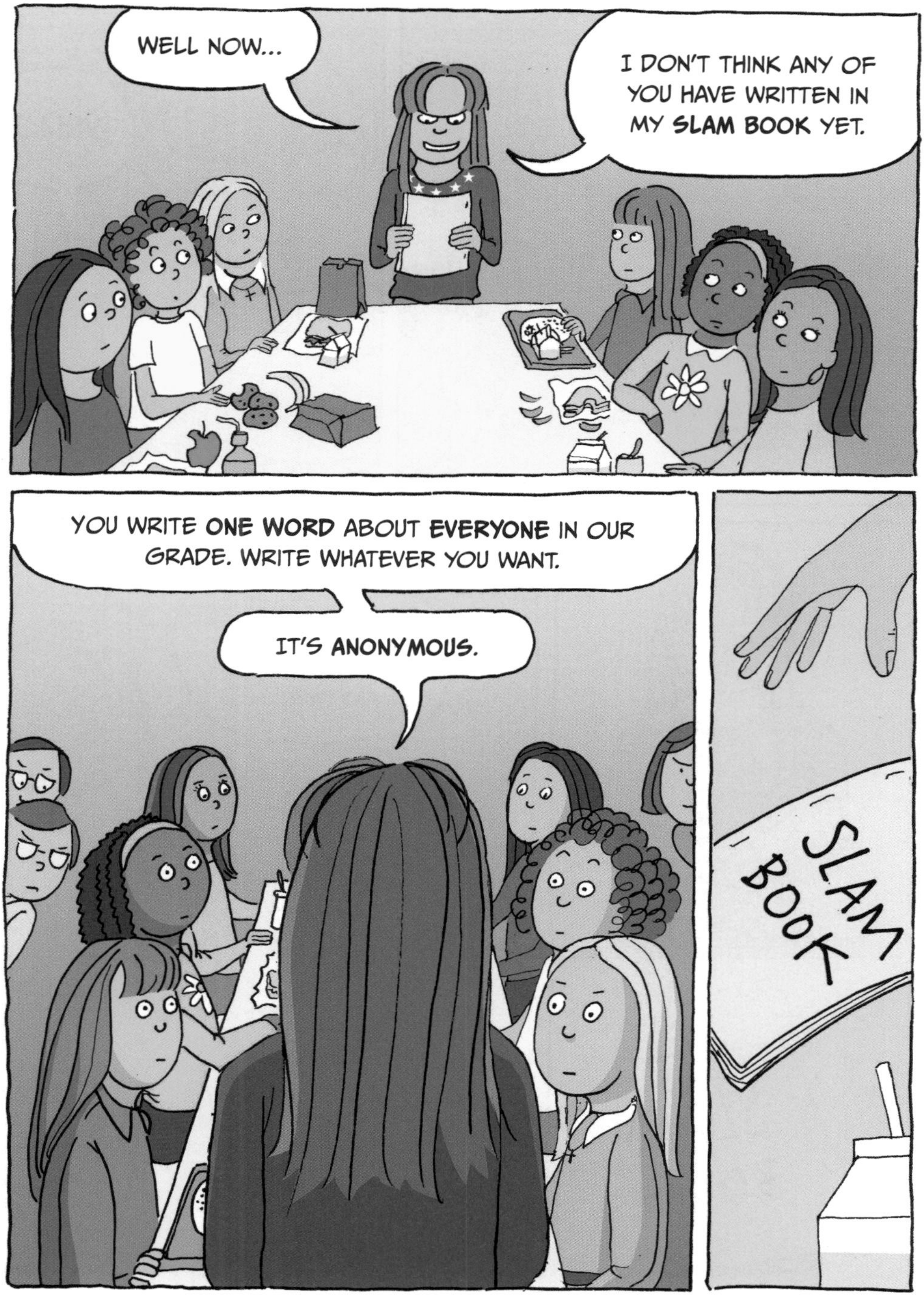
WELL NOW...
I DON'T THINK ANY OF YOU HAVE WRITTEN IN MY **SLAM BOOK** YET.
YOU WRITE **ONE WORD** ABOUT **EVERYONE** IN OUR GRADE. WRITE WHATEVER YOU WANT.
IT'S **ANONYMOUS.**
SLAM BOOK

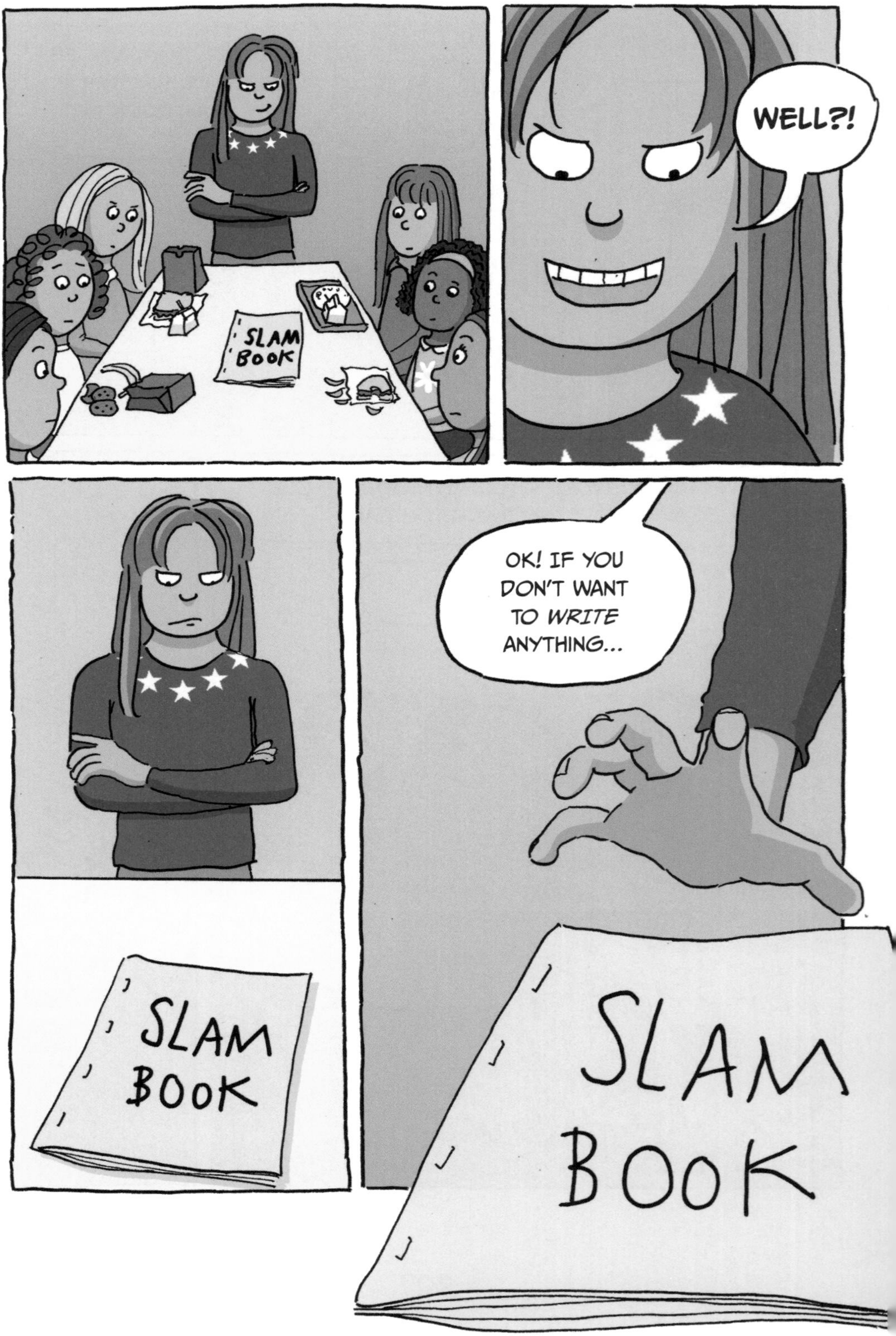
SLAM BOOK
WELL?!
SLAM BOOK
OK! IF YOU DON'T WANT TO *WRITE* ANYTHING...
SLAM BOOK

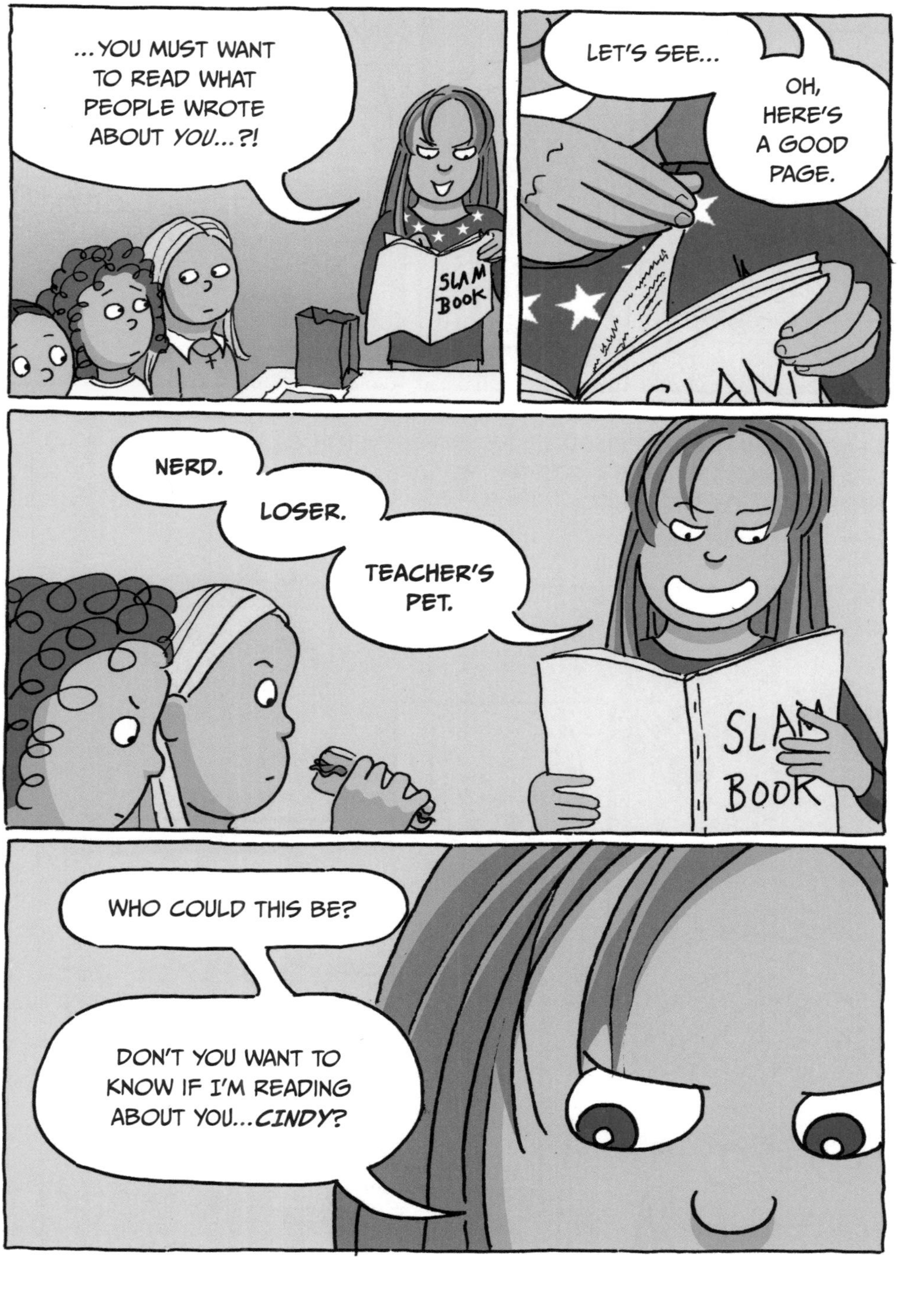
...YOU MUST WANT TO READ WHAT PEOPLE WROTE ABOUT *YOU*...?!
SLAM BOOK
LET'S SEE...
OH, HERE'S A GOOD PAGE.
NERD.
LOSER.
TEACHER'S PET.
SLAM BOOK
WHO COULD THIS BE?
DON'T YOU WANT TO KNOW IF I'M READING ABOUT YOU...*CINDY*?

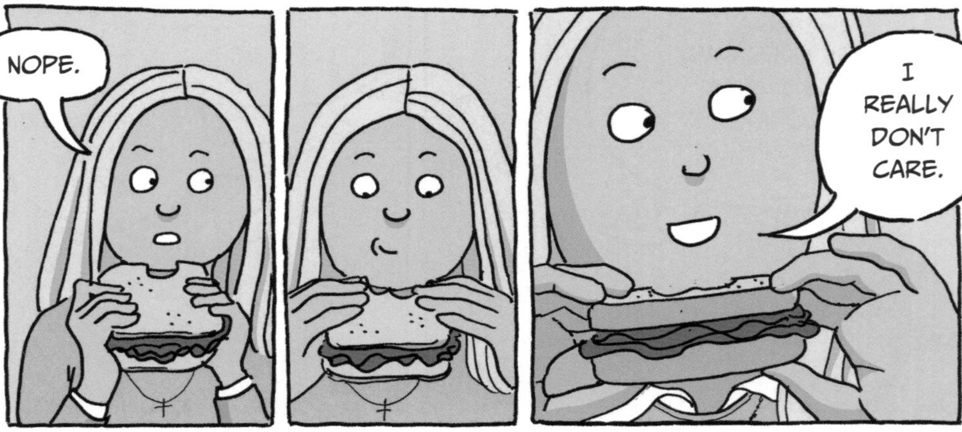
NOPE.
I REALLY DON'T CARE.

I KNOW HOW IT'S SUPPOSED TO WORK IN SEVENTH GRADE:
YOU ARE WHO THE OTHER KIDS SAY YOU ARE.
BUT I'M NOT OK WITH THAT.
I'LL SAY WHO I AM.

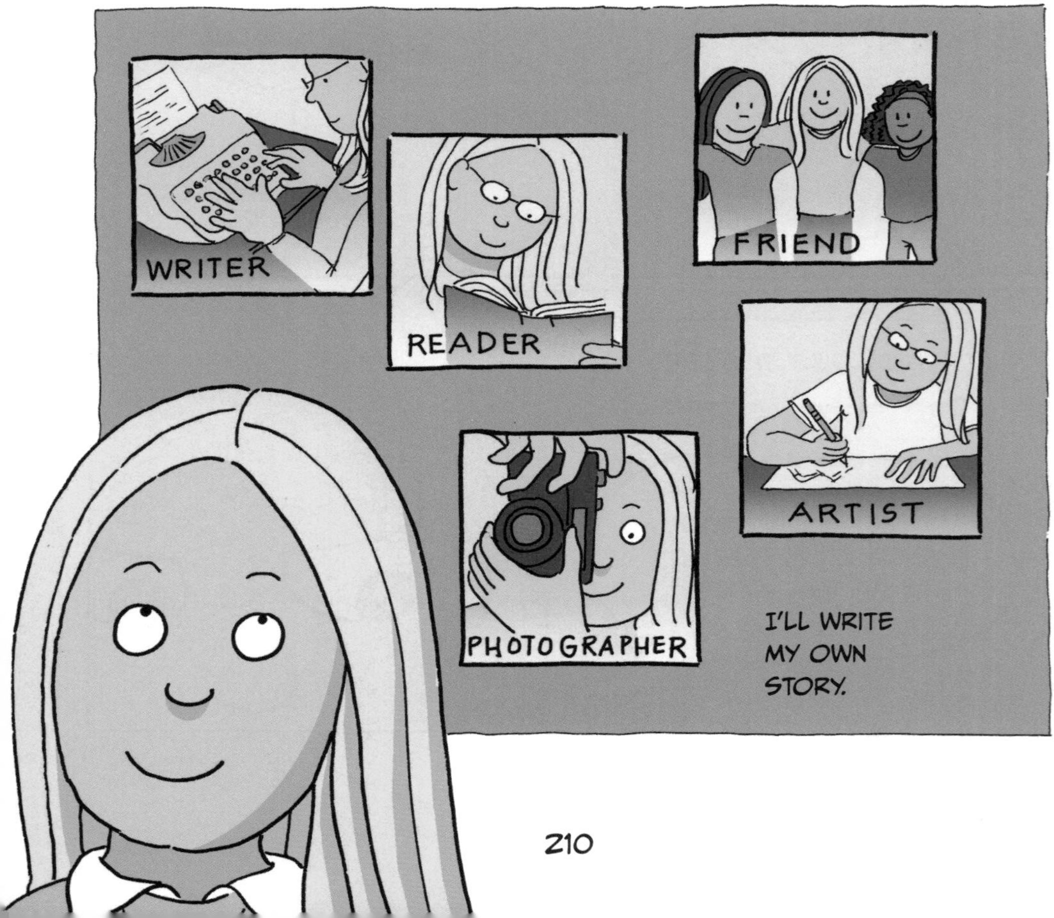
WRITER
READER
FRIEND
ARTIST
PHOTOGRAPHER
I'LL WRITE MY OWN STORY.

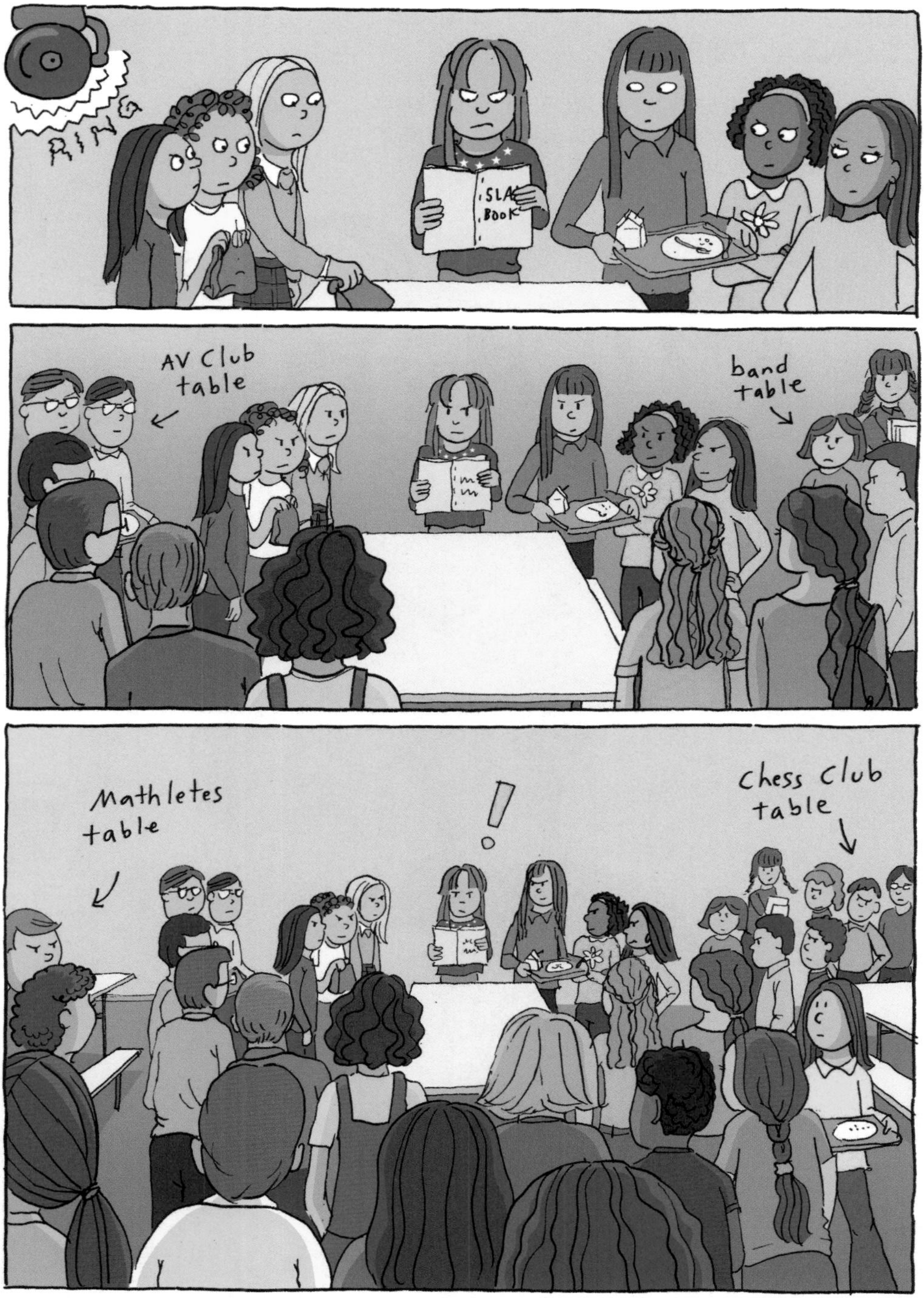
RING
SLA BOOK
AV Club table
band table
Mathletes table
!
Chess Club table

THERE IS *ONE MORE* DEFENSE PREY CAN USE:
COMMUNAL DEFENSE.

A PREY GROUP DEFENDS ITSELF BY STICKING TOGETHER AND MOBBING A PREDATOR RATHER THAN RUNNING AWAY.

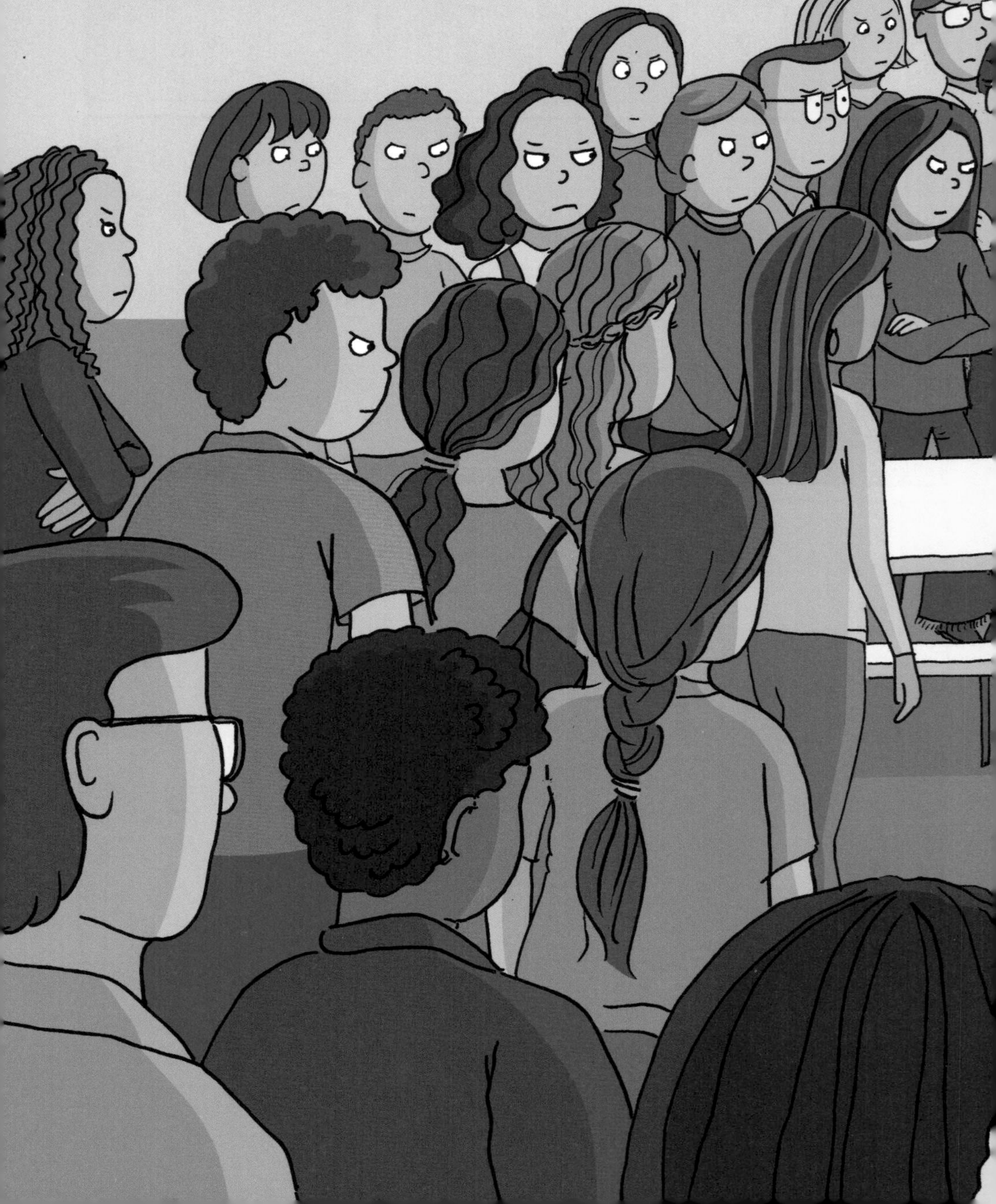

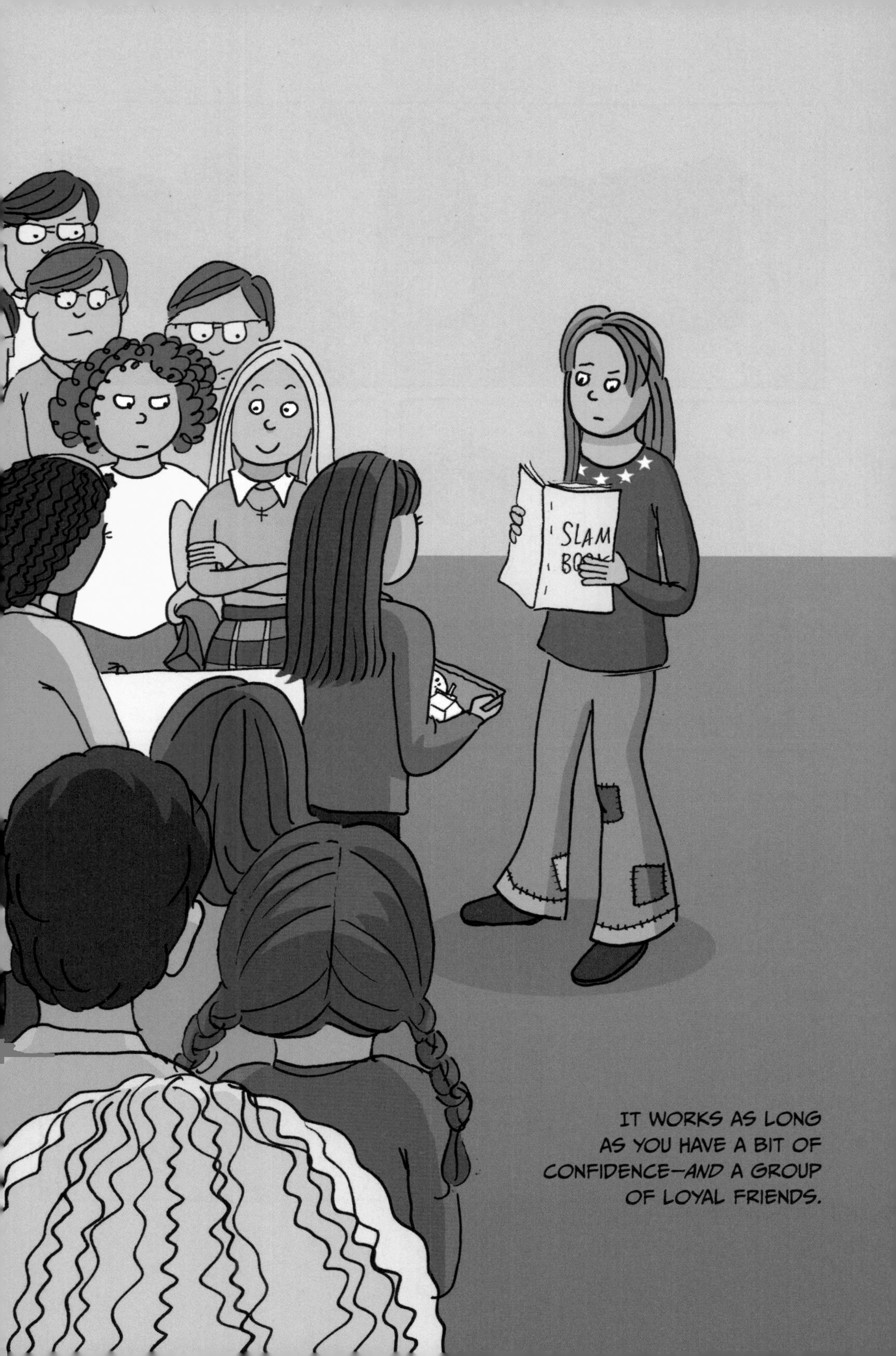
SLAM
IT WORKS AS LONG AS YOU HAVE A BIT OF CONFIDENCE—*AND* A GROUP OF LOYAL FRIENDS.

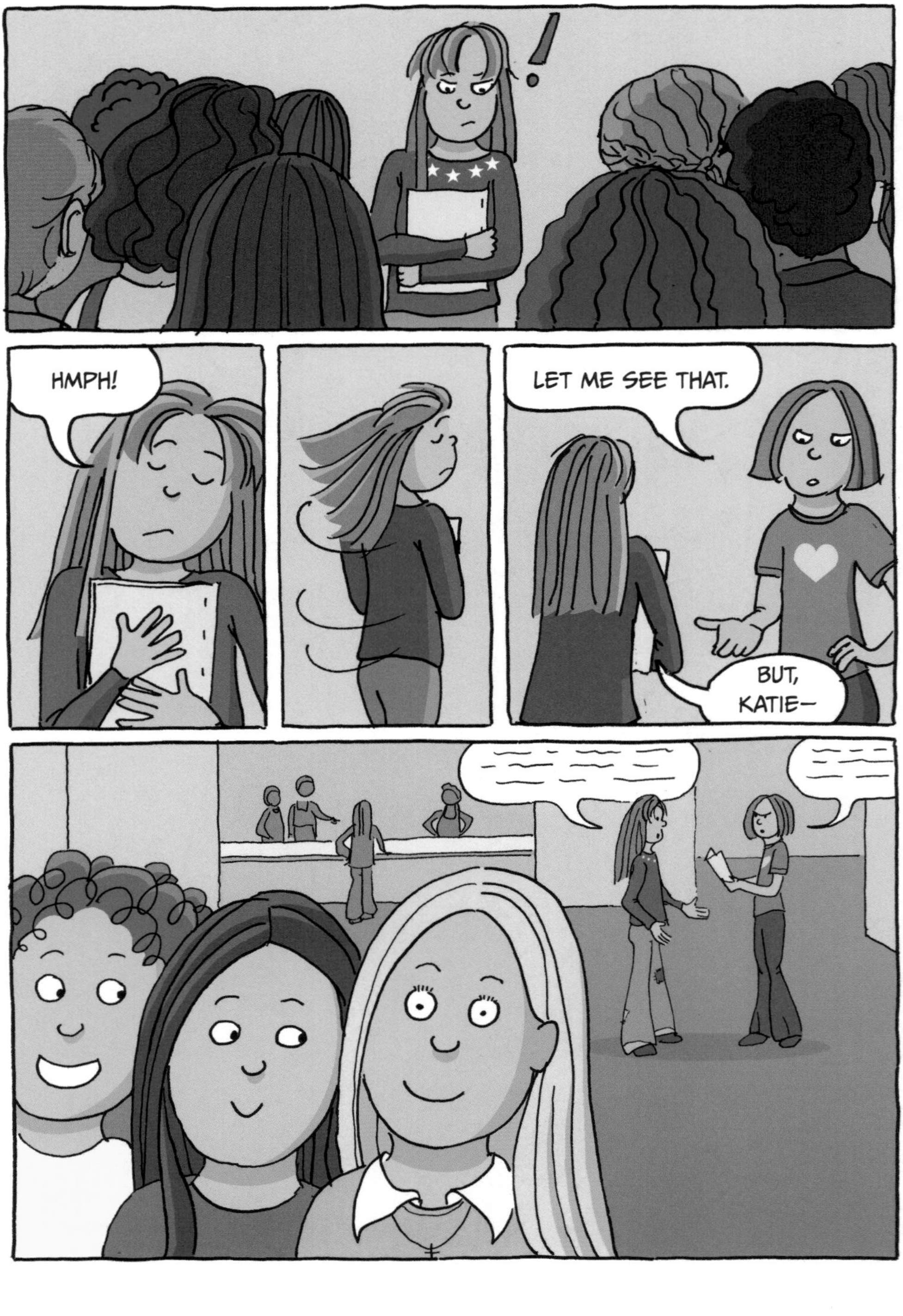
!
HMPH!
LET ME SEE THAT.
BUT, KATIE—

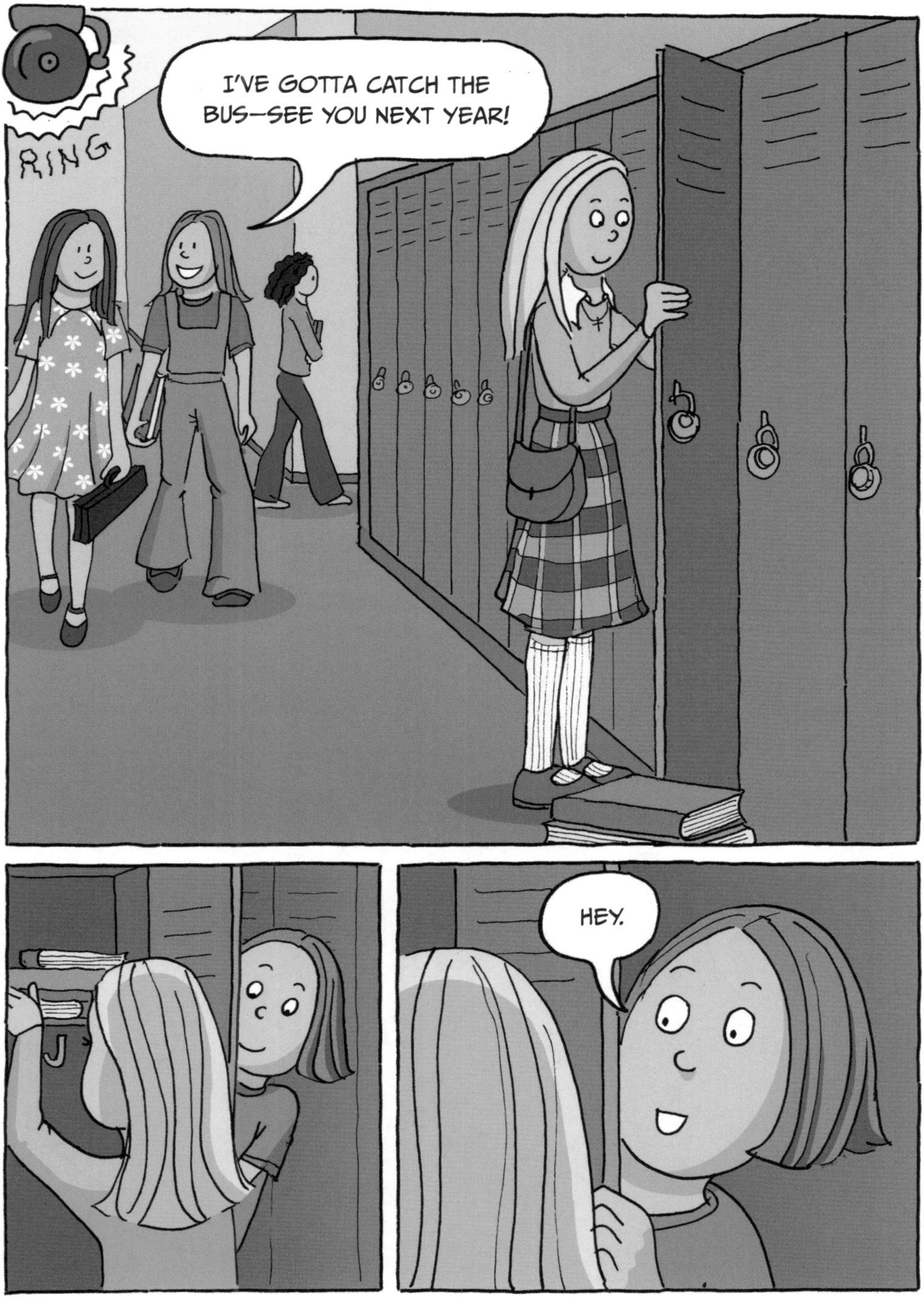
RING
I'VE GOTTA CATCH THE BUS—SEE YOU NEXT YEAR!
HEY.

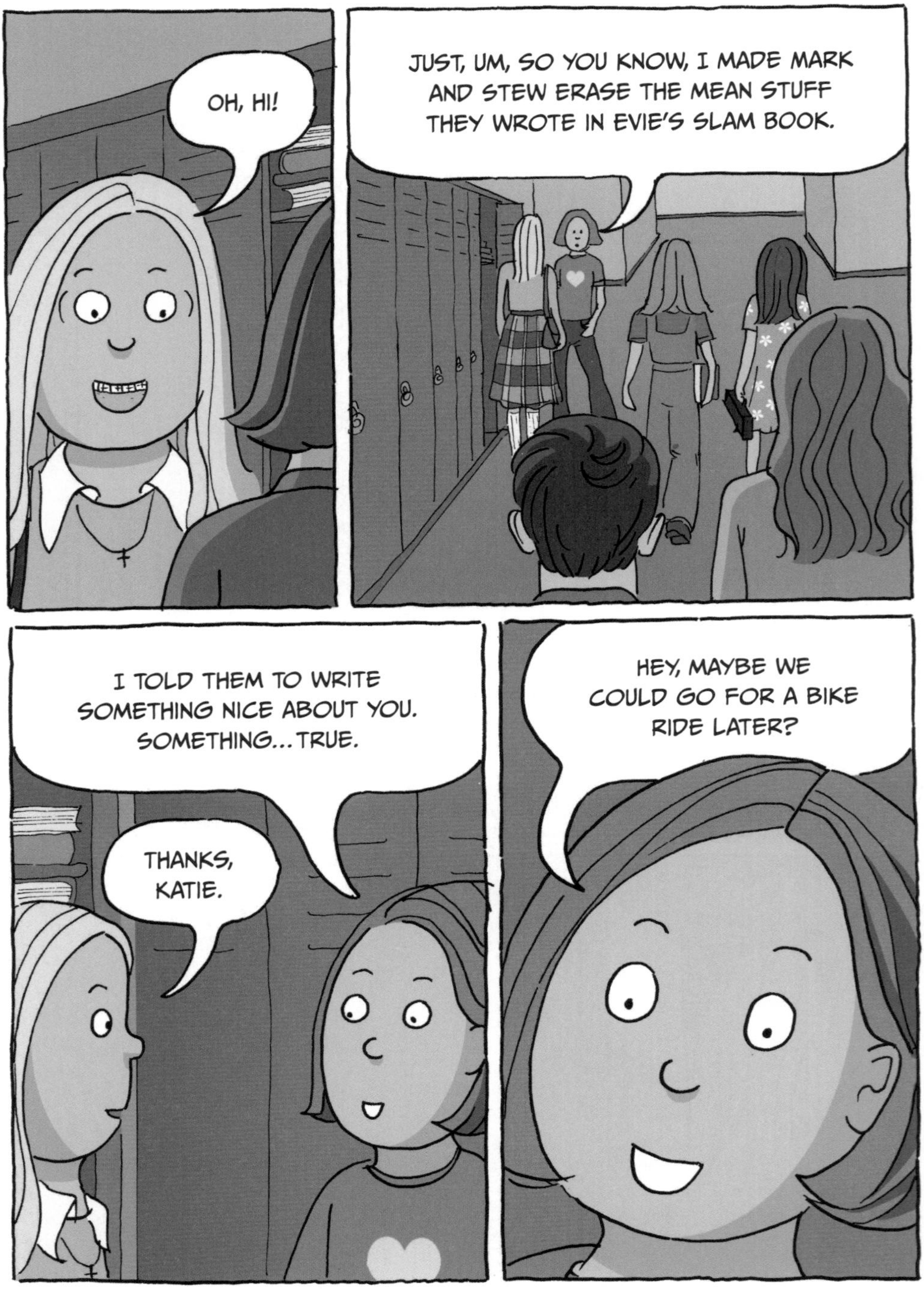
OH, HI!
JUST, UM, SO YOU KNOW, I MADE MARK AND STEW ERASE THE MEAN STUFF THEY WROTE IN EVIE'S SLAM BOOK.
I TOLD THEM TO WRITE SOMETHING NICE ABOUT YOU. SOMETHING... TRUE.
THANKS, KATIE.
HEY, MAYBE WE COULD GO FOR A BIKE RIDE LATER?

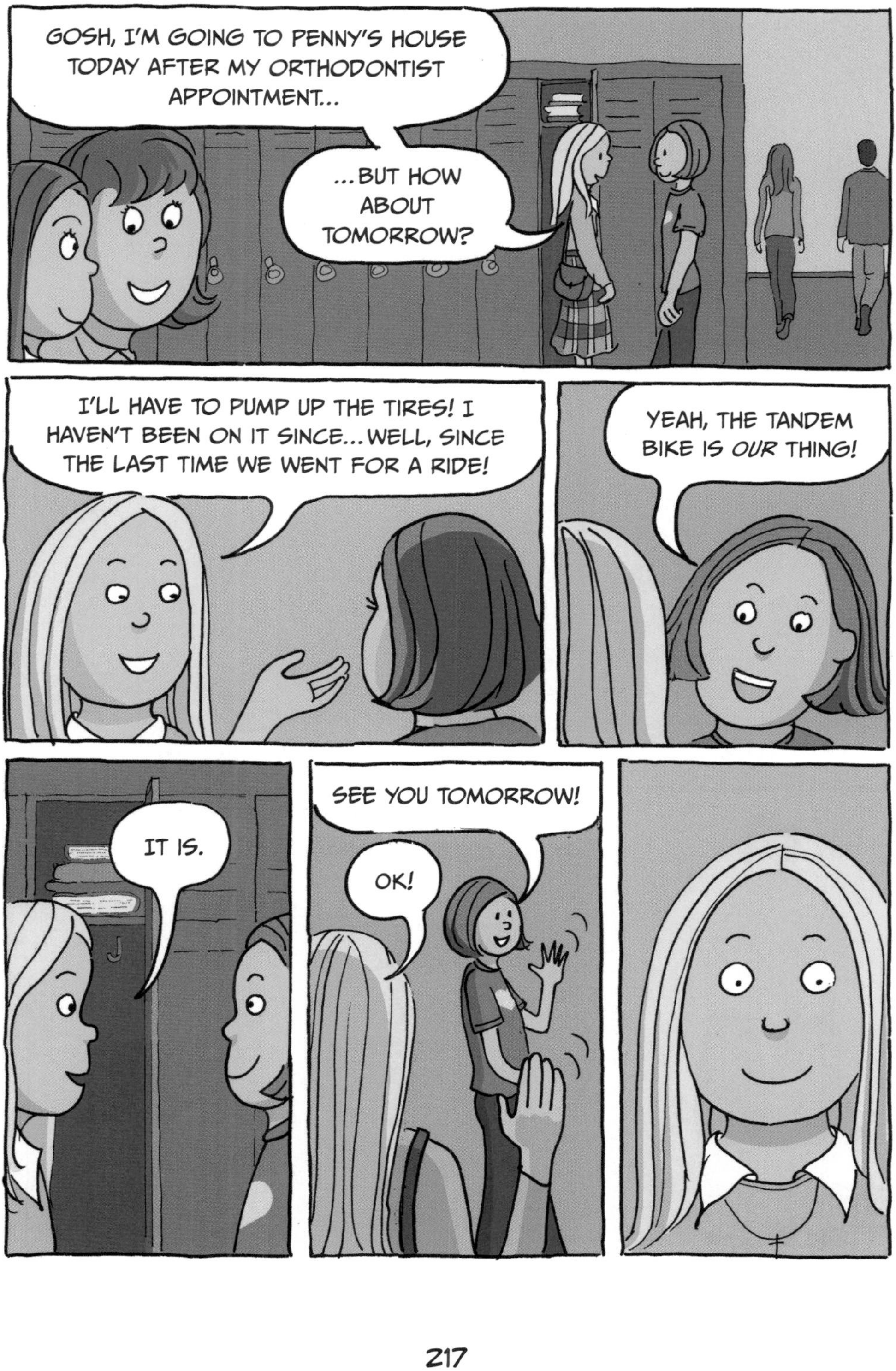
GOSH, I'M GOING TO PENNY'S HOUSE TODAY AFTER MY ORTHODONTIST APPOINTMENT...
...BUT HOW ABOUT TOMORROW?
I'LL HAVE TO PUMP UP THE TIRES! I HAVEN'T BEEN ON IT SINCE...WELL, SINCE THE LAST TIME WE WENT FOR A RIDE!
YEAH, THE TANDEM BIKE IS *OUR* THING!
IT IS.
SEE YOU TOMORROW!
OK!

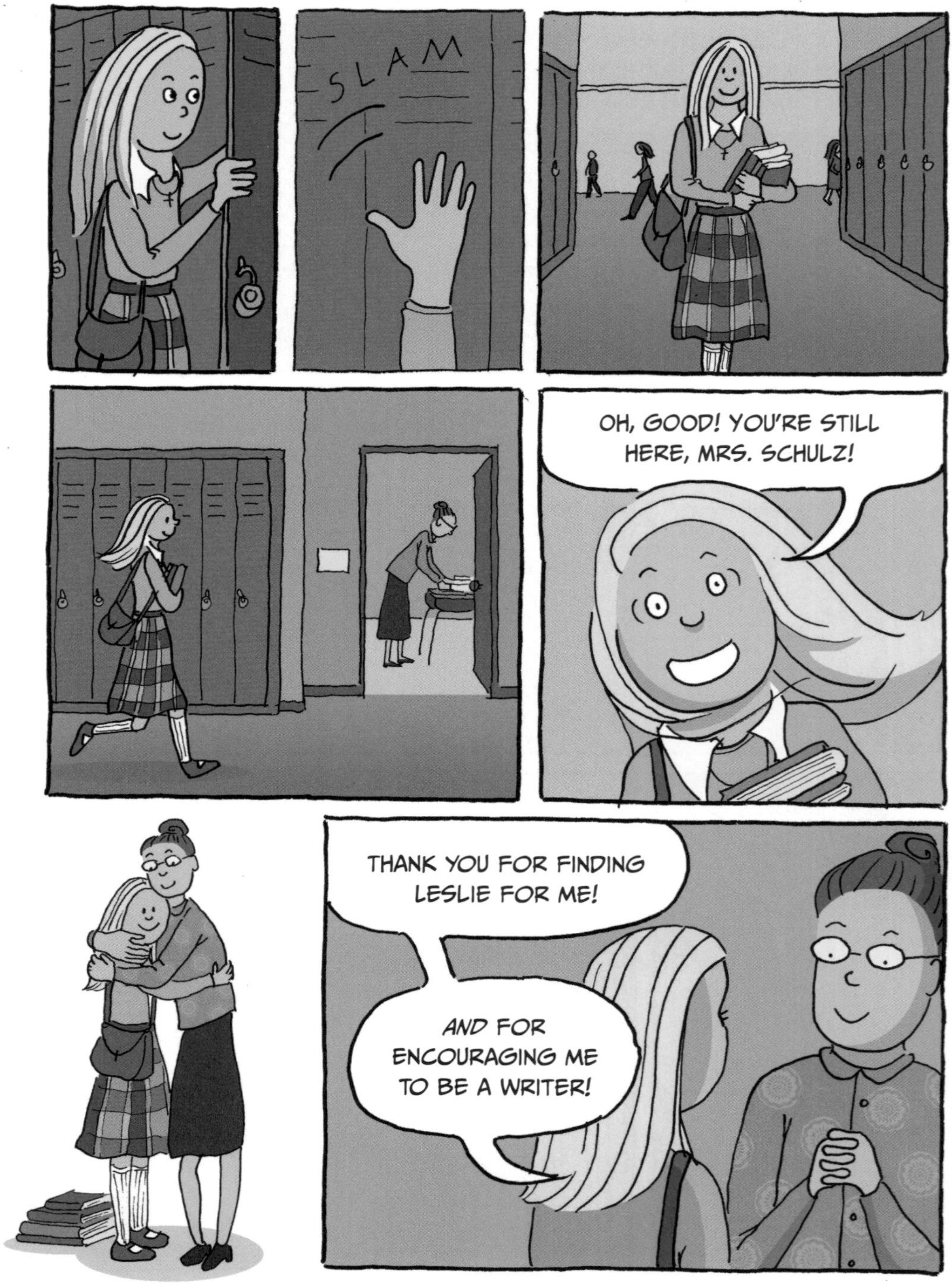
SLAM
OH, GOOD! YOU'RE STILL HERE, MRS. SCHULZ!
THANK YOU FOR FINDING LESLIE FOR ME!
AND FOR ENCOURAGING ME TO BE A WRITER!

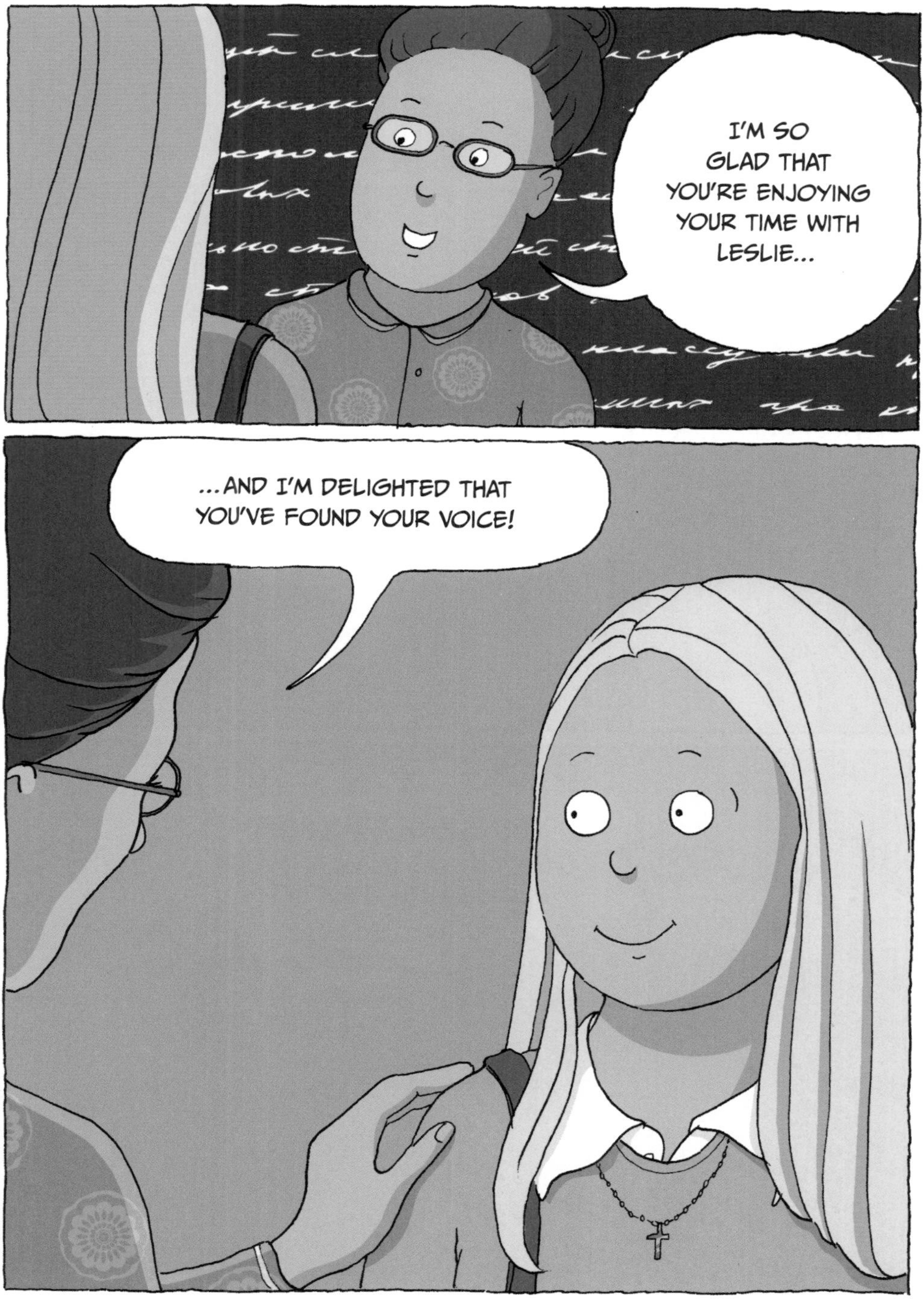
I'M SO GLAD THAT YOU'RE ENJOYING YOUR TIME WITH LESLIE...
...AND I'M DELIGHTED THAT YOU'VE FOUND YOUR VOICE!

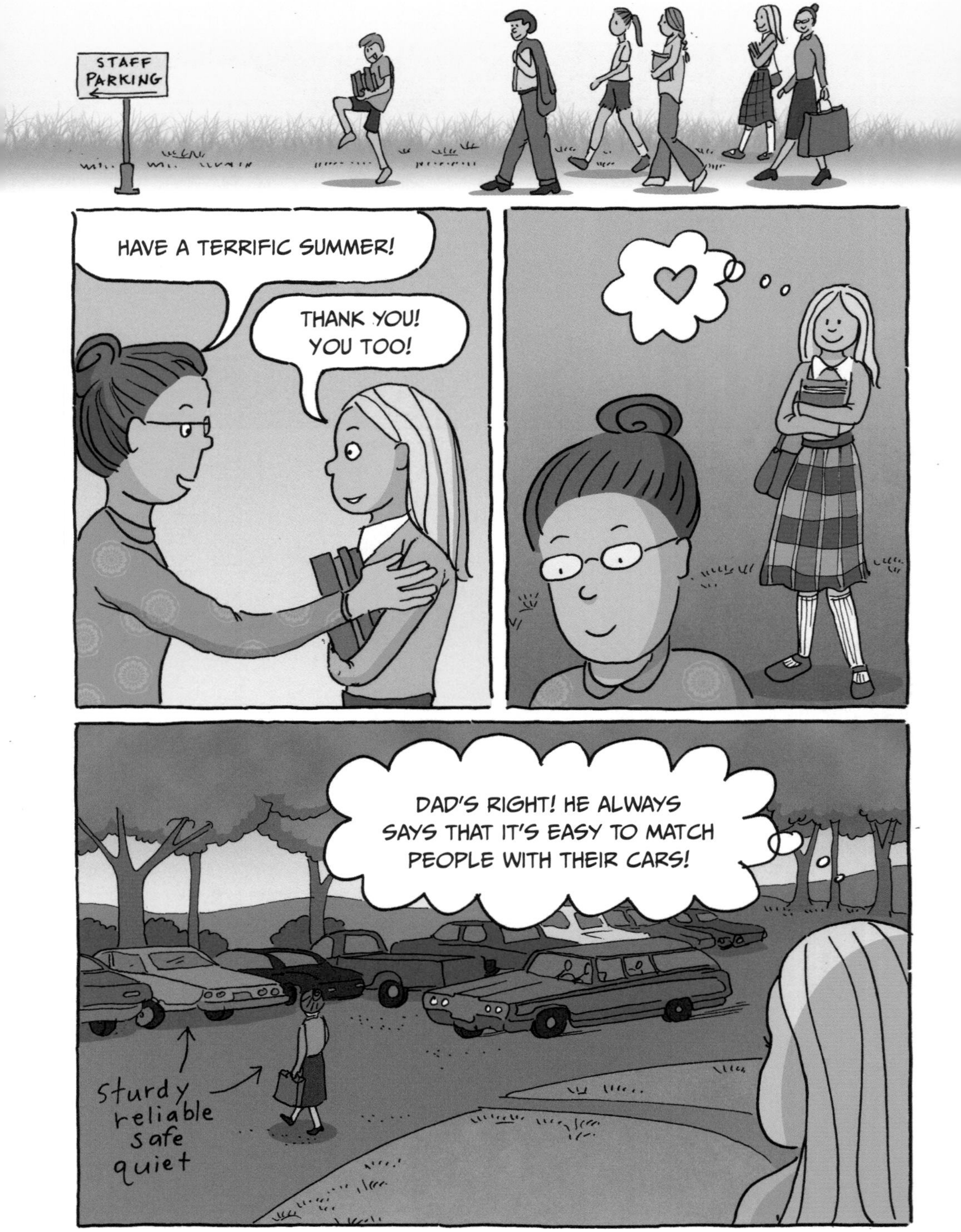
STAFF PARKING
HAVE A TERRIFIC SUMMER!
THANK YOU! YOU TOO!
DAD'S RIGHT! HE ALWAYS SAYS THAT IT'S EASY TO MATCH PEOPLE WITH THEIR CARS!
sturdy
reliable
safe
quiet

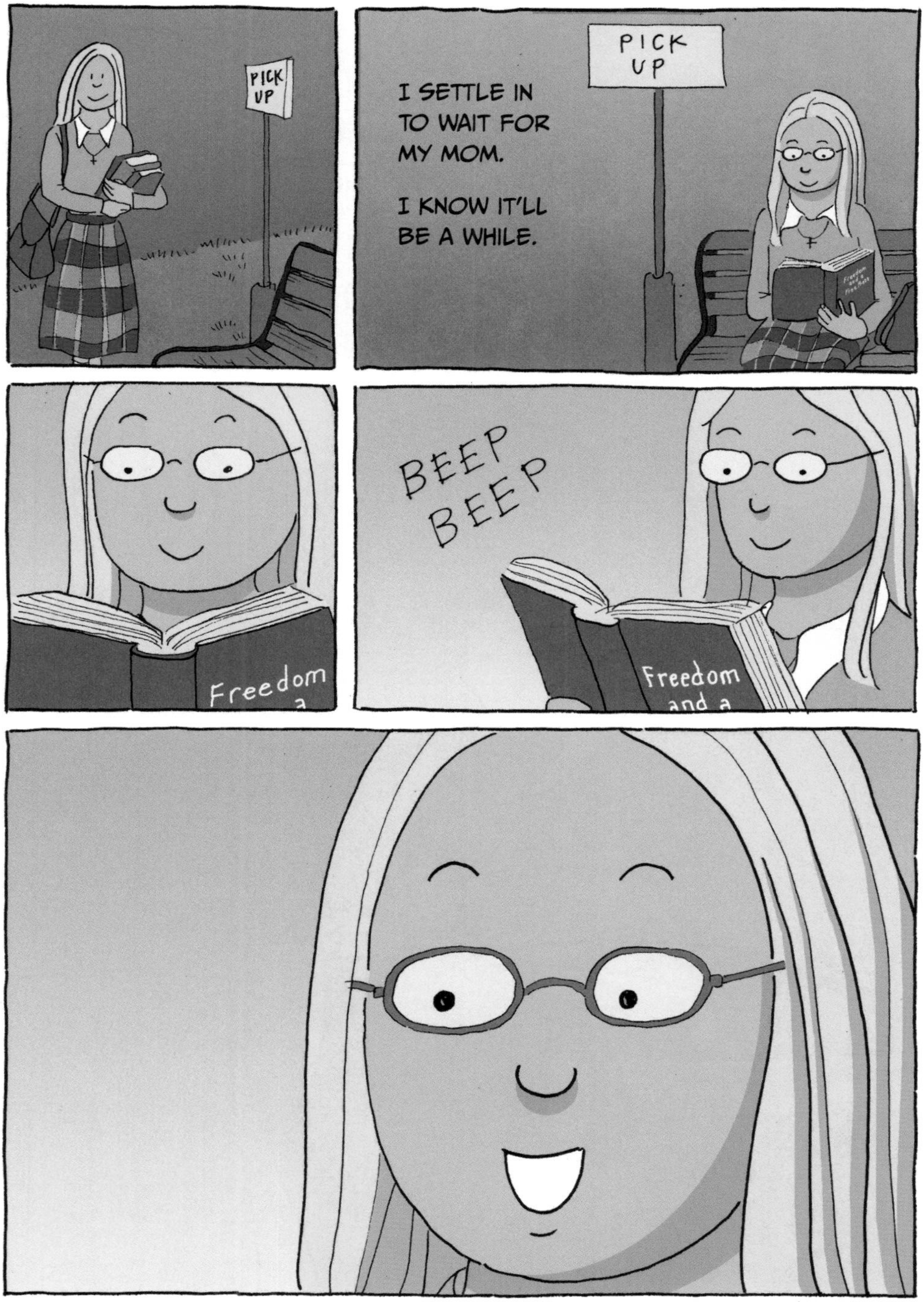
PICK UP
PICK UP
I SETTLE IN TO WAIT FOR MY MOM.
I KNOW IT'LL BE A WHILE.
Freedom a
BEEP BEEP
Freedom and a

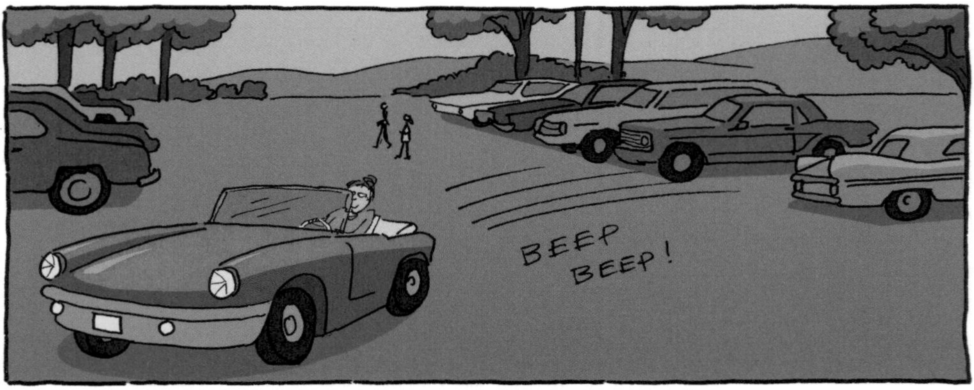
BEEP BEEP!

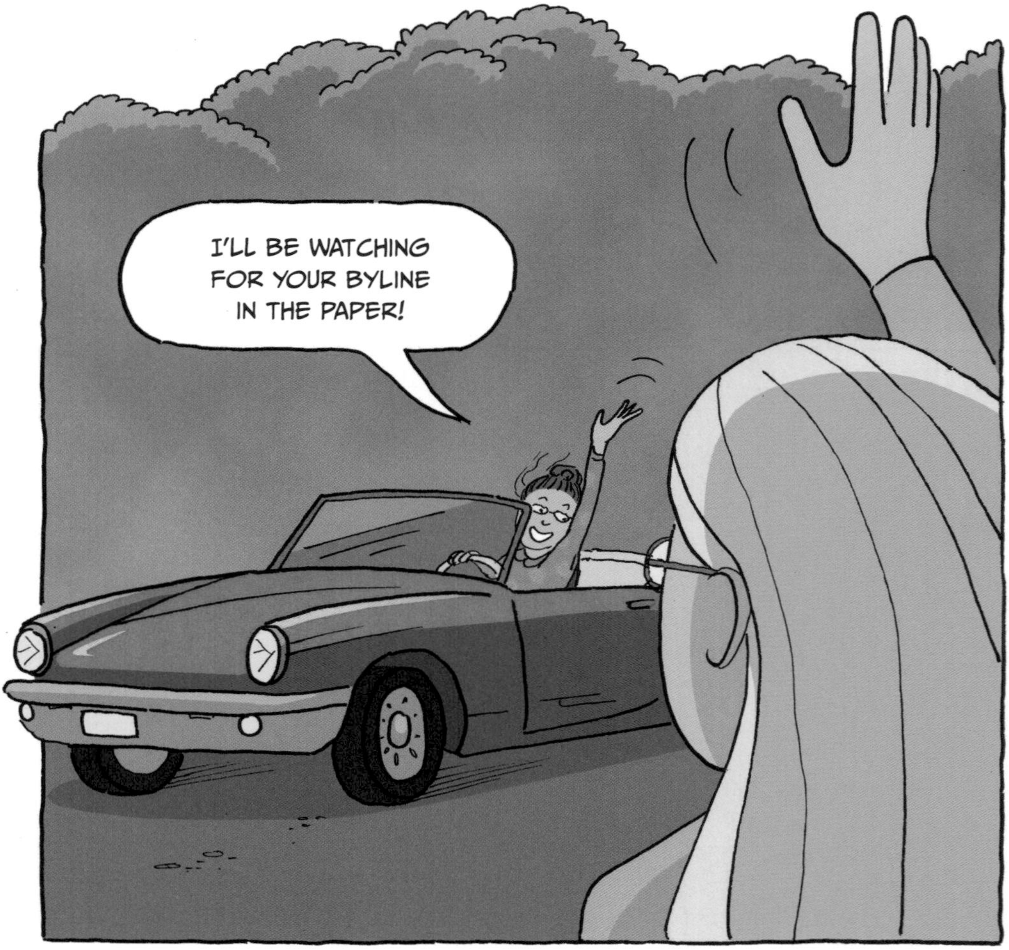
I'LL BE WATCHING FOR YOUR BYLINE IN THE PAPER!

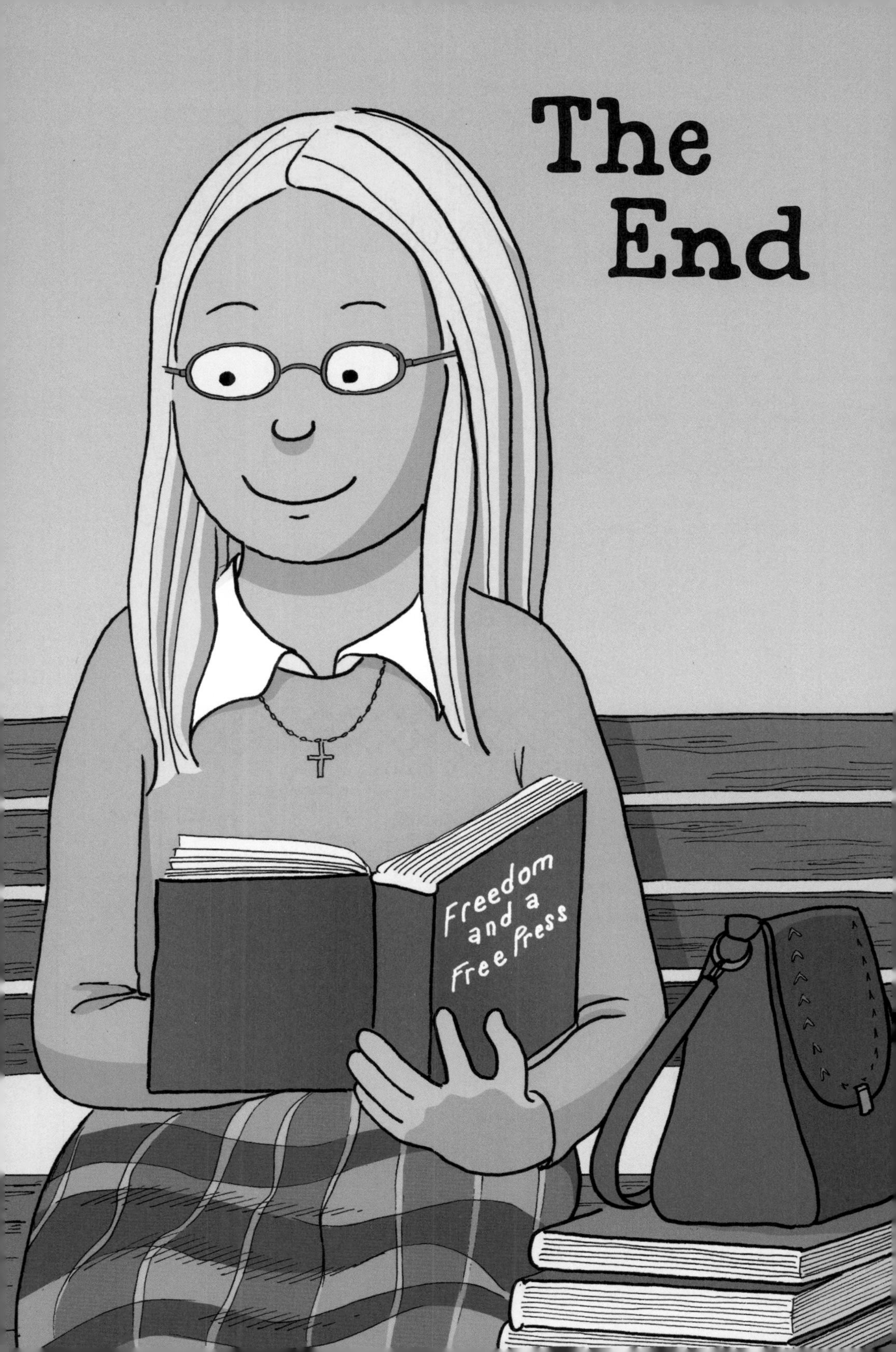
The End
Freedom and a Free Press

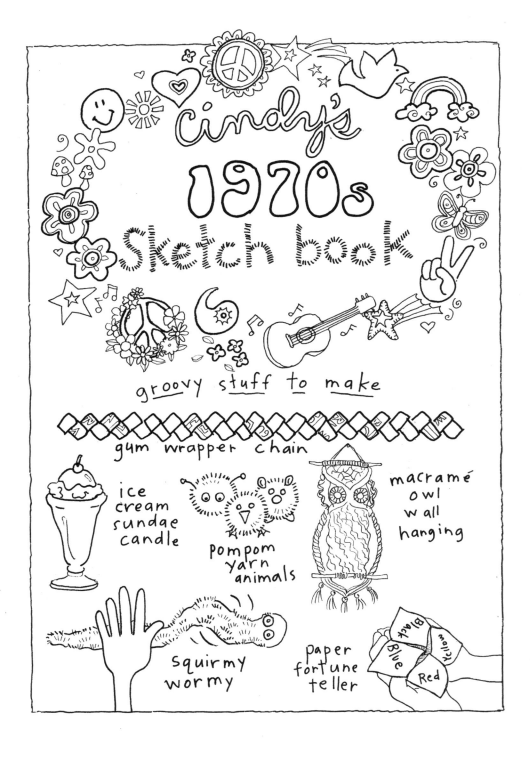

Cindy's 1970s Sketch book

groovy stuff to make

gum wrapper chain

ice cream sundae candle

pompom yarn animals

macramé owl wall hanging

squirmy wormy

paper fortune teller

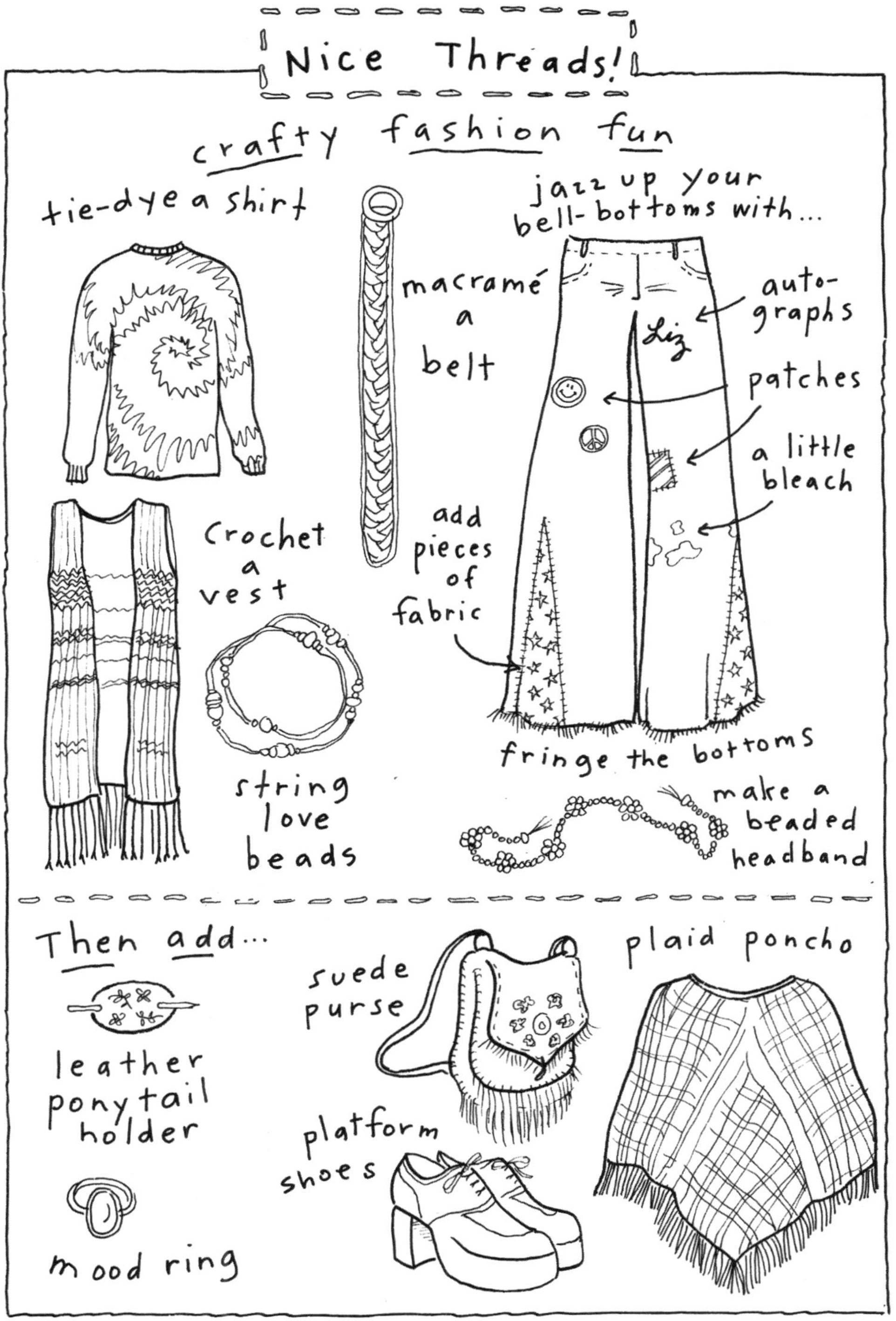
Nice Threads!
crafty fashion fun
tie-dye a shirt
macramé a belt
jazz up your bell-bottoms with...
auto-graphs
Liz
patches
a little bleach
add pieces of fabric
fringe the bottoms
Crochet a vest
string love beads
make a beaded headband
Then add...
leather ponytail holder
mood ring
suede purse
platform shoes
plaid poncho

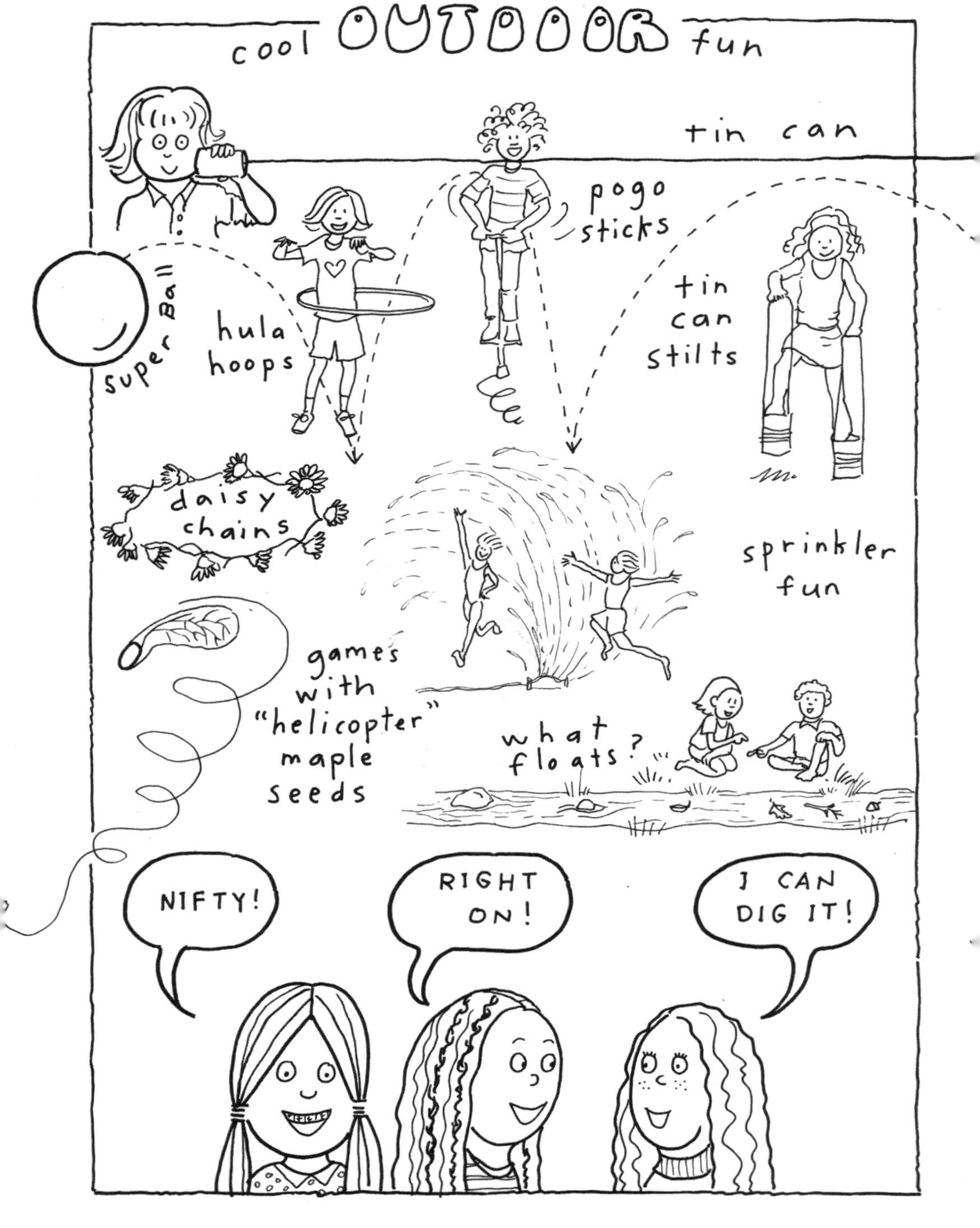
cool OUTDOOR fun
tin can
pogo sticks
Super Ball
hula hoops
tin can stilts
daisy chains
sprinkler fun
games with "helicopter" maple seeds
what floats?
NIFTY!
RIGHT ON!
I CAN DIG IT!

cool INDOOR fun
telephones
HA HA HA
Silly Putty Sunday comics
string games
Tiddlywinks
A
C
dots and boxes
Creepy Crawlers
Viewmaster
OUTTA SIGHT!
KEEP ON TRUCKIN'
FAR OUT!

AUTHOR'S NOTE

Cub is based on the true story of my time as a cub
reporter for a regional Connecticut newspaper, beginning
when I was in seventh grade. Many of the details
are true; for example, my work was published in the
newspaper, my dad built me a darkroom, and my drawings of
historic buildings appeared on crockery sold in town. I
lost my childhood best friend to a cool (and cruel) crowd
for a time and frequently hung out with my crush at the
secret fort we made on "the Island."

But real life rarely, if ever, unfolds in a way that
creates a perfect story. Like many memoirs, this one is
inspired by real events and maintains the essence of
what happened in my life, but incorporates changes for a
better reading experience. Some of the changes are mine,
and others were suggested by my editors.

I compressed the timeline in *Cub*, for instance, so
it would occur within one school year; in reality, I
continued to work with Leslie Jacobs into my high school
years. The newspaper headlines and articles in the book
are based on real ones that were published at that time,
and a lot of the meetings and events that Leslie and I
attend in the book were informed by the articles Leslie
wrote for the *Torrington Register* that year. Specific
details of meetings and interviews, however, are largely
fictional.

The challenge in writing about a historical time period—
especially for younger readers—is how authentically to
represent it. Is the book a time capsule, with language
and culture frozen in 1972 and accurately portrayed? Or
is it a modernized version, seen through a twenty-first-
century filter?

Cub is a bit of both. I hope that readers will notice
and discuss details like the all-boy AV club, kids riding

bikes without helmets, the number of adults smoking cigarettes, and the relatively homogeneous population, as well as the positive aspects of life in the seventies: lots of family meals and togetherness, the freedom (and free time) to explore the outdoors, the absence of intrusive social media, and the valued role of the town library. I also hope readers will notice how many of the issues we worried about all those years ago—equality for all, protecting the environment, corrupt politicians, attacks on a free press—are still topics of concern today.

Other than Mrs. Schulz, Leslie Jacobs, and my family members, I changed all the names and identifying details of characters in the book. Many of my classmates in Cub are composites of my friends from that time. The character called Katie remains a close friend to this day. In her childhood bedroom, the pencil lines where we—and yes, "Evie"—charted our growth are etched into the doorframe; the chalkboard in her attic still has the faintest markings from when we played school.

My beautiful hometown of Litchfield looks much as it did when this story took place. Kids still ride their bikes to Murphy's Pharmacy for candy, meet up at the cannon on the town green, and (I'm guessing) build secret forts on the Island.

It was a marvelous place to grow up. I was a lucky girl.

ACKNOWLEDGMENTS

Every book is a collaboration, and I'm deeply grateful to the talented and dedicated people on my team at Algonquin Young Readers, Workman Publishing, and Writers House.

My extraordinary agent, Dan Lazar, was instrumental in helping me shape and expand this story early on. His guidance—from the project's inception to its conclusion—was invaluable. I trust his instincts and always welcome his input.

Elise Howard, publisher of Algonquin Young Readers, provided wise and thoughtful edits. Her vision for *Cub* inspired and guided me, and I (gratefully) took every piece of advice she offered. I would have been lost without associate editor Sarah Alpert, who had a ready answer for every question I asked (and there were many!).

I was very fortunate to have had Neil Swaab design *Cub*; his was the calm voice of reason and reassurance over many months, and his subtle (delightful!) touches punctuate the book.

The contribution of Eisner-nominated colorist Ronda Pattison to the visual appeal of *Cub* can't be overstated. Ronda's talent and creative instincts brought my inked pages to life.

My daughter, Alex Carley, provided valuable feedback on the cover art and design and offered wisdom and encouragement throughout the many years it took to create *Cub*.

Many other exceptional people worked behind the scenes, playing important roles in *Cub*'s development: Laura Williams, Ashley Mason, Steve Godwin, Julie Primavera, and Janice Lee. Thanks to Megan Harley, Caitlin Rubinstein, and Carla Bruce-Eddings for seeing that young readers everywhere have a chance to discover *Cub*.

I've been part of the Workman Publishing family since 1993, when Peter Workman offered me my first significant book contract. I've always appreciated the support, respect, and attention the Workman group gives every one of its authors.

As for the experiences that inspired *Cub*, I'm indebted to Leslie Jacobs, who seemed so grown up when she was mentoring me, but was actually in her twenties. Idealistic and inspirational, she expanded my idea of what women's lives could look like, encouraging me to dream big.

Maureen Schulz, the exceptional English teacher whose phone call to the newspaper started it all, retired from teaching long ago. I recently wrote to her about *Cub*. She said that she read my note with tears in her eyes, having always wondered if she'd "left any positive mark" during her many years of teaching. I hope caring, compassionate teachers everywhere—including my beloved Mrs. Schulz—realize just how much of a lasting impact they have on their students.

I'm grateful most of all to my family, for providing me with my best memories and the happiest possible start in life. Growing up, my brothers made every day more fun (even when they were pestering me); now they are among my biggest supporters. My sweet mom, the family cheerleader, is still a whirlwind of happy energy. I'm thrilled that she was able to have a fulfilling career after we all left home—and has continued working into her eighties!

I dedicated *Cub* to my dad, who died before this book was finished. I hope his kind and gentle manner and devotion to his family come through in these pages. He was my fierce protector and biggest fan. I miss him every single day.

A. CLAYTON COPELAND

CYNTHIA L. COPELAND IS THE *NEW YORK TIMES* BESTSELLING AND AWARD-WINNING AUTHOR/ILLUSTRATOR OF MORE THAN 25 BOOKS FOR ADULTS AND CHILDREN. A GRADUATE OF SMITH COLLEGE, SHE LIVES IN NEW HAMPSHIRE WITH HER FAMILY. *CUB* IS HER FIRST GRAPHIC MEMOIR FOR YOUNG READERS.